Adam Smith and Rousseau

Edinburgh Studies in Scottish Philosophy

Series Editor: Gordon Graham
Center for the Study of Scottish Philosophy, Princeton Theological Seminary

Scottish Philosophy Through the Ages

This new series will cover the full range of Scottish philosophy over five centuries – from the medieval period through the Reformation and Enlightenment periods, to the nineteenth and early twentieth centuries.

The series will publish innovative studies on major figures and themes. It also aims to stimulate new work in less intensively studied areas, by a new generation of philosophers and intellectual historians. The books will combine historical sensitivity and philosophical substance which will serve to cast new light on the rich intellectual inheritance of Scottish philosophy.

Editorial Advisory Board

Books available

Adam Smith and Rousseau: Ethics, Politics, Economics edited by Maria Pia Paganelli, Dennis C. Rasmussen and Craig Smith
Thomas Reid and the Problem of Secondary Qualities by Christopher A. Shrock
Hume's Sceptical Enlightenment by Ryu Susato

Books forthcoming

Imagination in Hume's Philosophy: The Canvas of the Mind by Timothy M. Costelloe
Adam Ferguson and the Idea of Civil Society: Moral Science in the Scottish Enlightenment by Craig Smith
Essays on Hume, Smith and the Scottish Enlightenment by Christopher Berry
Eighteenth-Century Scottish Aesthetics: Not Just a Matter of Taste by Rachel Zuckert

www.edinburghuniversitypress.com/series/essp

Adam Smith and Rousseau

Ethics, Politics, Economics

Edited by Maria Pia Paganelli, Dennis C. Rasmussen
and Craig Smith

EDINBURGH
University Press

Edinburgh University Press is one of the leading university presses in the UK. We publish academic books and journals in our selected subject areas across the humanities and social sciences, combining cutting-edge scholarship with high editorial and production values to produce academic works of lasting importance. For more information visit our website: edinburghuniversitypress.com

Edinburgh University Press Ltd
The Tun – Holyrood Road, 12(2f) Jackson's Entry, Edinburgh EH8 8PJ

Typeset in 11/13 Adobe Sabon by
Servis Filmsetting Ltd, Stockport, Cheshire,
and printed and bound in Great Britain.

A CIP record for this book is available from the British Library

ISBN 978 1 4744 2285 7 (hardback)
ISBN 978 1 4744 2286 4 (webready PDF)
ISBN 978 1 4744 2287 1 (epub)

Contents

Acknowledgements

The genesis of this project was a joint meeting of the International Adam Smith Society and the Rousseau Association that was designed to foster further work on the intellectual connections between these two great thinkers. The meeting, held in July 2015 at the University of Glasgow and supported by a grant from the British Academy/Leverhulme fund, led to a series of highly productive discussions. The chapters collected in this volume were carefully selected and developed from the more than fifty papers prepared for the joint meeting.

The editors wish to acknowledge the assistance of the British Academy, the Leverhulme Trust, the International Adam Smith Society, the Rousseau Association, the Centre for the Study of Scottish Philosophy – in whose publication series this volume appears – and its director Professor Gordon Graham, and Edinburgh University Press, in particular Carol Macdonald and Ersev Ersoy. The editors are also grateful for the suggestions of the anonymous reviewers of the proposal.

Citations and Abbreviations

This volume uses the author/date in-text citation style with two exceptions. Scholars of Adam Smith have adopted a standard citation system to the Glasgow Edition of the Works of Adam Smith, published in hardback by Oxford University Press and in paperback by Liberty Fund Press, Indianapolis, and we have used this system in citations of Smith throughout the volume. Details of the standard abbreviations appear below.

For Rousseau, in the absence of a universally agreed standard English translation, we allowed the authors to select their own preferred translations (or indeed to make their own). In each case a note is offered to explain the editions and translations used. In several cases the citations are accompanied by reference to the French-language *Œuvres complètes*.

AL   *The Principles Which Lead and Direct Philosophical Enquiries; Illustrated by the History of the Ancient Logics and Metaphysics.* In EPS (cited by paragraph: page).

AP   *The Principles Which Lead and Direct Philosophical Enquiries; Illustrated by the History of the Ancient Physics.* In EPS (cited by paragraph: page).

CL   *Considerations Concerning the First Formation of Languages.* In LRBL (cited by paragraph: page).

Corr.   *Correspondence of Adam Smith.* Edited by E. Mossner and I. Ross (1987) (cited by letter: page).

ED   *Early Draft of Part of the Wealth of Nations.* In LJ (cited by paragraph: page).

EPS   *Essays on Philosophical Subjects.* Edited by W. Wightman, J. Bryce and I. Ross (1982).

ES   *Of the External Senses.* In EPS (cited by paragraph: page).

HA   *The Principles Which Lead and Direct Philosophical Enquiries; Illustrated by the History of Astronomy.* In EPS (cited by section. paragraph: page).

IA   *Of the Nature of that Imitation which takes place in what are called the Imitative Arts.* In EPS (cited by page).

Letter   *Letter to the Edinburgh Review.* In EPS (cited by page).

Life   *Account of the Life and Writings of Adam Smith, LL.D.* Dugald Stewart. In EPS (cited by page).

LJA   *Lectures on Jurisprudence 1762/3.* Edited by R. L. Meek, D. D. Raphael and P. G. Stein (1978) (cited by page).

LJB   *Lectures on Jurisprudence 1766.* Edited by R. L. Meek, D. D. Raphael and P. G. Stein (1978) (cited by page).

LRBL   *Lectures on Rhetoric and Belles Lettres.* Edited by J. Bryce (1985) (cited by section. paragraph: page).

TMS   *The Theory of Moral Sentiments.* Edited by A. L. Macfie and D. D. Raphael (1982) (cited by part. section. chapter. paragraph: page).

WN   *An Inquiry into the Nature and Causes of the Wealth of Nations.* Edited by R. H. Campbell and A. S. Skinner (1981) (cited by book. part. chapter. paragraph: page).

Series Editor's Introduction

It is widely acknowledged that the Scottish Enlightenment of the eighteenth century was one of the most fertile periods in British intellectual history, and that philosophy was the jewel in its crown. Yet, vibrant though this period was, it occurred within a long history that began with the creation of the Scottish universities in the fifteenth century. It also stretched into the nineteenth and twentieth centuries for as long as those universities continued to be a culturally distinctive and socially connected system of education and inquiry.

While the Scottish Enlightenment remains fertile ground for philosophical and historical investigation, these other four centuries of philosophy also warrant intellectual exploration. The purpose of this series is to maintain outstanding scholarly study of great thinkers like David Hume, Adam Smith and Thomas Reid, alongside sustained exploration of the less familiar figures who preceded them, and the impressive company of Scottish philosophers, once celebrated, now neglected, who followed them.

Gordon Graham

Part I

Adam Smith and Jean-Jacques Rousseau

Introduction

Maria Pia Paganelli, Dennis C. Rasmussen and Craig Smith

Jean-Jacques Rousseau and Adam Smith were two of the foremost figures of the European Enlightenment. They made seminal contributions to moral and political philosophy and shaped some of the key concepts of modern political economy. For some time there was a popular, if crude, notion that the two were in some sense opposites or even enemies. This crude reading of Smith as the advocate of liberalism, commercial society and progress as contrasted to Rousseau's advocacy of republicanism, the noble savage and a return to nature invited the unwary reader to see Smith as the champion of selfishness and progenitor of capitalism, in stark opposition to Rousseau as the champion of egalitarianism and the intellectual forefather of socialism. Fortunately the turn towards contextual and textual scholarship in the history of ideas has put paid to these stereotypes and has allowed the much more complex and rich connection between these thinkers to emerge. We are no longer dealing with caricatures where these two great thinkers are used as emblems for later intellectual developments, but we are still in the early stages of the exploration of their relationship. The present volume advances the analysis of their ideas by exploring a series of shared themes and preoccupations that can be traced in their writings.

This introduction sets the scene for the collection of essays that follows by briefly describing some of the biographical and textual elements of the Smith–Rousseau connection, and then providing a brief sketch of some of the recent scholarly work on the relationship between the two thinkers.

Rousseau and Smith: Some Context and Connections

Jean-Jacques Rousseau (1712–78) and Adam Smith (1723–90) were near contemporaries, but they never corresponded and probably never met one another. It is just possible that they met in Paris in late December 1765 or early January 1766, but the evidence seems to point against such a meeting (see Rasmussen 2008: 53–4). They did, however, have many mutual acquaintances and interlocutors among Europe's 'republic of letters'. Smith befriended a number of the leading *philosophes* during his stay in Paris in 1766 – Dugald Stewart, Smith's first biographer, singles out 'Turgot, Quesnai, Morellet, Necker, d'Alembert, Helvetius, Marmontel, Madame Riccoboni' (Life: 302–3) – and most of these figures knew Rousseau as well. The individual with the closest links to the two of them, however, was surely David Hume. Hume was Smith's best friend for more than a quarter of a century (see Rasmussen 2017), and his quarrel with Rousseau in 1766 created a considerable stir throughout the European literary world (see Zaretsky and Scott 2009). This quarrel occasioned a number of comments on Rousseau in the correspondence between Smith and Hume (see Corr. 90: 110; 93: 112–13; 96: 118; 103: 125; 109: 132; 111: 133–6; 112: 136–7). As might be expected, given the circumstances, these comments were mostly quite negative in tone. At one point Smith called Rousseau a 'great … Rascal' and a 'hypocritical Pedant' (Corr. 93: 112–13).

Rousseau never mentions Smith in any of his surviving letters or other writings, but Smith's references to Rousseau were not confined to his correspondence. In fact, one of Smith's earliest published works, an anonymous letter to the editors of the *Edinburgh Review* (1756), included a substantial review of Rousseau's *Discourse on the Origin of Inequality* (1755). In the letter Smith urged the *Review* to extend its ambit beyond Scottish publications and to bring news of the latest European works to Scottish readers. Smith's worry that Scotland's nascent cultural institutions ran the risk of becoming parochial indicates that he was aware that the intellectual life of Enlightenment Europe depended on the exchange and circulation of ideas (for analysis, see Lomonaco 2002). As an example of the sort of works that the *Review* should discuss, Smith turned to Rousseau's *Discourse*. He began by pointing to some unexpected parallels between Rousseau and Bernard Mandeville, the notorious defender of commercial vice, and then translated three long passages from the *Discourse* for the *Review*'s readers (Letter: 250–4). This letter demonstrates that Smith was actively engaged with Rousseau's thought from the early stages of his career, as he was writing *The Theory of Moral Sentiments* (1759). (The letter is discussed in more detail in a number of the contributions to this volume, particularly those of Hill, McHugh and Rasmussen.)

While the *Letter to the Edinburgh Review* was the earliest and most extensive of Smith's explicit discussions of Rousseau, it was not the only one. Smith also mentioned 'the ingenious and eloquent M. Rousseau of Geneva' in his *Considerations Concerning the First Formation of Languages* (1761), where he attempted to answer a question that Rousseau had raised in the *Discourse on Inequality*, that of how general names were first formed (see CL 2: 205). Smith also commented on Rousseau in a similar context in his lectures on rhetoric and *belles lettres* at Glasgow University in 1762–63 (see LRBL i.19: 9–10). Another reference to Rousseau can be found in Smith's essay *Of the Imitative Arts* (1795), in which he discussed Rousseau's argument in the *Dictionary of Music* (1768) that music has the power to imitate sights and events as well as sounds (see IA: 199–200). We have a record of a further comment by Smith on Rousseau from Barthélemy Faujas de Saint-Fond, a French geologist who visited Edinburgh in 1782. Smith 'spoke to me of Rousseau with a kind of religious respect', Saint-Fond reported: '"Voltaire," said he, "sought to correct the vices and the follies of mankind by laughing at them, and sometimes even getting angry with them; Rousseau, by the attraction of sentiment, and the force of conviction, drew the reader into the heart of reason. His *Contrat Social* will in time avenge him for all the persecutions he suffered"' (Saint-Fond 1907: 246). It is also worth noting that Smith owned many of Rousseau's works (in French), including the *Letter to M. d'Alembert on the Theater* (1758), the *Discourse on the Sciences and Arts* and Rousseau's replies to his critics, the *Letter on French Music*, his comic play *Narcisse*, his opera *Le Devin du village* (*The Village Soothsayer*), the *Encyclopédie* entry on *Political Economy*, and the *Discourse on Inequality* (all found in a collection of Rousseau's *Oeuvres diverses* from 1760), *Julie, or the New Heloïse* (1761), *Emile* (1762), *Letters Written from the Mountain* (1764), and a few miscellaneous volumes from later collections (see Mizuta 2000: 217–18).

Smith never mentions Rousseau by name in either of his books, *The Theory of Moral Sentiments* (1759) or *The Wealth of Nations*

(1776), but this omission is not particularly surprising: apart from Part VII of the former ('Of Systems of Moral Philosophy'), Smith rarely named any contemporaneous philosophers in these works, even the ones with whom he frequently and clearly engaged, such as Hume. Charles Griswold (1999: 47) suggests that Smith declined to explicitly name the thinkers with whom he engaged because he was 'intent on appealing directly to our everyday experience and reflection' and wanted to '[avoid] the impression that he wishes to debate another philosopher rather than engage the reflective reader in consideration of a view that naturally suggests itself'. In any event, there is good reason to believe that Smith had Rousseau in mind while writing several important passages in his books. Not only do some of his arguments appear to be directed at Rousseau, but at a few crucial junctures he also came close to duplicating phrases from Rousseau – phrases that, moreover, appeared in the very passages that he himself had translated in his *Letter to the Edinburgh Review*. As it happens, these paraphrases are found in some of the most famous passages in Smith's corpus.

The first of Smith's paraphrases of Rousseau appears in the passage on the ambitious 'poor man's son' in *The Theory of Moral Sentiments*. The poor man's son admires the advantages of the rich – their palaces, carriages, servants and so on – and imagines how much happier he would be if he were in their situation. Yet in the process of seeking these advantages for himself, he endures far more toil and anxiety than he would have endured by simply doing without them. In his attempt to distinguish himself, Smith writes, the poor man's son is forced to debase himself: 'he makes his court to all mankind; he serves those whom he hates, and is obsequious to those whom he despises' (TMS IV.1.8: 181). Similarly, in one of the passages from Rousseau's *Discourse on Inequality* that Smith translated for the *Edinburgh Review*, Rousseau declared that all too frequently the civilised individual 'makes his court to the great whom he hates, and to the rich whom he despises' (this is Smith's translation; see Letter: 253). The parallels here are too clear to miss.

The best-known of Smith's paraphrases of Rousseau – which is noted by the editors of the Glasgow Edition of *The Theory of Moral Sentiments* – comes just a few pages later, in the same paragraph as the only mention of the 'invisible hand' in that work. After dilating on the fact that people spend much of their lives striving for ever-more wealth and material goods, even though these things cannot guarantee true happiness and may even jeopardise it, Smith writes:

> And it is well that nature imposes upon us in this manner. It is this deception which rouses and keeps in continual motion the industry of mankind. It is this which first prompted them to cultivate the ground, to build houses, to found cities and commonwealths, and to invent and improve all the sciences and arts, which ennoble and embellish human life; which have entirely changed the whole face of the globe, have turned the rude forests of nature into agreeable and fertile plains ... (TMS IV.1.10: 183)

The last phrase of this quotation resembles another part of Rousseau's *Discourse* that Smith translated for the *Edinburgh Review*, in which Rousseau said that through the rise of civilisation 'the vast forests of nature were changed into agreeable plains' (Smith's translation; Letter: 252). As Michael Ignatieff (1986: 191) notes, this 'choice of words is so close to those of Rousseau ... that it cannot be mere coincidence'.

Still another parallel with Rousseau can be found in the famous 'butcher, brewer and baker' passage of *The Wealth of Nations*. Immediately before giving the example of the butcher, brewer and baker to prove his point, Smith remarks that it makes little sense for an individual in a commercial society to appeal to the benevolence of others in order to procure his needs. Instead, 'he will be more likely to prevail if he can interest their self-love in his favour, and shew them that it is for their own advantage to do for him what he requires of them' (WN I.ii.2: 26). In another passage from Rousseau's *Discourse* that Smith translated, Rousseau claimed that the rise of dependence in the modern world requires each individual to 'endeavour to interest [others] in his situation, and to make them find, either in reality or appearance, their advantage in labouring for his' (Smith's translation; Letter: 252). Smith did not duplicate Rousseau's language here to quite the extent that he did in the two passages from *The Theory of Moral Sentiments*, but some of the wording and much of the sentiment echo Rousseau's.

In these passages, and indeed throughout his corpus, Smith seemed to absorb some elements of Rousseau's views while simultaneously reacting against others. This complex blend of influence and reaction is part of what makes the Smith–Rousseau connection a subject ripe for further exploration.

Recent Scholarship on Rousseau and Smith

The scholarly literatures on Rousseau and Smith, taken individually, have long been, in the apt phrase of Frederick Neuhouser,
'unsurveyably vast' (2014: 15). Until fairly recently, however,
these literatures developed on parallel tracks, in almost complete
isolation from one another. Before the boom in Smith studies
that was set off by the bicentennial of *The Wealth of Nations*
and the publication of the Glasgow Edition of Smith's works in
1976, sustained examinations of Smith and Rousseau were very
few and far between (though see West 1971; Colletti 1972). A
handful of essays on the two appeared in the 1980s and 1990s
(see Ignatieff 1986; France 1989; Berry 1990; Barry 1995; Winch
1996), but the past decade and a half has seen an explosion
of scholarship on various aspects of this connection, including
studies on (inter alia) their assessments of commercial society,
Smith's 'sympathy' and Rousseau's 'pity', how they each envisioned the 'science of the legislator', and their respective views of
autonomy, civic republicanism, the division of labour, economics,
equality/inequality, human nature, morality/virtue, philosophy,
politics, poverty, progress, self-love and the theatre (see Pack
2000; Larrère 2002; Force 2003; Hurtado 2003; 2004; Berry
2004; Hanley 2006; 2008a; 2008b; 2009: 26–31, 36–42, 95–7,
102–9, 116–22, 137–40, 146, 157, 205; Rasmussen 2006; 2013;
Schliesser 2006; Neuhouser 2008: 230–2, 241–8, 262–3; Spector
2009; Vaughan 2009; Griswold 2010; Phillipson 2010: 145–57;
Kukathas 2014; Rathbone 2015; Stimson 2015; Niimura 2016;
Nazar forthcoming; Potkay 2017; Sagar forthcoming; Schwarze
and Scott working paper). There are also three book-length treatments of Smith and Rousseau. Those by Dennis C. Rasmussen
(2008) and Istvan Hont (2015) offer rather different interpretations of these thinkers' views of human nature and the virtues
and shortcomings of commercial society, while Charles Griswold
(2017) constructs a series of dialogues between Rousseau and
Smith on the human self and the problems that it faces, particularly in the modern world.

To this point much of the literature on the Smith–Rousseau connection has been authored by scholars who are primarily experts
on Smith, and they have tended to use Rousseau as something of a
foil with which to highlight or expose particular aspects of Smith's
outlook. The present volume includes a number of contributions

from scholars whose work focuses primarily on Rousseau and who therefore approach the relationship from the opposite direction. More broadly, the growing scholarly interest in the Smith–Rousseau connection makes this volume a timely one, particularly insofar as many of the contributions engage with – and occasionally challenge – the most recent developments in the field. As Hont notes,

> This is a good time to start . . . reconsidering the apparently opposite systems of Rousseau and Smith. We cannot but learn from the comparison. *Amour-propre*, the nation-state, and commerce are still the bread and butter of modern political theory, while *The Wealth of Nations* and *The Social Contract* are still among the most frequently mentioned books of modernity. (2015: 132)

The Present Volume

This volume brings together an international group of scholars working across the disciplines of philosophy, economics, political theory, literature and history. Each chapter explores an element of the moral and/or political philosophy of Rousseau and Smith.

The first section develops the themes of this Introduction with two essays engaging the latest scholarship on Rousseau and Smith. Ryan Patrick Hanley provides a critical engagement with one of the most important recent contributions to the topic, Istvan Hont's posthumously published *Politics in Commercial Society* (2015). Hanley considers the acute, and at times counter-intuitive, arguments that Hont develops in reaction to both the primary texts and the developing literature on the two thinkers. This is followed by a chapter from Mark Hulliung who offers a critical and cautionary note in light of the existing work on Rousseau and Smith. We should, Hulliung argues, be cautious when we compare and contrast two thinkers that we are not reading a conversation between them that may not, in reality, have taken place. This allows us to distinguish actual interlocutors from those who are made into interlocutors when their writings are compared and contrasted. This task of comparative Enlightenment studies provides another arena in which to consider Smith and Rousseau.

The remaining sections of the book are arranged thematically around key concepts that emerge from the work of Smith and Rousseau. In the second section, 'Self-interest and Sympathy', the essays explore the central tension between self-interest and sentimental sociability that marks such a significant shared concern of Rousseau and Smith. Christel Fricke continues the engagement with recent work by considering Ryan Hanley's and Frederick Neuhouser's apparently contrasting attempts to bring Smith and Rousseau together via their views on social comparison and its place in moral education. The apparent tension between the ideas of *amour-propre* and the danger of corruption from paying too much attention to the views of others creates a space in which to examine the idea of morality emerging from interpersonal comparison. Mark Hill follows with a chapter which discusses Rousseau and Smith in the context of a wider eighteenth-century debate. As noted above, Smith's first mention of Rousseau came in a review of the *Discourse on Inequality*, in which Smith compares Rousseau to Mandeville and situates him within a wider debate about the possibility of virtuous self-interest and its tension with the idea of socially directed morality. Hill examines Smith's reading of Rousseau and suggests an alternative account of Rousseau's place in the debate on self-interest and morality. In the final chapter in this section John McHugh continues the examination of Smith's analysis of Rousseau in the *Letter to the Edinburgh Review*. McHugh takes seriously the link between Rousseau and Mandeville that Smith makes in the letter. With it, he examines Smith's criticism of Mandeville in *The Theory of Moral Sentiments*, and reconstructs a Smithian response to Rousseau around the key issue of the corrupting or morally enhancing role of the desire for social approval.

The third section, 'Moral Sentiments and Spectatorship', continues the theme of interpersonal comparison but shifts the focus to the cultivation of the moral sentiments and the Smithian idea of an impartial spectator. Michael Schleeter examines the relationship between sympathy and virtue in Smith and Rousseau and questions the extent to which each thinker believed that commerce was in a position to erode sympathy and diminish virtue. He shifts the Rousseauian focus from the *Discourse* to *Emile* to explore the proposals for moral education that develop from the respective analyses of moral psychology. Tabitha Baker then expands the discussion to Rousseau's *Julie, or the New Heloïse*, arguing that it is through Rousseau's fiction that the complicated relationship between the two thinkers' ideas can be most evidently sourced. By examining Smithian themes in Rousseau's depiction of society and social interaction, Baker shows how Smithian concerns help us to understand the problems addressed by Rousseau and how these can be most acutely seen in the motif of the eighteenth-century English landscape garden developed in the novel. Adam Schoene then draws on the complex autobiographical approach of *Rousseau, Judge of Jean-Jacques: Dialogues* to examine the notion of the divided self and self-spectatorship that links Rousseau's search for self-awareness to Smith's notion of conscience as a voice within us that is produced by the socially evolved impartial spectator. By reading the *Dialogues* protagonist 'Rousseau's' plea to 'the Frenchman' for an unprejudiced witness in discourse with Smith's conception of the impartial spectator, in which satisfaction is derived from sympathy with the pleasure or pain of another, we come to see a shared conviction that justice is crucially dependent on the fair observation of others.

The fourth section, 'Commercial Society and Justice', continues the discussion of partiality, impartiality and justice in commercial society. Charles Griswold explores the intense concern with appearances and estrangement from one's true self that are often seen as characteristic of commercial society. He offers thoughts about what a dialogue between Rousseau and Smith about these issues might look like and how they shed light on contemporary notions of self-deception and authenticity. The chapter explores the social and political implications of this issue as each thinker seeks to deal with the idea of the role of self-deception in social life. Jimena Hurtado's chapter moves the discussion to the central social and political virtue of justice. She seeks to better understand Rousseau's and Smith's views of justice by placing them in dialogue with the traditional typology of justice – commutative, distributive and estimative – that we have inherited from Aristotle. Using Aristotle's framework, she furthers our understanding of the differences and coincidences between Smith and Rousseau, particularly as regards their view of justice in a commercial society and its relationship to the concept of equality.

In the final section, 'Politics and Freedom', Dennis C. Rasmussen reconsiders his earlier reading of Smith's reference to Rousseau as embodying 'the true spirit of a republican carried a little too far' (Letter: 251). Rasmussen explores the various senses in which someone could be understood as a republican in the eighteenth century and engages with those who have taken Smith's comment to refer to Rousseau's 'positive' or republican conception of liberty. He then uses Smith's reference as a way to reconsider Smith's and

Rousseau's respective conceptions of liberty. Jason Neidleman continues the focus on politics as he examines the role of the state in the formation of public opinion in the works of Smith and Rousseau. Both thinkers recognise the necessity of this endeavour, but both are troubled by its seeming incompatibility with the principles of personal liberty and popular sovereignty. Neidleman explores both thinkers' recognition of a legislator's paradox which leaves them with the task of reconciling political influence on public opinion with a desire to allow individual liberty. The crucial role of education and civic virtue for Rousseau sets his strategy for dealing with the paradox apart from Smith's more constrained understanding of the need for education and the rule of law. The volume concludes with a chapter by Neil Saccamano that investigates the problematic status of international relations in Rousseau and Smith. In particular it considers the implications for cosmopolitan politics that arise from the thinking of two writers who are so concerned about the social dimension of moral experience. Is an extended polity possible? Or does the constraint of particular sympathy or pity preclude so extensive a social order? Saccamano explores ideas of patriotism and belonging as they emerge from the accounts of sociability in Rousseau and Smith.

Bibliography

Barry, Norman (1995), 'Hume, Smith and Rousseau on Freedom', in Robert Wokler (ed.), *Rousseau and Liberty*, Manchester: Manchester University Press, 29–52.

Berry, Christopher J. (1990), 'Adam Smith: Commerce, Liberty and Modernity', in Peter Gilmour (ed.), *Philosophers of the Enlightenment*, Totowa, NJ: Barnes & Noble, 113–32.

Berry, Christopher J. (2004), 'Smith under Strain', *European Journal of Political Theory*, 3, 455–63.

Colletti, Lucio (1972), 'Mandeville, Rousseau and Smith', in *From Rousseau to Lenin: Studies in Ideology and Society*, trans. J. Merrington and J. White, New York: Monthly Review Press, 195–218.

Force, Pierre (2003), *Self-Interest before Adam Smith: A Genealogy of Economic Science*, Cambridge: Cambridge University Press.

France, Peter (1989), 'Rousseau, Adam Smith, and the Education of the Self', in George Craig and Margaret M. McGowan (eds), *Moy Qui Me Voy: The Writer and Self from Montaigne to Leiris*, Oxford: Oxford University Press, 30–51.

Griswold, Charles L. (1999), *Adam Smith and the Virtues of Enlightenment*, Cambridge: Cambridge University Press.

Griswold, Charles L. (2010), 'Smith and Rousseau in Dialogue: Sympathy, *Pitié*, Spectatorship and Narrative', in Vivienne Brown and Samuel Fleischacker (eds), *The Philosophy of Adam Smith*, London: Routledge, 59–84.

Griswold, Charles L. (2017), *Jean-Jacques Rousseau and Adam Smith: A Philosophical Encounter*, New York: Routledge.

Hanley, Ryan Patrick (2006), 'From Geneva to Glasgow: Rousseau and Adam Smith on the Theater and Commercial Society', *Studies in Eighteenth Century Culture*, 35, 177–202.

Hanley, Ryan Patrick (2008a), 'Commerce and Corruption: Rousseau's Diagnosis and Adam Smith's Cure', *European Journal of Political Theory*, 7, 137–58.

Hanley, Ryan Patrick (2008b), 'Enlightened Nation Building: The "Science of the Legislator" in Adam Smith and Rousseau', *American Journal of Political Science*, 52, 219–34.

Hanley, Ryan Patrick (2009), *Adam Smith and the Character of Virtue*, Cambridge: Cambridge University Press.

Hont, Istvan (2015), *Politics in Commercial Society*, ed. Béla Kapossy and Michael Sonenscher, Cambridge, MA: Harvard University Press.

Hurtado, Jimena (2003), 'The Risks of an Economic Agent: A Rousseauian Reading of Adam Smith', *Colombian Economic Journal*, 1, 194–220.

Hurtado, Jimena (2004), 'Bernard Mandeville's Heir: Adam Smith or Jean-Jacques Rousseau on the Possibility of Economic Analysis', *European Journal of the History of Economic Thought*, 11, 1–31.

Ignatieff, Michael (1986), 'Smith, Rousseau and the Republic of Needs', in T. C. Smout (ed.), *Scotland and Europe, 1200–1850*, Edinburgh: John Donald, 187–206.

Kukathas, Chandran (2014), 'Das Rousseau Problem: Adam Smith's Politics and Economics', *Adam Smith Review*, 7, 174–80.

Larrère, Catherine (2002), 'Adam Smith et Jean-Jacques Rousseau: sympathie et pitié', *Kairos*, 20, 73–94.

Lomonaco, Jeffrey (2002), 'Adam Smith's "Letter to the Authors of the *Edinburgh Review*"', *Journal of the History of Ideas*, 63, 659–76.

Mizuta, Hiroshi (ed.) (2000), *Adam Smith's Library: A Catalogue*, Oxford: Clarendon.

Nazar, Hina (forthcoming), 'The Eyes of Others: Rousseau and Adam Smith on Judgment and Autonomy', in Thomas Pfau and Vivasvan Soni (eds), *Judgment & Action: New Interdisciplinary Essays*, Evanston: Northwestern University Press.

Neuhouser, Frederick (2008), *Rousseau's Theodicy of Self-Love: Evil, Rationality, and the Drive for Recognition*, Oxford: Oxford University Press.

Neuhouser, Frederick (2014), *Rousseau's Critique of Inequality: Reconstructing the Second Discourse*, Cambridge: Cambridge University Press.

Niimura, Satoshi (2016), 'Adam Smith: Egalitarian or Anti-Egalitarian? His Responses to Hume and Rousseau's Critiques of Inequality', *International Journal of Social Economics*, 43, 888–903.

Pack, Spencer J. (2000), 'The Rousseau–Smith Connection: Towards an Understanding of Professor West's "Splenetic Smith"', *History of Economic Ideas*, 8, 35–62.

Phillipson, Nicholas (2010), *Adam Smith: An Enlightened Life*, New Haven, CT: Yale University Press.

Potkay, Adam (2017), 'Pity, Gratitude, and the Poor in Rousseau and Adam Smith', *Studies in Eighteenth-Century Culture*, 46, 162–82.

Rasmussen, Dennis C. (2006), 'Rousseau's "Philosophical Chemistry" and the Foundations of Adam Smith's Thought', *History of Political Thought*, 27, 620–41.

Rasmussen, Dennis C. (2008), *The Problems and Promise of Commercial Society: Adam Smith's Response to Rousseau*, University Park: Pennsylvania State University Press.

Rasmussen, Dennis C. (2013), 'Adam Smith and Rousseau: Enlightenment and Counter-Enlightenment', in Christopher J. Berry, Maria Pia Paganelli and Craig Smith (eds), *The Oxford Handbook of Adam Smith*, Oxford: Oxford University Press, 54–76.

Rasmussen, Dennis C. (2017), *The Infidel and the Professor: David Hume, Adam Smith, and the Friendship That Shaped Modern Thought*, Princeton: Princeton University Press.

Rathbone, Mark (2015), 'Love, Money and Madness: Money in the Economic Philosophies of Adam Smith and Jean-Jacques Rousseau', *South African Journal of Philosophy*, 3, 39–89.

Sagar, Paul (forthcoming), 'Smith and Rousseau, after Hume and Mandeville', *Political Theory*.

Saint-Fond, Barthélemy Faujas de (1907), *A Journey Through England and Scotland to the Hebrides in 1784*, trans. Sir Archibald Geikie, vol. 2, Glasgow: Hugh Hopkins.

Schliesser, Eric (2006), 'Adam Smith's Benevolent and Self-Interested Conception of Philosophy', in Leonidas Montes and Eric Schliesser (eds), *New Voices on Adam Smith*, New York: Routledge, 328–57.

Schwarze, Michelle A., and John T. Scott (working paper), 'Mutual Sympathy and the Moral Economy: Adam Smith Reviews Rousseau.'

Spector, Céline (2009), 'De Rousseau à Smith: esthétique démocratique de la sensibilité et théorie économiste de l'esthétique', in Jesper Rasmussen (ed.), *La Valeur de l'art: Exposition, marché, critique et public au dix-huitième siècle*, Paris: Champion, 215–44.

Stimson, Shannon C. (2015), 'The General Will after Rousseau: Smith and Rousseau on Sociability and Inequality', in James Farr and David Lay Williams (eds), *The General Will: The Evolution of a Concept*, Cambridge: Cambridge University Press, 350–81.

Vaughan, Sharon K. (2009), 'The Noble Poor: Jean Jacques Rousseau and Adam Smith', in *Poverty, Justice, and Western Political Thought*, Lanham, MD: Lexington, 63–104.

West, E. G. (1971), 'Adam Smith and Rousseau's *Discourse on Inequality*: Inspiration or Provocation?', *Journal of Economic Issues*, 5, 56–70.

Winch, Donald (1996), 'The Secret Concatenation', in *Riches and Poverty: An Intellectual History of Political Economy in Britain, 1750–1834*, Cambridge: Cambridge University Press, 57–89.

Zaretsky, Robert, and John T. Scott (2009), *The Philosophers' Quarrel: Rousseau, Hume, and the Limits of Human Understanding*, New Haven, CT: Yale University Press.

2

On the Place of Politics in Commercial Society

Ryan Patrick Hanley

Politics in Commercial Society (Hont 2015) is remarkable for at least two reasons. First, it is the final work of one of the twentieth century's great students of Adam Smith and the Scottish Enlightenment. Its author, the late Istvan Hont, was a pre-eminent voice in the scholarly debates on Smith and the Scots for many decades, and through both his consummately erudite published work and his teaching at Cambridge he did as much as any scholar in recent decades to shape our understanding of these subjects.

Politics in Commercial Society is also remarkable for a second reason. Its aim is to present a comparative study of the political theories of Smith and Rousseau – a subject that, as readers of this volume know well, has become a thriving industry in recent years. Hont himself was long interested in the Smith–Rousseau connection; his 2015 book owes its genesis to several sets of lectures on Rousseau and Smith that he delivered between 2009 and 2010 in Oxford, Boston and Jena.[1]

As a contribution to the comparative study of Smith and Rousseau, Hont's book is valuable on two fronts, one methodological and one substantive. Yet the book, it must be said, is far from the magnum opus for which some might have hoped. The author's untimely passing seems to have rendered it impossible for him to have added any citations to scholarship. The text also makes several substantive claims that one wonders whether he might not in time have revised or reworked, or at least provided further evidence to support. In light of this, what follows has three aims: first, to call attention to the work's most valuable substantive and methodological claims; second, to frame it by setting its claims in the context of recent scholarship; and third, to raise some questions regarding three of the book's core theses.

Hont's book begins with a striking claim. In its opening sentence we are told that it 'is about commercial society and how to understand politics in it' (1). The methodological significance of this claim deserves attention. The suggestion is that this is no mere exercise in the study of the history of political thought as it has been conventionally understood. The study of the history of political ideas is here being proposed, indeed, less as an end in itself than as a means to better understanding our political present; hence the claim in the following sentence that the aim of the work is 'to tease apart the different sorts of political vision that are currently relevant to us by using the history of political thought as a guide' (1). Hont's claims here are consistent with his previous work, likewise animated by a deep appreciation of the nature of and limits imposed by contemporary political and economic realities. But these claims also deserve our attention for the way in which they distinguish Hont's approach to the history of political thought from other approaches, especially those conventionally associated with the university of his employment. Hont's masterful grasp of the intellectual context of Smith and Rousseau's eighteenth-century world clearly distinguishes him even among the 'contextualists' of the Cambridge school. But to this grasp of context Hont joins a profound sensitivity to real politics today – a sensitivity that renders his work, to my mind, reminiscent less of the sort of history of political thought done at Cambridge than that done at Oxford by Isaiah Berlin.[2] In any case, what is clear is that Hont wants us to see Smith and Rousseau 'not just as authors of dead texts but also as presences in our contemporary theorizing' (24).

Hont is particularly concerned to employ the history of political thought to illuminate one specific aspect of our contemporary political world: namely our idea of the state. Indeed, the principal substantive aim of the work (which, he tells us, the title of the book is itself meant to suggest) is to delineate 'the problems involved in identifying the kind of state that might best complement a commercial society' (4). It is this concern that specifically animates Hont's turn to Rousseau and Smith. Hont regards the 'modern representative and commercial republic' as 'a result of a synthesis between the work of Rousseau and the work of Smith', and ultimately it is this belief that motivates his efforts to 'reconstruct the shape of the lost grand-political-theory projects of

Rousseau and Smith', in the hope that fuller appreciation of their contributions will enable us 'to pass judgment on this fusion and learn some of the inner secrets of modern statehood as understood after Hobbes' (24).

Hont's efforts on this front ultimately give rise to what is arguably the most valuable substantive element of the book. In order to uncover the modern state's origins, Hont turns to a careful examination of Smith's 'history of natural authority' (67), and in so doing he helpfully illuminates Smith's intricate and subtle account of the origins and genealogy of political authority and government. As he convincingly demonstrates, Smith's account centres on the emergence of political authority in the shepherding stage of the stadial evolution of society. Further, in this stage, wealth constituted 'the most important source of authority' (79), insofar as 'wealth could create dependency, which was the real source of power' (80). And it is here that the account becomes especially penetrating. As Smith went on to demonstrate, *contra* Rousseau – and as Hont goes on to show – the same evil that created both inequality and dependence, in time served to ameliorate the most pernicious aspects of inequality and dependence. Tracing Smith's genealogy of political authority in a manner that makes clear how Smith's stadial theory parallels the historical account of European economic development in Book III of *The Wealth of Nations*, Hont calls attention to the grounds of Smith's faith that 'the system of commercial society had a long-term beneficial tendency, creating more and more equality and material well-being for the majority' (53). And here, as Hont makes clear, lies Smith's key departure from Rousseau: whereas Rousseau saw the progress of commercial society as inevitably exacerbating the inequalities to which the birth of private property had given rise, Smith regarded the progress of commercial society as an engine of the mitigation and amelioration of precisely those economic inequalities and power asymmetries that so frightened Rousseau.

Hont is, of course, keenly aware how crucial this idea is for our contemporary political moment. For the most part he does not take this up explicitly, leaving it to others to think through how Smith and Rousseau might speak to our contemporary inequality debates.[3] Instead he focuses on other aspects of the political implications of commercial progress. One especially interesting aspect concerns Smith's analysis of the future political prospects of the commercial state. As Hont notes, Smith was deeply troubled by 'the loss of military capability in commercial society', regarding this as a 'systematic problem that still had relevance for the moderns' (82). Hont also helpfully calls attention to the fact that 'Smith explained repeatedly' that 'there was an incompatibility between economic development and warfare', as commercial occupations 'made the population disinclined to wage war' (84). As a consequence, the modern state faces a potential existential crisis as a direct result of its material progress – a theme that shaped Smith's 'republicanism' and which may also have relevance today.

Ultimately these two claims – that Smith valued commercial society for its capacity to relieve poverty and spread freedom, and that Smith's genealogy of the evolution of authority ran counter to Rousseau's in its final implications – are among the most valuable claims of Hont's book. Versions of them, of course, will already be familiar to readers of his previous work; both his agenda-setting introduction to his *Wealth and Virtue* (Hont and Ignatieff 1983) volume as well as his essay on Smith's political theory (Hont 2009) anticipate both claims to some degree. And this fact, again in light of the unfortunate absence of any references to the secondary literature, may lead readers to wonder how other claims made here situate themselves against other extant interpretations. It is clear that Hont himself regarded his study as an alternative to many of these other extant interpretations, and sought to advance an argument that would compel its audience to sit up and take notice. Thus in the first few pages of the book it is announced that he seeks 'to produce parallels and contrasts that are surprising' (1), to advance a set of claims regarding the Smith–Rousseau connection that 'look paradoxical' on their face and are likely to appear 'seemingly radical' when first encountered, and which the author himself suspects are likely to be regarded by some as evidence of an 'apparently perverse approach' (2–3).

Hont's 'surprising' or 'paradoxical' or 'radical' or 'perverse' claim is this: that while 'it is not unusual to contrast Rousseau and Smith, with the former seen as an enemy of, and the latter as an apologist for, modernity', the truth is that 'many of Smith's ideas were much closer to Rousseau's than is commonly thought' (1–2). The specific form this claim takes here is that 'Smith the political economist and Rousseau, political economy's arch critic, shared moral foundations' (21), even as they came to develop 'different political theories attached to the moral theory' (22; cf. 25). It is easy to imagine how radical and surprising such claims must have seemed to those generalist audiences fortunate to have heard these lectures a decade ago. But scholars familiar with the now-extensive literature on the Smith–Rousseau connection – to say nothing of the past two decades' scholarship on each of these thinkers taken independently – are likely to find these claims far from surprising or radical today.

This fact makes particularly regrettable the absence of references to current scholarship, as it renders it difficult for the reader to distinguish what may be novel here from what is already generally known and appreciated. It should be said that even in the absence of citations, Hont gives evidence of considerable familiarity with (and indeed disdain for) extant interpretations; thus a reading of Smith is dismissed as 'an inexplicable howler on the part of some modern interpreters' (34), and a reading advanced by 'some commentators' on Rousseau is said to have 'virtually no merit' (55). One wishes that Hont had had a chance to name names here; however much the philosophical discourses of Smith and Rousseau's day may have thrived on the indirect signalling that leaves targets identifiable only to those in the know, modern scholarship is hardly advanced by opacity. The absence of citations also renders it difficult for interested scholars to follow up on how other scholars have discussed these points. It is well beyond the scope of this essay to provide a comprehensive guide to the extant scholarship on all of the many insights contained in Hont's book. But to take a handful of examples from the book's opening pages, those intrigued by Hont's account of 'The Jean-Jacques Rousseau Problem' (1) will want to read an essay by Chandran Kukathas (2014). Those who find compelling the claim that the *Letter to the Edinburgh Review* 'offers an important key to a possible new reading of both Rousseau and Smith' (2) will do well to read several important studies by Dennis Rasmussen (2006; 2013). Those drawn to the claim that Rousseau too deserves to be regarded as 'a theorist of commercial society' (2) will want to consult a number of studies of Rousseau's political economy.[4] Those persuaded by the claim that 'what Smith wished to say was that their social relations within their own society became market-governed' (3) will do well to engage the authoritative study of this idea by James Otteson (2002). Those interested in how Smith's conception of commercial society compares to Hegel's vision of civil society (5) should consult Lisa Herzog's book (2013). Those who want to follow up on the claim that 'endorsing Hobbes's key

argument was one of the purposes of Rousseau's second *Discourse*'
(12) should compare this to, among others, recent studies of Robin
Douglass (2015) and Richard Tuck (2016). Those interested in
Smith's response to Rousseau's concept of pity in the opening
of *The Theory of Moral Sentiments* (27ff.) will want to consult
an indispensable study of Charles Griswold's (2010).[5] Those
who find compelling the claim that 'it is widely – but wrongly
– believed that for Rousseau, socially constructed self-love was
a purely negative agency in human history' (41) will want to
consult, among others, books by Laurence Cooper (1999) and
Frederick Neuhouser (2008).

Hont, of course, makes a number of genuinely novel claims, but
some readers are likely to find these contentious, or at least to think
that considerable additional evidence would need to be adduced in
order to render them persuasive. Three of the book's theses deserve
particular notice on this front. First is its characterisation of where
Smith is best placed on the continuum of self-love and sociability.
One of Hont's main theses in the book is that Smith should be
seen as closer to Hobbes than Hutcheson. In advancing this claim,
Hont in fact uses some of the strongest language to be found in the
book; in this vein Hutcheson is described as having offered Smith
'a doctrinal indoctrination into republican politics and Christian
neo-Stoic ethics, based on a visceral hatred of commercial society'
(17), and Smith, for his part, is said to have been 'a dissident pupil
of Hutcheson' (19) and to have 'rebelled against Hutcheson' (57).
This is, of course, a very different view of Smith's 'never-to-be-
forgotten' teacher and their relationship than that to which many
of us have grown accustomed. But what really matters for Hont is
that in distancing himself from Hutcheson, Smith came closer to
Hobbes. And hence we are strikingly told that Smith 'portrayed
himself as someone who had properly developed the Hobbesian
stream – that is the selfish system . . . to its proper conclusion', that
The Theory of Moral Sentiments is best regarded as 'a treatise in
enhanced Hobbism and Epicureanism' (32), and that the ultimate
goal of Smith and Rousseau alike was to return back 'to the more
pure and original Hobbesian (or Epicurean) idiom' (54).

Whether or not this rings true with what some readers may
hope to find in *The Theory of Moral Sentiments*, to be persuasive
it would need to be squared with Smith's forthright critiques
of the selfish system (e.g. TMS VII.ii.4) – which seem, on their
face, to read much more like rejections of this system rather than

efforts to refine it. Further, to render these claims convincing, one would need somehow to account for or explain away Smith's many discussions across *The Theory of Moral Sentiments* of such core ideas as the love of praiseworthiness, the pre-eminence of self-command, and indeed the very idea of virtue itself – ideas that seem only to have grown ever more significant as Smith revised his book over its several editions, and which would seem to place Smith squarely within the 'party of virtue' from which Hont is concerned to distance him (32). Take, for example, the reading of TMS III.iii.4 given here. As Hont rightly notes, Smith here dismisses what he calls the 'soft power of humanity' and the 'feeble spark of benevolence' as insufficient bulwarks against the sheer force of low self-love; these are indeed, as Hont says, 'feeble agents' (37). But what then restrains self-love? Smith's own claim is that it is rather 'a stronger love, a more powerful affection, which generally takes place upon such occasions; the love of what is honourable and noble, of the grandeur, and dignity, and superiority of our characters' (TMS III.iii.4: 136). It seems difficult to read this as evidence of an allegiance to Hobbesianism; to do so would require exclusively privileging the concept of 'superiority' (and indeed assuming that the sort of superiority to which Smith here refers is akin to the thymotic superiority Hobbes describes) in addition to dismissing or reading away Smith's explicit invocations of such anti-Hobbesian categories as 'the love of what is honourable and noble' and 'grandeur' and 'dignity'. What Hobbes sought to reject as the empty prattling of muddle-headed Peripatetics and Scholastics are for Smith real concepts that do real work.

Further, to render convincing the claim that Smith is, at the end of the day, best understood as an enhanced Hobbesian, more would also need to be done to justify the claim that Smith, like both Rousseau and Hobbes, rejects sociability. This is itself another core thesis of the book; when Hont refers to the common moral philosophy that formed the shared foundation of Smith's and Rousseau's projects, he has in mind 'their common denial of the natural sociability and morality of man' (48) – hence the claim that Smith and Rousseau both 'begin their modeling of the history of morality and government by taking Hobbes's anti-Aristotelian denial of primary human sociability as their starting points' (53). But this point needs to be handled carefully. It is most certainly the case that Smith does not use the language of natural sociability in any explicit sense, and this is hardly insignificant.[6] But it is not clear that the decision not to employ such language is tantamount to an embrace of Hobbesianism. Again, to make this convincing, we would need to see how this squares with other prominent and familiar claims in *The Theory of Moral Sentiments*. As readers of this volume know very well, Smith's book begins with the claim that 'how selfish soever man may be supposed, there are evidently some principles in his nature which interest him in the fortune of others, and render their happiness necessary to him' – a claim that is difficult to read on its face as anything but a repudiation of Hobbes (TMS I.i.1.1: 9). Thus here again, in order to render persuasive the strong claims being made with regard to Smith's ostensible Hobbesianism or Epicureanism, a significantly more extended argument would need to be given. In the absence of this, and given Smith's many obvious and clear borrowings from such diverse schools as Stoicism and Cynicism and Christian moralism, among so many others, it seems closer to the truth (and admittedly much less surprising and radical) to say, as others recently have, that Smith's own system is less an attempt to revive any one school than an attempt to synthesise elements of multiple schools in the manner of a modern Eclectic.[7] For all of these reasons, I find Hont more persuasive at those moments when, rather than distancing Smith from Hutcheson and aligning him with refined Hobbesian or Epicureanism, he portrays him as subscribing to the more moderate belief that 'self-regarding and other-regarding motives were not in opposition; they could be combined' (33), and as thinking that the key task is in fact to define 'the balance, or the propriety, one can establish between self-regarding and other-regarding sentiments' (38).[8]

A second thesis of the book demanding further scrutiny concerns Smith's orientation to 'natural history'. Hont's prominent focus on Smith's use of methods of analysis characteristic of natural history is an essential component of his project to distance Smith from Hutcheson. And in so doing, Hont not only means to bring Smith closer to Hobbes, but also closer to Hume. In this vein, Hont claims that the point of departure for Smith's ethics lies not simply in an embrace of 'Hobbes's anti-Aristotelian denial of primary human sociability', as noted above; perhaps more to the point, he says that 'Smith's starting point was Hume's skepticism toward the theories of Hutcheson' (41). This matters, it is suggested, not merely because of the way it shaped Smith's orientation to Hutcheson, but also because of the form and shape it gave to his moral philosophy. Specifically, Hont says, the consequence of this Humean influence is that *The Theory of Moral Sentiments* 'is best read as a natural or theoretical history of sympathy in the Humean mold' (35). This is perhaps the most frequently repeated claim in the book: namely that *The Theory of Moral Sentiments* is a 'natural history of sympathy' (35, 42, 47, 49, 56), indeed, one 'modeled on Hume's natural history of justice' (49). But this is, at the very least, contentious. Hont is clearly right to say that Smith hoped to execute a 'natural history of government' (49) akin to Hume's natural history of justice; what we have of his jurisprudence lectures bears ample witness to that. But the project of the *Lectures on Jurisprudence* seems very different from that of *The Theory of Moral Sentiments* – indeed so different that we may wish to pause before too readily accepting the claim that the 'natural history of government' that lies at the heart of the former can be readily analogised to the natural history of sympathy that is said to lie at the heart of the latter.

Without denying that *The Theory of Moral Sentiments* tells a developmental story, the story it tells is one of the development of the sentiments and the character of the individual rather than the evolutionary development of the needs and wants of the species. Thus, unless it can be shown that Smith subscribed to some version of the notion that ontogeny recapitulates phylogeny – a claim, I suspect, for which few would wish to argue – the suggestion that *The Theory of Moral Sentiments* can be understood as 'Smith's conjectural history of the origins of commercial society through sketching out the mechanisms underlying the rise of the sociable self' is at least questionable (35). Hont himself defines history as 'conceptual sequencing along a timeline' (52). If so, it would need to be shown that *The Theory of Moral Sentiments* in fact offers an account of sympathy across a timeline of the sort that Hume employs in his natural history of religion or elsewhere. Yet it is difficult for me to see evidence of such a timeline either in Hont's account of *The Theory of Moral Sentiments* or in the book itself. While reading these claims I was reminded of an interview that another eminent senior scholar of the history of eighteenth-century political ideas generously granted me nearly twenty years ago. In the course of conversation, that scholar asked me if I saw evidence of 'history' in *The Theory of Moral Sentiments*. I answered 'no'. Two additional decades of study have led me to rethink many of the positions to which that young student was then attached, but this is not one of them. All told, Hont's efforts to distance Smith and his political theory from the sort of 'analytical political-legal theory' with which later liberalism would come to be associated is welcome (75). Yet one wonders whether turning from ideal theory to historically inflected moral theory is the only route available, or the one that best captures the route in fact taken in *The Theory of Moral Sentiments*.

A third thesis central to Hont's book that deserves examination concerns its depiction of Smith's response to Rousseau's account of the origin of government. A principal claim of the work as a whole (and indeed, as noted above, one of its most valuable claims) is that Smith presented 'an alternative history of government and law than what Rousseau presented' (65). The key substantive claim on this front is that Smith's account of the sequential emergence of institutional authority is given in the form of a linear historical progression from executive to judicial to legislative power. This is said to be 'the reverse sequence from the one Rousseau used' (79), and Hont compellingly argues that in crafting this argument, and specifically with regard to the emergence of judicial power, Smith was 'consciously arguing against Rousseau' (51). This is an important and original claim, and Hont is right to call attention to it. Yet the way this claim is developed here has the potential to be misleading. And this matters not because the truth points in a direction different from Hont's thesis, but because it obscures the full force, and indeed the genuinely radical implications, of Hont's thesis pursued to its conclusion.

To see this requires reconstructing the way Hont presents the differences of Smith and Rousseau on this point. The main claim demanding attention is that regarding the two thinkers' respective orientations to what Hont calls the 'property first, government second, sequence' (69). This, as Hont makes clear with reference to Smith's own words in his *Letter to the Edinburgh Review*, is Rousseau's position; hence Smith describes both Rousseau and Mandeville as subscribing to the view that

> those laws of justice, which maintain the present inequality among mankind, were originally the inventions of the cunning and the power-ful, in order to maintain or acquire an unnatural and unjust superior-ity over the rest of their fellow creatures. (Letter: 251; quoted by Hont at 21–2)

In saying this, Smith clearly had in mind Rousseau's notorious claim in the *Second Discourse* (and perhaps also a parallel claim in Rousseau's *Discourse on Political Economy*) that the historical social contract that gave rise to government is merely a swindle of the poor by the rich.[9] As Hont notes, Rousseau's claim is that 'private property as a legalized system was born of a confidence trick' (52), in which the rich 'duped the poor into believing that the suppression of violence was in their interest too' in response to their recognition of the need to quell 'the anarchy preceding government', itself best understood 'as a conflict between two fundamental social classes, the "rich" and the "poor"' (72). As an account of Rousseau's position on the origin of government, this seems right. It also captures Smith's understanding of Rousseau's views on the origin of government. But how does it map on to Smith's own account of the origin of government?

Hont claims that Rousseau's and Smith's accounts are in total opposition on this front. Commenting on the quotation above in which Smith presents Rousseau's views, Hont immediately adds that 'Smith did not comment, but anybody who reads his works knows that he disapproved' (22). He repeats this claim later, even more strongly. At the start of his third chapter the block quotation above is repeated in full, and followed by the insistence that not only did Smith 'disagree' with this account of government's origin, but he in fact 'staked his entire later *oeuvre* on his disagreement with this account of the origins of justice' (49; cf. 69). But readers of Smith's *oeuvre* may be inclined to pause at this point. In fact, so far from rejecting this claim, Smith forthrightly and directly and repeatedly argued for precisely this claim in his own name. Indeed, the single most direct statement of the origin of government to be found in his published works is a restatement of this claim. Thus in Book Five of *The Wealth of Nations*, in the course of developing his claim that insofar as 'the affluence of the few supposes the indigence of the many', a means of defence needed to be contrived in preparation for that moment when 'the affluence of the rich excited the indignation of the poor' (WN V.i.b.2: 709). Herein lies the origin of government:

> civil government, so far as it is instituted for the security of property, is in reality instituted for the defence of the rich against the poor, or of those who have some property against those who have none at all. (WN V.i.b.12: 715)[10]

The same claim is advanced in the *Lectures on Jurisprudence* in its account of the conditions that rendered the establishment of government 'absolutely necessary'. Thus when

> some have great wealth and others nothing, it is necessary that the arm of authority should be continually stretched forth, and permanent laws or regulations made which may ascertain the property of the rich from the inroads of the poor, who would otherwise make incroachments upon it, and settle in what the infringement of this property consists and in what cases they will be liable to punishment. Laws and government may be considered in this and in every case a combination of the rich to oppress the poor, and preserve to themselves the inequality of the goods which would otherwise soon be destroyed by the attacks of the poor, who if not hindered by the government would soon reduce the others to an equality with themselves by open violence. (LJA: 22–3; cf. LJB: 19–20)

Taken together, Smith's two most direct statements on government's origin, so far from 'disagreeing' with Rousseau's property-first, government-second account, are in fact explicit affirmations of this claim. Hont is not unaware of Smith's position on this front, and alludes to the fact that in Smith's account 'the state starts with a very great, a brutally great, level of inequality' (80). Yet Hont makes no reference to either of these passages, which seem to demand response if the claim that Smith is rejecting Rousseau's account of the origin of government is to be persuasive.

This is a doubly a shame, because accounting for them would probably render Hont's ultimate argument stronger. His aim, again, is to illuminate Smith's response to Rousseau's account of the progress of the commercial state; where Rousseau sees only a state that is born in inequality and destined to reify those inequalities, Smith counters that the commercial state is capable of transcending the worst effects of those inequalities. Yet Smith's argument on this front only appears all the more remarkable in the light of the degree to which he shared Rousseau's concern that government was born out of property inequalities. Put somewhat differently, where Rousseau claims that commercial progress reifies political injustice, Smith's response is that commercial progress rectifies political injustice – in Hont's words, 'commerce created liberty' insofar as 'commerce created more equality in wealth than there had been at the beginning of the accumulation of wealth' (80). This, of course, is a claim that brings us back to the question of whether Smith believes that economic liberty will supplant political liberty. Joseph Cropsey – whose pioneering study of Smith's relationship to Hobbes has not been supplanted by Hont's analysis – long ago described Smith as advancing the 'eclipse' of political philosophy by economics.[11] Cropsey's account invites us to wonder whether in fact Smith laid the foundation for an economics that would in time eclipse not only political philosophy but politics itself. Put in the terms invited by Hont's study, the crucial but ultimately unanswered question of this study is whether in the long run politics in commercial society is ultimately either necessary or possible.

Notes

For helpful comments on this piece, the author is extremely grateful to Sam Fleischacker, Charles Griswold, Ralph Lerner, Eric Schliesser, John Scott and Craig Smith.

1. See Kapossy and Sonenscher (2015: ix and n. 1). Parenthetical citations are to Hont's text.
2. This is meant as a compliment, though no doubt critics of Berlin's contributions to the history of ideas are unlikely to see it as such. I elaborate on Berlin's approach in Hanley (forthcoming). On Hont's orientation to the Cambridge school, see Bourke (2016). Bourke also calls helpful attention to Hont's presentist intentions for the history of political thought (2016: 11).
3. For important studies in this vein, see especially Boucoyannis (2013), Neuhouser (2013) and Rasmussen (2016). Smith's and Rousseau's views on economic inequality each receive chapters in Williams (forthcoming).
4. See most recently Rousselière (2016). I treat much of the previous literature on Rousseau as political economist in Hanley (2013).
5. An expanded version of this argument will appear in Griswold's *Adam Smith and Jean-Jacques Rousseau: A Philosophical Encounter* (forthcoming). For additional helpful background on how Smith's claims in this opening chapter relate to Hobbes and Mandeville and especially Hume, see Fleischacker (2012). These should especially be read alongside Hont's claim regarding the 'generalization of the pity mechanism to every conceivable pattern of morality' (20).
6. The implications of this point promise to be helpfully developed in Griswold's *Smith and Rousseau: A Philosophical Encounter*.

7. On this claim, see e.g. Garrett and Hanley (2015: 278) and the works there cited.
8. Hont himself locates Rousseau and Smith 'in the middle of a moral and economic spectrum', but his spectrum's poles are ancient Cynicism and modern Epicureanism (91).
9. I address Smith's possible access to and engagement with Rousseau's political economy essay in Hanley (2016).
10. For helpful commentary on this passage, see Pack and Schliesser (2006).
11. Smith's relationship to Hobbes is a principal theme of Cropsey's *Polity and Economy: An Interpretation of the Principles of Adam Smith* (1957). The quotation is from Cropsey (1987: 635).

Bibliography

Boucoyannis, Deborah (2013), 'The Equalizing Hand: Why Adam Smith Thought the Market Should Produce Wealth Without Steep Inequality', *Perspectives on Politics*, 11, 1051–71.

Bourke, Richard (2016), 'Revising the Cambridge School: Republicanism Revisited', *Political Theory* (doi: 10.1177/0090591716672231; last accessed 3 December 2016).

Cooper, Laurence (1999), *Rousseau, Nature, and the Problem of the Good Life*, University Park: Penn State University Press.

Cropsey, Joseph (1957), *Polity and Economy: An Interpretation of the Principles of Adam Smith*, The Hague: Martinus Nijhoff.

Cropsey, Joseph (1987), 'Adam Smith', in J. Cropsey and L. Strauss (eds), *History of Political Philosophy*, 3rd edn, Chicago: University of Chicago Press, 607–30.

Douglass, Robin (2015), *Rousseau and Hobbes: Nature, Free Will and the Passions*, Oxford: Oxford University Press.

Fleischacker, Samuel (2012), 'Sympathy in Hume and Smith: A Contrast, Critique, and Reconstruction', in Christel Fricke and Dagfinn Føllesdall (eds), *Intersubjectivity and Objectivity in Adam Smith and Edmund Husserl*, Frankfurt: Ontos Verlag, 273–311.

Garrett, Aaron, and Ryan Hanley (2015), 'Adam Smith: History and Impartiality', in A. Garrett and J. A. Harris (eds), *Scottish Philosophy in the Eighteenth-Century, vol. 1: Morals, Politics, Art, Religion*, Oxford: Oxford University Press, 239–82.

Griswold, Charles (2010), 'Smith and Rousseau in Dialogue: Sympathy, *Pitié*, Spectatorship and Narrative', *Adam Smith Review*, 5, 59–84.

Griswold, Charles (forthcoming), *Adam Smith and Jean-Jacques Rousseau: A Philosophical Encounter*, London: Routledge.

Hanley, Ryan Patrick (2013), 'Political Economy and Individual Liberty', in Eve Grace and Christopher Kelly (eds), *The Challenge of Rousseau*, Cambridge: Cambridge University Press, 34–56.

Hanley, Ryan Patrick (2016), 'Adam Smith and the Encyclopédie', *Adam Smith Review*, 9, 218–36.

Hanley, Ryan Patrick (forthcoming), 'Berlin on the Nature and Purpose of the History of Ideas', in Joshua Cherniss and Steven B. Smith (eds), *The Cambridge Companion to Isaiah Berlin*, Cambridge: Cambridge University Press.

Herzog, Lisa (2013), *Inventing the Market: Smith, Hegel and Political Theory*, Oxford: Oxford University Press.

Hont, Istvan (2009), 'Adam Smith's History of Law and Government as Political Theory', in Richard Bourke and Raymond Geuss (eds). *Political Judgement: Essays for John Dunn*, Cambridge: Cambridge University Press, 131–71.

Hont, Istvan (2015), *Politics in Commercial Society: Jean-Jacques Rousseau and Adam Smith*, ed. Béla Kapossy and Michael Sonenscher, Cambridge, MA: Harvard University Press.

Hont, Istvan, and Michael Ignatieff (1983), 'Needs and Justice in the *Wealth of Nations*: An Introductory Essay', in Istvan Hont and Michael Ignatieff (eds), *Wealth and Virtue: The Shaping of Political Economy in the Scottish Enlightenment*, Cambridge: Cambridge University Press, 1–44.

Kapossy, Béla, and Michael Sonenscher (2015), 'Editors' Introduction', in Istvan Hont, *Politics in Commercial Society*, Cambridge, MA: Harvard University Press, xi–xix.

Kukathas, Chandran (2014), 'Das Rousseau Problem: Adam Smith's Politics and Economics', *Adam Smith Review*, 7, 174–80.

Neuhouser, Frederick (2008), *Rousseau's Theodicy of Self-Love: Evil, Rationality, and the Drive for Recognition*, Oxford: Oxford University Press.

Neuhouser, Frederick (2013), 'Rousseau's Critique of Economic Inequality', *Philosophy and Public Affairs*, 41, 193–225.

Otteson, James (2002), *Adam Smith's Marketplace of Life*, Cambridge: Cambridge University Press.

Pack, Spencer J., and Eric Schliesser (2006), 'Smith's Humean Critique of Hume's Account of Justice', *Journal of the History of Philosophy*, 44, 47–63.

Rasmussen, Dennis C. (2006), 'Rousseau's "Philosophical Chemistry" and the Foundations of Adam Smith's Thought', *History of Political Thought*, 27, 620–41.

Rasmussen, Dennis C. (2013), 'Adam Smith and Rousseau: Enlightenment and Counter-Enlightenment', in Christopher J. Berry, Maria Pia Paganelli and Craig Smith (eds), *The Oxford Handbook of Adam Smith*, Oxford: Oxford University Press, 54–68.

Rasmussen, Dennis C. (2016), 'Adam Smith on What is Wrong With Economic Inequality', *American Political Science Review*, 110, 342–52.

Rousselière, Geneviève (2016), 'Rousseau on Freedom in Commercial Society', *American Journal of Political Science*, 60, 352–63.

Tuck, Richard (2016), *The Sleeping Sovereign: The invention of Modern Democracy*, Cambridge: Cambridge University Press.

Williams, David Lay (forthcoming), *The Greatest of All Plagues: Economic Inequality in Western Political Thought*, Princeton: Princeton University Press.

3

Rousseau and the Scottish Enlightenment: Connections and Disconnections

Mark Hulliung

In recent years we have witnessed an outpouring of books and articles relating Rousseau to the Scots of his day, especially Adam Smith. Overwhelmingly it is students of Smith's thought, not Rousseau's, who are responsible for this spate of publications. One cannot read their works without noting their worthy intention of demonstrating that Smith was more than the champion of the emerging capitalist order – that he was also willing, where need be, to call attention to the problems that followed in its wake and to offer remedies. There would be every reason to applaud the efforts of the Smith scholars if, when they turned to Rousseau, their labours were directed to harvesting the benefits of comparative analysis. Regrettably, they are often unwilling to settle for comparisons; instead, they insist upon making the extremely dubious argument that Smith wrote in response to Rousseau and defeated him in a debate over 'commercial society'.[1]

Two decisive problems bedevil the scholarship as it now stands. The first is the paucity of the evidence presented by Smith scholars and their unwillingness to deal with disconfirming evidence. The second is their failure to treat Rousseau fairly: he is said to have lost an argument with Adam Smith over 'commercial society' which he could not possibly have won, since commercial society was not his primary focus. Rather, his fundamental target was nothing less than civilisation itself. In more ways than one Smith and Rousseau were not speaking the same language, so if we wish to juxtapose them we must realise that we are the ones engaging in comparisons and debates; they were not.

My intention in this essay is to question the claims that Rousseau wrote in response to commercial society and that a major concern of Smith in his most important works was to repudiate Rousseau. After that I shall suggest how we might rebuild and reclaim our scholarly endeavours by a comparative procedure that can begin with a discussion of Rousseau and Smith but which should end with an invitation to absorb Rousseau and the Scots into the larger framework of studying comparative Enlightenments, French and Scottish.

Rousseau and Commercial Society

Nothing is more common in the secondary literature written by Adam Smith scholars than to encounter the claim that Rousseau was a theorist of 'commercial society', its outspoken nay-sayer, hence the perfect opponent against whom the author of *The Wealth of Nations* could measure his achievement. Self-evident truths may be difficult to come by these days, but the notion that Smith wrote to refute Rousseau has been repeated so often in recent years, has been so much taken for granted, that no one bothers to raise long-overdue objections. Why, one wonders, did it take so long for Smith scholars to discover the Smith–Rousseau connection – their supposed debate – unless there was little or no connection waiting to be discovered? And why, if Rousseau wrote to challenge commercial society, has this highly significant intellectual event escaped the attention of Rousseau scholars?

No sooner do we examine the claim that Rousseau's focus was on commercial society than it crumbles for want of adequate evidence. That Rousseau was as relatively indifferent to discussions of commercial society as Smith was overwhelmingly preoccupied with the same topic may be observed time and again when comparing the two thinkers, beginning with this: while Adam Smith repeatedly and proudly proclaimed that he wrote about 'commercial society', Rousseau never says anything of the sort. Moreover, Rousseau has virtually nothing to say about the two noteworthy schools of economic thought in his day, mercantilism and physiocracy. Smith, by contrast, virtually gave the mercantilists their name, the better to criticise them relentlessly. As for the physiocrats, Smith's treatment is gentler: their theme of free trade is one he condones before firmly distancing himself from their strictly agrarian outlook. Put another way, he is for them before he is against them. When Rousseau briefly comments on the physiocrats in a letter written to the Marquis de Mirabeau in 1767, he dwells only on their theme of 'legal despotism' (Rousseau 1979), saying nothing about their economics.[2] Smith is as engaged in economic debate as Rousseau is oblivious to the same.

Also revealing are Rousseau's occasional comments on Holland and England. Unlike Smith or Montesquieu, who are preoccupied with the Dutch because of their commercial achievements, Rousseau rarely speaks of Holland, and when he does mention the Dutch, commerce is not on his mind. What draws Rousseau's attention is that, although revolution rarely succeeds, there have been a very few cases when it has freed an enslaved people, the Dutch providing one example. There are times, he explains, 'when horror of the past is equivalent to amnesia, and when the State, set afire by civil wars, is reborn . . . from its ashes and resumes the vigour of youth . . . Sparta in the time of Lycurgus and Rome after the Tarquins were like this, and among us so were Holland and Switzerland after the expulsion of the tyrants' (SC OC III: 385).[3]

If Adam Smith and Montesquieu spoke at length about Holland, all the more did they and other advocates of commercial society such as David Hume and Voltaire speak about England. Here again Rousseau is an exception: England is rarely present in his thoughts, and when he does mention that nation it is to discuss and criticise its politics, not its economics. Specifically, it is England's system of representative government that he condemns: 'The English people thinks it is free. It greatly deceives itself; it is free only during the election of members of Parliament. As soon as they are elected, it is a slave, it is nothing' (SC OC III: 430).[4]

Topics covered and topics ignored by Smith and Rousseau are quite revealing. Readers of *The Wealth of Nations* are not surprised to find themselves immersed in discussions of capital, markets, banks, interest, prices, wages, rents, manufactures, exports, wholesale and retail trades, among other topics dealing with an emerging modern economy. All such topics are conspicuously absent in Rousseau's works, a sure sign that the new world of commercial society was not his concern.

Given its title, one might anticipate that Rousseau's essay on 'Political Economy', published in the *Encyclopédie* (1755), would be a statement of his views on economics and commercial society. Nothing, however, could be further from the truth. The many topics he addresses in this essay have little or nothing to do with trade and markets. Instead, he is overwhelmingly preoccupied with several themes dear to his heart and to which he will return on many future occasions: civic education, the training of citizens, the need to avoid the extreme social and economic inequality which excludes the many from participation, and the distinction between proper and improper forms of the social contract. We may wish to draw the inference that he probably would have disapproved of commercial society, had he ever bothered to offer a thoroughgoing appraisal of its consequences. He did not do so. It is not so much commercial society as modernity in general, its possibilities and dilemmas, that is his concern (Hulliung 2016).

A few years after 'Political Economy' Rousseau published his most mature and systematic works, *Julie, ou La Nouvelle Héloïse* (1759), *Du contrat social* (1762) and *Emile* (1762). In none of those works does he offer anything beyond remarks in passing about commerce, which may explain why Adam Smith never saw fit to respond to any of them. Nor do Rousseau's earlier works, the *First* and *Second Discourses*, address the prospects and problems of commercial society. Not even his comments in the *Discourse on Inequality* about the deleterious effects of the division of labour are aimed directly at commercial society. What he has in mind in the *Second Discourse* is not the division of labour that to Smith's mind characterises modern history. No, Rousseau is thinking of something that happened a great many ages beyond the advent of recorded history. He discusses the division of labour in the course of pointing out the high price we pay for our transition from the animal to the social state.

The most that can be done is to infer that Rousseau would not have been the friend of commercial society, had he addressed that topic systematically. He briefly condemns luxury in the *First Discourse* and expresses his displeasure with time-saving machines in a few fragmentary, unpublished notes (OC III: 15, 516–25). Emile is tutored to escape from the ill effects of the division of labour by doing for himself rather than asking others to do for him (OC IV: 681). None of this, nor all of it, comes close to constituting a theory of commercial society.

Underlying the questionable view that Rousseau was responding to commercial society is ahistorical thinking: a failure to study texts in context. If Rousseau were a Scot he could not have escaped from conversations about the new economy and its social and political repercussions: discussions of commercial society are at the very centre of the Scottish Enlightenment. The same cannot be said of the French Enlightenment. When Rousseau lived in Paris during the 1750s and was in contact with Diderot, Condillac, d'Alembert, Holbach and other budding *philosophes*, the leading topics of debate rarely included commerce, and only a relatively few essays on economics had found their way at that time into the *Encyclopédie*.[5] Not until the 1770s, in response to Abbé Galiani's writings and Raynal's history of Europe in the two Indies, did Diderot take up the question of commerce. Rousseau's career burst upon the scene before discussions of trade and commerce had become fashionable in advanced French intellectual circles.

Why is it, we must ask, that scholars have been so insistent on forcing upon Rousseau the title of ardent critic of 'commercial society'? One obvious answer is that we are dealing with Smith scholars who want to provide Adam Smith with a convenient foil. Another explanation worth considering is that they may be indulging in anachronistic reasoning, reading back into the eighteenth century a nineteenth-century debate between liberals and socialists, with Smith figuring as the liberal and Rousseau, for want of a better candidate, forced into the pre-socialist category. The 'anticipation' fallacy lurks just beneath the surface (Rasmussen 2008: 48, 162, 174n).

Did Adam Smith and the Scots Write in Response to Rousseau?

Nowadays nothing is more common than to read that Rousseau was a major figure in the Scottish Enlightenment, that he was the author the Scots were especially keen to criticise, and that Adam Smith in particular wrote to refute him. If Rousseau sometimes fares slightly better, it is because Smith scholars, eager to point out that their man did not overlook the problems of commercial society, occasionally applaud Smith by crediting him with borrowing a critical point or two from Rousseau.[6] The problem with all these claims is that the supportive evidence could hardly be thinner.

One searches in vain for Rousseau's name in any of Smith's major works. Not a single mention of him is to be found in *The Theory of Moral Sentiments*, the *Lectures on Jurisprudence* or *The Wealth of Nations*. Throughout his most important writings, Smith repeatedly cites the authors he has in mind, whether to agree or disagree with them, whether to build upon or dismantle their work; even the names of writers only tangentially relevant to his arguments are occasionally mentioned. Why, then, if he was responding to him, is Rousseau missing from the texts of Smith's major works? And how, under these circumstances, is anyone entitled to proclaim that Smith was writing to refute Rousseau?[7]

The best that the scholars in Smith's camp can do to serve their cause when treating his major works is to ransack them in search of a passage here or there which reminds them of something in Rousseau. Implicitly recognising the severe limitations of this procedure, they turn for validation of their point of view to Smith's minor writings. Here, indeed, we do encounter several comments explicitly about Rousseau, but these scattered jottings do more to harm than to affirm the case of those who believe that Smith was deeply concerned with the remarkable Genevan. For what Smith unmistakably takes seriously in these minor writings is Rousseau's style of writing rather than his thought. Beyond favourable remarks about Rousseau's beautiful prose there is little on his reflections, except for the comment that emotional outpourings were more in evidence in his works than a capacity for sustained rational analysis.

It is Smith's *Letter to the Edinburgh Review* (1756) that today's scholars cite most frequently for proof that he was preoccupied with Rousseau. But in truth Smith's words about the *Discourse on Inequality*, if closely examined, give us little or no reason to conclude that he regarded Rousseau as a serious thinker, a foe worth answering. 'It would be to no purpose,' wrote Smith,

> to give an analysis [of the *Second Discourse*]; for none could give any just idea of a work which consists almost entirely of rhetoric and description. I shall endeavour to present your readers therefore with a specimen of his eloquence by translating one or two short passages. (Letter: 251)

In both the *Considerations Concerning the First Formation of Languages* (Smith 1963) and in another essay, *Of the Nature of that Imitation which takes place in what are called the Imitative Arts*, Smith continues to speak of 'the eloquent M. Rousseau', while adding the verdict, in the latter essay, that Rousseau was 'an Author, more capable of feeling strongly than of analysing accurately' (IA: 198–99). All in all, there is little or no reason to see Rousseau as more than a marginal figure in the publications of Adam Smith.

Marginal in Smith, it is telling that Rousseau was equally marginal or more so in the thought of Smith's close friend, David Hume. Concerned for the fate of 'men of letters', Hume generously provided Rousseau with shelter when the authorities in France and Geneva united against him. There are, however, few indications that Hume was deeply interested in Rousseau's writings either before or after he offered him a safe haven. In a letter of 1762 he expressed his concern for Rousseau's fate and called him 'a man whose character and talents I much admire'. That he had immersed himself in any of Rousseau's works is, however, far from obvious, and he sounds much like Smith when he remarks that 'For my part, I see some tincture of extravagance in all of them; [yet] I also think I see . . . much eloquence and force in imagination' (Hume 1983a I: 366). Rousseau the eloquent writer, not Rousseau the thinker, figures conspicuously in Hume's letters. In 1763, in response to a letter from the Comtesse de Boufflers soliciting his opinion, Hume again praised Rousseau 'on the head of eloquence' but complained that all his writings were somewhat compromised by 'some degree of extravagance'. 'Were it not for his frequent and earnest protestations to the contrary, one would be apt to suspect, that he chooses his topic less from persuasion, than from the pleasure of showing his invention, and surprising his readers by his paradoxes' (Hume 1983a I: 373).

Early in 1766 Hume tried to play genteel host to Rousseau, but then, a few months later, he abandoned his kind efforts and in exasperation denounced his guest as evil or mad. After the break, Hume continued to offer only summary treatments of Rousseau's works whenever his correspondents asked for his judgement – never providing an in-depth analysis of any of the books that, by his own account, were setting Europe astir. When on good terms with Rousseau, he had remarked repeatedly on his 'extreme sensibility'; on bad terms he wondered whether Rousseau was insane. On good terms, he had repeatedly underscored the 'eloquence' and 'extravagance' of Rousseau's writings; on bad terms, he told Turgot 'I always esteemed his Writings for their Eloquence alone and . . . I looked on them, at the bottom, as full of Extravagance and Sophistry' (Hume 1983a II: 91).[8] That is, Hume changed his favourite formula from the words 'eloquence and extravagance' to 'eloquence, extravagance, and sophistry'.

Moreover, even when on good terms in the early going, Hume had surmised that 'He has reflected, ... and studied very little; and has not indeed much Knowledge; He has only felt' (Hume 1983a II: 29). The parallel with Smith's views is striking, their negative assessments of Rousseau virtually identical: Rousseau is a remarkable rhetorician; a thinker he is not.

Neither Smith nor Hume give us reason to believe that Rousseau was a person of consequence in the Scottish Enlightenment. This conclusion, that Rousseau played a minor role at most in Scotland, becomes all the more compelling once we realise that not just Smith and Hume but none of the Scots ever said anything of consequence about Rousseau's novel, his book on education, or his treatise on the social contract. To the extent that any of the Scots said anything at all about Rousseau's *oeuvre*, they both began and ended with the *Discourse on Inequality*, never venturing any further.

A Deafening Silence: the Non-Response to *Du contrat social*

The absence of a Scottish response to two of Rousseau's most mature and systematic works, *Julie, ou La Nouvelle Héloïse* and *Emile, ou de l'Éducation*, is obviously incompatible with the claim that he was a figure at the centre rather than the periphery of the Scottish Enlightenment. Most revealing of all, however, is the non-response of the Scots to *Du contrat social*. For if there was one of Rousseau's books in particular that the Scots definitely should have answered if they took him seriously, it was his treatise on the social contract. After all, one of the most dominant themes of the Scots was their outspoken repudiation of social contract theory, of Hobbes and Locke especially. And yet they simply ignored Rousseau's remarkable treatise.

Everyone in Scotland was aware of the existence of Rousseau's 1762 tract on political philosophy, but no one addressed it in a formal publication. Hume revealed in a private letter that Rousseau 'himself told me that he valued most his *Contrat sociale* [*sic*]'. Nevertheless, no more than any of his Scottish brethren did Hume bother to answer Rousseau's political treatise. Instead, he offered the derogatory remark that Rousseau's suggestion that the *Social Contract* might be the most important of his writings was 'as preposterous a judgement as that of Milton, who preferred the

Paradise Regained to all his other Performances' (Hume 1983a II: 28). Never in public did Hume mention the *Social Contract*, nor did anyone else in Scotland. Glaringly absent from the many Scottish repudiations of social contract theory is an attack on Rousseau's version of that doctrine. It is difficult to imagine a more convincing demonstration of Rousseau's insignificance in Glasgow and Edinburgh than this refusal of the leading Scottish thinkers to comment publicly on the *Social Contract*.

Why the Scots were so intent on dismissing theories of the social contract was stated explicitly by Adam Smith in his *Lectures on Jurisprudence*: 'This was the prevailing and favourite doctrine from the year 1640 to 1660' (LJA: 297). It was the doctrine, that is, of the Puritan Revolution, which was the moment of history that the British were most eager to forget, the leading representatives of the Scottish Enlightenment taking the lead in imposing amnesia on the public. Adam Ferguson is a prime example. Speaking of the uprising against Charles I, he explicitly articulated the position that 'however beneficial its consequences have been, we should be grateful for what we enjoy, and not call to recollection a period full of horror' (Ferguson 1776: 36). If English history were to be represented as a tale of continuity, as the Scots frequently desired, the mid-seventeenth-century past would have to be forgotten, especially such episodes as the Agreement of the People (1647), that Leveller (and pre-Lockean) experiment in dangerous doctrines of natural rights and inalienable popular sovereignty. Many of the leading figures of the Scottish Enlightenment were ardently committed to burying from memory such mid-seventeenth-century adventures in transforming the idea of the social contract from theory to reality.

There is no reason to be surprised that the Scots chose to ignore *Du contrat social* once we recognise that for many years prior to the publication of Rousseau's treatise, and long afterwards, they made it a matter of principle to avoid discussions of political principles. Theories of the social contract raised the question of obligation, thereby rendering obedience problematical, which the anti-theoretical theorists of the Scottish Enlightenment deemed unacceptable. It had not always been this way, Hume reminded readers of his 'Of the Original Contract' (1748); ideas of a social contract had not always held sway: the ancient Greeks, assuming that we owe all we are to the socio-political order and are nothing outside it, never had to deal with the state of nature, the contract, or a problem of political obligation. Would that the moderns had never invented theories of the social contract with all the dangers such notions entail, as evidenced by the upheavals of the mid-seventeenth century.

As early as 1739, in his *Treatise of Human Nature*, Hume had sought to bury the social contract, and as late as 1776 Adam Ferguson, in the course of expressing his disgust for the rebellious Americans, placed substantial blame on theories of the social contract. The form of government rather than the legitimacy of government is the topic we might do well to consider, Ferguson made clear, and all such discussions of various forms should end with praise for the marvellous British Constitution. How dare the Americans, beneficiaries of the best government ever known, attempt to go their own way! Both Ferguson and Hume were especially concerned to keep the contract away from the many, the uneducated populace, or, what to them amounts to the same thing, the mob. If 'it is dangerous to enfeeble government by speculations', wrote Ferguson, 'how much more laudable to conceal from an unthinking multitude the source of government: the obedience due to authority ought never to be canvassed by the people' (Ferguson 1776: 36–7). Similarly Hume, decades before the American upheavals, had written that 'No maxim is more conformable, both to prudence and morals, than to submit quietly to the government which we find established in the country where we happen to live, without enquiring too curiously into its origin and first establishment' (Hume 1968: 558; see also Hume 1983b V: 544). Much later, upon hearing that Rousseau had questioned the authority of the Genevan government, Hume in a private letter labelled the *Lettres écrites de la montagne* a 'seditious' work (Hume 1983a I: 493).[9]

Both Hume and Smith objected to the notion of government based on the consent of the governed on the grounds that it would undermine the legitimacy of the absolutist regimes of France and Spain (Hume 1968: 549; Smith LJA: 323; LJB: 435). Hume's theme, stated early and repeated on various occasions, was that 'time and custom give authority to all forms of government' (Hume 1968: 566), to which he added in his anti-contract essay 'Of the Original Contract' the conclusion that 'new discoveries are not to be expected in these matters' (Hume 1985: 487). If a formula was needed to summarise the Scottish view, Ferguson was happy to provide it: 'we must take the world as it goes' (Ferguson 1776:

49). Revolution was what the Scots would do anything to avoid. Reform they sanctioned but only if undertaken with the greatest precaution because, as Ferguson warned, 'the most refined politicians do not always know whither they are leading the state by their projects' (Ferguson 1995: 119).

Taking into account their unwillingness to grant Locke's *Second Treatise of Government* a serious hearing, it is only to be expected that the Scots would simply ignore Rousseau's more radical *Social Contract*. Adam Smith found the means to defuse Locke's doctrine of the social contract by treating its universalistic argument as something hopelessly provincial: 'this doctrine of obedience founded on contract', he wrote, 'is confined to Britain and has never been heard of in any other country, so that [elsewhere] it cannot be the foundation of the obedience of the people; and even here it can have influence with a very small part of the people, such as have read Locke' (LJA: 316). In addition, Smith joined Hume in misreading Locke: both argued against Locke that even if there were an original contract, it could not bind subsequent generations – failing to understand that Locke, and Rousseau as well, made no such claim (Hume 1985: 471). Quite the contrary, for Locke, and even more markedly for Rousseau, no generation could bind the generations to follow. The consent of the people could be withdrawn at any time, especially if the government was oppressive, and the ever sovereign people could demand that the social contract be renegotiated – consent was not once and for all. Theory became practice when the American 'people', rather than inheriting a constitution in good British fashion, willed one into being – and with the understanding that their sovereign authority would never end.

All of the foregoing is to say, of course, that the Scots were ill prepared for the new era of the American and French Revolutions. Ferguson in 1776 issued a fiery polemic against Richard Price who had dared to support the Americans. Almost everything Edmund Burke said in his polemic against Price in 1789–90, in the famous *Reflections on the Revolution in France*, may be found in embryo at least in Ferguson's earlier pamphlet. Neither Ferguson nor Burke, who had so to speak gone to school with the Scots, had the slightest appreciation of social contract theory – or Jean-Jacques Rousseau.

The Scots might have gained enormously from taking Rousseau's *Social Contract* seriously, whether to answer the challenge it presented to their outlook or to reconsider their anti-social contract position. Had they done so they might have been much better prepared to recognise the great events of the late eighteenth century in America and France as something new, rather than a re-enactment of the Puritan Revolution. Alas, Rousseau was so tangential to their concerns, their indifference or hostility to social contract theory so adamant, that they completely ignored his greatest work of political philosophy. This may well be the most significant of all the disconnections between Rousseau and the Scottish Enlightenment.

Scholars today have overlooked the failure of the Scots to answer *Du contrat social*. On a larger scale they have neglected the Scottish dismissal of all social contract theory, perhaps because they are often preoccupied with finding in the Scots an 'anticipation' of nineteenth-century sociology.[10]

Reconsidering the *Letter to the Edinburgh Review*

Adam Smith scholars, as noted earlier, searching for a meaningful link between Smith and Rousseau but finding no mention of the Citizen of Geneva in *The Theory of Moral Sentiments*, the *Lectures on Jurisprudence* or *The Wealth of Nations*, have been reduced to reading great significance into brief comments in Smith's minor works. Most often they turn to Smith's comments on the *Discourse on Inequality* at the end of his *Letter to the Edinburgh Review*. Typically, they read deep meanings into Smith's few words, taking such liberties in interpretation that one cannot help but suspect that Smith would be quite surprised to hear he had meant anything of the kind.

What they omit is that Smith links his short commentary on Rousseau with remarks on Bernard Mandeville, author of the famous and infamous *The Fable of the Bees: Or Private Vices, Publick Benefits*. In Smith's major works, where Rousseau is absent, Mandeville is very much present. *The Theory of Moral Sentiments* includes a critique of 'the system of Dr. Mandeville', and Mandeville's name also appears in the *Lectures on Jurisprudence* (TMS VII.ii.6–13: 308–13; LJA: 393; LJB: 513). When the editors of Smith's major works point out what they regard as allusions to *The Fable of the Bees*, Mandeville's name crops up some thirty-five or so times, Rousseau's name only twice.[11] The evidence, direct and circumstantial, points to Mandeville, not Rousseau, as one of Smith's favourite targets.

Mandeville appears in Smith so often because he figures everywhere in the Scottish Enlightenment as the thinker who must be answered, his formula of 'private vices, public benefits' repudiated. Francis Hutcheson, who was Adam Smith's teacher at Glasgow in the late 1730s, made it his special mission to refute Mandeville. David Hume was also intent on saving moral philosophy from Mandeville's deliciously perverse and joyously scandalous philosophy. Likewise Smith, as fully as any figure of the Scottish Enlightenment, was intent on pushing Mandeville off the public stage. It was Mandeville, not Rousseau, who mattered greatly to the Scots; Mandeville was the thinker who had to be answered and defeated.

Mandeville was a serious threat because he had presented in a highly provocative and disturbing form, totally unacceptable to the Scots, many of the positions they wished to make their own. On matters concerning trade and commerce, Mandeville in the early eighteenth century, long before the Scots penned their writings, had set forth views that were decidedly progressive. Several times, moreover, he seemed to allude to what Smith would later term the 'division of labour' (Mandeville 1988: 197, 226, 367). Smith's optimistic statement that under modern economic conditions 'universal opulence ... extends itself to the lowest ranks of society' (WN I.i: 22), and that the European peasant is better off than an African king, were also in effect restatements of Mandeville (WN I.i: 24). One of Smith's most quotable lines, that 'it is not from the benevolence of the butcher, the brewer, or the baker that we expect our dinner, but from their regard to their own interest', is yet another duplication, whether deliberate or inadvertent, of Mandeville, as is Smith's statement that 'by pursuing his own interest he frequently promotes that of the society more effectively than when he really intends to promote it' (WN I.ii: 27; WN IV.ii: 456; Mandeville 1988: 169).

Despite significant overlap with Mandeville, the Scots condemned *The Fable of the Bees* for fear that his scandalous treatise might bring their work into public disfavour. Self-interest and self-love, central to Mandeville's treatise, also played a central role in Scottish thought, but could only serve the cause of enlightenment if disassociated from Mandeville. It was Mandeville's undertaking to deflate all our pretensions, to show that even our most seemingly selfless actions are self-promoting. Why, he asks, does anyone risk his very life on the battlefield? And he answers that the soldier is so 'intoxicated with the fumes of vanity', so preoccupied with 'the praises that shall be paid his memory . . . as to neglect his present life' (Mandeville 1988: 213–14). Virtue in Mandeville's world is never more than a disguised expression of vanity (Mandeville 1988: 57).

Sometimes the Scots distanced themselves from Mandeville as Hume did in his *Treatise*, by assuring his readers that the formula of universal selfishness was 'as wide of nature as any accounts of monsters which we meet with in fables and romances' (Hume 1968: 486–7). Or, like Smith in his *Theory of Moral Sentiments*, they held that a narrow preoccupation with self-interest in economics did not entail the same in moral discourse pertaining to society and politics. But their single most important move was to save the word 'virtue' from Mandeville's criticisms. Much like their French counterparts, the *philosophes*, the Scots devoted their efforts to showing that interest sustains virtue, is its complement rather than its opposite.[12] Down with the repressive virtue of the Church; up with the virtue that is no less virtuous because it brings us happiness and enhances our being. Mandeville was no better than the most dogmatic clergyman in failing to understand that our satisfaction in doing good strengthens rather than undermines virtue. There is no reason why self-love and love of others cannot be one, with virtue enhanced rather than virtue diminished.

Smith's comments on the *Discourse on Inequality* in his *Letter to the Edinburgh Review* are unremarkable and were not developed into anything meaningful at a later date in his major works. Nor do Smith's remarks about Mandeville in the same letter amount to anything in themselves. But throughout Smith's career, Mandeville was always on his mind, most notably when he wrote such major works as *The Theory of Moral Sentiments* and again when he delivered his *Lectures on Jurisprudence*, which explains why, even when discussing Rousseau in the *Letter*, he cannot refrain from speaking of Mandeville.

Rousseau and the Scots: Alternative Approaches

If the scholarship on Rousseau and Smith, or more broadly Rousseau and the Scots, has taken a wrong turn, what can we do to set it on a more promising path? How can it be restructured and reclaimed? One possibility would be for scholars to admit frankly that they have not been thinking as historians but rather as political theorists. They might concede that the links they have suggested between Rousseau and Smith are their own theoretical creation rather than their historical discovery. They could acknowledge that theirs is the response that to their minds Smith might have made or perhaps should have made to Rousseau. Alternatively, they might settle upon arguing that they are in fact historians but that theirs is an exercise in comparative history rather than a historical recreation of an argument that actually took place between Smith and Rousseau. Much of the current scholarship could be reclaimed if the investigators were to transform their publications into a comparative historical framework; placing Smith and Rousseau side by side may yield noteworthy results.

There is yet another way by which we might rebuild the scholarship. With so many books and essays in existence that are best read as tales of how Smith could have answered Rousseau, it is only right that someone should indicate how Rousseau might have answered Smith and the Scots. Turnabout is fair play. No sooner do we ask ourselves how Rousseau would have answered the Scots than a great many possibilities spring to mind. For present purposes one will do: keeping to our previous themes, let us confine ourselves to the question of how Rousseau might have responded to the Scottish banishment of social contract theory.

Rousseau was unfamiliar with the writings of the Scots, but had he read them he would surely have noted that Smith's references to Grotius were as plentiful as those to Locke were sparing, and that his comments on Grotius never betray any of the hostility that is always on display when Locke is the topic of discussion.[13] Ever suspicious of Locke, whose doctrine of inalienable natural rights, popular sovereignty and social contract might be the source of upheaval, the Scots were untroubled by Grotius, presumably because he held that our natural rights and sovereignty had been alienated and transferred to the government in a social contract signed long ago. For the Scots, Grotius was an authority to whom they might turn for information about this or that topic; to Rousseau he was the well-known public figure who 'spares no pains to rob the people of all their rights and transfers them to kings in the most artful manner' (SC OC III: 370).

Forever deciding what ought to be on the basis of what is and has been, Grotius sanctioned such evils as slavery, provided it was based on a contractual agreement, as in the case of a prisoner of war (Grotius 1925: 690). The Scots, of course, were anti-slavery, but they ignored Grotius in this matter rather than call him out. Rousseau, by contrast, did insist on holding Grotius accountable: 'His most persistent mode of reasoning is always to establish right by fact. One could use a more rational method but not one more favourable to tyrants' (SC OC III: 353). The explicit intent of Rousseau in his *Discourse on Inequality* was 'to test the facts by right' (SD OC III: 182). One can well imagine what he would have thought of Ferguson's recommendation, so typical of the political conservatism of the Scots, to 'take the world as it goes'.[14] From the standpoint of Rousseau, the Scots all too readily established right by fact, rather than testing the facts by right.

Finally, by way of reconstituting the scholarship, we might be well advised to consider a strategy of beginning with a discussion of Rousseau and the Scots but only as a prelude to something potentially more satisfying, a series of studies of the Scottish and French Enlightenments in transnational and comparative perspective. A promising way to initiate this more comprehensive endeavour is to review Adam Ferguson's attack on Rousseau's discussion of a 'state of nature' at the outset of *An Essay on the History of Civil Society*. Far more than Smith in the *Letter to the Edinburgh Review*, Ferguson attempts to offer a significant response to Rousseau. No matter how disappointing Ferguson's critique, no matter how inadequately argued, it has the accidental advantage of providing us with a springboard from which to move on to a more ambitious comparison of Enlightenment in two countries, Scotland and France.

Ferguson, in his chapter 'Of the Question of the State of Nature', never mentions Rousseau by name, but there can be no doubt that the author of the *Second Discourse* is the thinker he is inviting his readers to hold in contempt. In common with the other Scots who had little or no use for the concept of a state of nature, Ferguson demanded that in studying human nature we should never look beyond how the human creature 'has always appeared within the reach of our own observation, and in the records of history' (Ferguson 1995: 8). Because Rousseau had cited Buffon, Ferguson takes up the theme of natural history and affirms that 'the natural historian thinks himself obliged to collect facts, not to offer conjectures. When he treats of any particular species of animals, he supposes that their present dispositions and instincts are the same as they originally had.' Ferguson was especially horrified by Rousseau's conjecture that orang-utans today may be as all humans once were. To quote Ferguson, Rousseau was guilty of taking 'as the model of our nature in its original state, some of the animals whose shape has the greatest resemblance to ours' (Ferguson 1995: 11; SD OC III: 211). Only a fool or a charlatan, he assures us, could offer such a conjecture.

Ferguson's critique was far more remarkable as a display of dogmatism than as an effort to respond fairly to an intellectual challenge. For when he, against Rousseau, proclaimed language something given by nature to man, likening it to 'his reason ... and the erect position of his body' (Ferguson 1995: 9), which he deemed also given by nature, he placed himself unwittingly at odds with Locke's developmental psychology, possibly at odds as well with Adam Smith's *Considerations Concerning the First Formation of Languages* and even at odds with his own thoughts in his much later work, *Principles of Moral and Political Science.*[15] Moreover, his condemnation of conjecture was arguably another unacknowledged break with the Scottish Enlightenment: his pupil Dugald Stewart, for instance, held that 'in this want of direct evidence, we are under a necessity of supplying the place of fact by conjecture' and expressed respect for 'Theoretical or Conjectural History' (Life: 293). It is tempting to conclude that Rousseau brought out the worst in Ferguson, whose hits at his Genevan nemesis were more unfaithful to his beloved Scottish Enlightenment than effective against Rousseau.

No matter how unimpressive Ferguson's denunciations of Rousseau, they do have their uses in raising a larger point. What they bring to mind – the generalisation they invite – is that while Enlightenment everywhere counted strongly on science, in Scotland science meant Newtonian physics, whereas in France there was a major effort, after absorbing Newton, to move on to the bold new world of the life sciences. Rousseau's uses of Buffon, his conjectures on the orang-utan, were an exercise in transforming 'natural history' into the history of nature, quite unlike the Scottish preoccupation with timeless modern physics. Other French intellectuals, Diderot most famously, were raising the question of whether species come in and go out of existence. Not so in Scotland, where even Hume, who did not share the Scottish devotion to 'natural religion', opined that 'there appears not to be any single species which has yet been extinguished in the universe' (Hume 1977: 75).

In *De l'interprétation de la nature* (1753) Diderot made a major effort to ground scientific research in the outlook of Francis Bacon.

But even as Diderot undertook his labour to import Bacon to the Continent, he also offered a major revision of the *New Organon*. Bacon had insisted that the interpretation of nature could only be undermined by flights of the imagination: 'The conclusions of human reason as ordinarily applied in matter of nature, I call ... *Anticipations of Nature* (as a thing rash or premature). That reason which is elicited from facts by a just and methodical process, I call *Interpretation of Nature*' (Bacon 1960: Bk. I, No. xxvi). Diderot, in marked contrast, preoccupied with the emerging life sciences, insisted that pure empiricism was inadequate as a method of discovery. Imagination was as essential in science as in the arts; therefore his book abounds with 'conjectures', with 'reveries', and, later, one of his most important contributions to the philosophy of science would be a volume bearing the title *D'Alembert's Dream*.

Ernst Cassirer, with his focus on Kant, offered a universalistic account of Enlightenment in his famous study of 1932, *The Philosophy of the Enlightenment*. In 1981 Roy Porter and Mikulas Teich edited a noteworthy volume of essays on *The Enlightenment in National Context*. Against Cassirer, they pointed out that however cosmopolitan and universal its ideals, there was not one Enlightenment but many, each needing to be studied in its distinctive national context. We may add that it is necessary to take matters one step further, to study the French and Scottish Enlightenments in *comparative* national and *transnational* context. Our studies may begin but should not end with Smith and Rousseau.[16]

Notes

1. For example Rasmussen (2008), Hont (2015) and Hanley (2008).
2. Rousseau to Marquis de Mirabeau, 26 July 1767.
3. References to Rousseau are taken from the *Oeuvres complètes*. SC is *Social Contract* and SD *Second Discourse*.
4. More favourable comments on England may be found in the ninth of the *Lettres écrites de la montagne*, OC III: 874–9.
5. Quesnay contributed two articles, Forbannais several on economic themes.
6. Rasmussen (2008: 7). See also Hanley (2006).
7. It is true, however, that Smith sometimes alludes to, without citing, Hume.
8. Hume to Turgot, letter 351, late September 1766.

9. Hume to Comtesse du Boufflers, letter 269, January or February 1765.
10. The 'anticipation' of sociology claim is especially marked in the somewhat older literature, for example Lehmann (1979), originally published in 1960.
11. I refer to the editors of the Liberty Classics editions.
12. See the discussion in Hulliung (1994) ch. 1, 'The Virtue of Selfishness'.
13. E.g., TMS VII.ii.10: 269; VII.iv.37: 341–2. LJA: 36, 72, 104, 136, 138, 150; LJB: 397, 552.
14. The link between Adam Smith and Edmund Burke was quite strong. Burke, for instance, publicly recommended *The Theory of Moral Sentiments*, and Smith supported Burke and the Rockingham Whigs during the constitutional crisis of 1782.
15. See Ferguson (1975: I, 39–46). Even here, however, he asserts (43) that language has always existed.
16. I wish to thank Craig Smith for his thoughtful comments on the penultimate draft of this chapter.

Bibliography

Bacon, Francis (1960) [1620], *The New Organon*, New York: Library of Liberal Arts.

Diderot, Denis (1995) [1770], *Apologie de l'Abbé Galiani*, in *Oeuvres de Diderot*, ed. Laurent Versini, Paris: Robert Laffont, Vol. III, 123–60.

Ferguson, Adam (1776), *Remarks on Dr. Price's Observations on the Nature of Civil Liberty*, London: Printed for G. Kearsley.

Ferguson, Adam (1975) [1792], *Principles of Moral and Political Science*, New York: Garland Publishing.

Ferguson, Adam (1995) [1767], *An Essay on the History of Civil Society*, Cambridge: Cambridge University Press.

Grotius, Hugo (1925) [1625], *The Law of War and Peace*, Indianapolis: Bobbs-Merrill.

Hanley, Ryan Patrick (2006), 'From Geneva to Glasgow: Rousseau and Adam Smith on the Theater and Commercial Society', *Studies in Eighteenth-Century Culture*, 35, 177–202.

Hanley, Ryan Patrick (2008), 'Commerce and Corruption: Rousseau's Diagnosis and Adam Smith's Cure', *European Journal of Political Theory*, 7, 137–58.

Hont, Istvan (2015), *Politics in a Commercial Society: Jean-Jacques Rousseau and Adam Smith*, Cambridge, MA: Harvard University Press.

Hulliung, Mark (1994), *The Autocritique of Enlightenment: Rousseau and the Philosophes*, Cambridge, MA: Harvard University Press.

Hulliung, Mark (ed.) (2016), *Rousseau and the Dilemmas of Modernity*, New Brunswick, NJ: Transaction Publishers.

Hume, David (1968) [1738], *A Treatise of Human Nature*, Oxford: Clarendon Press.

Hume, David (1977) [1779], *Dialogues Concerning Natural Religion*, New York: Hafner Press.

Hume, David (1983a), *The Letters of David Hume*, ed. J. Y. T. Grieg, New York: Garland Publishing.

Hume, David (1983b) [1762], *The History of England*, Indianapolis: Liberty Classics.

Hume, David (1985) [1748], 'Of the Original Contract', in *Essays: Moral, Political, and Literary*, ed. E. F. Miller, Indianapolis: Liberty Fund, 465–87.

Lehmann, William C. (1979) [1960], *John Millar of Glasgow*, New York: Arno Press.

Mandeville, Bernard (1988) [1714], *The Fable of the Bees: Or Private Vices, Publick Benefits*, Indianapolis: Liberty Fund.

Rasmussen, Dennis C. (2008), *The Problems and Promise of Commercial Society: Adam Smith's Response to Rousseau*, University Park: Pennsylvania State University Press.

Rousseau, Jean-Jacques (1979) [1767], Letter to Marquis de Mirabeau, 26 July 1767, in *Correspondence complètes de Jean Jacques Rousseau*, ed. R. A. Leigh, Oxford: Voltaire Foundation, vol. XXXIII, 242–4.

Rousseau, Jean-Jacques (1959–95), *Oeuvres complètes*, ed. Bernard Gagnebin and Marcel Raymond, 5 vols, Paris: Gallimard, Bibliothèque de la Pléiade.

Smith, Adam (1963) [1761], *Considerations Concerning the First Formation of Languages*, in *Works of Adam Smith*, vol. 5, Aalen: Otto Zeller.

Part II

Self-interest and Sympathy

4

The Role of Interpersonal Comparisons in Moral Learning and the Sources of Recognition Respect: Jean-Jacques Rousseau's *amour-propre* and Adam Smith's Sympathy

Christel Fricke

Jean-Jacques Rousseau was one of the eighteenth century's sharpest critics of commercial society and of the socio-economic inequalities it imposed on its members. Since he saw humans as naturally provided with freedom and equality, he denied the possibility of their flourishing under conditions of dependency, domination and servility. We know – from Adam Smith's *Letter to the Edinburgh Review* (Letter: 242–54) – that Smith had read Rousseau's 1754 *Discourse on the Origin of Inequality and the Foundations of Inequality among Men*. Indeed, Smith owed the inspiration for some of his harshest criticisms of the physical, social and moral impact of commercial society on its members in general, and on the labourers at the lower end of society in particular, to Rousseau (Rasmussen 2008: 51–90; Neuhouser 2013; 2014). Not only was he sensitive to the misery of the poor; like Rousseau, he objected to the socio-economic inequalities of commercial society on moral grounds. Morality carries a commitment to the equality of all people and is thus at odds with socio-economic inequalities, inequalities furthermore that do not originate in naturally given differences between humans.[1]

Neither Rousseau nor Smith argued in favour of a commercial revolution aimed at a radically egalitarian redistribution of wealth. Rousseau developed a utopian political solution to the problem of socio-economic inequality in the shape of a state based on a social contract. Smith did not endorse this solution.[2] He suggested a more pragmatic way of alleviating the lot of the poor, relying on a cost-benefit analysis of the socio-economic effects of commercial society.[3] Smith was convinced that no single human being could flourish (morally or otherwise) without a certain degree of material wealth and that commercial society produced more wealth than any other kind of society. So although the wealth that commercial society produces comes at a price – namely, substantive socio-economic inequalities – in the light of the economic alternative of an agricultural society (not to mention a society of hunter-gatherers or shepherds) and the poverty that it would impose on the vast majority of its members, this price is worth paying: 'it may be true . . . that the accommodation of a European prince does not always so much exceed that of an industrious and frugal peasant, as the accommodation of the latter exceeds that of many an African king, the absolute master of the lives and liberties of ten thousand naked savages' (WN I.i.11: 24). Still, commercial society should not be committed to the production of wealth exclusively and turn a blind eye to the way it is distributed and invested; it should promote the common good, attend to concerns of national security and invest in public institutions. These include institutions for infrastructure (such as roads, bridges and canals as means for facilitating commerce), institutions for justice and institutions providing education for all, including in particular the common people or members of the class of labourers (WN V.i.f.54: 785–6). Smith argues extensively for the claim that the state 'derives no inconsiderable advantage from their [the common people's] instruction' (WN V.i.f.61: 788).[4] This argument carries an important message. In commercial society, nobody, not even the labourers with the lowest wages, should be too poor to have a decent life:

> A man must always live by his work, and his wages must at least be sufficient to maintain him. They must even upon most occasions be somewhat more; otherwise it would be impossible for him to bring up a family, and the race of such workmen could not last beyond the first generation. (WN I.viii.15: 85)[5]

Smith is aware of the fact that a person's socio-economic status has a strong impact on their prospects in life: their education, their opportunities to discover and develop their talents, and their moral flourishing depend on their access to sufficient resources (WN V.i.f.61: 788). In commercial society, socio-economic inequalities provide the framework in which people interact. How can a person learn to be virtuous and to respect all other people as his or her moral equals if what he or she discovers when making interpersonal comparisons are substantial differences in socio-economic status as well as in education, in talents, and in the part they have in the omnipresent relations of dominance and servility?

Rousseau and Smith shared an interest in this question. Smith's account of the dynamics of social interaction and interpersonal comparisons in his *Theory of Moral Sentiments* (1759/1790) was certainly inspired by his reading of Rousseau's *Discourse on the Origin and the Foundations of Inequality among Men* (1754), his so-called 'Second Discourse'. But inspiration can manifest itself in different ways. The question is whether and to what extent Smith *followed* Rousseau in the conclusions he drew. Obviously, the answer to this question depends on the underlying readings of Rousseau's and Smith's views of the matter. Recently, two scholars have answered this question in the positive, though based on very different readings of Rousseau's and Smith's views on moral matters. Ryan Hanley has proposed a reading of Smith as a virtue ethicist whose account of moral judgement gives pride of place to the individual person's conscientious practical reasoning. Against the background of this reading, he claims that Smith followed Rousseau both in his diagnosis of a moral disease arising from social interaction and interpersonal comparisons, and in his recommended remedy: social interaction provides a constant challenge to the development and flourishing of an individual person's moral character, and the way to avoid these challenges is moral solipsism (Hanley 2009; 2015). Frederick Neuhouser rejects the traditional and mostly misanthropic reading of Rousseau. He explores Rousseau's accounts of *pitié* and *amour-propre* in depth and claims to discover, under the many layers of more or less narcissistic interpersonal competition to which *amour-propre* can give rise, a source of recognition of all other people as moral equals. He reads Rousseau as the first philosopher to provide us with an account of universal and egalitarian moral recognition as a requirement of virtue. Accordingly, he concludes that Smith was among the 'appropriators' of Rousseau's account of recognition, together with Hegel and Freud and, though to a lesser degree, Kant, Mead, Sartre, Habermas and Rawls.[6]

In the following, I shall briefly present my own readings of Rousseau's and Smith's respective accounts of social interaction and interpersonal comparisons, of their role in processes of moral learning, and of the challenges they represent. I shall then discuss Hanley's and Neuhouser's assimilating readings of Rousseau's and Smith's views. Finally, I shall argue in favour of a more sceptical account of Smith's appropriation of, and agreement with, Rousseau. My claim is that Smith's response to Rousseau's account of social interaction and interpersonal comparisons, not unlike his response to the Humean account of these phenomena, was a straightforward 'Yes, but . . .'[7] Whereas Rousseau was among the philosophers who inspired Smith's account of social interaction and its contribution to moral flourishing, he did not follow Rousseau either in the details of his analysis or in the conclusions he drew. Smith provides us with an account of moral development that attributes a key role to social interaction and interpersonal comparison in the process of a person's learning to be moral and in his or her acquisition of a moral character. This account is more optimistic than the one proposed by Rousseau.

Rousseau on Social Interaction and Interpersonal Comparisons

Rousseau attributes three emotional and motivational dispositions to people: *amour de soi* (self-love), *pitié* (pity) and *amour-propre* (sometimes translated as pride).[8] Whereas the former two dispositions are natural, the third is an acquired or 'artificial' disposition. Humans share their self-loving nature with other animals: self-love is an animal's instinct-based disposition to protect and defend itself, to provide for itself, to seek pleasure and avoid pain. No animal could survive without self-love, and human animals are no exception. Self-love is not morally objectionable. Originally, it gives rise only to needs and interests that can be satisfied by consuming what nature provides.

Pity is the disposition to empathise with those in distress and to try and come to their assistance:

> Setting aside . . . all scientific books that teach us only to see men as they have made themselves, and mediating on the first and simplest operations of the human soul, I believe I perceive in it two principles preceding reason, one of which interests us ardently in our well-being and our self-preservation, and the other of which inspires in us a natural repugnance to see any sensitive being, and principally our fellow-humans, perish or suffer. (Rousseau 2014: 54)

Whereas pity is not entirely absent from the animal world (Rousseau 2014: 83), what definitely distinguishes humans from non-human animals is *amour-propre*. Creatures can only acquire it if they have 'reason', the capacity to think, to be conscious of themselves, and to distinguish themselves from other people. It is this disposition that induces us to pay attention to other people, to their naturally given and culturally acquired differences and, what is most important for their rational capacities, to their opinions on matters both factual and evaluative, including their opinions on ourselves as moral agents. This disposition depends on reason in so far as it depends on the capacity to look at matters of factual and evaluative judgement from a plurality of viewpoints. It allows us to discover the multiplicity of perspectives as well as the limitations of our own perspective on the world. Without it, we could not distinguish between appearance and reality. Furthermore, this disposition has a motivational function; it gives rise to a desire to be loved, liked, appreciated, esteemed, recognised and praised by other people.

As members of a society, we cannot help but compare ourselves to others. This comparison allows us to discover the differences between people. Indeed, people are different as to their physical properties and their socio-economic status and corresponding lifestyles. Whereas physical differences are 'natural', differences in lifestyle are 'conventional' (Rousseau 2014: 61). Physical differences are merely aggravated by society: conventional differences, however, are constituted by society, and in commercial society their impact on people is particularly devastating. In commercial society, under the influence of their *amour-propre*, people acquire new, non-natural needs, needs which cannot be satisfied by what nature provides. Indeed, *amour-propre* plays a key role in Rousseau's account of social inequality and its destructive consequences for human flourishing:

> having previously been free and independent, here is man, subjected, so to speak, by a multitude of new needs to all of nature and especially to his fellow humans, whose slave he in a sense becomes even in becoming their master. Rich, he needs their services; poor, he needs their help, and being in a middling condition does not enable him to do without them. He therefore constantly has to seek to interest them in his fate and to make them find their own advantage, in reality or appearance, in working for his. This makes him deceitful, treacherous,

and artful with some, imperious and harsh with others, and makes it necessary for him to mislead all those he needs when he cannot get them to fear him and when he does not find it in his interest to make himself useful to them. (Rousseau 2014: 100)

The aspects that people mostly focus on when making these comparisons are 'wealth, nobility or rank, power, and personal merit'; these are 'the principal distinctions by which one is measured in society' (Rousseau 2014: 113). The effect of *amour-propre* is that 'every individual ... attach[es] more importance to himself than to anyone else'; it 'inspires in men all the harm they do to one another, and that is the true source of honor' (Rousseau 2014: 147 n. xv).

By allowing themselves to be 'measured in society' and by letting society determine the respective measure, people make themselves dependent on others' appraisal: they make their self-esteem depend on others' praise of their superior merits. Rather than recognition by others as people with equal moral worth, that is, 'recognition respect', they seek 'appraisal respect' from people they consider their equals, if not their superiors.[9] Nobody cares much about being appraised as superior by those judged as inferior. It is this dynamic of appraisal respect, of actual praise and the self-esteem depending on it, that gives rise to the morally devastating impact of *amour-propre*: the desire to be praised and esteemed as a person with superior social status and merit cannot be satisfied, because it is a desire for praise and respect from people who are either equal or superior in social status and merit (that is, status and merit according to conventional standards). Every time people find themselves praised by others, this praise is devalued by the fact that it comes from people who thereby express their own inferiority. Due to the negative dynamics of *amour-propre*, actual praise leads to further efforts to gain the praise of others not yet recognised as inferior, rather than to the satisfaction of a desire for recognition respect. Indeed, Rousseau's account of the impact of *amour-propre* on members of a commercial society reads like a psychological account of the features characteristic of a narcissistic personality.[10] It may reveal much of what Rousseau felt himself as a person of low social origins and little education who, as a child, had not experienced much love or encouragement, when he finally moved among the French and British intellectuals and aristocrats of his time.

Since *amour-propre* is not a natural but an artificial disposition, the suffering it imposes on people is not without a remedy.
As Dennis Rasmussen has argued, Rousseau explores three kinds
of remedy or 'escape routes' from the problems to which *amour-
propre* gives rise once people live in commercial society: a political
remedy (in his *Social Contract*), a personal remedy (exemplified
in his own life as a *Solitary Walker*) and an educational remedy
(in his *Emile*) (Rasmussen 2008: 41). However, none of these
remedies promises individual recovery, since none of them is
within reach of the individual member of commercial society in
the grip of a narcissistic desire for appraisal. The first remedy
aims at reducing the impact of conventional socio-economic
differences between people by providing a counterbalance of
political equality and freedom from dependence relations, dominance and servility. Citizens of a state based on a social contract
are free, equally autonomous, and therefore political and legal
equals; their political freedom and equality do not fuel narcissistic dispositions. But for the individual member of commercial
society, the construction of a state based on a social contract
is utopian. The second remedy aims at avoiding interpersonal
comparisons: those who live a solitary life deprive themselves
of the opportunity of comparing themselves to others and thus
stay away from all that could trigger their narcissistic *amour-
propre* to unfold its destructive force. By choosing a solitary life,
a person returns, so to say, to the state of freedom and equality as proto-humans enjoyed it in the original 'state of nature'.
The third remedy is preventive in kind. If a child is brought up
with a great amount of love and care, in a way that strengthens
its trust in the love and protection of other people as well as
in its own worthiness of this love, it will acquire a self-esteem
independent of appraisal respect for merits defined in terms of
conventional socio-economic standards. A child brought up in
such a loving and self-trust enforcing way will be less vulnerable
to the devastating impact of *amour-propre*. Such a preventive
measure will evidently not be available to an adult already in
the grip of narcissistic *amour-propre*. Nevertheless, Rousseau,
in his treatise on education, reveals deep insights into the conditions of emotional stability and happiness as necessary traits of
a moral character. He anticipates findings by contemporary neu-
robiologists and psychologists who confirm the importance of
love and care for newborn children as the foundations of future

emotional stability, social competence, self-trust, self-esteem and the disposition to feel and act in a morally proper way.[11]

Given the utopian nature of a state based on a social contract as Rousseau envisioned it and the impossibility of having a new, more promising start in life, one might be tempted to conclude that the only available remedy for the members of commercial society who find themselves in the grip of narcissistic desire for appraisal respect is to withdraw from society and to live a solitary life, similar to that of our ancestors, those pre-human, animal-like creatures who lived in the state of nature. But whereas Rousseau himself followed this way of life at a certain point in his career and experienced some peace of mind as a solitary walker on the Ile de St-Pierre, he did not generally recommend it. Sociability is an intrinsic human need and nobody can be really happy without it.

Indeed, even though Rousseau described human life in a pre-social state of nature as a state of equality and freedom and deplored the loss of these values in commercial society, he made it very clear that those naturally free and equal creatures were not humans in the full sense of the term. Rather, they were proto-humans, living almost like animals, innocent but not properly moral. And while they did not suffer from the narcissistic and morally destructive impact of *amour-propre*, they did not enjoy any of the charms that only a properly human, self-conscious life can provide: 'love and leisure' (Rousseau 2014: 95). Of all the stages of human development, it was not the state of nature that Rousseau considered to have been the happiest; rather, it was the state of 'nascent society', when reason had started to develop and when people had become sensible to the charm of sociability. Their *amour-propre* had been awoken, but it was not yet fully developed: 'this period of the development of human faculties, occupying a golden mean between the indolence of the primitive state and the petulant activity of our pride, must have been the happiest and most durable epoch' (Rousseau 2014: 97).

For members of commercial society, returning to this happy stage of nascent society is no more an option than returning to the state of nature.[12] Thus, none of the above-mentioned escape routes is open to them. What then can they do in order to minimise the devastating impact of *amour-propre*, in order to avoid making their self-esteem dependent on others' praise and thus engaging in an endless competition with others, a competition that nobody can win? How can they find a way to learn to become virtuous and flourish as moral beings? How can they, in a society of endless competition and comparison, where everyone seeks to be recognised as superior to others, learn to recognise others as their moral equals? Does Rousseau provide a convincing answer to these questions? Or does his overall outlook on human life and on the prospects of virtue and happiness remain mostly pessimistic?

Both Hanley and Neuhouser have suggested readings of Rousseau's work according to which Rousseau did not draw exclusively pessimistic conclusions from his psychological inquiry into the nature and dynamics of *amour-propre* in commercial society. And, since they attribute a somewhat more optimistic view about the prospects of humans' moral flourishing to Rousseau, they conclude that his work not only provided a source of inspiration for Adam Smith's moral theory, but that Smith followed Rousseau in his account of the dynamics of social interaction, interpersonal comparison and its contribution to the shaping of a person's moral character.

Smith on Social Interaction and Interpersonal Comparisons

Smith's account of humans' natural emotional and motivational dispositions both follows and departs from that which he found in Rousseau's work. Generally speaking, it provides us with an outlook on social life that is more optimistic than Rousseau's. Like Rousseau, Smith attributes self-love to humans, a natural disposition to provide for themselves, for their survival, well-being and happiness. The second natural disposition he attributes to humans, namely 'sympathy', includes elements both of Rousseau's pity and of his *amour-propre*. But in the details of his analysis of sympathy, Smith departs from Rousseauian views. Sympathy is, according to Smith, a natural disposition to be interested 'in the fortune of others' (TMS I.i.1.1: 9). It is a disposition to empathise with others, either by a mere transfusion of feelings (TMS I.i.1.6: 11) or by one's imaginatively taking the point of view of another person in order to understand either what this person actually feels or what one would feel if exposed to the same circumstances (TMS I.i.1.2ff: 9–12). It resembles Rousseau's pity to a limited extent.[13] Rousseau stresses the motivational impact of pity (it triggers helping behaviour); Smith is more interested in sympathy as a disposition with a cognitive function. Sympathy allows us to discover the multiplicity of human perspectives on the world, the limitations of our own perspective, and the need to distinguish between appearance and reality in moral matters. As such, it bears affinities to Rousseau's account of *amour-propre* and its connection to reason.

As a result of our sympathy, we make interpersonal comparisons. But Smith departs from Rousseau in his account both of the focus and function of these comparisons. He does not deny what Rousseau so eloquently described, namely people's interest in social praise, their disposition to admire those who enjoy a high status in socio-economic terms, and their attempt to acquire such a status themselves. And he shares Rousseau's criticism of this interest and guiding force. After all, 'the pursuit of wealth, of power, and pre-eminence' (TMS I.iii.2.1: 50) does not facilitate the acquisition either of proper moral understanding or of a moral character.[14] But Smith's claim is that this is not all we do when making interpersonal comparisons, and it is certainly not what we should do. But what else could we focus on when making interpersonal comparisons?

According to Smith, when relying on our sympathy, we pay attention to other people's judgements on moral matters and to their judgements on the moral propriety or impropriety of our own behaviour in particular. We make comparisons between others' and our own moral judgements. And we seek unanimity with others in our moral judgements, both in our judgements about other people and in those about ourselves. There are two reasons for this interest in the unanimity of our own moral judgements with those of others, one psychological and the other cognitive or justificatory in kind. On the one hand, such unanimity reveals agreement on moral matters and such an agreement gives rise to mutual sympathy, an essential condition for human happiness (see TMS I.i.2.1ff: 13–16). On the other hand, we are interested in making proper moral judgements, judgements with which other people have reason to agree. Thus, whenever we encounter moral disagreement with others, we take this to reveal that at least one of the disagreeing parties is in the wrong. We then have to try and identify the party who is in the wrong and eliminate the mistake in moral judgement that this party has made. For this purpose, we have to engage in a sympathetic process, a process of communication in the course of which we try to empathise with each other; we exchange points of view in order to learn what a certain circumstance looks and feels like from another person's point of view. We share relevant factual knowledge as it is available from the various points of view, and we try to identify and eliminate sources of evaluative prejudice that might distort the respective moral judgements.

The aim of such a process of communication is to establish unanimity in matters of moral judgement and thus lay the foundations for mutual sympathy. According to Smith, unanimity in matters of moral judgement among people can be a justificatory reason for them to trust that they hold morally proper judgements. But not just any kind of unanimity will provide such a reason. People who accidentally find themselves in agreement on matters of moral judgement have no more reason to trust in the propriety of their judgement than those who disagree with each other. Only a unanimity brought about by a sympathetic process provides a reason to trust in the propriety of the respective judgement. This is because this particular, sympathy-based way of coming to an agreement about a moral judgement justifies this judgement as morally proper. Or, to put this point in Smith's terms, actual praise of an action does not reveal the action's moral propriety: only praiseworthy actions are morally proper. And in order to inquire into an action's praiseworthiness, we have to engage in a sympathetic process (see TMS III.2.25: 126).

People who engage in a sympathetic process thereby acquire the faculty of moral conscience. Moral conscience is, according to Smith, a faculty of moral self-assessment. This faculty is crucial for people interested in holding properly justified moral judgements. They have to take a critical attitude to their own moral judgements and to their own moral self-judgements in particular; after all, these judgements may be made from too limited a point of view. Without such a critical attitude, they could not recognise the limitations of their own points of view and the lack of justification of the moral judgements made from these limited points of view. According to Smith, conscientious moral self-assessment is not a matter of listening to the voice of a transcendent and absolute authority, as Ryan Hanley has argued.[15] Rather, it requests engagement in an imaginary sympathetic process in which the conscientious person imaginatively takes the points of view of all parties involved (see TMS III.1.6: 113).

According to Smith, the justification of a particular moral judgement can be provided in two different ways: by engaging in a sympathetic process with other people who exchange their respective and equally limited points of view, or by conscientiously engaging in an imaginative sympathetic process and taking the points of view of all the relevant parties. Smith does not give preference to either of these procedures; both have their pros and cons and neither can provide absolute certainty of the propriety of the respective moral judgement. When engaging in such a process with actual people, there is always the danger that these people will pursue other goals rather than that of joining forces with others as equals in order to find out how to properly judge the moral goodness or badness of an agent's action. They might simply try to manipulate the others and make them agree with them, by bribing them or by other means (see TMS III.2.24: 126). They might be stubborn and not accept any criticism or they might refuse any revision of their own moral opinions for fear of being exposed as less morally competent than others. But conscience-based moral judgements are not without their challenges either. The main challenge for moral self-assessment and the engagement in a merely imaginary sympathetic process is that these procedures can be blurred by ignorance, including the ignorance of the limitations of one's own perspective, and self-deceit, the 'fatal weakness of mankind' (TMS III.4.6: 158).[16]

Independently of whether a sympathetic process is actual or imaginative and virtual, it can only provide justification for a moral judgement if all relevant perspectives, the perspectives of all the people who are directly or indirectly affected by the matter at stake, are included or taken into account. The participants in this process meet each other with recognition respect as it is due equally to all people. Smith's account of the sympathetic process as a procedural way of justifying a moral judgement implies an account of the origin of recognition respect. This respect is an essential part of our interest in the propriety of moral judgements, that is, the justification of their claims to unrestrained authority. Since all people have their individual point of view and since all individual points of view are equally limited, they can only achieve a proper, a properly justified, moral judgement if they share the relevant information from all points of view. People who recognise the need to join forces in order to understand which moral judgements are justified cannot exclude anybody from participating in this process: otherwise they run the risk of arbitrarily excluding those who might provide relevant information not available to anybody else.

Engaging in sympathetic processes is, according to Smith, an essential part of moral learning. It is through sympathy-based interaction and interpersonal comparisons of moral judgements that people learn who they are, that they acquire self-awareness and conscience, that they learn about the limitations of their own point of view and outlook on the world, and that they acquire the skill of distinguishing between unjustified and properly justified judgements (including moral judgements). Whereas Smith did not ignore the psychological challenges of interpersonal comparisons as Rousseau had described them, he pointed out that such comparisons could focus on different aspects and serve different functions than those Rousseau had mainly been interested in. Smith focused on the justificatory potential of interpersonal comparisons of moral judgements; he saw interpersonal comparisons as an essential tool of moral justification and of learning to become a moral person, a person who lets him or herself be guided by sympathy and properly justified moral judgements.

Thus, it seems that there is a substantial discrepancy between Rousseau's and Smith's accounts of the function of interpersonal comparisons in matters of moral learning and action. Nevertheless, both Ryan Hanley and Frederick Neuhouser have argued in favour of the claim that Smith and Rousseau shared more than criticism of the socio-economic inequalities between members of commercial society and an interest in the psychological nature and dynamics of social interaction and interpersonal comparisons. Both Hanley and Neuhouser focus in their respective arguments on Rousseau's account of *amour-propre*. But whereas Hanley's claim is that Smith followed Rousseau's view of the psychological nature and dynamics of social interaction as morally challenging and counter-productive, Neuhouser's claim goes in the opposite direction. He attributes to Rousseau an account of the dynamics and prospects of social interaction and interpersonal comparison according to which it is the source of recognition respect, and concludes that, as far as the origin of recognition respect is concerned, Rousseau did not leave much for Smith to add.

Ryan Hanley's Assimilating Reading of Rousseau and Smith

According to Ryan Hanley, Smith agreed with Rousseau's claim that social interaction among the members of commercial society represents a constant threat to an individual's moral flourishing and that the only remedy or escape route available was to ignore other people's opinions as much as possible and to make one's moral judgement and decisions regarding action independently of them (Hanley 2015). His claim is that Smith's inquiry into the sympathetic process is merely a psychological account of the acquisition of conscience. Whereas a child depends on interacting with at least some people in order to develop and become a proper human being, to acquire reason, self-consciousness and conscience, once it has reached this level of intellectual and emotional development it no longer depends on social interaction to learn to be virtuous and to flourish as a moral being. Moral development requires 'a shift from intersubjectivity to self-sufficiency' of the reflective person (Hanley 2009: 136 n. 9), a shift from 'conventional' to 'true' morality (Hanley 2015: 143).[17] Underlying this is the claim that the only source of proper moral understanding, according to Smith, is conscience. Conscience is the 'mechanism' of the impartial spectator (Hanley 2015: 136). It enables a person 'to become a self-spectator' (Hanley 2015: 136) and to 'transcend the solicitude of the opinion of others which might otherwise promote conformity or homogeneity' (Hanley 2015: 137).[18] Hanley implies that conscientious practical reasoning could rightly command a superior moral authority than any agreement reached through a sympathetic process with other actual people. He finds this reading of Smith confirmed by a passage in *The Theory of Moral Sentiments* where Smith does indeed claim that conscientious moral judgements are informed by 'a much higher tribunal' (TMS III.2.32: 130) than any tribunal actual people can provide (Hanley 2015:143).

According to Hanley,

> Smith's system of practical ethics . . . takes such processes [social constructions and reciprocal adjustments of ethical behaviour via a train of self-conscious exchanges of observations and judgements between actors and spectators] as a departure point, but . . . its goal is not merely the establishment of an intersubjective ethics of mutual recognition but the transcendence of a dependence of recognition via the cultivation of the love of virtue. (Hanley 2009: 99)

Whereas he can refer to a limited number of passages from Smith's *Theory of Moral Sentiments*, other passages speak against the claim that conscience can rightly command superior authority.[19] And as far as Hanley's reading of Rousseau is concerned, it ignores Rousseau's own denial of the claim that a solitary life was a morally promising option for fully developed human beings. Rousseau did not recommend it even to members of commercial society suffering from a narcissistic desire for appraisal. He himself withdrew to the Ile de St-Pierre not in order to avoid the narcissistic impact of *amour-propre*, but rather to escape persecution after having been accused of blasphemy. Hanley is, however, aware of Smith's not following Rousseau's account of a fully morally self-sufficient lifestyle in all its aspects: the virtuous man, as Smith sees him, 'transcends opinions only and not the duties expected of the virtuous', duties such as active beneficence (Hanley 2015: 149).[20]

Frederick Neuhouser's Assimilating Reading of Rousseau and Smith

Frederick Neuhouser has suggested a reading of Rousseau's *amour-propre* according to which this disposition is not only the source of all moral evil but also of the remedy to this evil. It is, according to Neuhouser, the origin of people's disposition to respect others as their moral equals (Neuhouser 2008: 2, 3, 15, 187, 218). Indeed, Rousseau says explicitly that the effect of *amour-propre* is not exclusively negative:

> If this were the place to go into details . . . I would show that it is this ardor to be talked about, this frenzy to distinguish ourselves that almost always keeps us outside ourselves, to which we owe what is best and worst among men, our virtues and our vices, our sciences and our errors, our conquerors and our philosophers – that is, a multitude of bad things as against a small number of good ones. (Rousseau 2014: 113)

What are the good things that would not exist without people being driven by *amour-propre*? In the passage quoted, Rousseau mentions 'science' and 'philosophy', implying that it is because of our *amour-propre* that we make an effort to improve our knowledge of the world and of ourselves in the world. Without the wish to excel ourselves, we would not have been motivated to develop our specifically human talents, namely the sciences and the arts. Indeed, narcissists are typically ambitious, since their self-esteem depends on other people's praise of their merits; they work hard to achieve those merits and a corresponding social status as defined by conventional standards. Neuhouser, however, attributes a further positive impact to *amour-propre*; he sees it as the main source of recognition respect, and thus of our intrinsic commitment to virtue. To defend his reading, he draws not only on the *Discourse on Inequality*, but also on *Emile* and on the *Social Contract*.

But how can people's *amour-propre* be the source of their mutual recognition as moral equals? For his answer to this question, Neuhouser distinguishes between two shapes that *amour-propre* can take: 'non-inflamed' and 'inflamed' (Neuhouser 2008: 116). Only the latter is narcissistic or pathological. Independently of the particular shape it takes, *amour-propre* is the disposition of a person to compare themselves to others, to value the merits of themselves and others by comparison, and to desire praise and esteem from other people for the merits they assume themselves to have. But only if *amour-propre* is inflamed does it induce a person to desire praise and esteem for having superior merits, and thereby give rise to the negative dynamics that are characteristic of a narcissistic personality. Only if driven by inflamed *amour-propre* does a person lose his or her integrity and freedom and become dependent on others, alienated and self-estranged (Neuhouser 2008: 99, 82–3).

The characteristic feature of a person whose *amour-propre* is not inflamed or narcissistic is that they can rely on a firm self-esteem, based on a warranted trust in their own merits. Neuhouser does not raise the question of how Rousseau accounts for the 'objectivity' or 'well-groundedness' of this trust; he seems to imply that Rousseau is a realist about personal merits that warrant self-trust (Neuhouser 2008: 97). A person who has such objective merits will still seek appraisal and esteem from other people; the psychological need of such appraisal is induced by their *amour-propre*. But he or she seeks this appraisal from those people in particular who can actually recognise his or her objective merit, that is, from people who share his or her evaluative standards. And the appraisal they seek is therefore not appraisal as a person superior to those who esteem them, but rather as a person who is their equal in merit. Thus, Neuhouser concludes that *amour-propre* as a psychic disposition of a person who can rely on a firm and objectively warranted self-esteem is constitutive of this person's recognition of other people as their equals. Strictly speaking it would be unrealistic for such a person to expect the appraisal of all people: too many people may be in the grip of inflamed *amour-propre* and blinded to others' objective merits. Nevertheless, he or she can justifiably claim the appraisal of all people because his or her objective merits warrant this appraisal (see Neuhouser 2008: 80–1, 84, 97).

Neuhouser admits that Rousseau himself is not very explicit about the structure and implications of non-inflamed *amour-propre*. In his reconstruction of non-inflamed *amour-propre* as the origin of universal recognition respect, he relies on Hegelian inspirations (see Neuhouser 2008: 98). Furthermore, his claim is that Smith's 'naturalistic account of the formation of a moral character' (Neuhouser 2008: 12) is the account of a character of a person who recognises all others as their moral equals and expects and requests to be themselves recognised accordingly, and that this is 'heavily indebted to' and 'indeed an extension of' Rousseau's (Neuhouser 2008: 231 n. 19).

Some aspects of Neuhouser's reconstruction of Rousseau's psychological account of the origin of recognition respect in non-inflamed *amour-propre* are indeed reminiscent of Smith's account of the way people communicate in a sympathetic process. He attributes to Rousseau the claim that people's *amour-propre*-induced concern for the opinions of others cannot be limited to their need of praise and social recognition. Rather, it is an intrinsic aspect of their rationality, since it gives rise to an individual's awareness of her or his own opinion as just one among many others. This awareness helps, according to Neuhouser, 'to foster rational agency . . . by providing individuals with an incentive to learn to view and judge *themselves* – their own actions and qualities – from an external perspective', and he stresses the importance of this point: '*amour-propre* impels us to recognize others not merely as sentient, passive beings – sufferers of pleasure and pain – but as active, judging subjects who adopt an evaluative stance to their world, including to other subjects' (Neuhouser 2008: 225).

Indeed, Neuhouser interprets Rousseau's account of *amour-propre* as an account of a desire all people share, namely the desire to be recognised as a worthy person in the eyes of others who are equally worthy. And from this he concludes that Rousseau's account of *amour-propre* is a forerunner not only of Smith's naturalistic moral theory but also of Kant's rationalistic morality and of the Categorical Imperative in particular (Neuhouser 2008: 53).

However, according to Neuhouser, non-inflamed *amour-propre* is not the only source of people's recognition of all others as equals: he also attributes an important role to pity (Neuhouser 2008: 176). Indeed, as Rousseau points out in *Emile*,

> we are attached to our fellows . . . by the sentiment of their pains, for we see . . . in . . . [their pains] the identity of our natures with theirs and the guarantees of their attachment to us. If our common needs unite us by interest, our common miseries unite us by affection . . . who does not pity the unhappy man whom he sees suffering? Who would not want to deliver him from his ills if it only cost a wish for that? Imagination puts us in the place of the miserable man rather than in that of the happy man . . . Pity is sweet because, in putting ourselves in the place of the one who suffers, we nevertheless feel the pleasure of not suffering as he does. (Rousseau 1991: 221)

Thus, according to Neuhouser, we can identify two sources of people's disposition to recognise others as their equals: in experiencing pity, they recognise others as equally vulnerable and as equally in need of help as themselves; and in their desire to be esteemed and valued for their objective merits by other people, they recognise others as people equally committed to objective merits but with opinions on these merits different from their own.

Neuhouser is not of the opinion that pity and non-inflamed *amour-propre* are sufficient to counterbalance the negative impact that inflamed *amour-propre* can have on people. Further educational measures are needed to provide a person with the means and strength to resist the temptation of engaging in an endless competition for the recognition of their superiority by others. And in order to really enjoy equality and freedom, people have to live as members of a state constituted by a social contract. This is because only as an equal participant in a general will can a person enjoy equal legal respect and equal recognition as a bearer of rights (Neuhouser 2008: 166–8).

Recognition Respect and its Origin: Rousseau, Smith and Kant

The question to be raised is whether pity and the non-inflamed *amour-propre*-based desire for esteem and self-esteem, warranted by a person's objective merits, as Rousseau describes them, are indeed constitutive of the particularly moral kind of recognition respect Neuhouser claims them to be. Did Rousseau really provide a convincing account of the origin of moral recognition respect and thereby anticipate both Smith's and Kant's accounts? Smith's and Kant's respective accounts of the origin of recognition respect may not be the same. But they agree on one point: recognition respect is not due to a person because of any particular merits that he or she may have. It is due to all people unconditionally, that is, independently of their particular merits. As such, it cannot arise from any interpersonal comparisons that focus on the merits people have achieved, whether these merits are objective or not.

According to Smith, we have to recognise all people as potential subjects of sympathy and sympathy-based moral judgements; while it may turn out that some people are more sensitive to morally relevant matters than others, and thus more important partners in a sympathetic process, we do not have any non-arbitrary criteria for assessing people's moral sensitivity before we have actually engaged in a sympathetic process with them. Our interest in making proper moral judgements commits us to recognising all people as partners in a sympathetic process. Otherwise, the standards of moral propriety constituted in such a process could not rightly request unlimited authority, that is, the authority to guide the behaviour of all people, or at least of all those people who are not mentally retarded and who are capable of exercising some control over their actions.

Kant provides us with an account of moral recognition and its origin that is different from Smith's. According to Kant, properly moral recognition respect is not only supposed to be universal, including all people independently of their natural properties and socio-economic status; it is also due to people because of their intrinsically equal moral worth, which originates in their rationality. Rationality distinguishes people from non-human animals. As embodied creatures provided with reason, humans resemble both non-human animals and divine, namely purely rational, creatures. In respecting another person as one's equal, one recognises both one's own and the other person's resemblance to the divine. The right of a person to be recognised as a moral equal does not depend on their actual moral merit. Nor does it depend on how smart this person is. Whereas one person can address another and thereby express his or her recognition respect of the other's moral worth, people do not depend for their moral worth on others paying recognition respect to them. The moral worth of a person and his or her awareness of it differs from the psychological state of self-esteem, which is indeed dependent on the experience of being respected by others.

Rousseau does anticipate Smithian views in his attribution of a kind of empathy to all people, namely the disposition to imagine themselves in the position of others and to share their feelings of happiness and distress. But, according to Rousseau, reason and reflection, once acquired, reduce the impact of pity on our desires rather than giving rise to recognition respect. Pity provides more of a counterpart to self-love and the selfish desires arising from it than to *amour-propre* and the narcissistic desires to which it gives rise when inflamed. And finally, under the influence of *amour-propre*, the experience of pity can lead to an increased awareness of the comparative inferiority of the one in distress who is the object of pity:

> Indeed, commiseration will be all the more energetic to the extent that the onlooking animal identifies more intimately with the suffering animal. Now, it is obvious that this identification must have been infinitely closer in the state of nature than in the state of reasoning. It is reason that engenders pride [*amour-propre*], and it is reflection that fortifies it. It is reason that turns man back upon himself. It is reason that separates him from everything that bothers and afflicts him. It is philosophy that isolates him; it is by means of it that he secretly says at the sight of a suffering man: perish if you will, I am safe. (Rousseau 2014: 84)

Is the kind of recognition that Neuhouser finds originating in Rousseau's *amour-propre*, if properly guided and not inflamed, intrinsically moral? People do not need recognition from *all* people to satisfy their psychic desire for self-esteem and the social esteem on which it depends. On the contrary, the esteem they need for this purpose has to come from those they consider their equals, if not their superiors, since nobody cares much about esteem from inferiors, be they inferior in socio-economic status or in objective moral merit.

The same point can be put in terms of Darwall's distinction between recognition respect and appraisal respect (Darwall 1977; 2006: 122–6). Whereas appraisal respect is due to people by virtue of certain merits that they have, recognition respect is due to people by virtue of their being people, of their having intrinsic moral worth, a kind of moral status that they can neither merit nor lose. What Neuhouser finds in Rousseau's *amour-propre* is 'appraisal respect': people want to be valued and praised for their – apparent or real – merits, whatever it is that counts as a merit. But valuing and recognising people for their merits is not the same as recognising them as people who have intrinsic moral worth.[21]

Conclusion

It is difficult to agree with either Hanley or Neuhouser and their different but equally assimilating readings of Rousseau's and Smith's thought about human morality. Hanley reads both Rousseau and Smith as proponents of a moral ideal of social independence and moral self-sufficiency, that is, of an ideal of moral solipsism. He thereby minimises Rousseau's and Smith's unanimous commitment to the claim that human nature is essentially social and that humans depend on others for their virtue and happiness. Neuhouser reads Rousseau's accounts of pity and non-inflamed *amour-propre* as mutually dependent origins of people's motivation to help others in need, and to recognise them as equally vulnerable and worthy of respect, as a forerunner of Smith's and Kant's accounts of moral recognition respect. According to Smith and Kant, recognition respect is due to all humans: it is intrinsically unconditional and therefore non-comparative. For neither Kant nor Smith is recognition respect merely a psychic disposition to feel pity for other people or to appraise them and to request their appraisal. According to Kant, recognition respect is due to all people unconditionally because of their *a priori* moral worth. According to Smith, recognising all other people as one's equals is a rational requirement originating in our commitment to moral propriety and its justification. We have no access to moral merit independently of what we agree upon through sympathetic processes. Smith's account of recognition respect and its origin is a valuable alternative to the Kantian account. The same does not apply to Rousseau's psychological account of pity and non-inflamed *amour-propre* as reconstructed by Neuhouser.

Notes

1. See WN V.i.f.51: 783: 'Every man does, or is capable of doing, almost every thing which any other man does, or is capable of

doing.' On Smith's criticism of socio-economic inequalities, see also Rækstad (2017).

2. On Smith's departure from Rousseauian views on republicanism, see Fleischacker (2004: 246–9).

3. Here I follow Rasmussen (2008: 9), who speaks of Smith's response to Rousseau's criticism of commercial society in terms of a 'cost-benefit analysis'. On this topic, see also Anderson (2016).

4. For the details of his argument, see WN V.i.f.48–61: 781–8.

5. On Smith's account of commercial societies' commitment to justice and fairness, see also Sen (2009: 44).

6. See Neuhouser (2008: 12). Historically speaking, Smith's 'appropriation' of Rousseauian views in his *Theory of Moral Sentiments* has to be limited to those views that were made public before 1759. Thus, Rousseau's *Emile* (1762), on which Neuhouser relies extensively, cannot have been appropriated by Smith, at least not in the first edition of *The Theory of Moral Sentiments*. As for the later editions of *The Theory of Moral Sentiments*, the 6th edition from 1790 in particular, they reveal Smith's growing scepticism concerning the possibility of moral flourishing under non-egalitarian socio-economic conditions. Whereas this development may reveal the influence of Rousseauian misanthropic views, these are not the views that Neuhouser is mostly interested in when inquiring into Rousseau's account of *amour-propre*.

7. For similar readings of Smith's response to Rousseau, see West (1971) and Rasmussen (2008). However, West and Rasmussen focus on Smith's defence of economic society rather than on his moral theory.

8. The question of how to translate *amour-propre* into English is a difficult one. Apart from 'pride', one might use 'conceit'; but these translations have exclusively negative connotations and block the path to more neutral or even positive interpretations of *amour-propre* as they have recently been put forward by Frederick Neuhouser (2008; 2013). Given these difficulties of translation, I shall continue to use the original French term *amour-propre*.

9. For the distinction between 'recognition respect' and 'appraisal respect', see Darwall (1977; 2006: 122–6).

10. See Neuhouser (2008: 86). On the negative dynamics of *amour-propre*, see also Dent (1988), Cohen (1997) and Neuhouser (2008: 60, 75–6).

11. For the psychological work to which I refer here, see Narvaez (2014).

12. On this point, see Lovejoy (1923) and Neuhouser (2008: 85–6).

13. For a detailed comparison between Rousseau's notion of 'pity' and Smith's notion of 'sympathy', see Force (2003: 20–47).

14. See also TMS I.iii.3: 61–6 and IV.1.8: 181–3.

15. See Hanley (2009: 97–9). For my criticism of this reading of Smith's account of conscience, see Fricke (2013).

16. For a more detailed defence of this phenomenological reading of Smith's moral theory, see Fricke (2012; 2013).

17. See also Hanley (2015: 146): 'Smith agrees with Rousseau that man's proper aim is the recovery of his self-sufficiency.'

18. Amartya Sen distinguishes between two ways of reading the role of Smith's impartial spectator. One can understand this role as that of an 'arbitrator' or as that of someone 'whose reading and assessment help us to achieve a less partial understanding of the ethics and justice of a problem' (Sen 2009: 131). While Hanley endorses the first reading, Sen endorses the second (as do I).

19. See Fricke (2013). Hanley (2015: 150) grants this to some extent when he talks of the 'social aspects of self-sufficiency' as Smith requests it of the virtuous man.

20. For a somewhat revised reading of Smith's view of moral deliberation and judgement that does not entirely reject the usefulness of interaction and communication with others, see Hanley (2016).

21. Neuhouser refers to Darwall's distinction between appraisal respect and recognition respect, but claims that his distinction between an *amour-propre*-based desire for esteem as a person with superior merits and an *amour-propre*-based desire for recognition as a person with actual moral merits does not match Darwall's distinction. See Neuhouser (2008: 62 n. 11).

Bibliography

Anderson, Elizabeth (2016), 'Adam Smith on Equality', in Ryan Patrick Hanley (ed.), *Adam Smith. His Life, Thought, and Legacy*, Princeton: Princeton University Press, 157–72.

Cohen, Joshua (1997), 'The Natural Goodness of Humanity', in A. Reath, B. Herman and C. M. Korsgaard (eds), *Reclaiming the History of Ethics*, Cambridge: Cambridge University Press, 102–39.

Darwall, Stephen (1977), 'Two Kinds of Respect', *Ethics*, 88, 36–49.

Darwall, Stephen (2006), *The Second Person Standpoint*, Cambridge, MA: Harvard University Press.

Dent, N. J. H. (1988), *Rousseau*, Oxford: Basil Blackwell.

Fleischacker, Samuel (2004), *On Adam Smith's 'Wealth of Nations'*, Princeton: Princeton University Press.

Force, Pierre (2003), *Self-interest before Adam Smith. A Genealogy of Economic Science*, Cambridge: Cambridge University Press.

Fricke, Christel (2012), 'Overcoming Disagreement – Adam Smith and Edmund Husserl on Strategies of Justifying Descriptive and Evaluative Judgments', in Christel Fricke and Dagfinn Føllesdal (eds), *Intersubjectivity and Objectivity in Adam Smith and Edmund Husserl*, Frankfurt: Ontos Verlag, 171–241.

Fricke, Christel (2013), 'Adam Smith: The Sympathetic Process and the Origin and Function of Conscience', in Christopher Berry, Maria Pia Paganelli Craig Smith (eds), *The Oxford Handbook of Adam Smith*, Oxford: Oxford University Press, 177–200.

Hanley, Ryan Patrick (2009), *Adam Smith and the Character of Virtue*, Cambridge: Cambridge University Press.

Hanley, Ryan Patrick (2015), 'Commerce and Corruption. Rousseau's Diagnosis and Adam Smith's Cure', *European Journal of Political Theory*, 7.2, 137–58.

Hanley, Ryan Patrick (2016), 'Adam Smith on Living a Life', in Ryan Patrick Hanley (ed.), *Adam Smith. His Life, Thought, and Legacy*, Princeton: Princeton University Press, 123–37.

Lovejoy, Arthur O. (1923), 'The Supposed Primitivism of Rousseau's Discourse on Inequality', *Modern Philology*, XXI, 165–86.

Narvaez, Darcia (2014), *Neurobiology and the Development of Human Morality*, New York: W.W. Norton.

Neuhouser, Frederick (2008), *Rousseau's Theodicy of Self-Love. Evil, Rationality, and the Drive for Recognition*, Oxford: Oxford University Press.

Neuhouser, Frederick (2013), 'Rousseau's Critique of Inequality', *Philosophy and Public Affairs*, 41.3, 193–225.

Neuhouser, Frederick (2014), *Rousseau's Critique of Inequality. Reconstructing the Second Discourse*, Cambridge: Cambridge University Press.

Rækstad, Paul (2017), 'Human Development and Social Stratification in Adam Smith', *The Adam Smith Review*, 9, 275–94.

Rasmussen, Dennis C. (2006), 'Rousseau's "Philosophical Chemistry" and the Foundations of Adam Smith's Thought', *History of Political Thought*, XXVII.4, 620–41.

Rasmussen, Dennis C. (2008), *The Problems and Promise of Commercial Society. Adam Smith's Response to Rousseau*, University Park: Pennsylvania State University Press.

Rousseau, Jean-Jacques (1991) [1762], *Emile, or On Education*, trans. and ed. Allan Bloom, London: Penguin.

Rousseau, Jean-Jacques (2014) [1754], 'Discourse on the Origin, and the Foundations of Inequality Among Men', in *The Major Political Writings of Jean-Jacques Rousseau. The Two Discourses and The Social Contract*, trans. and ed. John T. Scott, Chicago: University of Chicago Press, 37–151.

Sen, Amartya (2009), *The Idea of Justice*, London: Penguin.

West, E. G. (1971), 'Adam Smith and Rousseau's Discourse on Inequality: Inspiration or Provocation?', *Journal of Economic Issues*, 5.2, 56–70.

5

Actors and Spectators: Rousseau's Contribution to the Eighteenth-century Debate on Self-interest

Mark J. Hill

A debate between the virtue of self-interest and social conceptions of morality emerged in the seventeenth century. Aspects of the historical narrative of these ideas have been touched on by Franco Venturi (1971), Albert O. Hirschman (1977), Pierre Force (2003) and Eric MacGilvray (2011), among others, but broadly one can recognise two camps which ossified during the eighteenth century: those who saw public utility in self-interest emerge from the positive externalities of commerce, and those who had serious concerns over the political implications of entangling commerce and virtue. This chapter locates, primarily, Rousseau within this debate, and by looking at how his moral philosophy interacts with his political thought, argues that he is distinct from contemporary thinkers (in particular, Adam Smith), but in an often confused way: while some have been tempted to view Rousseau as a republican moralist, he is in fact a philosopher of the political and social good of self-interest.[1]

To make this argument, this chapter opens with a brief exploration of Adam Smith's position and the 'impartial spectator', arguing that Smith is a moral sentimentalist and moral rationalist.[2] That is to say, first, moral ideas are born from moral sentiments, and these truths are discoverable through reason. The chapter then examines the source of morality and moral action in Rousseau's thought.[3] It is argued that he is not a moral realist and instead agrees with Hobbes that morality comes to exist only with society (although he denies that this lack of morality is the equivalent to immorality – he is not a moral realist) (*Second Discourse* 1997a: 151/OC III: 153).[4] Specifically, morality emerges due to perfectibility – the confluence of pity and reason result in moral concepts being developed. Thus, it is shown that Rousseau is a moral rationalist. However, this position is complicated by Rousseau's belief that moral rationalism is, by itself, incapable of ensuring moral actions. The chapter goes on to demonstrate that the source of this problem is, in fact, reason itself. He is, therefore, a moral rationalist in terms of source, but is sceptical of reason as a moral motivator.

How Rousseau solves this problem is the topic of the second part of this chapter. It is argued that he has two approaches: first, he turns to something akin to theological voluntarism to legitimise structures which encourage (or force) moral action – a theory in which the political self dictates what is moral through the general will, and thus the legal obligations which follow are considered to spring internally from our own will. However, while this may legitimise moral laws, it does not go far enough to ensure moral actions in everyday life. To resolve this problem Rousseau turns to self-interest. That is, Rousseau both rejected the 'selfish hypothesis', but also envisioned moral motivation emerging through something akin to Mandeville's egoism – a conclusion not entirely dissimilar from the one Smith came to in his review of Rousseau's *Second Discourse* for the *Edinburgh Review* – that is, a system in which we see it as our interest to act morally, but we do not see self-interest itself as moral (i.e. *doux commerce*). This is done by encouraging social institutions which make use of our *amour-propre* so as to transform self-interest into something which can be used to motivate virtuous actions.

That is to say, this chapter argues that Smith develops a moral philosophy in which one must be a spectator capable of selfless and impartial rational reflection in order to will moral ends as an individual, while Rousseau argues that one must have an interest in a situation if one is to be a moral actor.

Adam Smith, Morality and Self-interest

'It is not from the benevolence of the butcher, the brewer, or the baker, that we expect our dinner, but from their regard to their own interest' (WN I.ii.2: 26–7). This is perhaps the most oft-used quote to demonstrate Smith's position on *why* we act, and his views on the virtue of self-interest. However, while there is meaning here in relation to his views on economic activity (and specifically the division of labour), it ignores an important question that Marçal has recently asked: who cooked Adam Smith's dinner? The answer is, in fact, his mother. This is not offered as criticism of Smith. Instead, it highlights how the quote – and self-interested economic activity generally – is insufficient when it comes to explaining Smith's moral philosophy. For that, one must turn to his *Theory of Moral Sentiments*.

Smith explicitly claimed that human relationships have their origin outside of self-interest, and that sociability emerges from, and exists because of, 'pity or compassion, the emotion which we feel for the misery of others'. However, while these sympathies are universal natural sentiments, they are not *entirely* motivational. Smith acknowledges this in the same section: 'For this sentiment, like all of the other original passions of human nature, is by no means confined to the virtuous and humane ... The greatest ruffian, the most hardened violator of the laws of society, is not altogether without it' (TMS I.i.1.1: 9). Thus, while sociability is in some way related to sympathy for fellow humans, moral motivation is decidedly more complicated than natural sentiments encouraging sociable action – how else could the existence of 'ruffians' be explained?

Sympathy is instead an instinct which begins the imaginative process of putting oneself in the position of another:

> As we have no immediate experience of what other men feel, we can form no idea of the manner in which they are affected, but by conceiving what we ourselves should feel in the like situation. Though our brother is upon the rack, as long as we ourselves are at our ease our senses will never inform us of what he suffers ... By the imagination we place ourselves in his situation, we conceive ourselves enduring all the same torments, we enter, as it were, into his body and become in some measure the same person with him; and then form some idea of his sensations. (TMS I.i.1.2: 9)

It is in a similar manner that we make moral judgements: 'We either approve or disapprove of the conduct of another man according as we feel that, when we bring his case home to ourselves, we either can or cannot entirely sympathize with the sentiments and motives which directed it' (TMS I.iii.1.2: 109). However, judging the morality of an action is different from motivating moral actions – not least of all because, when we are the subject, we are likely to have an interest in a given situation. To address this problem Smith turned to the impartial spectator:

> We can never survey our own sentiments and motives, we can never form any judgment concerning them; unless we remove ourselves, as it were, from our own natural station, and endeavour to view them as at a certain distance from us ... We endeavour to examine our own conduct as we imagine any other fair and impartial spectator would examine it. If, upon placing ourselves in his situation, we thoroughly enter into all the passions and motives which influenced it, we approve of it, by sympathy with the approbation of this supposed equitable judge. If otherwise, we enter into his disapprobation, and condemn it. (TMS I.iii.1.3: 110)

By making use of this impartial spectator within us, we disconnect any interest the self may have in an outcome from the process of judging one's own actions. What is more, unlike the condition in which we judge others – that is, where a lack of perfect information can result in incorrect conclusions – the impartial spectator is aware of our intentions, our relationships and our interests. This makes it, as Driver claims, an 'ideal observer' which 'possesses qualities that prevent mistakes' by being 'all-knowing with respect to the non-normative facts' (2013: 371).

However, there is a potential issue with Smith's theory. By acknowledging the direct relationship between public judgements and personal judgements one may be led to conclude that the impartial spectator is simply a representation of one's understanding of public morality (or worse: opinion). That is to say, regardless of being a *better* judge, the standard by which one judges seems to come from an external set of rules – the public – and the inclination to be moral may actually be born out of a self-interested desire to be esteemed by peers. This, however, is the opposite of the argument Smith wants to make.[5] Instead, he argues that the impartial spectator should be capable of overcoming such vanity (of wanting to be praised by others), and in the most extreme cases 'despise the censure of the world' (TMS I.iii.1.5: 112). This is possible due to human beings' underlying natural sentiments: 'Nature, accordingly, has endowed him, not only with a desire of being approved of, but with a desire of being what ought to be approved of; or of being what he himself approves of in other men' (TMS I.iii.2.7: 117). The idea of there being something which 'ought' to be approved of outside of social relationships, however, may mean that morality is in some way objective, and that Smith is, in his own way, a moral realist.

Debes argues that Smith sidesteps the issue of moral realism as he 'seems to suspend judgement on all ultimate questions of "reality" [and thus] there are no grounds to attribute definitively to Smith moral realism' (2014: 518). However, Driver argues that, for Smith, moral properties are objective in that, in a sense, they are 'stance-independent' (2013: 371) and Otteson argues that Smith's 'interactive process of judgement-sharing and negotiation gives rise to intersubjectively objective standards' (2013: 439). For our purposes it is enough to note that there is evidence to claim that Smith is a weak moral realist, and that it is by making reference to these objective moral facts that the impartial spectator can overrule the desire for public esteem and 'the natural misrepresentations of self-love' (TMS I.iii.5.4: 137).

This also means that the construction of our moral faculty is learned, and as it improves we become better at moral reasoning (TMS I.iii.3.21–5: 145–7). Raphael notes:

> A child . . . first learns to control emotion in order to gain the favour and avoid the contempt of his schoolfellows. A man of weak character is like a child; in misfortune he can control his feelings only when others are present. A man of greater firmness remains under the influence of the impartial spectator at all times, so much so that the division of the self into two persons, the imagined spectator and the agent, almost disappears; imagination virtually takes over from reality. (2007: 40)

Thus, the desire to be esteemed may indeed exist, but the impartial spectator is, or will become, aware of it, and rebuke us for such desires. While morality begins with sympathy (Smith writes: 'These first perceptions, as well as all other experiments upon which any general rules are founded, cannot be the object of reason, but of immediate sense and feeling'), and it may initially be buttressed by social interactions, ultimately we are capable of independent moral judgements. Reason establishes 'general rules of justice by which we ought to regulate our actions', 'ideas of what is prudent', 'decent' and 'generous and noble'. That is: 'The general maxims of morality are formed, like all other general maxims, from experience and induction' (TMS VII.iii.2.6–7: 319–20).

There is an important upshot from this position: our moral calculations can be wrong, be it as individuals miscalculating how we should act (for example, individuals becoming 'ruffians' or acting to obtain praise), or society miscalculating what should be praised. Thus, imposing moral rules, rather than allowing for communal self-discovery, could infringe on this natural, yet objective, emerging moral order. That is not to say that there is no role for remonstrating clearly immoral acts – Smith is not a utopian thinker, and as he acknowledges, ruffians exist. However, to create an *a priori* moral order would be wrong, as morality – and therefore moral laws – are *a posteriori* constructions. As Otteson argues: 'Our strong desire for mutual sympathy of sentiments can . . . lead to reciprocity and mutual seeking of sympathy, thereby generating, via an invisible-hand mechanism, commonly shared standards of behaviour and judgement and even a shared system of morality' (2013: 423–4). This means there may be serious political implications in Smith's moral position: lest morality itself be risked, there must be limits to state paternalism. The freedom to make moral judgements as an individual is also the freedom necessary to be virtuous. As we will see, Rousseau's position differs quite substantially.

The Source of Morality in Rousseau

Rousseau's reflections on morality are, like much of his work, difficult. As he wrote himself: 'Regardless of what the Moralists say about it, human understanding owes much to the Passions which, as is commonly admitted, also owe much to [human understanding]' (1997a: 142/OC III: 143). It is this position which led Remy Debes, in his study of eighteenth-century conceptions of morality, to side-line Rousseau from his study – he did not clearly fit categorisation precisely due to the way that 'elements of rationalism and sentimentalism are subtly blended' (2014: 526). It is this relationship, then, which signposts where an investigation must begin.

No Morality in Nature

Moral realism was a position, as held by eighteenth-century thinkers, which argued 'that moral judgments purport to be true or report facts' and therefore 'there are moral facts in light of which our moral judgments are true or false' (Debes 2014: 502). This is a position which Rousseau seems to explicitly deny in the *Second*

Discourse: 'Savages are not wicked precisely because they do not know what it is to be good' (1997a: 151/OC III: 154). This is not simply a claim as to their own understanding of their actions, which in itself would not dismiss moral realism, only moral culpability. Instead, it is also a claim which denies the existence of moral relationships and obligations which, if morality were objectively true, would allow *us* to assign moral blame to the actions of primitive men. This is the error, Rousseau claims, Hobbes made by retroactively applying moral principles to people who could not share them. Instead, Rousseau argued that while humans may be naturally good, they are not naturally moral; nature itself is amoral. However, if morality does exist, its source must be discoverable in something unique to humans – specifically reason and pity.

In the *Second Discourse* Rousseau writes that 'Nature alone does everything in the operations of the Beast, whereas man contributes to his operations in his capacity as a free agent' (1997a: 140/OC III: 141). This freedom, Rousseau will go on to argue, is perfectibility, the faculty which 'is the source of all of man's miseries ... causing his enlightenment and his errors, his vices and his virtues to bloom' (1997a: 141/OC III: 142). More specifically, perfectibility makes possible rational reflection in particular circumstances which can result in behaviours different from those which nature would have imposed. Of course, this alone is not enough for morality to emerge. In fact, perfectibility alone would, Rousseau argues, result in the Hobbesian state of nature (1997a: 151/OC III: 154). However, humans are given pity in addition to reason which 'tempers [human] ardour for well-being with an innate repugnance to see his kind suffer'; it is that which, 'in the state of nature, takes the place of Laws, morals, and virtue' (1997a: 152, 154/OC III: 154, 156).

Pity, however, is not morality. Instead, it is a sentiment which motivates action without reflection or reason playing a role, and is therefore an instinct not worthy of (moral) praise.[6] It is only when reason and pity are combined that morality can emerge – when one decides to act on the instinct. This is the truth which Rousseau claimed contributors to the selfish hypothesis missed or denied: 'Mandeville clearly sensed that, for all their morality, men would never have been anything but monsters if Nature had not given them pity in support of reason: but he did not see that from this single attribute flow all the social virtues he wants to deny in men'

(1997a: 153/OC III: 155). Reason combined with pity, therefore, allows morality to emerge.

Rousseau's Moral Rationalism

Moral rationalism is the view that morality is born out of, or understood through, reason. Debes argues that in the eighteenth century the concept 'edged increasingly to the claim that reason itself can *motivate* us to act' (2014: 502). It will be shown that the former may be true for Rousseau, but the latter is not.

The problem from a Rousseauian perspective is that it is not universally true that reason will result in all people coming to understand morality, that those who do will come to the same conclusions, or that people will be motivated to act because of their reasoned moral conclusions. While reason may allow for *humankind* to discover morality, it does not guarantee anything with regard to individuals: 'While Socrates and minds of his stamp may be able to acquire virtue through reason, mankind would long ago have ceased to be if its preservation had depended solely on the reasonings of those who make it up' (*Second Discourse* 1997a: 154/OC III: 156–7). The reason for this is reason itself.

There are at least four identifiable parts to Rousseau's concern with reason. The first is that reason has historically been politically divisive. As argued in the *First Discourse*, enlightenment requires knowledge, and knowledge requires leisure; one man's leisure requires another man to do twice his share of work, the loss of universal self-sufficiency, and ultimately freedom. Secondly, reason can overpower man's naturally social passion: pity. As Rousseau put it:

> It is reason that engenders *amour-propre*, and reflection that reinforces it; reason that turns man back upon himself; reason that separates him from everything that troubles and afflicts him: It is Philosophy that isolates him; by means of Philosophy he secretly says, at the sight of a suffering man, perish if you wish, I am safe. (1997a: 153/OC III: 156)

Thirdly, although reason is treated as universal and objective, Rousseau argues that it is no such thing. Instead, he writes that 'when a man cannot believe what he finds absurd, it is not his fault; it is that of reason', and that 'human reason has no well-determined common measure and . . . it is unjust for any man to give his own as the rule of that of others' (1960: 11/OC V: 11). This leads to the fourth problem. In his reply to Stanisław's observations on the *First Discourse*, Rousseau noted that whenever reason is an issue of contention between men they are returned to their natural equality and the freedoms given to all men by the right of nature (1997a: 32/OC III: 35). Thus, reason can lead to conflict.

While these concerns make it incredibly difficult for reason to lead to consensus, they also make it impossible to claim that Rousseau is a typical moral rationalist: reason may tell us something about morality, but reason is also the cause of our fallibility on moral issues. The problem, Rousseau writes, is one of misguided self-interest. In the *Discours sur la vertu du héros* he writes:

> Men are more blind than wicked; and there is more weakness than malice in their vices. We deceive ourselves before deceiving others, and our faults are solely due to our errors; we almost only commit any because we allow ourselves to get caught up by petty present interests which makes us forget more important and more remote things ... Our most formidable enemies are within ourselves. (1997a: 315/OC II: 1273)

The problem is epistemological: those who would gain from rational arguments proving the utility of moral laws (for example, Grotius's natural laws – or what Rousseau calls 'la loi de raison') need to have already achieved a level of rationality which would allow them to understand the proofs. However, if they already have this level of rationality, and if these laws were truly natural, the conclusions should have already been discovered and should have motivated moral actions (as they would for the likes of, as Rousseau notes, Socrates). If they are instead capable of this level of rationality, but have failed to embrace the same conclusions – or worse, purposely ignored them – their reason is likely to have already become anti-social and their *amour-propre* inflamed. Any further attempts to encourage morality through reason will fall on deaf ears.

This is a descriptive, rather than normative, point. As Force wrote, in Rousseau's conception of civilisation 'the selfish hypothesis is fully operational. Self-interest is the only engine of human behaviour' (2003: 41). In nature the power of pity is its disconnection from 'personal interest'. Reason and society, however, problematise this. When one leaves the state of nature and becomes socialised, one grows concerned with one's own social needs – *amour-propre* replaces *amour-de-soi*. At this point reason is put to use to gain personal advantages at the expense of others. Thus, the outcome is, ironically, immoral rationalism.

Immoral Rationalism

While Rousseau does not deny moral rationalism, he also does not deny that it may appear to be rational to be immoral:

> No doubt there is a universal justice emanating from reason alone; but this justice, to be admitted among us, has to be reciprocal. Considering things in human terms, the laws of justice are vain among men for want of natural sanctions; they only bring good to the wicked and evil to the just when he observes them toward everyone while no one observes them toward him. (*Social Contract* 1997b: 66/OC III: 378)

There is, therefore, a tension between reason and morality.

It is worth turning to three examples of this tension, each of which offers a slightly different lesson: first, that recognising the rationality of morality may be difficult; secondly, that even if we recognise morality, there may be nothing which motivates us to act; and finally, that rationality may actually inform us that it is rational to be immoral.[7]

In *Emile* Rousseau offers La Fontaine's fable *The Crow and the Fox* as a negative example to would-be tutors and parents.

Master Crow, on a tree perched,
Held in his beak a cheese.
Master Fox by the odor atticed
Made to him a speech of this kind.
Well, good day, Monsieur Crow!
How charming you are! How handsome you seem to me!
Without lying, if your song
Corresponds to your plumage,
You would be the Phoenix of the landlords of these woods.
At these words the Crow cannot contain his joy.
And to show his fine voice
He opens his big beak, lets fall his prey.
The fox grabs it and says: My good monsieur,

Learn that every flatterer
Lives at the expense of the one who listens to him.
This lesson is doubtless worth a cheese.
The Crow, ashamed and embarrassed,
Swore, but a little late, that he would not be caught that way again.
   (1979: 113–15/OC IV: 353–5)

While the moral may appear obvious to adults, Rousseau argues that, first of all, understanding the allegorical – and therefore moral – lesson is beyond the capability of the young, and they are, therefore, more likely to take its lessons literally. That is, what may actually be taught is much more problematic: that there are bad people in the world, and you are better off being a clever and well-fed fox than a naïve, hungry and humiliated crow; that there is utility to flattery and lying, and that one can benefit from deceit. This, Rousseau argues, is not because children are naturally bad, but because it is what naturally follows. However, it was not only children who were at risk.

In the *Letter to d'Alembert*, Rousseau engages with the claim that the theatre could be used in Geneva to aid morality. To counter this position, he argues that a theatre is an inherently solitary place, and thus members of the audience are in a relationship which, at first, seems strikingly similar to Smith's impartial spectator:

> The heart of a man is always right concerning that which has no personal relation to himself. In the quarrels at which we are purely spectators, we immediately take the side of justice, and there is no act of viciousness which does not give us a lively sentiment of indignation so long as we receive no profit from it. (TMS I.iii.1.3: 110)

Rousseau continues by noting that these are not useful moral lessons: 'when our interest is involved, our sentiments are soon corrupted. And it is only then that we prefer the evil which is useful to us to the good that nature makes us love' (1960: 24/OC V: 22). Rousseau claims that while *spectating* allows the audience to feel moral – and congratulate themselves for such feelings – it does not engender *action* outside of that particular sphere. The weakness of the impartial spectator in encouraging moral action is that it is both impartial and a spectator. It may feed some natural sentimentalism in man, and thus placate some instinctual desire, but it does little else:

In the final accounting, when a man has gone to admire fine actions in stories and to cry for imaginary miseries, what more can be asked of him? Is he not satisfied with himself? Does he not applaud his fine soul? Has he not acquitted himself of all that he owes to virtue by the homage which he has just rendered it? What more could one want of him? That he practice it himself? He has no role to play; he is no actor. (1960: 25/OC V: 23–4)

Unlike the example of *The Fox and the Crow*, the theatregoer understands the moral lesson, and is able to make some psychological use of it, but it does little else. However, like La Fontaine's fable, there may even be immoral lessons one could make use of (especially in the case of comedies).[8] This leads to the third example of the tension between morality and reason in Rousseau's thought.

The immoral use of reason was addressed explicitly in the 'Geneva Manuscript' through the voice of a would-be rational citizen. There it is argued that, even though one may accept all the 'advantages of the social law', these truths are not sufficient reason to obey social laws; without assurance that everyone else observes the law, it may be in one's interest to defect. That is to say, reason goes so far as to tell us that, even if we are convinced that we should accept precepts that dictate that it is best that all men live according to a set of shared moral rules, even if we are ourselves convinced by these moral principles, by obliging ourselves to follow them we risk harming ourselves. Thus, even if an individual is not naturally inclined to act selfishly, it becomes rational – and potentially an imperative – that they do so.

This is the crux of Rousseau's scepticism of reason: it teaches us to do what is in our interest. The goal of politics, then, is to overcome this tension between collective and individual interest. To do this Rousseau turns to voluntarism and self-interest.

The Engendering of Morality

The second part of this chapter examines the implications of Rousseau's moral philosophy for his political thought. In particular, it examines how he turns to voluntarism and the general will to legitimise public morality. It then offers an examination of the use of self-interest as a way to motivate moral actions in daily life.

Voluntarism

If morality is born from reason, yet reason does not motivate moral action, how is one to encourage morality? One solution is to turn to legal obligation – a system in which immoral actions are tempered by external enforcement. However, moral action cannot emerge from dictates. Rousseau, therefore, moves to develop a system in which moral actions are enforced externally, but these obligations are authorised internally. That is, he turns to a form of voluntarism.

Theological voluntarism was a concept Rousseau would have been familiar with. It existed, to some extent, in the works of Jean Calvin, and was a topic debated among the intellectual classes of Geneva.[9] The argument, briefly, is that God's will binds all equally, and that which God willed is, by virtue of being divine, righteous. Therefore, to accept the will of God as one's own will is to will morally. This idea was integrated into Calvin's political thought by arguing that all communities of Christians found themselves bound by God's will to obey their political superiors (Calvin 1560: IV. XX. 8–9). Thus, one also willed oneself into a political submission which was divinely sanctioned as just. While this sort of willing looks an awful lot like obedience, it was nonetheless born out of a decision being made by the one willing: one could rebel, but by accepting the tenets of the Church (and therefore the laws of the state) one instead found oneself in a situation morally akin to having willed the relevant laws oneself. In a situation where individuals cannot be expected to come to moral conclusions through reason alone, this begins to looks like a sufficient solution. To return to the metaphor of theatre, while one has not written the script, one has nonetheless, self-consciously, decided to act it out.

The claim that morality could emerge from voluntarism was contested, however. Debes highlights three concerns found in the eighteenth century. First, some denied the possibility of voluntarism and moral rationalism coexisting: 'rationalists hold that if morality is necessarily true it must originate in reason alone, not in an act of [God or anyone else's] will, as voluntarism claims. Indeed, if moral laws are beyond human comprehension, then moral rationalism is ruled out *per force*' (2014: 504). This position, while perhaps applicable to theological voluntarism, is too forceful. As has been shown, Rousseau accepts that morality emerges through reason, but dismisses both the universality of these discoveries and the motivational force of them. Therefore, one needs to be open to other avenues if humans are to be moral. Secondly, Debes highlights the issue of intention: if one only volunteers to act morally to avoid punishment, can it truly be considered moral (or perhaps even voluntary)? If so, then 'voluntarism has succeeded in tyrannising morality itself by confusing what it really is – or rather, what it is not. Morality is not prudence' (Debes 2014: 504). Rousseau would agree, but perhaps add that although morality is not prudence, it is prudent – despite what reason may tell us at times – to be moral. This position, however, can be re-stated more firmly, as seen in the third concern:

> Anti-voluntarists were eventually to argue that the reduction of the moral motive to a consideration of external sanctions made morality impossible. The only way to make morality genuinely *obligating*, it would be argued, was if its authority and binding force sprang *internally* from within the moral agent. And many thought that the only way to secure such internalism was through the power of reason. (Debes 2014: 504–5)

Rousseau agreed that the source must be taken into account – and if voluntarism is to be legitimised, the source must be ourselves rather than God or a monarch. That is to say, Rousseau does not break with the position put forward by anti-voluntarists. Instead, he accepted that internalism is necessary for obligations to be moral (rather than simply prudent). His solution to the tension between internalism and voluntarism was found with the general will – it is in this way that Rousseau was able to develop a theory which allowed one to be 'forced to be free'.[10]

The General Will

It has thus far been shown that Rousseau is a moral rationalist, but that he does not believe people can be trusted to reach moral conclusions through reason. Further, while voluntarism can go some way to legitimising moral obligations, it is difficult to understand how it can also be self-imposed and thus fulfil the criteria of internalism.[11] Rousseau attempted to overcome this problem by arguing that a rational source of both self-imposed (internal) and therefore legitimately obligatory (voluntary) public morality was to be found in the general will.[12]

There are two parts worth noting in Rousseau's development of the general will which attempt to meet the criteria of being both self-imposed and obligatory: the unification of *citizens* into a single 'moral person' and the disentanglement of *subjects* from this 'persona ficta'.[13] That is, there is an act of association which 'involves a reciprocal engagement between the public and private individuals' in which 'each individual, by contracting, so to speak, with himself, finds himself engaged in a two-fold relation: namely, as a member of the Sovereign toward private individuals, and as a member of the State toward the Sovereign' (*Social Contract* 1997b: 51/OC III: 362–4). The aim is to create a new unity which has a singular and shared interest among all parties in the state. In this way the problem of self-interest and reason – at the political level – dissolves; rational reflection aiding the self-interest of the state becomes the goal.

To achieve this, people assemble, forming one body, to vote on particular issues. Before this moment there is to be no discussion or outside deliberation, there are to be no parties or factions. They are not assembled as representatives of their own personal or collective interest (as subjects), but as part of the sovereign. One is not asked whether one approves of the proposals put forward, but whether one believes them to be in conformity with the general will. In this way, Rousseau argues, one never expresses a view which is contrary to the general will, only a view which shows that one was either correct or mistaken as to what the general will is (1997b: 124/OC III: 441). This is what allows Rousseau to claim that the general will cannot err, but that individuals can be mistaken. This is important, as it means that, were one to have been wrong, the enforcement of the decision does not run contrary to the idea of individual internalism on two counts: the individual never expressed a contrary position and they were still a part of the expression of the general will.

What is more, since people answer this question as part of the sovereign, it is entirely possible for the general will to be in opposition with one's particular will. However, the laws which are expressed by the people-as-sovereign oblige all through self-imposed sanctions. In doing this, one is actualising one's own morality by both being author as sovereign (internalism) and voluntarily accepting the laws as subject (voluntarism). That is to say, it is this ability to take part in public reasoning, to be mistaken, yet still accept the outcome as one's own will that allows Rousseau to develop self-imposed obligations. However, this does not resolve the problem of moral action.

In his *Encyclopédie* article 'Political Economy', Rousseau writes that, after the institution of a political system in which the general will can be discovered, the population's adherence to it is the next maxim of good government. Since the general will is the legitimate source of morality for the state, 'virtue is nothing but this conformity of the particular will to the general will' (1997b: 13/ OC III: 252). Thus, the problem of ensuring moral action did not end when a method of creating moral and binding laws was satisfied. To argue otherwise would be both idealistic and impractical. However, it must be remembered that Rousseau's concern in the *Social Contract* was how one *legitimises* political obligation, not how one ensures it (1997b: 41/OC III: 351). Again, Rousseau recognised that two categories – the general and the particular – do not always converge, and therefore we are returned to a familiar problem: it is not always in one's interest – it is not always even rational – to accept the moral impositions of the state:

> Each individual may, as a man, have a particular will contrary to or different from the general will he has as a Citizen. His particular interest may speak to him quite differently from the common interest; his absolute and naturally independent existence may lead him to look upon what he owes to the common cause as a gratuitous contribution, the loss of which will harm others less than its payment burdens him and, by considering the moral person that constitutes the State as a being of reason because it is not a man, he would enjoy the rights of a citizen without being willing to fulfil the duties of a subject; an injustice, the progress of which would cause the ruin of the body politic. (1997b: 52–3/OC III: 363)

So while the general will may attempt to resolve the philosophical problem of moral rationalism, voluntarism and internalism, it does very little in terms of actually encouraging moral actions: if morality is determined through public reason, and is both established and legitimised by self-obligating law, yet it has no guaranteed motivational force beyond sanction, how is one to establish a virtuous society? Rousseau tells us that the answer is self-interest.

Self-interest

On 15 September 1761 Grimprel d'Offreville wrote to Rousseau and asked the 'wise and virtuous man, a Superior being animated by the desire of human happiness' (Rousseau 1965–98 IX: 1494) to respond to those who claim that every human action is motivated by outcomes considered relative to oneself – the selfish hypothesis. Rousseau responded on 4 October, and began by restating the question: how, he asked, does he respond to those who argue that 'even in the most sublime acts of virtue, even in the purest works of charity, everyone relates everything to himself?'

> I must admit to you that I am of your adversary's opinion. For when we act, we have to have a motive for acting, and this motive cannot be extrinsic to ourselves, since it is ourselves it sets to work . . . Is it not true that if you were told that a body is being pushed without anything touching it, you would say that is not conceivable? The same holds regarding morality, when one believes oneself to be acting without any interest. (Rousseau 1965–98 IX: 1500)

Self-interest, therefore, was always seen as a motivational force in Rousseau's thought (in contrast to Smith, who argued that sympathy, and therefore morality, is not 'in any sense' a 'selfish principle' (TMS VII.iii.1.4: 317)). We are offered further evidence of Rousseau's position in his *Letter to d'Alembert*, where he states that there are 'only three instruments with which we can act on the morals of a people: the force of the laws, the empire of opinions, and the appeal of pleasure' (1960: 22/OC V: 20–1). Let us examine these options.

The problem with the first option – laws – can be traced back to Rousseau's criticisms of reason and its inability to internally motivate moral action already discussed. As Rousseau wrote in a fragment: 'Law acts only externally and rules actions; only [morals] penetrate internally and direct wills' (OC III: 555). Thus, laws only act negatively on an individual – they discourage.

There is a larger concern here, for Rousseau. The morals of a people are a part of their unwritten constitution – a law which he calls 'the most important of all', one which is 'graven not in marble or bronze, but in the hearts of the Citizens; which is the State's genuine constitution; which daily gathers new force; which, when the other laws age or die out, revives or replaces them, and imperceptibly substitutes the force of habit for that of authority' (*Social Contract* 1997b: 81/OC III: 394). This law cannot be changed, and to attempt to do so with contrary laws will fail.[14]

The third method of acting upon a people's morals noted by Rousseau was pleasure. This, unsurprisingly, is also problematic. Pleasure is not *de facto* bad, but the things which we gain pleasure from may have an imprudent impact upon our social relationships. While in the state of nature, pleasure is satisfied through the fulfil-ment of the necessities of life (*amour de soi*); in society, however, *amour-propre* makes more serious demands upon individuals. In its primitive form, pleasure is a reaction to necessities, and a moti-vational force or desire which is forgotten as soon as it is satisfied. In its more problematic formulation it can become a tyrant – both over one's fellow citizens and oneself (*Second Discourse* 1997a: 155–6, 170–1/OC III: 157–8, 174–6). This criticism emerges most clearly in Rousseau's critiques of commerce.

Doux commerce was the belief that our collective self-interest creates a more peaceful world through trade and interdepend-ence. Montesquieu put it this way: 'Commerce cures destructive prejudices and it is almost a general rule that, wherever one finds soft morals, one finds commerce; and that wherever one finds commerce, they find soft [*douces*] morals' (1748: xx.i). This was a problematic principle for Rousseau. Instead, he argued that commerce was a form of competition which resulted in a loss of freedom: individually for the people who found themselves entangled by unhealthy and unending desires, for the poor who came to find themselves enslaved by the rich, and for states which found themselves at the receiving end of the commercial interests of larger neighbours (Hont 2005: 24).

Rousseau, therefore, turned to the second option – public opinion and the self-interested desire to be esteemed by one's peers – to 'get a hold on' morals; as Shklar noted: 'Pleasure calls us, laws coerce us, but it is opinion that rules' (1969: 75). To do this, however, he had to embrace the thing which was most clearly responsible for corrupted man: *amour-propre*.

This position should not be seen as problematic. Much has been written in the past two decades on the potentially false dichotomy between the 'good' *amour-de-soi* and 'bad' *amour-propre* (see Bertram 2013). As Dent noted: 'it is *not* his view that we need to suppress, transmute etc. *amour-propre*, in its character as a desire to occupy the first rank among men . . . Rousseau, rather, argues that it is inevitable that we all shall want the first rank and standing' (1998: 63–4). When this position is accepted the question of *amour-propre* shifts; it is no longer one of escaping it, but controlling it. Instead, it becomes a question of directing one's self-interest towards politically beneficial ends. As Cohen has noted, when living under a set of just and egalitarian institutions (for example, those organised so as to meet the criteria of 'political right' set out in the *Social Contract*), *amour-propre* becomes 'instrumentally reasonable' and 'unlike the view of oneself as of greater worth, it can genuinely (without affectation) be upheld by others, and so need not be a source of discontent and misery' (Cohen 2010: 102). This, then, is why public opinion is turned to – to 'make virtue reign' (*Political Economy* 1997b: 13/OC III: 252). To see *how* Rousseau believes this can be done we can turn to two examples: social clubs and class systems.

Genevan *Cercles*

In the *Letter to d'Alembert*, Rousseau writes that there is 'no well-constituted state in which practices are not to be found which are linked to the form of government and which help to preserve it'. He specifically reflects on practices and traditions he experienced as a child in republican Geneva, such as the 'exercise of arms which brings us together every spring, the various prizes which are awarded during one part of the year, the military festivals which these prizes occasion, the taste for the hunt common to all the Genevans'. These, he argued, gave 'them the occasion to form among themselves dining societies, country outings and, finally, *bonds of friendship*' (1960: 99/OC V: 90).[15] What was important, however, was the way in which these relationships could aid in self-interested moral action. Rousseau offers a specific example of this in the Genevan *cercle*.

Cercles were associations of twelve to fifteen members who met to gamble, chat, read, drink and smoke. Rousseau compared them to the clubs found in London during the seventeenth and early eighteenth centuries – institutions which provided 'simple and innocent' amusements, but were also able to 'preserve some image of ancient morals'. In the case of *cercles*, they were safe spaces which allowed men (so long as women were not present) 'to speak of country and virtue'. Discussions, Rousseau argued, were combative, with some form of psychological well-being on the line:

> If the turn of conversation becomes less polished, reasons take on more weight; they are not satisfied by jokes or compliments. They cannot get away with fine phrases for answer. They do not humor one another in dispute; each, feeling himself attacked by all the forces of his adversary, is obliged to use all his own to defend himself. (1960: 105/OC V: 96)

They were, therefore, spheres in which *amour-propre* could be satisfied by demonstrating superior dedication to the public good. These were, Rousseau argued, practices which could maintain a people suited to republican morals: 'these honest and innocent institutions bring together all which can contribute to forming men as friends, citizens, soldiers, and consequently, all that is best suited for a free people' (1960: 105/OC V: 96).[16]

It was more than simply the topic and method of discussion, however, which pleased Rousseau. The *cercles* brought people together and encouraged friendships, while keeping them in the view of the public – and thus concerned about what that public was seeing. This was, importantly, the opposite of what Rousseau recognised the theatre as doing:

> People think they come together in the theatre, and it is there that they are isolated. It is there that they go to forget their friends, neighbours, and relations in order to concern themselves with fables, in order to cry for the misfortunes of the dead, or to laugh at the expense of the living. (1960: 16–17/OC V: 16)

He therefore feared that the establishment of a theatre in Geneva would kill off the *cercles*, and with them, Geneva's republican and civic morality. Thus, Rousseau concluded:

> Let us, if need be, permit men to spend the night drinking who, without that, might spend it doing worse . . . The excess of wine degrades man, at the least alienates his reason for a time, and in the long run, brutalizes it. But after all, the taste for wine is not a crime and rarely causes one to be committed; it makes man stupid, not evil. For every fleeting quarrel it causes, it forms a hundred durable attachments. Speaking generally, drinkers are cordial and frank; they are almost all good,

upright, just, faithful, brave, and decent men except for their single failing. (1960: 108–9/OC V: 99)

Rousseau does not a call for Spartan austerity to enforce virtue, but instead attempts to encourage virtue through correct institutions – institutions which are to be managed: 'The people's interest shouldn't just be left to run rampant. This will lead to excess.' People will simply choose the amusements which 'promote their penchants, whereas what is needed are entertainments which would moderate them' (1960: 18/OC V: 17). Self-interest, therefore, remains problematic, but Rousseau does not move to deaden it, nor let it run wild. Instead, institutions must be crafted which allow morality and self-interest to converge; through the skill of the legislator (here we may recognise similarities with Mandeville's 'skilful politician'), self-interest must be directed.

Again, Rousseau argued that there was 'no well-constituted state in which practices are not to be found which are linked to the form of government and which help to preserve it' (1960: 98/ OC V: 90). In the case of Geneva, Rousseau was being descriptive. When it comes to his propositional political thought, however, we can see the 'skilful politician' at work.

Class in Corsica and Poland

To see how self-interest can be used to ensure moral actions in practice, one can turn to Rousseau's reflections on class systems. Specifically, we can identify three aspects worth noting: a class system open to all citizens; qualifications based on public good; and the use of *amour-propre*.

Openness

Rousseau sets limits on class distinctions in the *Social Contract*: 'the law can very well state that there will be privileges, but it cannot confer them on any one by name; the law can create several Classes of Citizens, it can even specify the qualifications that entitle to membership in these classes, but it cannot nominate this person or that for admission to them' (1997b: 67/OC III: 379). Thus, while classes are in essence structures of inequality, Rousseau allows for them so long they are not entirely closed.

In practice, this can be seen in Rousseau's proposals. For Corsica, Rousseau developed three classes: 'aspirants', open to all men of twenty years or older; 'patriots', made up of aspirants who held property; and 'citizens', married patriots with at least two living children. Ignoring the inherent inequalities born out of natural characteristics, the system is one through which every male Corsican would have the opportunity to progress. A similar system is proposed for the Polish nobility – class distinctions which are born out of achievements rather than inheritance. In both cases, Rousseau's concern for inequality is tempered by guarantees that benefits can be, potentially, enjoyed by all. These are structural criteria, however; to understand the benefits provided one must look at these classes in more detail.

Qualifications Based on Public Good

Rousseau's proposed three-tier class system for Poland makes a much more explicit nod to the social duties attached. The first class, 'servants of the state', was to be made up of those who had worked as 'Lawyers, Assessors, even as lower court judges; as managers of some portion of the public monies, and in general in all the lower posts which provide those who occupy them with the opportunity to exhibit their merit, their ability, their accuracy, and above all their integrity'. The second class, 'citizens elect', would be offered to those servants of the state who had been elected to the Diet on at least three occasions, and thus had obtained the approval of their peers. They would also form the body from which senators could be elected. In addition, upon becoming a citizen elect one would take on a role in public education as a principal or inspector. Finally, the third class, 'guardians of the laws', would be open to those who had been senators on three occasions. While not holding public office, they would also form the 'college of Administrators of education', again playing an important role in state-sponsored public education (1997b: 239–42/OC III: 1020–3).

In the case of Corsica, classes were to attach the people to their land, discourage commerce and create a life which was 'happy in its mediocrity, respectable in its simplicity. Furnishing all the needs of life, all the public tributes without sales and without trafficking, all the means for consideration' (2005: 143/OC III: 925). While the practices are more austere, the intentions are nonetheless similar: to enshrine a sense of unity and membership in the public sphere while encouraging good public deeds. However, and again, as was the case with the *cercles*, Rousseau recognised the necessity of having recourse to *amour-propre* to motivate these actions.

Making Use of amour-propre

Rousseau specifically linked his class systems to the human desire for esteem. In the case of Corsica he wrote that the natural urge to want to 'distinguish oneself' would result in the desire to fulfil the duties attached to particular class positions in a manner 'better than others'. That is:

> to make larger harvests, to furnish stronger contingent to the state, to deserve the people's votes in elections. Large families well nourished and well clothed will bring honor to leaders; and, since real abundance will be the sole object of luxury, each will want to distinguish himself by that sort of luxury. As long as the human heart remains what it is such establishments will not produce laziness. (2005: 144/OC III: 925)

As long as the 'human heart' loves itself – is encouraged by *amour-propre* – the Corsicans would find themselves encouraged to cultivate land and grow their families, and thus ensure that they met the basic necessities for the state's self-sufficiency and self-defence.

In the case of Poland – a nation with a much more established conception of class distinction – Rousseau allowed for outward expressions of rank via 'distinctive insignia' – although he noted that they were effectively worthless 'baubles' which would satisfy *amour-propre* – the vanity of wanting to be judged by others as being respectable – without putting any strain on the state (1997b: 240/OC III: 1020).[17] However, there was a much more pressing issue than medals and chevrons for Poland.

Poland had a very old and well-established class system – one in which over 70 per cent of the population were living in serfdom (Bideleux and Jeffries 1998: 154). In the face of this problem, Rousseau wrote: 'What I fear is not only poorly understood interest, the *amour-propre* and the prejudices of the masters. Once this obstacle is overcome, I would fear the vices and the cowardice of the serfs' (2005: 185/OC III: 974). Again, a misunderstanding of what is really in one's interest was the problem – both with regard to the nobles and the peasants. The solution, however, was again found in the power of opinion: Rousseau accepted that there must be a method of emancipating the serfs – to satisfy natural right – but this must also contribute to the public good. To this end he proposed a system by which those peasants who, 'based on faithful memoranda and on well-verified reports of the public voice', 'distinguish themselves by good conduct, good cultivation, good morals, by the care of their family, by all the duties of the station' would be freed (2005: 228/OC III: 1026). In this way, even (especially) the peasants would find it to be in their interest to work towards the public good, if only to enhance their reputation among others.

These are the grand schemes Rousseau turned to in the hope of uniting *amour-propre* with the interests of the state – which was, of course, also the interest of the individual. As Neuhouser put it:

> Rousseau's point when he later calls society (and the passion that accompanies it, *amour-propre*) artificial is not that social relations (or *amour-propre*) necessarily corrupt humans, nor that they are foreign to our 'true,' or ideal, nature. His point, rather, is that society is something humans help to make, which is to say, something that is always partly the product of human belief and will. (Neuhouser 2014: 31)

By allowing for a method by which one can distinguish oneself – and thus satisfy *amour-propre* – through patriotic duties, Rousseau attempted to establish a system which would ensure moral outcomes through self-interested actions.[18]

Conclusion

The aim of this chapter has been to develop an understanding of what Rousseau conceptualised morality as (its origins), and how he felt it could be put into practice politically (its engendering) – both in terms of legitimising the state and encouraging the populace. To this end it has been argued that Rousseau was a moral rationalist who felt that the weakening of pity, due to reason, had left man in a state in which being immoral could be seen as rational. To overcome this, he developed a political system which morally legitimised a state's dictates by their being born from citizens themselves; a form of public rationality which allowed for self-obligating laws. Accepting that this was not enough, Rousseau went further to argue that *amour-propre* could be used to encourage individuals to see their own interests as the same as the state's. To achieve this he turned to the wise arrangement of political institutions and rules. Thus, Rousseau took a position in which morality was not born from self-interest, but instead one in which being moral was in one's self-interest. On the other hand, Adam Smith argues that self-interest on the whole is a positive thing for the community, but this not a moral concept. Instead, moral action comes from an individual's own self-reflection via the impartial spectator. That is, for Rousseau, man must be forced (by the many) to be free (as an individual). For Smith, the individual must be free (from the many) to be forced (by the self).

Notes

1. For the most thorough investigation into Rousseau and moralism, see Hendel (1934).
2. By addressing Smith before Rousseau, no claims are being made with regard to influence. While I accept that Smith was, in some cases, developing ideas in response to Rousseau (Force 2003; Rasmussen 2008), the goal of this essay is not to highlight this relationship (for more on this topic, see McHugh's and Rasmussen's contributions to this volume).
3. This chapter follows Gourevitch (Rousseau 1997a) in translating *moeurs* as 'morals' (see Gourevitch's 'A note on the translations' in the *Discourses*).
4. References to Rousseau are to the Pléiade *Œuvres complètes* (OC), highlighting volume and page number. English translations, when available and accurate, are taken from editions noted in the bibliography.
5. This is made explicit in the exchange between Smith and Sir Gilbert Elliot after the publication of the first edition of *The Theory of Moral Sentiments*. For more on this, see Raphael (2007).
6. Rousseau appears to be picking up on a position clearly expressed by Shaftesbury, whose *Inquiry Concerning Virtue and Merit*, translated by Diderot and published in 1745, was known to Rousseau (Richebourg 1932: 243): '[I]f a creature be generous, kind, constant, compassionate; yet if he cannot reflect on what he himself does, or sees others do, so as to take notice of what is worthy or honest and make that notice or conception of worth and honesty to be an object of his affection, he has not the character of being virtuous. For thus, and no otherwise, he is capable of having a sense of right or wrong,

a sentiment or judgment of what is done, through just, equal, and good affection, or the contrary' (Shaftesbury 1999: 173).

7. A further point worth examining is offered in the *Social Contract*, although he does not go into explicit detail (1997b: 43; OC III: 353), when Rousseau draws attention to Plutarch's 'That Beasts Use Reason', a tale in which Ulysses' crew, having been transformed into beasts by Circe, come to recognise their lives as better without human rationality.

8. On Molière, Rousseau wrote: 'His greatest care is to ridicule good-ness and simplicity and to present treachery and falsehood so that they arouse our interest and sympathy. His decent people only talk; his vicious characters act, and the most brilliant successes accompany them most of the time. Finally, the honor of applause is reserved rarely for those who are the most respectable, and goes almost always to the cleverest' (1960: 34; OC V: 31–2).

9. Whether Calvin was a voluntarist is debated; whether voluntarist ideas exist in his work is less so. For more on this discussion, see Helm (2004) and Rosenblatt (1997).

10. The legitimacy – from Rousseau's perspective – of the voluntary acceptance of the rational or moral lessons of others is seen explicitly at the end of *Emile*, when the student acknowledges that he would remain what Rousseau-the-tutor had made him, and voluntarily add no further chains (OC IV: 855).

11. These concerns were not unique to Rousseau. There was a broader discussion taking place among eighteenth-century republicans who were interested in a public morality which could emerge through public reason rather than private interest (MacGilvray 2011: 45).

12. This is a characteristically republican point. Obeying laws – it is argued – is inherently different when you had a part in, or were free to, draft them. In this way freedom and virtue are inherently linked, as both are related to being able to choose to act morally, in accordance with the general will, and potentially in contrast to the particular will (or the will of a foreign power).

13. Interestingly, the attributes which made morality problematic in the theatre are turned to in the creation of the general will: the disconnection between the object of investigation and the will of the individual.

14. Rousseau makes this point explicit when writing for Poland: 'if Poland is already at the point where everything is venal and rotten to the core, then it is in vain that it seeks to reform its laws' (1997b: 242; OC III: 1022).

15. Italics mine. For a more fleshed-out example, see Rousseau's reflections on the festival of the Regiment of St Gervais (1960: 135–6; OC V: 123–4).

16. The response Rousseau received from Genevans after he praised the *cercles* may reflect his intellectual break with the city. His fellow countrymen were 'shocked' at this endorsement (Coleman 2011: 136). On the side of the government, Tronchin wrote a letter to Rousseau arguing that 'This country, my friend, is not what you imagine.' Instead, he argued that the *cercles* caused degeneration, distraction, loss of time and weakened education. He concludes by noting that 'what was good for the Greek Republics is no longer suitable for ours' (Rousseau 1965–98 V: 734). From the Church, Rousseau received letters from Jean Perdriau and Jacob Vernet, the former telling him not to believe everything he wrote about the *cercles* as they were in reality a source of great abuse, and the latter stating his doubt that the *cercles* could be 'politically useful' and instead claimed that the young men who attended them were morally questionable (Rousseau 1965–98 V: 742).

17. For more on the importance of symbols of rank, see Rousseau's reflections on the *épée* in in his *Confessions* (OC I: 269).

18. For more on Rousseau's Corsican proposals, see Hill (2017).

Bibliography

Bertram, Chris (2013), 'Rousseau and Ethics', in R. Crisp (ed.), *The Oxford Handbook of the History of Ethics*, Oxford: Oxford University Press, 280–91.

Bideleux, Robert, and Ian Jeffries (1998), *A History of Eastern Europe: Crisis and Change*, London: Routledge.

Calvin, Jean (1560), *Institution de la religion chrestienne*, Geneva: Jean Crespin.

Cohen, Joshua (2010), *Rousseau: A Free Community of Equals*, Oxford: Oxford University Press.

Coleman, Patrick (2011), *Anger, Gratitude, and the Enlightenment Writer*, Oxford: Oxford University Press.

Debes, Remy (2014), 'Moral Rationalism and Moral Realism', in Aaron Garrett (ed.), *The Routledge Companion to Eighteenth Century Philosophy*, New York: Routledge, 500–34.

Dent, N. J. H. (1998), 'Rousseau on *Amour-Propre*', *Aristotelian Society Supplementary*, 72.1, 57–74.

Driver, Julia (2013), 'Moral Sense and Sentimentalism', in R. Crisp (ed.),

The Oxford Handbook of the History of Ethics, Oxford: Oxford University Press, 358–75.

de Fénelon, F. (1717), *Les avantures de Telemaque fils d'Ulysse*, Paris: Jacques Estienne.

Force, Pierre (2003), *Self-interest before Adam Smith*, Cambridge: Cambridge University Press.

Helm, Paul (2004), *John Calvin's Ideas*, Oxford: Oxford University Press.

Hendel, C. W. (1934), *Jean-Jacques Rousseau: Moralist*, Oxford: Oxford University Press.

Hill, Mark J. (2017), 'Enlightened "Savages": Rousseau's *Social Contract* and the "Brave People" of Corsica', *History of Political Thought*, 38.3, 462–93.

Hirschman, Albert O. (1977), *The Passions and the Interests: Political Arguments for Capitalism before its Triumph*, Princeton: Princeton University Press.

Hont, István (2005), *Jealousy of Trade: International Competition and the Nation-state in Historical Perspective*, Cambridge, MA: Harvard University Press.

MacGilvray, Eric (2011), *The Invention of Market Freedom*, Cambridge: Cambridge University Press.

Marçal, Katrine (2015), *Who Cooked Adam Smith's Dinner: A Story about Women and Economics*, London: Portobello Books.

Montesquieu, Charles-Louis de Secondat (1748), *L'esprit des loix*, Geneva: Barillot & Fils.

Neuhouser, Frederick (2014), *Rousseau's Critique of Inequality: Reconstructing the Second Discourse*, Cambridge: Cambridge University Press.

O'Hagan, Timothy (1999), *Rousseau*, London: Routledge.

Otteson, James (2013), 'Adam Smith', in R. Crisp (ed.), *The Oxford Handbook of the History of Ethics*, Oxford: Oxford University Press, 421–40.

Plutarch (1874), 'That Brute Beasts Make Use of Reason', in Plutarch, *Plutarch's Morals*, ed. W. W. Goodwin, Boston: Little, Brown, vol. 5, 218–33.

Rasmussen, Dennis C. (2008), *The Problems and Promise of Commercial Society: Adam Smith's Response to Rousseau*, University Park: Penn State University Press.

Raphael, D. D. (2007), *The Impartial Spectator: Adam Smith's Moral Philosophy*, Oxford: Oxford University Press.

Richebourg, M. (1932), 'La Bibliothèque de Jean-Jacques Rousseau', *Annales de la société Jean-Jacques Rousseau*, 21, 181–250.

Rosenblatt, Helena (1997), *Rousseau and Geneva: From the First Discourse to The Social Contract, 1749–1762*, Cambridge: Cambridge University Press.

Rousseau, Jean-Jacques (1959–95), *Œuvres complètes*, ed. B. Gagnebin and M. Raymond, 5 vols, Paris: Bibliothèque de la Pléiade.

Rousseau, Jean-Jacques (1960) [1758], *Politics and the Arts: Letter to M. d'Alembert on the Theatre*, trans. Allan Bloom, Ithaca, NY: Cornell University Press.

Rousseau, Jean-Jacques (1965–98), *Correspondance complète de Jean-Jacques Rousseau*, ed. R. A. Leigh, 52 vols, Oxford: Voltaire Foundation.

Rousseau, Jean-Jacques (1979) [1762], *Emile, or On education*, trans. Allan Bloom, New York: Basic Books.

Rousseau, Jean-Jacques (1997a), *The Discourses and Other Early Political Writings*, ed. V. Gourevitch, Cambridge: Cambridge University Press.

Rousseau, Jean-Jacques (1997b), *The Social Contract and Other Later Political Writings*, ed. V. Gourevitch, Cambridge: Cambridge University Press.

Rousseau, Jean-Jacques (2005), *The Plan for Perpetual Peace, On the Government of Poland, and Other Writings on History and Politics*, ed. Christopher Kelly, trans. Christopher Kelly and Judith Bush, Lebanon, NH: Dartmouth University Press.

Shaftesbury, Anthony Ashley Cooper, 1st Earl of (1999) [1711], *Characteristicks of Men, Manners, Opinions, Times*, ed. P. Ayres, 2 vols, Oxford: Oxford University Press.

Shklar, Judith (1969), *Men and Citizens: A Study of Rousseau's Social Theory*, Cambridge: Cambridge University Press.

Venturi, Franco (1971), *Utopia and Reform in the Enlightenment*, Cambridge: Cambridge University Press.

Voltaire (1771), 'Cérémonies, Titres, Prééminence, etc', in Voltaire, *Questions sur l'encyclopédie*, Geneva: Cramer.

6

Pursuing Sympathy without Vanity: Interpreting Smith's Critique of Rousseau through Smith's Critique of Mandeville

John McHugh

One of the most remarkable things about Smith's 1756 review of Rousseau's *Discourse on the Origin of Inequality* is how assuredly it identifies Rousseau's conception of human nature with Bernard Mandeville's. When read in combination with Smith's attack on Mandeville in *The Theory of Moral Sentiments*, the review also identifies the causes of Rousseau's appeal with the causes of Mandeville's. In the review, Smith comments that Rousseau's *Discourse* 'consists almost entirely of rhetoric and description', rather than honest argument (Letter: 251).[1] Similarly, in *The Theory of Moral Sentiments*, Smith claims that a major reason why Mandeville's 'erroneous . . . notions' have an 'air of truth and probability' and thus are 'very apt to impose upon the unskilful' is that they are 'described and exaggerated by . . . lively and humorous, though coarse and rustic eloquence' (TMS VII.ii.4.6: 308).

Another remarkable thing about Smith's review is that it contains almost no philosophical content. While the treatment of Mandeville in *The Theory of Moral Sentiments* actually argues against his view, the review's discussion of Rousseau says almost nothing about where he goes wrong. Perhaps a reason for this is that Smith's engagement with Rousseau's ideas was far too extensive and complex to fit into the space of a review; several scholars have recently argued that the place to look in Smith's writing for his philosophically critical thoughts on Rousseau is *everywhere*, as he is a principal target of Smith's general defence of commercial society (see, e.g. Rasmussen 2008; Hanley 2009: esp. 15–52; Griswold 2010). But even if Smith's thinking about Rousseau reached too far and ran too deep to be distilled into a few measly pages, it remains rather odd that the review makes almost *no* substantial philosophical points. And since the review contains one of only two explicit references to Rousseau in works that Smith published in his lifetime,[2] this is unfortunate for those who believe that Smith saw Rousseau as one of his main interlocutors.

I certainly do not wish to call this view into question; it has been firmly established in spite of this obstacle. On the contrary, my goal in this chapter is to contribute to the development of this view by paying careful attention to Smith's explicit critique of Mandeville in *The Theory of Moral Sentiments*. Given the evident connection in Smith's thinking between the two philosophers, this critique can plausibly be treated as an approximate critique of Rousseau;[3] thus, I try to translate Smith's critique of Mandeville into a critique of Rousseau. In the first section of the chapter, I flesh out the position on human sociality that Smith attributes to both Mandeville and Rousseau. In the second section, I explicate Smith's explicit response to Mandeville's version of this position. In the third section, I attempt to reconstruct a Smithian response to Rousseau on the basis of this response to Mandeville. Invoking Smith's sympathy-based account of approval, which, I argue, underlies his response to Mandeville, I ultimately argue that his disagreement with Rousseau can be understood as centring on the very nature of our concern with winning sympathy from others.[4] The chapter closes with two brief reflections on how this reading might impact the ongoing project of further clarifying the overall relationship between Smith and Rousseau.

Smith on Mandeville and Rousseau on Human Sociality

The position on human sociality that Smith's review attributes to both Mandeville and Rousseau is that while pity is natural to us, 'there is in man no powerful instinct which necessarily determines him to seek society for its own sake' (Letter: 250). Pity, for Smith, is 'the emotion which we feel for the misery of others' (TMS I.i.1.1: 9). Generally, it is an aversion to seeing other people in pain, which may prevent us from hurting them or even lead us to help them when they are in need. Thus, it acts as a motive mainly in a negative sense, one that leads us *not* to do something, to *prevent* something from happening, or to make something *stop*; it does not, in Smith's words, really lead us to 'seek' anything. But if both Mandeville and Rousseau deny that we have a positive motive 'to seek society', how do they explain the fact that we end up living socially?

According to the review, for Mandeville, the 'misery of our original state compelled [us] to have recourse to [the] otherwise disagreeable remedy' of social living; in other words, even though we don't naturally like having other people around, we decided to live with them out of concern for our own interest in things like the safety that grouping together provides (Letter: 250). Our association with others is then strengthened by the 'laws of justice,' which were 'originally the inventions of the cunning and the powerful in order to maintain or to acquire an unnatural and unjust superiority over the rest of their fellow-creatures' (Letter: 251). As the discussion of Mandeville in *The Theory of Moral Sentiments* points out, our obedience to these laws and other group-solidifying social mores is furthered buttressed by our love of the praise we receive when we follow them, which people give to each other in accordance with their collectively inculcated delusion that such actions are 'entirely disinterested' (TMS VII.ii.4.7–8: 308–9).

Rousseau's explanation for how naturally non-social creatures end up living socially differs mainly with respect to its understanding of the non-social, natural state. According to the review, Rousseau thinks that the isolated, 'primitive state of mankind' is not miserable but 'the happiest and most suitable to his nature'. Thus, unlike Mandeville, Rousseau does not think that human beings really need to group together; rather, he thinks that we more or less end up doing so due to 'some unfortunate accidents'.[5] The main psychological impact of these accidents is the 'birth [of] the unnatural passions of ambition and the vain desire of superiority' (Letter: 250). Thus, while Rousseau disagrees with Mandeville's claim that social living is conducive to our interests and originates at least partly in our awareness of this fact, he agrees with Mandeville that the psychological force that ends up holding society together is vanity. For both, once we begin living in settled groups for other reasons and/or from other causes, we end up positively 'seeking' association with others because we want their praise. Thus, since praise tends to be an exclusive prize, both conceive of society as a domain in which people are, almost paradoxically, united by their struggle to one-up each other for attention and power. Mandeville might have thought the benefits of society worth the costs of this permanent strife, while Rousseau, famously, probably did not.

Smith's review calls attention to one more noteworthy difference between Rousseau and Mandeville. Rousseau believes that pity is strong enough to be 'capable of producing all those virtues, whose reality Dr. Mandeville denies'.[6] Thus, Rousseau does not hold the position that Smith attributes to Mandeville in *The Theory of Moral Sentiments* of '[taking] away altogether the distinction between vice and virtue' (TMS VII.ii.4.6: 308). Rousseau's belief in the reality of virtue must be what leads Smith to observe that in his 'system', 'the principles of the English author are softened, improved, and embellished, and stript of all that tendency to corruption and licentiousness which has disgraced them in their original author' (Letter: 250). However, this does not mean that Smith took Rousseau to have provided an adequate account of virtue; for Smith, a trait such as self-command is a virtue, but it could not grow out of pity alone.[7] Nor does Smith's reference to this difference between Mandeville and Rousseau imply that he read the latter as arguing against the former that society is held together by pity-based virtue. As we shall see in more detail below, the three paragraphs Smith quotes and translates from Rousseau in the review focus mainly on the misery that accrues to human beings once they start caring about others' estimations of them; thus, as he did for Mandeville, Smith believed that, for Rousseau, vanity is the defining characteristic of socialised human beings (Letter: 251–4).

Having laid out Smith's understanding of the positions Rousseau and Mandeville adopt on human sociality, I turn now to consider his philosophical attitude towards each. I begin with Smith's attack on Mandeville and then use this attack to reconstruct a Smithian attack on Rousseau.

Smith *contra* Mandeville

Smith's goal in attacking Mandeville is to '[establish] the reality of virtue', understood not in terms of the disposition to feel pity or some other kind of other-directed concern, but in terms of the disposition to 'desire . . . doing what is honourable and noble' for its own sake (TMS VII.ii.4.8: 309). In other words, Smith believes that Mandeville's account of moral motivation fails not because it underestimates the power of human altruism but because it confuses the desire to do the right thing with vanity. This mistake is tough to spot, Smith argues, because there is a 'certain remote affinity among' the love of praise 'at any rate' (or the love of praise *per se*), 'the love of true glory' (or the love of deserved praise) and 'the love of virtue' (or the love of doing/becoming what is honourable and noble) (TMS VII.ii.4.9–10: 310–11). This affinity between the three loves, which is what makes it possible for Mandeville to use the term 'vanity' for all of them, lies in the fact that they all involve 'some reference to the sentiments of others' (TMS VII.ii.4.10: 310).

The 'affinity between vanity and the love of true glory' is obvious, 'as both these passions aim at acquiring esteem and approbation'. The latter differs from the former only insofar as it is a desire for 'what [one] is justly entitled to, and what cannot be refused to [one] without some sort of injury' (TMS VII.ii.4.9: 310). According to Smith, although Mandeville's overly broad use of the term 'vanity' fudges this distinction, he should have no problem recognising it, as his account of the socialisation process includes the development of an above-mentioned collective delusion regarding our motives; thus, Mandevillian agents actually believe that they deserve the praise that they seek (TMS VII.ii.4.7: 308–9). Smith's main objection, then, must be that Mandeville fails to recognise the existence of the love of virtue *per se*.

The affinity between this love and the second one is obvious, in that both involve '[aiming] at *really being* what is honourable and estimable' (Smith TMS VII.ii.4.10: 310, emphasis added). But Smith thinks that the love of virtue is also like the other two loves in that it too has 'some reference to the sentiments of others'. One might think that Smith understands this 'reference' only to be an *epistemic* one, meaning that others' sentiments are essential to the pursuit of virtue as sources of evidence regarding one's progress; such an interpretation would fit nicely with Smith's well-known discussion of the way in which society provides the mirror necessary for self-evaluation (TMS III.1.3–7: 110–13). However, Smith seems to think of this 'reference' in more *psychological* terms. He writes:

> The man of the greatest magnanimity, who desires virtue for its own sake, and is most indifferent about what actually are the opinions of mankind with regard to him, is still, however, delighted with the

thoughts of what they should be, with the consciousness that though he may neither be honoured nor applauded, he is still the proper object of honour and applause, and that if mankind were cool and candid and consistent with themselves, and properly informed of the motives and circumstances of his conduct, they would not fail to honour and applaud him. Though he despises the opinions which are actually entertained of him, he has the highest value for those which ought to be entertained of him. That he might think himself worthy of those honourable sentiments, and, whatever was the idea which other men might conceive of his character, that when he should put himself in their situation, and consider, not what was, but what ought to be their opinion, he should always have the highest idea of it himself, was the great and exalted motive of his conduct. As even in the love of virtue, therefore, there is still some reference, though not to what is, yet to what in reason and propriety ought to be, the opinion of others, there is even in this respect some affinity between it, and the love of true glory. (TMS VII.ii.4.10: 311)

Smith believes that a reference to some other's sentiments, albeit an idealised one, is somehow built into the love of virtue for its own sake. This is a position that Smith took very seriously. Elsewhere in *The Theory of Moral Sentiments*, he observes that all self-directed moral sentiments 'suppose the idea of some other being, who is the natural judge of the person that feels them; and it is only by sympathy with the decisions of this arbiter of his conduct, that [one] can conceive, either the triumph of self-applause, or the shame of self-condemnation' (TMS IV.2.12: 193). And in a letter to his friend Gilbert Elliot, Smith expresses unwillingness to give up his '*Doctrine* that our judgments concerning our own conduct have always a reference to the sentiments of some other being', despite any philosophical trouble it invites (Corr. 40: 48–9, emphasis added).

This position follows from Smith's sympathy-based account of other-directed evaluation. In that same letter to Elliot, Smith observes that 'it would seem very odd if we judged of our own conduct by one principle and of that of other men by another' (Corr. 40: 49). According to Smith, 'to approve of the passions of another . . . as suitable to their objects, is the same thing as to observe that we entirely sympathize with them' (TMS I.i.3.1: 16). Thus, to avoid oddness, Smith concludes that since judgement of others requires attempting to sympathise with them, judgement of ourselves must require imagining if others could sympathise with us (cf. TMS III.1.2: 109–10).

Smith's belief that all self-directed moral sentiments must bear some reference to another person also seems to follow from a combination of tacit theoretical commitments regarding the natures of value and identity. Smith seems to think it impossible to assign value to things such as sentiments, motives, traits, etc. without referring to a valuing subject. He claims that 'virtue is not said to be amiable, or to be meritorious, because it is the object of its own love, or of its own gratitude; but because it excites those sentiments in other men' (TMS III.1.7: 113). Thus, evaluation of one's own sentiments, motives, traits, etc. requires consideration of how some other subject would feel about them. The second relevant commitment explains more fully why this evaluating subject cannot, strictly speaking, be identical to the agent being evaluated. Smith seems to believe that the moment one adopts a reflective, critical stance upon oneself, one must become, in some respect, another person. He claims:

> We can never survey our own sentiments and motives, we can never form any judgment concerning them; unless we remove ourselves, as it were, from our own natural station, and endeavour to view them as at a certain distance from us. But we can do this in no other way than by endeavouring to view them with the eyes of other people. (TMS III.1.2: 110)

Smith even goes so far as to imply that this reference to another person's perspective is not just a psychological but also a *logical* requirement: 'that the judge should, in every respect, be the same with the person judged of, is as impossible, as that the cause should, in every respect, be the same with the effect' (TMS III.1.6: 113). Thus, he concludes, 'whatever judgment we can form concerning [ourselves], accordingly, must always bear some secret reference, either to what are, or to what, upon a certain condition, would be, or to what, we imagine, ought to be the judgment of others' (TMS III.1.2: 110).

Regardless of both *why* he believes that moral self-evaluation must have a reference to another person's sentiments and *how he understands the nature of* this reference, the sheer fact that Smith believes this reference is built into the pursuit of virtue for its own sake is striking. Of course, one thing that distinguishes this pursuit and the pursuit of praise *per se* is that the former involves reference to an *idealised* other with *corrected* sentiments. Clearly, Smith owes us an account of how we develop and attach ourselves to this concept. Rather than push him on this point here, however, I would like to focus on the fact that his attack on Mandeville boils down to the very general claim that he gets something wrong about the way in which we care about others' opinions of us. As we shall see in the next section, this feature of the attack is what makes it most relevant to Smith's attitude towards Rousseau.

A Reconstruction of Smith *contra* Rousseau

After comparing Rousseau to Mandeville and explaining Rousseau's rhetorical allure in terms of his 'agreeable' exhibition of the pre-social, 'savage life as the happiest of any', Smith quotes and translates three paragraphs from the *Discourse* (Letter: 251–4). Collectively, these three paragraphs explain and lament the development of relationships of dependence between human beings.[8] The first paragraph explains how the 'sweets of an *independent* society' that people initially gain from living together gradually disappear once the division of labour and the recognition of private property give rise to relations of economic dependence (Letter: 252, emphasis added). The second paragraph explains that as these dependence relations develop, 'man [goes] from being free and independent' to being 'subjected ... above all to his fellow creatures', whom he now must persuade that 'either in reality or appearance, their advantage [is found] in labouring for his' (Letter: 252). According to the third paragraph, this process culminates in total psychological dependency; as human beings in the 'civilized state' come to require others' approval for its own sake, they become 'a species of [beings] who count for something the looks of the rest of the universe; who can be happy and contented with themselves upon the testimony of another, rather than upon their own' (Letter: 253).

In these passages, Rousseau hints at several reasons why he thinks the development of this kind of dependency should be lamented. One is that living independently or 'in [oneself]' rather than 'out of [oneself]' is a more natural and thus preferable way to live (Letter: 253). Another is that the kind of dependency he has in mind leads us to worry more about how we *appear* to others than about how we actually *are*; thus, socialisation makes us insincere and even deceptive. A third is that because our pursuit of others' praise takes the form of 'an insatiable ambition, an ardour to raise [our] relative fortune, not so much from any real necessity, as to set [ourselves] above others', it necessarily leads to conflict; after all, 'superiority' is an exclusive prize won only in zero-sum competitions (Letter: 252).

To show that Rousseau is wrong about the nature and value of sociality, Smith needs to take on all three of these claims. He would obviously reject the first one out of hand; he believes that human beings are naturally social in the way that Rousseau denies. Smith's response to Mandeville can help us piece together a response to the next two. As Dennis Rasmussen has pointed out, Smith's appeal against Mandeville to the distinction between loving praise and loving virtue speaks directly to Rousseau's concerns about the prioritisation of appearing virtuous over being virtuous (Rasmussen 2008: 118–19). But can Smith offer more in response to Rousseau than just this potentially *ad hoc* distinction?

As we saw above, one of the most striking things about Smith's conception of the pursuit of virtue for its own sake is that it, like the pursuit of praise, involves reference to some other person's sentiments, albeit an idealised one. Again, Smith must explain how we come to think of and desire this idealised other's praise. But no matter how such an account might work, it must take the form of an explanation of how the love of an idealised other's praise develops out of or from the love of actual others' praise.[9] In order to see how this development is even possible, we must consider what the love of praise itself *means* for Smith. Doing so will reveal that Smith has the resources to claim more generally that Rousseau gets something fundamentally wrong about what it means to care about others' evaluative sentiments. Doing so will also help us both to fill out Rasmussen's Smithian response to Rousseau's second claim and to generate a distinct Smithian response to Rousseau's third claim.

If to win others' praise is to win their approval, then, on Smith's moral psychology, to win others' praise is to win their sympathy, for, as we saw above, Smith believes that sympathy *is* approval.[10] Thus, the effort to attain others' praise amounts to the effort to get them to feel the same sentiments, desires, etc., to the same degree that we do. Now, if sociality consists primarily in having this aim, then Rousseau might be right to identify sociality with the struggle for attention and dominance rather than with the achievement of virtue-constituting harmony; it is easy to interpret the pursuit of others' sympathy as a manifestation of Rousseauian claim three's troublesome 'insatiable ambition . . . to set [ourselves] above others' (Letter: 252).[11] Rousseau could argue that we pursue others' sympathy because we want them to subjugate their sentimental evaluations to our own, out of recognition of our superiority. Rousseau could then use this interpretation of the pursuit of sympathy to undermine Smith's supposedly harmony-explaining model of the process by which it is often achieved. On this Rousseauian reading, when our attempts to win sympathy from others do not work, we either subjugate our sentiments to theirs or, more likely, negotiate with them in such a way that neither of us ends up as happy with the result as we otherwise would have been (see TMS I.i.4.5–10: 20–3). If widespread iterations of these negotiations are what generate social norms,[12] Rousseau's negotiators will only ever be committed to them begrudgingly and insincerely, as inferior means of satisfying their hidden but lingering desires to dominate each other's sentiments (see McHugh 2016). Thus, if the standard of virtue is fixed in this way and agents are praised for caring about virtue for its own sake, then, at least with respect to this concern, they are necessarily guilty of the kind of dissimulation diagnosed by Rousseau's second claim.

It is well documented that Smith had Rousseauian concerns at least broadly similar to these about commercial society in general and about the pursuit of sympathy in particular; thus, in line with his similar attitude towards Mandeville, Smith believes that Rousseau's views 'in some respects bordered upon the truth' (TMS VII.ii.4.14: 313).[13] Smith's versions of these concerns appear most explicitly in his treatment of the corrupting influence of fame and wealth, the pursuit of which he takes to be rooted in our desire 'to be observed, to be attended to, to be taken notice of with sympathy, complacency, and approbation' (TMS I.iii.2.1: 50). But, as we have seen, Smith also believed that the sincere love of virtue is real and rooted in the pursuit of sympathy. Thus, Smith cannot mean that human beings *only* pursue sympathy in the way just outlined.

Perhaps, then, he means that we can pursue sympathy with the goal of establishing and observing sentimental agreement *per se*, not just that of getting others to agree with us. Having this goal involves seeing other people as equals, with legitimate claims to having a say in the harmony that results from our interaction with them.[14] Thus, pursuit of sympathy in this way is not reducible to the desire 'to set [ourselves] above others', *contra* Rousseau's third claim (Letter: 252). And attachment to the harmony that results from this pursuit would be sincere, *contra* Rousseau's second claim. Most importantly, however, by invoking this way of pursuing sympathy, we can render Smith's appeal to the love of virtue less *ad hoc* and shed some light on how this appeal might be able to develop out of the love of praise. To pursue sympathy with an *idealised* other, a person who is 'cool', 'candid', '[self-]consistent' (TMS VII.ii.4.10: 311), 'equitable' (TMS II.iii.3.6: 108), 'well-informed' and 'impartial' (TMS III.2.32: 130), is to pursue sympathy with an attitude that does not give special priority to any individual, including oneself; hence Smith's description of the idealised spectator as a 'man in general' (TMS III.2.31: 129, ed. note). Once again, Smith owes us an account of *how* one comes to value sympathy in this way, with this idealised other. But the fact that the natural pursuit of sympathy *can* take this form constitutes the heart of his response to Rousseau, which we can now reconstruct as follows.[15]

Rousseau's reduction of all concern about what others think of us to 'ambition and the vain desire of superiority' is mistaken for the same reason that Mandeville's similar reduction of all such concern to vanity is mistaken (Letter: 250). Neither thinker realises that these reductions only take into account one way of pursuing others' sympathy. We can also pursue others' sympathy not for egocentric reasons but simply because we value sentimental agreement. This kind of pursuit of sympathy is behind what Smith identifies, in response to Mandeville, as the love of virtue. Since the Smithian love of virtue must be rooted in the love of sympathy with others, it must involve a reference to others' sentiments; this reference is to an idealised other, with whom we non-egocentrically seek sympathy. So, according to Smith, Rousseau was right in believing *both* that self-estimation derives from a concern for what others think of us *and* that this concern often takes the form of an egocentric desire for their worship; Smith explicitly acknowledges in his attack on Mandeville that the pursuit of sympathy 'seldom' takes the idealised form (TMS VII.ii.4.10: 311). But Smith thinks Rousseau was wrong in believing that sociality, understood merely in terms of the concern that others sympathise with and therefore approve of our sentiments, is not just unnatural but also could not naturally generate an impersonal love of virtue, understood as a love of sentimental harmony *per se*.

Interpretive Upshots of this Reconstruction

If my understanding both of Smith's review of Rousseau's *Discourse* and of Smith's overall moral psychology is correct, it gives rise to at least two additional interpretive tasks. The first is to consider how Smith's proposed solutions to the problems Rousseau diagnoses with commercial society – solutions outlined extensively by Ryan Hanley (2009: 53–208) and Rasmussen (2008: 91–158) – might assist the development of the kind of pursuit of mutual sympathy I have identified. It would be worth considering, for example, how the plan of education in *The Wealth of Nations* to which so many of Smith's defenders appeal might actually shape the ways in which Smithian moral agents pursue sympathy. The second task is to investigate how Smith's non-egocentric-sympathy-based conception of the love of virtue relates to Rousseau's own solution – i.e. the concept of the general will – with respect to each's broad normative orientation and concrete, first-order ethical and political implications.[16]

Notes

1. This essay was much improved as a result of questions and comments from attendees at the conference 'Themes from Smith and Rousseau', held at the University of Glasgow in July 2015. The same is true regarding attendees at the panel at which it was given at the annual of the American Political Science Association, held in Philadelphia in August 2016. Special thanks goes to Brandon Turner who, in comments on that presentation, rightly pointed out that getting clear on the overall relationship between Smith and Rousseau, as well as between both and Mandeville, will also require investigation of whether the philosophers read each other *accurately*. This, however, is a project for another occasion. Thanks to Maura Sharkey for copy-editing assistance.

    In the essay, *Of the Nature of that Imitation which takes place in what are called the Imitative Arts*, Smith levels this charge more broadly, describing Rousseau as 'an Author, more capable of feeling strongly than of analysing accurately' (IA: 198).

2. The other reference is in the essay, *Considerations Concerning the First Formation of Languages* (CL 2: 205). Thanks to Michelle Schwarze for reminding me of this.

3. Rasmussen makes a similar observation (2008: 119). I hope to develop this way of understanding the relationship between the

review and the discussion of Mandeville in *The Theory of Moral Sentiments* more fully.

4. Thus, the reading I offer here differs from Griswold's, which centres on epistemic rather than conative aspects of sympathy. According to Griswold, Smith, unlike Rousseau, believes that we are capable of truly *understanding* each other (Griswold 2010). I, on the other hand, argue that Smith takes Rousseau to have too limited a conception of what it means to *seek* what Smith calls 'mutual sympathy' (TMS I.i.2: 13). In doing so, I make distinctions between ways of desiring mutual sympathy that are more fully worked out, without connection to Rousseau, in McHugh (2016).

5. In the *Discourse*, Rousseau suggests that 'accidents' such as 'great floods or earthquakes surrounded the inhabited areas with water or precipices' and thereby 'brought [people] together and forced [them] to live together' (Rousseau 1987: 63).

6. In the *Discourse*, Rousseau argues that the following virtues are derived from 'the force of natural pity': 'generosity', 'mercy', 'humanity', 'benevolence' and 'even friendship' (Rousseau 1987: 54).

7. Smith believes that self-command is rooted in a 'regard to the sentiments of other people' towards oneself, a source that, as we shall see below, Rousseau would not see as a natural wellspring of virtue (TMS VI.concl.1: 262).

8. Though I think I have identified a major theme running through Smith's selections, I do not mean to imply that my reading exhausts the content of these rich passages. For a treatment that is more exhaustive, see Rasmussen (2008: 68–90).

9. I assume here that Smith places the love of praise and the love of virtue, the love of praiseworthiness, etc. (see TMS III.2: 113–34) on a developmental continuum. In other words, I am reading Smith not as positing the existence of distinct drives towards the right and/ or the good, but as trying to explain how such drives grow out of our more basic social ones. This position needs to be defended, but I trust that it is plausible enough to be assumed for the present purposes. For more on this issue, see McHugh (2016).

10. This feature of Smith's conception of sympathy is what makes it possible to say, perhaps awkwardly, that Smithian sympathy is the kind of thing one can *pursue*. Thanks to the editors of the present volume for requesting some clarification on this point.

11. In *Discourse* passages that Smith does not quote, Rousseau grounds this ambition in what he calls *amour-propre*, helpfully translated by Donald Cress as 'egocentrism', an artificial 'sentiment which has its

source in comparisons' and 'moves each individual to value himself more than anyone else' (Rousseau 1987: 106). I employ Cress's term below.

12. For an extended treatment of Smith's own version of how this process would work, see Otteson (2002).

13. See Rasmussen (2008: 51–90) and Hanley (2009: 15–52). Also see Fleischacker (2004: 104–22).

14. Thus, my interpretation is in broad agreement with much recent work developing Smith's egalitarianism. See Darwall (1999: 139–64), Fleischacker (2004: 72–80) and Debes (2012: 109–40).

15. The way of reading Smith suggested in this paragraph is much more fully developed and defended in McHugh (2016).

16. Such an investigation would be particularly worthwhile because we have reason to believe that Smith thought highly of Rousseau's *Social Contract*. Upon visiting Smith in 1784, the French scientist Barthélemy Faujas de Saint-Fond commented that 'he spoke . . . of Rousseau with a kind of religious respect' and remarked that the *Social Contract* 'will in time avenge him for all the persecutions he suffered' (quoted in Ross 2014: 241; and in Rasmussen 2008: 56).

Bibliography

Darwall, Stephen (1999), 'Sympathetic Liberalism: Recent Work on Adam Smith', *Philosophy and Public Affairs*, 28.2, 139–64.

Debes, Remy (2012), 'Adam Smith on Dignity and Equality', *British Journal for the History of Philosophy*, 20.1, 109–40.

Fleischacker, Samuel (2004), *On Adam Smith's Wealth of Nations: A Philosophical Companion*, Princeton: Princeton University Press.

Griswold, Charles L. (2010), 'Smith and Rousseau in Dialogue: Sympathy, *Pitié*, Spectatorship and Narrative', in V. Brown and S. Fleischacker (eds), *The Philosophy of Adam Smith: The Adam Smith Review, Volume 5*, London: Routledge, 59–84.

Hanley, Ryan P. (2009), *Adam Smith and the Character of Virtue*, Cambridge: Cambridge University Press.

McHugh, John (2016), 'Ways of Desiring Mutual Sympathy in Adam Smith's Moral Philosophy', *British Journal for the History of Philosophy*, 24.4, 614–34.

Mossner, E. C., and I. S. Ross (eds) (1987), *Correspondence of Adam Smith*, Indianapolis: Liberty Press.

Otteson, James (2002), *Adam Smith's Marketplace of Life*, Cambridge: Cambridge University Press.

Rasmussen, Dennis C. (2008), *The Problems and Promise of Commercial Society: Adam Smith's Response to Rousseau*, University Park: Penn State University Press.

Ross, Ian S. (2014), 'The Philosopher, the Geologist and the Piobaireachd Competition: Adam Smith's Musical Experiment', in F. Forman (ed.), *The Adam Smith Review*, Vol. 7, London: Routledge, 239–49.

Rousseau, Jean-Jacques (1987) [1755], 'Discourse on the Origin of Inequality', in *The Basic Political Writings*, ed. and trans. D. Cress, Indianapolis: Hackett, 25–110.

Part III

Moral Sentiments and Spectatorship

7

Adam Smith and Jean-Jacques Rousseau on the Vices of the Marketplace

Michael Schleeter

In October 2008 a humbled Alan Greenspan sat before the United States House Committee on Oversight and Government Reform. The former Federal Reserve Chairman – who in past years had been dubbed 'Maestro' by journalist Bob Woodward and been one of the leading advocates for the deregulation of financial markets – had been called before the committee to give testimony in the wake of the global financial crisis, which had been precipitated by the collapse of the American and European housing markets. In his testimony, Greenspan admitted, 'those of us who have looked to the self-interest of lending institutions to protect shareholders' equity, myself especially, are in a state of shocked disbelief' (Financial Crisis 2008). And, later on, 'I found a flaw. I don't know how significant or permanent it is, but I have been very distressed by that fact' (Financial Crisis 2008). The 'flaw' that Greenspan had found was in what he called his 'ideology', the 'conceptual framework' or 'model that [he had] perceived [to be] the critical functioning structure that defines how the world works', which entailed that self-interest alone would compel marketplace actors not to jeopardise their own long-term credibility or solvency by, for example, creating securities backed by risky sub-prime mortgages, paying ratings agencies to assign them high investment grades, and selling them off to unwitting investors around the world (having sometimes also 'insured' these securities with credit default swaps purchased from firms with insufficient capital reserves to pay out if the securities were to fail) (Financial Crisis 2008).

The Maestro's confidence in the power of self-interest to discourage immoderate behaviour within the marketplace had been severely shaken. And so had been the confidence – such as it was – of many others, which created openings for reformers and revolutionaries alike. For example, it created an opening for Congressman Barney Frank, Senator Chris Dodd and President Barack Obama to pass and sign legislation that significantly increased federal regulation of the financial services sector. And it also created an opening for Kalle Lasn and Micah White, the instigators of the first Occupy Wall Street protest in Zuccotti Park, to spark a movement wherein hundreds of thousands worldwide organised and mobilised, in order, as Tahrir Square protester Raimundo Viejo put it, 'to attack the system ... [as] one big swarm of people', and, as Micah White put it, to 'propel us toward the radical democracy of the future' (Original Email 2014). More broadly, though, this widespread crisis in confidence created an opening for individuals to begin to ask fundamental questions about the marketplace and the motivations of its actors, such as: to what extent and in what ways does self-interest in fact encourage, rather than discourage, immoderate behaviour within the marketplace? Put differently, to what extent and in what ways does self-interest in fact encourage, rather than discourage, vicious behaviour within the marketplace? And what, if anything, can be done to address the problem?

In what follows, I want to explore these questions within the context of the thought of Adam Smith and Jean-Jacques Rousseau. More specifically, I want to explore them primarily within the context of their thought as it was developed in Smith's *An Inquiry into the Nature and Causes of the Wealth of Nations* (1776) and Rousseau's *Emile, or On Education* (1762). For the former provides valuable insights into both the extent to which, and the specific ways in which, self-interest may encourage marketplace actors to engage in immoderate or vicious behaviour. And the latter provides valuable insights, which supplement those of the former, into some possible remedies for some of the worst of these activities.

Adam Smith on the Marketplace

In his *Wealth of Nations*, Adam Smith advocated for the establishment of what he called a 'system of natural liberty', both within and between nations (WN IV.ix.5 1: 687). Such a system, he argued, would enable each individual within it 'to pursue his own interest his own way' by instituting and safeguarding a set of basic rights and freedoms, not only political and civil, but also economic, such as the right to hold and the freedom to exchange private property (WN IV.ix.51: 687). For Smith, these latter rights and freedoms, if properly instituted and safeguarded, would ensure that, in general, individuals would not be subjected to force, constraint or fraud in their exchanges with one another – whether of their labour or of their other property – and would thereby create the framework for a properly functioning marketplace.[1]

Smith did allow for two important exceptions to the above, however. For he argued that, even within a system of natural economic liberty, individuals could be subjected to force or constraint in their exchanges if doing so were necessary either for the preservation of liberty itself or for the promotion of some other vital public good that could not otherwise be achieved. For example, Smith argued that individuals could be forced to pay taxes in order to support a 'military force' as well as the various governmental institutions required for what he called 'an exact administration of justice', all of which he thought were necessary for the preservation of liberty itself (WN V.i.a.1: 689; WN IV.ix.51: 687). And he further argued that they could be forced to pay taxes in order to erect and maintain basic infrastructure (roads, canals, bridges, etc.), post offices and schools, all of which he thought were necessary for the promotion of commerce, communication and scientific and religious instruction, three vital public goods that he thought could not otherwise be achieved, 'because the profit [of erecting and maintaining them] could never repay the expense to any individual or small number of individuals', although, he added, 'it may frequently do much more than repay it to a great society' (WN IV.ix.51: 688).

Along similar lines, Smith argued that individuals could be constrained in their exchanges if doing so were necessary either to prevent exchanges that might 'endanger the security of the whole society', such as exchanges between prospective borrowers and lenders with insufficient capital reserves to back up their promissory notes, or to encourage 'dangerous and expensive experiment[s], of which the publick is afterwards to reap the benefit', through the granting of temporary monopolies – or 'letters patent' – to merchants, inventors and authors on their respective trades, discoveries and writings (WN II.ii.94: 324; WN V.i.e.30: 754). For Smith, such exceptions were entirely compatible with a system of natural economic liberty.

Smith assumed that individuals within a system of natural economic liberty would be motivated in their exchanges primarily by a species of self-interest that he called 'the desire of bettering our condition, a desire which, though generally calm and dispassionate, comes with us from the womb, and never leaves us till we go into the grave' (WN II.iii.28: 341). And he continued,

> In the whole interval which separates those two moments, there is scarce perhaps a single instant in which any man is so perfectly and completely satisfied with his situation, as to be without any wish of alteration or improvement, of any kind. An augmentation of fortune is the means by which the greater part of men propose and wish to better their condition. (WN II.iii.28: 341)

Smith thus assumed that 'the greater part' of individuals would be motivated in their exchanges primarily by the desire to augment their fortunes, which he thought would lead them, first, to increase their productivity by entering into the division of labour and creating new technologies (i.e. by specialising and innovating) and, secondly, to participate only in exchanges that were to their advantage – with butchers, brewers, bakers and the like, who would themselves be similarly motivated (WN I.ii.2: 26–7).

Smith argued that, by increasing their productivity and participating only in exchanges that were to their advantage, individuals within a system of natural economic liberty would, irrespective of their conscious intentions, promote two additional public goods: widespread material prosperity and, in fact, a species of material equality. Indeed, Smith insisted that specialisation, innovation and exchanges for mutual benefit would, in 'a well-governed society', ultimately occasion a 'universal opulence which extends itself to the lowest ranks of the people' (WN I.i.10: 22). For, in such a society, he explained,

> Every workman has a great quantity of his own work to dispose of beyond what he himself has occasion for; and every other workman being exactly in the same situation, he is enabled to exchange a great quantity of his own goods for a great quantity . . . of theirs. He supplies them abundantly with what they have occasion for, and they accommodate him as amply with what he has occasion for, and a general plenty diffuses itself through all the different ranks of society. (WN I.i.10: 22)

In this way, Smith argued that individuals, motivated primarily by the desire to augment their fortunes, would, in a well-governed society, promote the public good of widespread material prosperity.[2]

Smith also insisted that exchanges for mutual benefit, such as exchanges of, for example, labour for wages, would, in 'a society where ... there was perfect liberty, and where every man was perfectly free both to chuse what occupation he thought proper, and to change it as often as he thought proper', ultimately occasion a perfect equality – or, at least, a tendency towards it – in the 'whole of the advantages and disadvantages of the different employments of labour and stock' (WN I.x.a.1: 116). For, in such a society, he explained,

> If in the same neighbourhood, there was any employment evidently either more or less advantageous than the rest, so many people would crowd into it in the one case, and so many would desert it in the other, that its advantages would soon return to the level of other employments ... Every man's interest would prompt him to seek the advantageous, and to shun the disadvantageous employment. (WN I.x.a.1: 116)

Smith's point here was that, if, for example, an employment of labour were to arise in a given labour market with all of the advantages of the most advantageous employments (e.g. high compensation, prestige, etc.) but with none of the disadvantages (e.g. high barriers to entry, stress levels, etc.), so many individuals would be driven by self-interest to enter into the former, that its balance of advantages and disadvantages would eventually achieve parity with the latter. In this way, Smith argued that individuals, motivated primarily by the desire to augment their fortunes, would, in a society where there was perfect liberty, promote the public good of a species of material equality.

Adam Smith on the Vices of the Marketplace

Smith acknowledged that self-interest within the context of a properly functioning marketplace could encourage behaviour that was industrious, ingenious, parsimonious, frugal and sober. However, he also observed that it could encourage behaviour that was immoderate or – if Aristotle's equation of immoderation, which can find expression in both excessive and deficient behaviour, and vice may be granted – vicious in nature. And this in at least two senses. For Smith suggested that individuals could be motivated by self-interest to engage in activities that were, indeed, immoderate or vicious, but that did not violate the economic liberties of others, as well as in activities that did violate the economic liberties of others, and that were, for precisely this reason, immoderate or vicious. In this way, he suggested that individuals could be driven by self-interest to succumb to what may be called 'liberal' as well as 'illiberal' vices.

In his *Wealth of Nations*, Smith described a rather large number of liberal vices, but only a few of them were of the kind to which individuals could be driven to succumb specifically by the desire to augment their fortunes. Perhaps the two most notable of these vices were ones to which he thought members of the class of 'those who live by wages', or the class of labourers, were particularly susceptible (WN I.xi.p.7: 265). The first was a vice to which the members of this class who were 'liberally paid by the piece' were especially vulnerable (WN I.viii.44: 100). As Smith explained, workmen who were paid per piece of work done were 'very apt to over-work themselves, and to ruin their health and constitution in a few years' (WN I.viii.44: 100). Similarly, soldiers who were paid per task performed were 'frequently prompted' by 'mutual emulation and the desire of greater gain . . . to over-work themselves, and to hurt their health by excessive labour' (WN I.viii.44: 100). Such individuals could thus be motivated by the desire to augment their fortunes to engage in activities that were excessive in nature, and that were, in this way, immoderate or vicious.

The second of these vices was one to which all of the members of this class were especially vulnerable, since all of them would be motivated to increase their productivity by entering into the division of labour. As Smith explained,

In the progress of the division of labour, the employment of the far greater part of those who live by labour, that is, of the great body of the people, comes to be confined to a few very simple operations; frequently to one or two. But the understandings of the greater part of men are necessarily formed by their ordinary employments. The man whose whole life is spent in performing a few very simple operations . . . has no occasion to exert his understanding . . . He naturally loses, therefore, the habit of such exertion, and generally becomes as stupid

and ignorant as it is possible for a human creature to become ...
His dexterity at his own particular trade seems, in this manner, to be
acquired at the expense of his intellectual, social, and martial virtues.
But in every improved and civilized society this is the state into which
the labouring poor, that is, the great body of the people, must necessarily fall, unless government takes some pains to prevent it. (WN
V.i.f.50: 781–2)

Smith's point here was that, by specialising, individuals were very
apt to stop exercising certain important capacities that lay outside
the scope of their specific tasks within the division of labour, and
that, as a result, these capacities would start to atrophy. Such
individuals could thus be motivated by the desire to augment their
fortunes to engage in activities that were deficient in nature, and
that were, in this way, immoderate or vicious.

Smith suggested a remedy for each of these liberal vices. The
remedy for the first, the vice which found expression in excessive
labour, was one that ultimately aimed to reshape the external conditions of those who might succumb to it, and thereby to moderate
their behaviour from without. For Smith suggested that this vice
could best be addressed by enjoining the masters of labourers to
'listen to the dictates of reason and humanity', and 'rather to moderate, than to animate the application of many of their workman'
(WN I.viii.44: 100). By doing this, Smith argued, both the masters
and the labourers would benefit, since 'the man who works so
moderately, as to be able to work constantly, not only preserves
his health the longest, but ... executes the greatest quantity of
work' (WN I.viii.44: 100).

The remedy for the second, the vice which found expression
in deficient exercise of certain important capacities, was one that
ultimately aimed to reshape the 'internal conditions' of those who
might succumb to it – to reshape their characters – and thereby
to moderate their behaviour from within. For Smith suggested
that it could best be addressed by enjoining the public to establish
'in every parish or district a little school, where children may be
taught for a reward so moderate, that even a common labourer
may afford it', and thereby to 'facilitate ... encourage, and ...
even impose upon almost the whole body of the people, the necessity of acquiring those most essential parts of education' (WN
V.i.f.54–5: 785). By doing this, Smith argued, the public could
effectively mitigate 'the gross ignorance and stupidity which, in a

civilized society, seem so frequently to benumb the understandings of all the inferior ranks of people' (WN V.i.f.61: 788).

Although Smith described a rather large number of liberal vices in his *Wealth of Nations*, he focused to a far greater extent in this text on the illiberal vices, to which he thought members of the class of 'those who live by profit', or the class of merchants and manufacturers, were particularly susceptible (WN I.xi.p.7: 265). Indeed, Smith insisted that members of this class were frequently motivated by the desire to augment their fortunes to violate the economic liberties of others, and thus to engage in activities that were, for precisely this reason, immoderate or vicious. In particular, he insisted that they were frequently motivated by this desire to manipulate commercial policy so that individuals, both within and between nations, could be subjected to both force and constraint in their exchanges with one another (and in ways that were necessary neither for the preservation of liberty itself nor for the promotion of some other vital public good that could not otherwise be achieved).

Indeed, Smith insisted that the merchants and manufacturers of his day were 'the contrivers' and 'by far the principal architects' of commercial policy, and that their 'private interests ... may, perhaps, have extorted from the legislature ... the greater part of [the nation's] commercial regulations' (WN IV.viii.54: 661; WN IV.viii.3: 643). And, further, he insisted that they had manipulated commercial policy in ways that violated the economic liberties of others. For example, Smith observed, they had manipulated it so that individuals could be forced to pay taxes in order to support bounties and drawbacks on various imports and exports as well as to support public subsidies for the training of certain professionals. And they had manipulated it so that individuals could be constrained in their exchanges by 'high duties' and 'absolute prohibitions' on certain imports and exports as well as by corporate monopolies and restrictive apprenticeship rules in various trades. In fact, Smith argued that it was precisely because they had done so that 'the policy of Europe' was such that it 'no-where leaves things at perfect liberty' (WN I.x.a.2: 116).

For Smith, to violate the economic liberties of others in these ways was no small matter. He claimed, for example, that the merchants and manufacturers of his day who had manipulated commercial policy so that individuals could be subjected to constraint in their exchanges had, in general, succumbed to what he called 'the

corporation spirit' or, alternatively, 'the wretched spirit of monop-
oly' (WN I.x.c.6: 136; WN IV.ii.21: 461). Moreover, he claimed
that those who had manipulated it specifically so that individuals could be constrained by restrictive apprenticeship rules, which
prevented masters from taking on more than a specified number of
apprentices and/or releasing them from service before the passage
of a specified number of years, had manipulated commercial policy
in a way that not only represented 'a manifest encroachment upon
the just liberty both of the workman, and of those who might be
disposed to employ him', but also, since the 'property which every
man has in his own labour . . . is the most sacred and inviolable',
represented 'a plain violation of this most sacred property' (WN
I.x.c.12: 138). In this way, such commercial regulations functioned
to diminish economic liberty in a very significant way.

    And, for Smith, insofar as such commercial regulations func-
tioned to diminish economic liberty, they also functioned to diminish prosperity and equality. In fact, he argued that it was precisely
because such regulations functioned to diminish equality that the
merchants and manufacturers of his day had manipulated commercial policy in these ways in the first place. As Smith explained,
such regulations had occasioned 'a very important inequality in
the whole of the advantages and disadvantages of the different
employments of labour and stock' (WN I.x.c.3: 135). And, he
continued, it was precisely 'to prevent [a] reduction in price, and
consequently of wages and profit, by restraining that free competition which would most certainly occasion it, that all corporations,
and the greater part of corporation laws, have been established'
(WN I.x.c.17: 140). More generally, Smith observed,

> The interest of the dealers . . . in any particular branch of trade or
> manufactures, is always in some respects different from, and even
> opposite to, that of the publick. To widen the market and to narrow
> the competition, is always the interest of the dealers. To widen the
> market may frequently be agreeable enough to the interest of the
> publick; but to narrow the competition must always be against it, and
> can serve only to enable the dealers, by raising their profits above what
> they naturally would be, to levy, for their own benefit, an absurd tax
> upon the rest of their fellow-citizens. (WN I.xi.p.10: 267)

Smith's point here was that commercial regulations that subjected individuals to constraint in their exchanges functioned to

diminish equality by effecting a transfer of wealth from those who had been so subjected, on the one hand, to those with whom they were constrained to exchange, on the other. And this was true for commercial regulations that subjected individuals to force in their exchanges as well. Indeed, it was for precisely this reason that, as Smith observed, in all such regulations, 'the interest of our manufacturers has been most peculiarly attended to' (WN IV.viii.54: 662).

Smith suggested a remedy for these illiberal vices, as well – one that ultimately aimed to reshape the external conditions of those who might succumb to them, and thereby to moderate their behaviour from without. As he explained, 'the mean rapacity, the monopolizing spirit of merchants and manufacturers . . . though it cannot perhaps be corrected, may very easily be prevented from disturbing the tranquility of any body but themselves' (WN IV.iii.c.9: 493). Smith suggested that the mean rapacity of merchants and manufacturers, though perhaps finally incorrigible, could best be addressed by enjoining the public to subject their preferred commercial regulations to intense scrutiny. As he explained,

> The proposal of any new law or regulation of commerce which comes from this order, ought always to be listened to with great precaution, and ought never to be adopted till after having been long and carefully examined, not only with the most scrupulous, but with the most suspicious attention. It comes from an order of men, whose interest is never exactly the same with that of the publick, who have generally an interest to deceive and even to oppress the publick, and who accordingly have, upon many occasions, both deceived and oppressed it. (WN I.xi.p.10: 267)

Smith noted that such intense public scrutiny was particularly needful to overcome 'the clamour and sophistry of merchants and manufacturers', which could, in its absence, 'easily persuade [the public] that the private interest of a part, and of a subordinate part of the society, is the general interest of the whole' (WN I.x.c.25: 144).

Interestingly, Smith never explained exactly why the mean rapacity of merchants and manufacturers was perhaps finally incorrigible, or exactly why the remedy for the illiberal vices should be one that ultimately aimed only to reshape the external conditions of those who might succumb to them, and thereby only to moderate their behaviour from without. And, indeed, it is unclear why either of these should be the case. For if education could effectively mitigate the gross ignorance and stupidity of labourers, and thereby play a role in cultivating their intellectual, social and martial virtues, why could it not also effectively mitigate the mean rapacity of merchants and manufacturers, which might lead them to violate the economic liberties of others? Put differently, why could education not also play a role in cultivating their capacity to feel compassion for others, particularly those whose liberty, prosperity and equality their preferred commercial regulations had diminished?

In his *Theory of Moral Sentiments*, Smith claimed that even the 'greatest ruffian, the most hardened violator of the laws of society, [was] not altogether without' compassion, 'the emotion which we feel for the misery of others, when we either see it, or are made to conceive it in a very lively manner' (TMS I.i.1.1: 9). More precisely, he claimed that we feel compassion when we identify in our imaginations with others, in their suffering as they themselves experience it (TMS VII.iii.1.4: 317). As he explained,

> By the imagination we place ourselves in his situation, we conceive ourselves enduring all the same torments, we enter as it were into his body, and become in some measure the same person with him, and thence form some idea of his sensations, and even feel something which, though weaker in degree, is not altogether unlike them. (TMS I.i.1.2: 9)

A remedy for the illiberal vices that would ultimately aim to reshape the 'internal conditions' of those who might succumb to them – to reshape their characters – and thereby to moderate their behaviour from within, could involve a programme of education that would play a role in cultivating the capacity of individuals to identify in their imaginations with others, particularly with the poor and oppressed, in their suffering as they themselves experience it, and thereby their capacity to feel compassion for them. What would such a programme of education entail? In order to begin to answer this question, I want to turn to the work of Jean-Jacques Rousseau, and specifically to his *Emile*, which provides valuable insights into this issue.

Jean-Jacques Rousseau on a Potential Remedy for the Illiberal Vices

In his *Emile*, Rousseau outlined a programme of education for his titular student, which spans from infancy to young adulthood. Of particular interest here is the stage of this programme that begins at puberty, or at Emile's 'second birth' (Rousseau 1979: 212). For it is at this stage that Emile's nascent moral sentiments begin to develop, first among them pity and, eventually, compassion. Like Smith, Rousseau claimed that we feel these sentiments when we identify in our imaginations with others, in their suffering as they themselves experience it. As Rousseau explained,

> In fact, how do we let ourselves be moved by pity if not by transporting ourselves outside of ourselves and identifying with the suffering animal, by leaving, as it were, our own being to take on its being? We suffer only so much as we judge that it suffers. It is not in ourselves, it is in him that we suffer. Thus, no one becomes sensitive until his imagination is animated and begins to transport him out of himself. (Rousseau 1979: 222–3)

For Rousseau, what is true of our pity for 'the suffering animal' is also true of our pity for other human beings, for whom we feel this sentiment when we transport ourselves out of ourselves and leave our being to take on theirs in our imaginations, when we thereby identify with them, in their suffering, not as it exists in ourselves, but as it exists in them.

Rousseau claimed that our capacity to identify in our imaginations with others, in their suffering, is at first limited to those whose suffering is of a sort that we have ourselves experienced, and that we feel we could experience again. He expressed this through the following maxim: 'One pities in others only those ills from which one does not feel oneself exempt' (Rousseau 1979: 224). And he further claimed that pity gives way to compassion when our capacity to identify with others, in their suffering, is no longer limited in this way – when it finally extends to those whose suffering is of a sort that we have not ourselves experienced, but that we feel we could experience someday. As he explained, young people 'can pity only ills they know, and this apparent insensibility, which comes only from ignorance, is soon changed into compassion when they begin to feel that there are in human life countless pains they do not know' (Rousseau 1979: 227).

For Rousseau, then, our capacity to feel both pity and compassion for others rests upon our ability to see the suffering of others as suffering that we could ourselves experience. And he observed that the rich and powerful were often lacking in precisely this ability with respect to the poor and oppressed. As he explained,

> Why are kings without pity for their subjects? Because they count on never being mere men. Why are the rich so hard toward the poor? It is because they have no fear of becoming poor. Why does the nobility have so great a contempt for the people? It is because a noble will never be a commoner. (Rousseau 1979: 224)

Rousseau's point here was that, if the rich and powerful see themselves as being entirely incapable of ever becoming poor and oppressed, they will be unable to see the suffering of the poor and oppressed as suffering that they could themselves experience. Consequently, the rich and powerful will be unable to identify in their imaginations with the poor and oppressed, in their suffering, and will thus be unable to feel pity or compassion for them. In this way, the rich, for example, will find it easier to be 'hard toward the poor', and, indeed, to violate their economic liberties and further diminish their prosperity and equality.

Rousseau suggested that our capacity to feel both pity and compassion for others should be actively cultivated, beginning in early adolescence. In the programme of education he outlined for Emile, and specifically at the stage of this programme that begins at puberty, Rousseau stressed that his student would be exposed first-hand to 'the sufferings of the unfortunate and the labors of the poor'. And he enjoined any teacher who followed this programme to:

> Make [the student] understand well that the fate of these unhappy men can be his, that all their ills are there in the ground beneath his feet, that countless unforeseen and inevitable events can plunge him into them from one moment to the next. Teach him to count on neither birth nor health nor riches. Show him all the vicissitudes of fortune. Seek out for him examples, always too frequent, of people who, from a station higher than his, have fallen beneath these unhappy men. (Rousseau 1979: 224)

Emile would thus be taught to see himself as entirely capable of becoming poor and oppressed, and thereby to see their suffering as suffering that he could himself experience. More generally, he would be taught that '[men] are not naturally kings, or lords, or courtiers, or rich men', that '[all] are born naked and poor', that 'all are subject to the miseries of life, to sorrows, ills, needs, and pains of every kind' and that 'all are condemned to death', and would thus be taught 'what truly belongs to man' and 'what is most inseparable from' human nature (Rousseau 1979: 222). In this way, Emile's capacity to identify in his imagination with the poor and oppressed, in their suffering, and thereby his capacity to feel pity and compassion for them would be actively cultivated.

What significance does the programme of education Rousseau outlined for Emile, either in whole or in part, have for us today? If nothing else, it provides valuable insights into at least one element of a remedy for the illiberal vices that would ultimately aim to reshape not only the external conditions, but also the 'internal conditions' of those who might succumb to them – a remedy that would thereby aim to moderate their behaviour not only from without, but also from within. And, indeed, such a remedy may prove needful, for the illiberal vices are extremely prevalent today, and it is not clear that public scrutiny alone, no matter how intense, either has been or will be sufficient to address them.

Indeed, the marketplace actors who were most deeply responsible for the global financial crisis, for example, were not the ones who created or sold risky securities, or the ones who paid ratings agencies to assign them high investment grades – they were not the ones whom Alan Greenspan claimed, rightly or wrongly, that 'the markets have already punished' (Financial Crisis 2008). Rather, the ones who were most deeply responsible for the global financial crisis were the marketplace actors who were motivated by the desire to augment their fortunes to manipulate commercial policy in ways that made it possible to engage in these activities in the first place – the actors within the financial services industry who used their enormous resources to contribute to political campaigns and lobby members of Congress in order, first, to fight regulations that were designed to prevent exchanges that might 'endanger the security of the whole society', and were therefore necessary for the preservation of liberty itself, and, second, to push through legislation by means of which the public was forced to support a massive bailout of the financial services sector. All of these efforts functioned not only to diminish economic liberty, but also to diminish prosperity and equality. And, it is worth noting, intense public scrutiny proved insufficient to address them. The bailout legislation, for example, was met with overwhelming public opposition, but ultimately passed despite that opposition.

If intense public scrutiny neither has been nor will be sufficient to address the liberal vices, perhaps a remedy that would ultimately aim to reshape the characters of those who might succumb to them is required. Such a remedy could involve a programme of education that would not only expose individuals, perhaps beginning in early adolescence, first-hand to the suffering of the poor and oppressed, but also teach them to see the suffering of the poor and oppressed as suffering that they could themselves experience. In this way, the capacity of those who eventually become merchants and manufacturers to identify in their imaginations with those whose liberty, prosperity and equality their preferred commercial regulations would diminish, and thereby their capacity to feel pity and compassion for them, would be actively cultivated. Perhaps such a programme of education would render the mean rapacity of which Adam Smith was so critical rather more corrigible than he imagined.

Notes

1. Interestingly, Smith also suggested that, within the framework of a properly functioning marketplace, individuals would not be subjected to what might today be called 'exploitation', for he suggested that, within such a framework, individuals would not be driven into exchanges of their labour for wages in which they would not participate were they not desperate for the basic necessities of life (WN I.viii.11–12: 83–4).

2. At one point, Smith put the matter even more plainly: 'The natural effort of every individual to better his own condition, when suffered to exert itself with freedom and security, is so powerful a principle, that it is alone, and without any assistance . . . capable of carrying on the society to wealth and prosperity' (WN IV.v.b.43: 540).

Bibliography

The Financial Crisis and the Role of Federal Regulators: Hearing before the Committee on Oversight and Government Reform,

House of Representatives, 110th Congress 2 (2008) (testimony of Alan Greenspan), https://archive.org/stream/gov.gpo.fdsys.CHRG-110hhrg55764/CHRG-110hhrg55764#page/n19/mode/2up/search/equity (accessed 31 August 2017).

The Original Email that Started Occupy Wall Street (2014), https://economicsociology.org/2014/12/27/the-original-email-that-started-occupy-wall-street/ (accessed 31 August 2017).

Rousseau, Jean-Jacques (1979) [1762], *Emile, or On Education*, trans. Allan Bloom, New York: Basic Books.

8

Julie's Garden and the Impartial Spectator: An Examination of Smithian Themes in Rousseau's *La Nouvelle Héloïse*

Tabitha Baker

Traditionally thought of as opponents with irreconcilable ideologies, Jean-Jacques Rousseau and Adam Smith can be said to represent two very different views of the progress of eighteenth-century society. Rousseau's *Discours sur l'origine de l'inégalité parmi les hommes* abhors the inequality and corruption that has arisen in society as a result of commercial progress, and he channels these criticisms into his proposal for a more equal and enlightened society in *Du contrat social*. In contrast, Smith's *The Wealth of Nations*, and to a certain extent *The Theory of Moral Sentiments*, are often thought of as an exaltation of the capitalist society which Rousseau deplores. Yet an examination of their respective discourses reveals a striking similarity between certain aspects of their thought; as important commentators on modern commercial society, we can see that both are equally concerned with the threat that such a society posed to equality and morality. It is thus their similarities rather than their differences which form the focus of this chapter.

Scholars who have compared Rousseau and Smith and sought to re-examine their traditional opposition include Dennis C. Rasmussen (2008), Pierre Force (2003), Michael Ignatieff (1986), Donald Winch (1996: 66–75), Ryan Patrick Hanley (2008), Daniel Luban (2012), Harvey Mitchell (1989) and to some extent Maureen Harkin (2005). As far back as 1938 Richard B. Sewall stated that 'the first paragraph of [*The Theory of Moral Sentiments*] is little more than a restatement of Rousseau's conception of pity' (1938: 98). To date, comparative scholarship on Rousseau and Smith has concentrated on Smith's *Theory of Moral*

Sentiments as a response to Rousseau's many criticisms of modern commercial society, in particular those set forth in *Discours sur l'origine de l'inégalité parmi les hommes* and *Du contrat social*. That the two thinkers share a similar idea of pity (or in Smith's case, sympathy) is one of the fundamental theories which link Rousseau and Smith; for both it could be said that the capacity to empathise with others is an intrinsically natural mechanism and the fundamental basis of humanity.

Indeed, research which compares the discourses of Rousseau and Smith suggests that there is very real basis for considering the two thinkers as complementary, yet the majority of scholarly work is concentrated on Smith's response to Rousseau's theoretical works. Much work therefore remains to be done on how Rousseau's fictional works can be seen to further inform and be informed by Smith's theories, and this chapter seeks to go some way to filling this gap in the current scholarship. To date, no comprehensive study has examined Rousseau's novel in isolation with Smith's theories as set forth in *The Theory of Moral Sentiments* and *The Wealth of Nations*, yet I argue that it is through Rousseau's fiction that the complicated relationship between the two thinkers' thought can be most evidently sourced.

In particular, it is in *La Nouvelle Héloïse* that the traditional differences between Smith and Rousseau become blurred. *La Nouvelle Héloïse*, published in 1761, illustrates Rousseau's criticisms of contemporary society and seeks to propose a way in which virtue and morality can be upheld in a new, enlightened society. I argue that Rousseau's novel can be seen as inherently Smithian in nature due to the way in which moral and economic themes are treated. To analyse the novel as a Smithian piece of fiction in its complete form would be beyond the scope of this chapter, but for now I will demonstrate how the Smithian aspects of the novel can be most acutely seen in the motif of the eighteenth-century English landscape garden in the fourth part of the novel. I will argue that it is in this space that Rousseau's novel seems to reflect Smith's principles of arriving at moral behaviour and true virtue, and it is here that Rousseau's and Smith's theories seem to be reconciled in order to produce a blended social model in which Smith provides responses to Rousseau's failed utopia. By using Smith as a lens through which to reconsider the garden, it is evident that the traditional opposition between Rousseau and Smith is not as clear cut as hitherto thought.

Both Rousseau and Smith are preoccupied with the conceptions of self-interest and vanity in modern society; it is for this reason that I have chosen to anchor my comparison of their thought in the motif of the landscape garden, not least because of the microcosm of society which the garden space can be seen to represent. Similarly concerned with the idea of vanity and how this could be re-channelled in order to create a more liberal and egalitarian space were the designers and proprietors of the eighteenth-century English landscape garden. As a contested space in the eighteenth century, the garden went through a period of tumultuous change alongside politics and philosophy. A preoccupation with the values of liberty saw a so-called 'gardening revolution' occur during this epoch, and the move away from the formal French style championed during the seventeenth century and characterised by its straight lines and axial alleys, signified a rejection of tyrannical and monarchical absolutism. The new style which was to emerge out of this political stance, with a return to nature and more simplistic designs, was to become known as the 'English landscape garden', which was largely attributed to the genius of Lancelot 'Capability' Brown and the aristocratic owners of gardens such as Stowe. Gardens which represented seventeenth-century formal design principles, particularly those of Versailles, attracted much contemporary criticism, with Alexander Pope (1963: 131) famously chastising the creators of 'proud Versailles'[1] for their vanity and fixation with glory. Indeed, the gardens of Versailles were synonymous with political and territorial power, and were a mark of seventeenth-century political absolutism. Painstakingly designed and crafted over a period that spanned almost the entirety of Louis XIV's reign, the expertise and cost involved in the creation of the gardens was extortionate and stood in stark contrast to the adherence to nature and utility which the new eighteenth-century English landscape garden was seen to represent. Smith himself addresses the differences between French and English gardens in his essay on the imitative arts, discussing evolutions in the fashion for topiary: 'It was some years ago the fashion to ornament a garden with yew and holly trees, clipped into the artificial shapes of pyramids, and columns, and vases, and obelisks. It is now the fashion to ridicule this taste as unnatural' (IA: 183). For Smith, the act of gardening is to consciously display one's allegiance to a certain fashion, and this is in turn more deeply connected to one's economic status. The French nobility, Smith suggests, have continued to employ topiary ornamentation in their gardens because the lower ranks of society cannot afford to follow suit (IA: 184). Louis XIV's gardens were certainly designed to impress and elicit exactly the kind of sentiment which Smith suggests is the corruptible force in society:

> This disposition to admire, and almost to worship, the rich and the powerful, and to despise, or, at least, to neglect persons of poor and mean condition, though necessary both to establish and to maintain the distinction of ranks and the order of society, is, at the same time, the great and most universal cause of the corruption of our moral sentiments. (TMS I.iii.1.1: 61)

Consequently, gardens which were formal in design came to represent a corrupting force in society if we are to read them in Smithian terms as the source of admiration, vanity and pride (TMS VII.ii.4.9–10: 310–11). Smith's moral philosophy is a useful paradigm for analysing the concept of the landscape garden as it allows for an in-depth analysis of both the motivation behind the creation of the garden and the sentiments elicited in the individual through their experience of the garden. It is therefore significant that as an avid defender of equality and liberty, Rousseau chose to incorporate a garden in the new style into his work of fiction; the closed and private garden of Julie in *La Nouvelle Héloïse* suggests a desire to move away from the aggressive land management of the nobility and establish a more virtuous and moral approach to the control of the estate.

Through an examination of *La Nouvelle Héloïse* alongside Smith's *Theory of Moral Sentiments* it will become apparent that the symbol of the landscape garden in Rousseau's novel is an experimental setting in which Rousseau's and Smith's theories can be reconciled. This chapter will explore the significance of the dichotomies of public and private in landscape garden design and demonstrate how public and private society can be seen to underline both Smith's and Rousseau's thought. Beginning with a discussion of Smith's 'impartial spectator', this chapter will demonstrate how such a concept is important to understanding how moral behaviour is appropriated within the public and private garden; this will be followed by an exploration of how vanity is encouraged in the public garden through eliciting the desire to gain the approbation of others, and how Rousseau attempts to negate such behaviour through the creation of the private garden. An exploration of proximity and distance in the garden will conclude this chapter, where I will demonstrate how Smith's thoughts on moral regulation are distorted by Rousseau in *La Nouvelle Héloïse* and necessitate the failure of Rousseau's vision of utopian society.

The Impartial Spectator

It is first important to establish the role of Smith's impartial spectator, a notion which can be explained as a regulator of moral conduct and moderation: 'the man within the breast' (TMS VI.i.11: 215) is part of our imaginative faculty that enables a process in which we imagine how others perceive us and then imagine how they think we should act. While this becomes a significant part of the act of moderating our sentiments and behaviour which will be explored later, for now this awareness of how we appear to others will form the basis of my exploration of vanity and the desire to obtain admiration in the garden, providing contextualisation for my examination of the private Elysée garden in *La Nouvelle Héloïse*. As a shared public space, the eighteenth-century public garden can be seen to intensify Smithian notions of approbation and spectatorship, as individuals come together to consciously display what they perceive to be socially acceptable forms of morality, virtue and sympathy. Gardens that were completely open to the public, particularly pleasure gardens such as Vauxhall and Ranelagh in England, encouraged a culture of seeing and being seen, and naturally favoured the upper and more wealthy classes. Smith explains:

> The fortunate and the proud wonder at the insolence of human wretchedness, that it should dare to present itself before them, and with the loathsome aspect of its misery presume to disturb the serenity of their happiness. The man of rank and distinction, on the contrary, is observed by all the world. Every body is eager to look at him, and to conceive, at least by sympathy, that joy and exaltation with which his circumstances naturally inspire him. His actions are the objects of the public care. (TMS I.iii.2.1: 51)

Here Smith suggests that we are naturally inclined to look to those who are highly placed in society as we assume that their wealth and position make them happy, and we in turn empathise more strongly with the upper classes because of their more favourable social position. Moreover, Smith tells us that 'It is because mankind are disposed to sympathize more entirely with our joy than with our sorrow, that we make parade of our riches, and conceal our poverty' (TMS I.iii.2.1: 50). This in turn encourages a fashion-led culture within the confines of the public garden which both Rousseau and Smith suggest is incompatible with eighteenth-century ideals of noble virtue. Rousseau's contempt for such vanity found in the formal garden is channelled through Monsieur de Wolmar, who says 'I merely see in these grounds, which are so vast and so richly decorated, the vanity of the landowner and that of the artist' (Rousseau 1967: 360).[2] Through a desire to imitate the more fortunate, then, one has a tendency to 'abandon the paths of virtue; for unhappily, the road which leads to the one, and that which leads to the other, lie sometimes in very opposite directions' (TMS I.iii.3.8: 64). The straight axial alley of the formal public garden can here be interpreted as the path to immorality and vanity, as the public garden increases our awareness of the opinions of others and of our own appearance. Smith tells us that as a result,

> The desire of becoming the proper objects of this respect, of deserving and obtaining this credit and rank among our equals, is, perhaps, the strongest of all our desires, and our anxiety to obtain the advantages of fortune is accordingly much more excited and irritated by this desire, than by that of supplying all the necessities and conveniencies of the body, which are always very easily supplied. (TMS VI.i.3: 213)

However, Harkin (1995: 183) suggests that, for Smith, 'sympathy with the wealthy or powerful performs a socially useful task, first of all, by consolidating support for the social order'. It is here that we can see a tension beginning to emerge between both Smith's and Rousseau's theories and the design of the public and private landscape garden. If Smith's assertion that our tendency to emulate and sympathise with the wealthy is merely another form of legitimation for the existing social order, it would seem that the public garden, through its encouragement of *amour-propre* and vanity, would also correspond in part to this theory. In contrast, the incorporation of a private landscape garden in the new English style in *La Nouvelle Héloïse* suggests a desire to escape this kind of social reinforcement and create a private space away from the scrutiny of others, where *amour-propre* and vanity can hold no legitimate place. An exploration of the nature of the public garden in eighteenth-century England complicates this further, as reinforcement of the social order can similarly be seen through the control of admission to the garden. Unlike the pleasure gardens of eighteenth-century London, which incidentally were often in the seventeenth-century French formal style, the landscape parks of the landowning aristocracy had more selective entry requirements. The pseudo-public nature of the English landscape garden in the eighteenth century formed part of the emergence of 'polite culture', whereby the private gardens of wealthy landowners were opened up to members of the emerging middle classes such as professionals and the mercantile class. However, the restricted access to gardens such as Stowe reflected the *intellectual* inaccessibility of the gardens, which required a classical education with a strong grip on Latin and philosophy in order to decipher their meaning. Guidebooks were on hand to provide discourse and instruction to promeneurs, but through the emblematic motifs and notions of association, the complicated allegory of the landscape park was often lost on the lesser-educated visitor. The landscape parks of the wealthy in eighteenth-century England were private gardens, but 'private' in the sense that their meaning was closed to all who did not have access to the same classical education, philosophical ideas and fashionable taste that the landowning classes held. The eighteenth-century English landscape garden became another tool with which to exclude the lower classes and sanctify the political and intellectual position of the aristocracy; a far cry from the values of liberty with which the eighteenth-century landscape garden is traditionally associated.

Received notions of taste can therefore be seen as a consolidation of the social order, and it is here again that we are able to see the preoccupations of Smith and Rousseau as manifest in the landscape garden, particularly in the public garden. Karen Valihora's interpretation of Smith's impartial spectator is useful for understanding the extent to which this feature of Smith's thought also reinforced the codes of taste: 'The impartial spectator exemplifies the dynamics of an appeal to "common sense" or "good taste" as a principle of judgement; it does not represent a set of principles, but a stance on the world' (Valihora 2013: 138). Taste was an important principle in contemporary garden design, and in this way the landscape garden can be seen as a space in which visitor and creator alike attempted to attain the correct 'stance on the world' through anticipating what the other imagines to be 'good taste'. Although Smith would suggest that this is a positive mechanism, the vanity that is associated with a preoccupation with the opinion of others reappears, and it is here that we can see Rousseau's critique of modern society underline the more conceited tendencies of the impartial spectator. As David Marshall acknowledges, such elitist predispositions in the new style of gardening meant that gardens became 'complex texts that had to be deciphered. Composed in a private and soon almost illegible language of emblems, influenced by newer principles of association derived from Hobbes and Locke, they were criticized for being unnatural and for failing to provide an aesthetic experience' (Marshall 2002: 417).

We find no such restriction in Julie's garden, where Saint-Preux wanders with curiosity and explains, 'I was more eager to see objects rather than to examine their meaning, and I enjoyed succumbing to this charming observation without the trouble of having to think' (Rousseau 1967: 356).[3] The private Elysée garden thus becomes a space in which hierarchical values of taste seem to be abandoned, and Saint-Preux's contentment in not having to think or analyse the meaning of Julie's garden reflects Thomas Whately's sentiment, that the enjoyment of a landscape garden should 'not [be] fought for, not laboured; and have the force of a metaphor, free from the detail of an allegory' (1982: 151) . Writing in 1770, Whately complains in *Observations on Modern Gardening* that the revolution in garden design in eighteenth-century England was leading to complicated 'allegories' which had to be 'examined, compared, perhaps explained, before the whole design of them is well understood' (1982: 151), which inevitably detracted from the visitor's enjoyment. This kind of social exclusion, whereby the 'polite spectator could be distinguished from the vulgar interloper, the person of taste from the pretender to taste' (Denney 2005: 494), therefore indicates a form of reinforcement of the social order, where rank and class position could be preserved.[4]

What this further highlights is the notion that the desire to gain approbation from others is intensified within the confines of a garden, as visitor and creator seek to emulate the good taste of a certain social group. While the private garden in *La Nouvelle Héloïse* seeks to redirect such desires, the public garden becomes synonymous with ostentatious displays of wealth which in turn attract admiration, jealousy and thus that morally corruptible force in society, vanity. As described earlier, it is this sentiment of jealousy created by wealth and power which Smith deems to be 'the great and most universal cause of the corruption of our moral sentiments'. This in turn poses the question of how to avoid the displays of excess which inevitably lead to such a sentiment; the creation of the private garden. The tension between public and private is manifest in *La Nouvelle Héloïse* long before the garden at Clarens is introduced in Part IV, Letter XI. For the purpose of aligning public society with moral corruption, Rousseau sets up Paris as distinct from the country, or private society, and through its effects on Saint-Preux we are able to see the dangers that Smith warns against. The tension between public and private society is further highlighted in the garden scene where Saint-Preux muses on the contrast between the French formal garden and Julie's natural, or English landscape, garden:

> I imagine, I said, a rich man from Paris or London, master of this house, and bringing with him a dearly paid architect to spoil nature. With what disdain he would enter this simple and humble place! With what contempt he would tear out these tatters! The straight alignments that he would make! The perfect paths he would impose! (Rousseau 1967: 360)[5]

Here, money and public society are associated with artifice, the straight lines of the seventeenth-century French formal garden, and the costs involved in achieving such undesirable effects. Compared to the designer of the formal garden whom Saint-Preux imagines to be 'dearly paid', Rousseau emphasises the economy involved in the creation of the Elysée garden, which enhances the sense of morality and virtue that one finds in Julie's private sanctuary. Pope similarly appreciates economy and rationality in the expenditure of wealth in the garden, as can be seen in his praise of Lord Burlington, proprietor of Stow:

> Oft have you hinted to your Brother Peer,
> A certain Truth, which may buy too dear:
> Something there is, more needful of Expence,
> And something previous ev'n to Taste – 'Tis *Sense*;
> Good Sense, which only is the Gift of Heav'n,
> And tho' no Science, fairly worth the Seven.
> A Light, which in *yourself* you must perceive;
> *Jones* and *Le Nôtre* have it not to give. (Pope 1963: 130)

Sense, then, is what Pope suggests gardens such as Versailles are lacking, and it is this which sets the eighteenth-century English landscape garden apart from the seventeenth-century French formal garden. Moreover, the type of admiration that excites vanity in the formal garden can be seen to be juxtaposed with the admiration that is elicited by the eighteenth-century English landscape garden. The design of this garden seems to advocate a new, enlightened form of admiration, which is prompted by the garden designer's good taste, sense and use of nature, rather than a simple display of wealth and ornament. While the visitor to the garden is naturally inclined to approve of those who share his or her appreciation of the beauty of the landscape, this mutual admiration of an object does not elicit sympathy or 'the most perfect harmony of sentiments and affections'. Rather, it is only when one can enter into a state of surprise and wonder upon seeing someone else share our sense of taste in a way that does not correspond entirely to our own that we are able to give that person a heightened sense of approbation which itself is not linked to vanity. For Smith, 'approbation heightened by wonder and surprise, constitutes the sentiment which is properly called admiration', and he explains further that

> when [the sentiments of our companion] not only coincide with our own, but lead and direct our own; when in forming them he appears to have attended to many things which we had overlooked, and to have adjusted them to all the various circumstances of their objects; we not only approve of them, but wonder and are surprised at their uncommon and unexpected acuteness and comprehensiveness, and he appears to deserve a very high degree of admiration and applause. (TMS I.i.4.3: 20)

It is this sentiment that is elicited by the public gardens at Stowe, which prompts Pope to elevate the designer above that of Versailles (Le Nôtre). More acutely, deserved approbation in the Smithian sense as demonstrated above is given over entirely to Julie by Saint-Preux through his appreciation of the garden at Clarens when he marvels that 'Yet there is here . . . something that I cannot understand; that a place so different to what it once was could become what it is with only cultivation and care' (Rousseau 1967: 359).[6] A wealth of criticism pertaining to eighteenth-century garden design is dedicated to the observation that 'utility' was the great difference between the French formal garden and the English landscape park, which elevated the latter to a position of superior beauty and taste; indeed the greater part of *Epistle to Burlington* is dedicated to the idea of utility and good sense forming our appreciation of another's taste. However, Smith suggests that utility is not what first encourages us to admire a person's taste, although the acknowledgement of this quality may give it a 'new value' (TMS I.i.4.4: 20); rather, it is in recognising someone else's judgement as coinciding with our own, that we are encouraged to 'approve' of another's sense of taste and judgement. In this way, the eighteenth-century landscape garden in *La Nouvelle Héloïse* can be seen as a space in which Julie's ideas of truth, reason and virtue can be seen to correspond to those of Saint-Preux, and in turn, Rousseau's judgement is aligned with that of the reader as the sentiments of approbation, surprise and wonder are elicited in the reader. Both the public and the private garden in the eighteenth century can therefore be seen as a space in which the desire to gain approbation from others is elicited, albeit in contrasting ways.

It can thus be argued that the drive to acquire the esteem of others can be seen as part of Rousseau's own motivation for writing the novel. Desire to gain the approbation of one's readers, and even one's contemporaries, is consequently a further aspect to note in Rousseau's incorporation of an English landscape garden into the novel. The importance of England in *La Nouvelle Héloïse* can be seen to correspond to eighteenth-century ideals of liberty and democratic government, and Rasmussen notes that

> nearly all of the *philosophes* favoured a modern commercial society similar to the one that in the mid-eighteenth century was beginning to take root in England – a country that many of them greatly admired for this very reason. They believed that freedom and commerce went hand in hand and reinforced each other. (Rasmussen 2008: 18)[7]

Rousseau himself declares in *Du contrat social* that the English are 'closer to liberty than all others' (Rousseau 1962: 244),[8] and his incorporation of an *English* landscape garden can thus be seen as a means of attracting the admiration of a contemporary readership.[9] England, and the English estate, represent a private space in *La Nouvelle Héloïse* away from public society where Julie and Saint-Preux's relationship can be 'made legitimate' (Rousseau 1967: 138),[10] or indeed attract the approbation of the English public.

In the second part of the novel, Milord Edouard offers his estate in England to the two lovers as a private exile where they can be married in a public where 'our wise laws do not repeal those of nature' (Rousseau 1967: 139).[11] England is thus aligned with the ideals of sentimentality where the possibility of reordering the social hierarchy would enable Julie and Saint-Preux to escape the social prejudices of their own tyrannical society and be true to their natural passions. Milord Edouard emphasises the natural and virtuous love between Julie and Saint-Preux by aligning it with the laws of England, and describes how his estate will complement their progressive relationship:

> I have in the Duchy of York quite a considerable estate, which was for a long time, the residence of my ancestors. The house is old, but decent and comfortable; the surroundings are solitary, but pleasant and diverse. The River Ouse, which flows past the end of the park, offers at the same time a charming view, and a simple outlet for commodities. The produce of the land is adequate for the needs of the master, and can double before his eyes. Odious prejudice has no place in this happy land; here the peaceful habitant still preserves the simple way of life from the earliest times, and here one finds the image of the Valais described in such a touching way by your friend's pen! This land is yours, Julie. (Rousseau 1967: 138)[12]

The seat of Milord Edouard here demonstrates several notions of the English landscape garden tradition. First, a sense of nostalgia is invoked through his insistence on the age of the estate and the fact that it has been in his family for several generations; the nostalgia generated in this way legitimises England as the source of rational thinking and the reader is convinced of the social stability that the country would provide the two lovers, as although it may be 'old', it is welcoming and liberal. A common trend in contemporary landscape design was to incorporate ruins and old-style buildings into gardens to provoke sentiments of nostalgia and to celebrate England's intellectual and political history. For example, the Gothic Temple at Stowe was designed in such a manner that it served as a reminder of England's strong heritage and stimulated the Romantic sentiments of the sublime and nostalgia. The emphasis on the size of the estate and the reference to Milord Edouard's 'ancestors' suggests that the family and estate form part of public society, yet the fact that the house and gardens are 'solitary' does not indicate the same kind of extravagant display of wealth and power so often associated with the French château and gardens. More importantly, Milord Edouard insists that the estate is free from social prejudice and that the inhabitants are able to live their lives away from such traits of public life, where they are able to form a simple community which has echoes of Rousseau's utopian ideals of primitive society.

The exploration of Milord Edouard's estate and gardens in England is subsequently important to our understanding of the creation of Julie's garden at Clarens in Part IV of the novel. The dichotomy between public and private society in Milord Edouard's letter, whereby he suggests that the lovers' relationship will be legitimate in the eyes of the English public and yet they are able to carry on their relationship within the confines of a private estate, indicates a need to be accepted by society in order to lead a virtuous existence in private. Julie and Saint-Preux never follow Milord Edouard's advice, yet echoes of English society reappear in the later parts of the novel, where the private, familial community at Clarens seems to reflect ideals of individual liberty, rational estate management and self-sufficiency. Perhaps the most striking feature of Clarens is the garden, which I would like to suggest is a manifestation of Milord Edouard's estate and garden in England as described in Part II, Letter III. The estate at Clarens is similarly 'old', and it could be said that Julie has transposed Milord Edouard's English landscape garden into her Elysée, where she has been able to incorporate features of English society into the society that she felt unable to leave, thus indicating her desire to be accepted by the public, or indeed her desire to gain the approbation of others. The incorporation of an English landscape garden into the novel consequently exemplifies the desire of both the author and the heroine to elicit the admiration of others, and thus highlights the similarities between Rousseau's and Smith's thoughts on such a conception. Nevertheless, it is the reclusive nature of the Elysée garden that problematises the relationship between public and private, and indeed between Rousseau and Smith, particularly if this is to be understood in terms of the theories expressed in Smith's *Theory of Moral Sentiments* which will be explored in the subsequent section of this chapter.

The Society of Strangers

An important part of Smith's theories on sympathy and approbation relates to our proximity to other people and how this controls the acuteness of our moral sentiments; in this section I will examine how this forms an important part of public and private society, and thus the corresponding gardens. It is the particularly private nature of Rousseau's fictional garden that most evidently provides a basis for such an exploration. Both Rousseau and Smith comment on the role of proximity in contemporary society, with Rousseau suggesting that our concern for others is more concentrated by our proximity to them, and highlighting that this renews our strength of humanity (Rousseau 2016). Smith demonstrates in *The Theory of Moral Sentiments* that the closer we are to one another, the easier it is to share our feelings; but that as this distance increases, so too does the difficulty with which we control our passions. Maria Pia Paganelli suggests that it is this distance and practice of our self-command which 'is the foundation of moral development', and further, that 'we learn impartiality and morality by observing a situation at the appropriate distance and by practicing a command of our passions. Being too close or too far away from a situation does not adequately constrain the violence of our passions; it distorts one's judgement, hindering moral development' (Paganelli 2010: 425–41; see also Forman-Barzilai 2005: 189–217). Like Paganelli, I intend to demonstrate how distance and proximity in Smith's thought can be seen to be at work in the landscape garden, and in particular how such a 'distortion' occurs throughout *La Nouvelle Héloïse*, particularly in the garden.

Notions of distance, space and proximity are important design aspects to consider when creating a garden. For example, the seventeenth-century formal garden was designed such that it created the illusion of space and displayed the extent of the owner's wealth and ownership over the land, as can be seen at Versailles; whereas the eighteenth-century English landscape garden sought to create a feeling of intimacy through the illusion of small, enclosed spaces alongside large open spaces (Neumeyer 1947: 190). It is this utilisation of space which I suggest mirrors Smith's theories on commercial society and our distance from others. Indeed, the role of distance is an important aspect of both Rousseau's and Smith's discourses on society, and it is first necessary to examine the extent to which they differ on this subject. For Rousseau, it is the widening of the gaps in social relationships as a result of the development of commercial society that has produced the type of inequality and immorality that he condemns; the greater number of people that the individual has to interact with in modern society is what Rousseau suggests has led to the development of *amour-propre* and our preoccupation with the opinions of others. Yet it is precisely this multiplication in our relationships with other people that Smith believes renders commercial society 'the most fertile ground for moral development' (Paganelli 2010: 425–6). This has led to what many critics call Smith's 'society of strangers', a concept that I will apply to the culture of gardening in the eighteenth century, and more specifically, to the Elysée garden in *La Nouvelle Héloïse*.

First, it can be argued that it is Smith's 'society of strangers' that forms the basis for polite culture in eighteenth-century England and that subsequently acts as an important form of self-command and a way of regulating moral conduct in the eighteenth-century English landscape garden. As we have seen, the landscape parks of the aristocracy were governed by a culture of 'politeness', and it could be said that the open access to the gardens that encouraged this interaction of 'strangers' ensured the moral conduct of its visitors, as Smith says happens in commercial society. In Frances Burney's 1778 novel *Evelina*, the eponymous heroine is subject to a number of mishaps as she learns to navigate her way through social customs and behaviours; it is worth dwelling on the role the public garden plays in this particular novel in order to compare how Rousseau's landscape garden both utilises and rejects Smith's theories on distance. It is in the formal, public gardens of Vauxhall that Evelina must overcome incidents that pose a threat to her virtue, and it is perhaps no coincidence that the gardens were laid out in the French formal style, conceivably drawing inspiration from Versailles, as suggested when Evelina complains of the design of Vauxhall as being 'too formal; I should have been better pleased, had it consisted less of strait walks' (Burney 2008: 195).[13] As a 'new site of social exchange' (Harvey 2001: 159), open access to the public garden can thus be seen to represent a microcosm of commercial society, where Smith's 'society of strangers' manifests itself through new opportunities for interaction between men and women, and between members of different social groups. An appropriate measure of distance between strangers in the public gardens is maintained and it is this reflection of social behaviour that demonstrates how the garden can be seen as a space in which moral behaviour is practised and perfected.

In the case of *Evelina*, the heroine is able to successfully navigate her way out of the French formal garden style and, more importantly, any lasting damage to her reputation; the triumph of Evelina's virtue is facilitated through her continual exposure to strangers, both in and out of the public garden. Of Smith's views on interaction between strangers, Paganelli explains: 'the more we interact with strangers, the more we develop self-command, and the more self-command we have the more virtuous we are. It is this effort, consistently repeated, that will develop into solid self-command that is the foundation of moral development. Practice and habit will make the impartiality stick' (Paganelli 2010: 434). This can indeed be seen in *Evelina*: the heroine develops virtue through the 'practice and habit' of being around strangers and channelling her passions appropriately, and it is this idea of 'practice' and regular exposure to strangers in public society that can be seen to provide the fundamental difference between the fates of Burney's Evelina and Rousseau's Julie. The public garden and its opportunities for interaction with strangers thus supports Smith's assertion that this type of exposure is essential to creating a society that is both morally and economically progressive.

In contrast, Rousseau's fictional garden does not allow for such opportunities: closed to the public, the private garden at Clarens is described as an impervious space to all who do not have permission to access it. Saint-Preux exclaims that it is 'so well hidden by the covered path which separates them, that it cannot be glimpsed from anywhere. The thick foliage which surrounds it does not allow the eye to penetrate, and it is always carefully locked' (Rousseau 1967: 353).[14] Rousseau incorporates an extreme form of private society[15] in the form of the Elysée garden in order to rectify the damage done to the individual as a result of their exposure to public society; yet if we examine Smith's view, we can see that it is the *private* nature of the garden that is in fact problematic. Let us here return to Paganelli's interpretation of Smith, that 'commerce breaks the boundaries of small and closed communities. Commercial societies allow for, and are based on, interactions among strangers. And the continuous exposure to strangers can facilitate the moralizing process' (Paganelli 2010: 425). Julie's garden is locked to the outside and therefore to exposure to strangers; Wolmar tells Saint-Preux, 'I admit that one must not bring strangers here with ceremony; but on the other hand one can take pleasure in it, without showing it to anybody' (Rousseau 1967: 363).[16] Nevertheless, this desire to avoid public displays of ceremony by restricting access to the garden and encouraging the activity of private pleasure can be said to naturally hinder the moralising process, and could go some way to explaining the breakdown of the society at Clarens.

Moreover, the distortion of distance – in which Smith offers 'if we are at all masters of ourselves, the presence of a mere acquaintance will really compose us, still more than that of a friend; and that of an assembly of strangers still more than that of an acquaintance' (TMS I.i.4.9: 23) – can therefore be seen to be at work in *La Nouvelle Héloïse*. This is first indicated through the very genre of the novel, the epistolary form. The communication through letters seems to manipulate the sentiments of both Julie and Saint-Preux, as the distance created through this form of communication should in theory diminish the strength of their sentiments; yet we can see that in actual fact the letters amplify their passions and they are unable to exhibit the kind of 'self-command' that Smith suggests distance encourages. Rousseau immediately introduces us to this particular tension in Saint-Preux's first letter to Julie:

> I dare to ask you, how can you be so playful in public, and so serious when we are alone? I presumed it to be the opposite, and that one must control one's behaviour in proportion to the number of spectators. Instead, I am equally perplexed by the tone of ceremony which you use with me in private and a familiar one in front of everybody: deign to be more constant, perhaps then I would be less tormented. (Rousseau 1967: 11)[17]

Here we can see that a distortion of distance is beginning to take root in *La Nouvelle Héloïse* which anticipates that which will be encountered in Julie's garden. The restraint of passions that Julie observes in the private company of someone familiar to her is inconsistent with Smith's thoughts on proximity, and it could be said that it is this distortion that upsets the balance of Rousseau's ideal society. Furthermore, the private garden does not encourage exposure to strangers, and the characters in *La Nouvelle Héloïse* risk another distortion of distance; they are now too close to each other. The intense privacy of the Elysée garden is heightened by its size and spatial layout, and their reconciliation in the Elysée garden means that their intense closeness in such a small space ensures that their passions are heightened in a new way. Julie herself suggests that the unique privacy of the society at Clarens, particularly when all the staff are excluded from breakfast, means that 'here we do not constrain any of our feelings' (Rousseau 1967: 366).[18] And it is exactly this excess of passions and outpouring of feeling among friends that Smith believes distorts our moral sentiments. It can thus be suggested that here Smith's theories would provide the antidote to the breakdown of Rousseau's fictional society at Clarens, which itself can be attributed to the distortion of distance that Smith warns against.

We must therefore ask why such a distortion occurs in *La Nouvelle Héloïse*, and it is in Rousseau's theoretical works that we can find the answer. Rousseau suggests that the ideal conditions for a democracy to thrive would be where the state is 'very small, where the population is easy to gather together, and where each citizen can easily know all the others' (Rousseau 1962: 280–1).[19] This explains Rousseau's choice of a tight-knit community at Clarens, where the size of the community would provide the requisite foundations for such a democracy to exist. Here again we can see that proximity is distorted in the Smithian sense, even in Rousseau's theoretical works; for a society where everybody knows each other well indicates that there is no need to regulate one's passions as strictly as if they were operating in commercial society, where as 'strangers' they must 'endeavour to bring down [their] passion to that pitch' (TMS I.i.4.9: 23). Nevertheless, Rousseau himself recognises that these conditions are rare when he says 'these conditions which are difficult to combine do not guarantee such a government!' (Rousseau 1962: 280).[20] It seems that even Rousseau himself recognises that such a society is difficult to sustain in modern times, and that in order to be successful, the new kind of society which he encourages must have some degree of openness and exposure to the public.

Conclusion

The reconciliation of the ideas of Rousseau and Smith in *La Nouvelle Héloïse* is complicated through Rousseau's apparent reluctance to conform to the Smithian ideas that can be seen to underlie the entire novel. As we have seen, certain aspects of the novel are inherently Smithian in nature, and these are particularly acute in the motif of the English landscape garden in the fourth part. Rousseau's and Smith's thought is reconciled through their preoccupation with morality rather than political economy, as can most evidently be seen through Rousseau's attempt to re-channel vanity through the creation of the garden, which in turn reflects Smith's recognition of the need to deflect such sentiments in commercial society.

I suggest that the inadequacy of Clarens as a progressive society can be attributed to the fact that Rousseau does not go far enough in incorporating Smithian thought in his fictional society. Rather, where Rousseau does not fully develop the ideas that are overtly Smithian, this leads to the demise of the society at Clarens. Smith himself is ultimately concerned with the economic progress of society, yet his *Theory of Moral Sentiments*, if read alongside *The Wealth of Nations*, goes some way to suggesting how society can be both moral and economically progressive; it is therefore the more commercial aspects of Smith's theories that Rousseau seems to take issue with. For example, the Smithian notions of distance and proximity in commercial society are rejected by Rousseau because of his belief that interaction with strangers has led to the moral corruption of civilisation. Nevertheless, the distortion of distance that is created in *La Nouvelle Héloïse* necessitates the failure of the society that Rousseau envisions precisely because the characters are unable to exercise the type of moral regulation that Smith suggests is encouraged by commercial society. *La Nouvelle Héloïse* can thus be seen to legitimise Smith's theories, despite the fact that Rousseau cannot bring himself to fully realise them.

Notes

1. Created around 1713, Stowe has often been cited as possible inspiration for Rousseau's fictional garden in *La Nouvelle Héloïse* (see Willis 1972).
2. The English translations of Rousseau in this chapter are the author's own. The original French text of the passages cited is given in the notes. 'Je ne vois dans ces terrains si vastes et si richement ornés que la vanité du propriétaire et de l'artiste.'
3. 'J'étais plus empressé de voir les objets que d'examiner leurs impressions, et j'aimais à me livrer à cette charmante contemplation sans prendre la peine de penser.'

4. See Bending (1992). Bending suggests that the public nature of the eighteenth-century landscape garden and its interpretation relied on a 'shared' knowledge: 'The design is predicated upon a confidence in shared knowledge, yet, equally, that knowledge is of a deliberately exclusive and excluding nature' (1992: 384).

5. 'Je me figure, leur dis-je, un homme riche de Paris ou de Londres, maître de cette maison, et amenant avec lui un architecte chèrement payé pour gâter la nature. Avec quel dédain il entrerait dans ce lieu simple et mesquin! Avec quel mépris il ferait arracher toutes ces guenilles! Les beaux alignements qu'il prendrait! Les belles allées qu'il ferait percer!'

6. 'Il y a pourtant ici ... une chose que je ne puis comprendre; c'est qu'un lieu si différent de ce qu'il était ne peut être devenu ce qu'il est qu'avec de la culture et du soin.'

7. For a comprehensive discussion of the *philosophes* and their admiration of England, see Grieder (1985: 119).

8. 'plus près de la liberté que tous les autres'.

9. Rousseau's desire to be admired is well documented by Anne Srabian de Fabry, who suggests that 'nous savons par les *Confessions* et les *Dialogues* quelle a été l'ambition la plus constante de Jean-Jacques: il voulait être universellement admiré, estimé et respecté, c'est-à-dire qu'il voulait être aimé *à sa guise*' (Fabry 1977: 63).

10. 'rend[u] légitime'.

11. 'nos sages lois n'abrogent point celles de la nature'.

12. 'J'ai dans le duché d'York une terre assez considérable, qui fut longtemps le séjour de mes ancêtres. Le château est ancien, mais bon et commode; les environs sont solitaires, mais agréables et variés. La rivière d'Ouse, qui passe au bout du parc, offre à la fois une perspective charmante à la vue, et un débouché facile aux denrées. Le produit de la terre suffit pour l'honnête entretien du maître, et peut doubler sous ses yeux. L'odieux préjugé n'a point d'accès dans cette heureuse contrée; l'habitant paisible y conserve encore les mœurs simples des premiers temps, et l'on y trouve une image du Valais décrit avec des traits si touchants par la plume de votre ami! Cette terre est à vous, Julie . . .'

13. Here Burney references the criticisms of Versailles from Pope's *Epistle to Burlington*, highlighting further the extent to which Versailles would have been a model for English pleasure gardens and the moral danger that the design of these gardens posed to the virtue of young, sensible heroines.

14. 'tellement caché par l'allée couverte qui l'en sépare, qu'on ne l'aperçoit de nulle part. L'épais feuillage qui l'environne ne permet

point à l'œil d'y pénétrer, et il est toujours soigneusement fermé à clef.'

15. For a comprehensive study of Rousseau's extreme antidotes of public society and private society in his theoretical works, see Cladis (2000).

16. 'J'avoue qu'il n'y faut pas amener en pompe les étrangers; mais en revanche on s'y peut plaire soi-même, sans le montrer à personne.'

17. 'J'ose vous le demander, comment pouvez-vous être si folâtre en public, et si grave dans le tête-à-tête? Je pensais que ce devait être tout le contraire, et qu'il fallait composer son maintien à proportion du nombre des spectateurs. Au lieu de cela, je vous vois, toujours avec une égale perplexité de ma part, le ton de cérémonie en particulier et le ton familier devant tout le monde: daignez être plus égale, peut-être serai-je moins tourmenté.'

18. 'on n'y contraint aucun de ses sentiments'.

19. 'très petit, où le peuple soit facile à rassembler, et où chaque citoyen puisse aisément connoître tous les autres'.

20. 'que de choses difficiles à réunir ne suppose pas ce gouvernement!'

Bibliography

Bending, Stephen (1992), 'Re-Reading the Eighteenth-Century English Landscape Garden', in *An English Arcadia: Landscape and Architecture in Britain and America*, San Marino: Huntington Library, 379–99.

Burney, Frances (2008) [1778], *Evelina or the History of a Young Lady's Entrance into the World*, Oxford: Oxford University Press.

Cladis, Mark S. (2000), 'Redeeming Love: Rousseau and Eighteenth-Century Moral Philosophy', *The Journal of Religious Ethics*, 28, 221–51.

Denney, Peter (2005), '"Unpleasant, Tho' Arcadian Spots": Plebeian Poetry, Polite Culture, and the Sentimental Economy of the Landscape Park', *Criticism*, 47, 493–514.

Fabry, Anne Srabian de (1977), *Etudes autour de La Nouvelle Héloïse*, Québec: Editions Naaman de Sherbrooke.

Force, Pierre (2003), *Self-Interest before Adam Smith: A Genealogy of Economic Science*, Cambridge: Cambridge University Press.

Forman-Barzilai, Fonna (2005), 'Sympathy in Space(s): Adam Smith on Proximity', *Political Theory*, 33, 189–217.

Grieder, Josephine (1985), *Anglomania in France 1740–1789: Fact, Fiction, and Political Discourse*, Geneva: Librairie Droz.

Hanley, Ryan Patrick (2008), 'Enlightened Nation Building: The "Science of the Legislator" in Adam Smith and Rousseau', *American Journal of Political Science*, 52, 219–34.

Harkin, Maureen (1995), 'Smith's *The Theory of Moral Sentiments*: Sympathy, Women, and Emulation', *Studies in Eighteenth-Century Culture*, 24, 175–90.

Harkin, Maureen (2005), 'Adam Smith's Missing History: Primitives, Progress, and Problems of Genre', *ELH*, 72, 429–51.

Harvey, Karen (2001), 'Gender, Space and Modernity in Eighteenth-Century England: A Place Called Sex', *History Workshop Journal*, 51, 158–79.

Ignatieff, Michael (1986), 'Smith, Rousseau and the Republic of Needs', in T. C. Smout (ed.), *Scotland and Europe 1200–1850*, Edinburgh: John Donald, 187–206.

Luban, Daniel (2012), 'Adam Smith on Vanity, Domination, and History', *Modern Intellectual History*, 9, 275–302.

Marshall, David (2002), 'The Problem of the Picturesque', *Eighteenth-Century Studies*, 35, 413–37.

Mitchell, Harvey (1989), 'The Social Construction and Deconstruction of Morality: Montesquieu, Rousseau and Adam Smith on Deception', *Studies on Voltaire and the Eighteenth Century*, 263, 500–3.

Neumeyer, Eva M. (1947), 'The Landscape Garden as a Symbol in Rousseau, Goethe and Flaubert', *Journal of the History of Ideas*, 8, 187–217.

Paganelli, Maria Pia (2010), 'The Moralizing Role of Distance in Adam Smith: *The Theory of Moral Sentiments* as Possible Praise of Commerce', *History of Political Economy*, 42, 425–41.

Pope, Alexander (1963) [1731], 'Epistle IV to Richard Boyle, Earl of Burlington', in *Epistles to Several Persons (Moral Essays)*, ed. James E. Wellington, Coral Gables: University of Miami Press, 129–34.

Rasmussen, Dennis C. (2008), *The Problems and Promise of Commercial Society: Adam Smith's Response to Rousseau*, University Park: Pennsylvania State University Press.

Rousseau, Jean-Jacques (1962) [1762], *Du contrat social, ou principes du droit politique*, Paris: Éditions Garnier.

Rousseau, Jean-Jacques (1967) [1761], *Julie, ou La Nouvelle Héloïse*, Paris: Garnier-Flammarion.

Rousseau, Jean-Jacques (2016) [1751–88], 'Economie ou oeconomie', in *Encyclopédie ou dictionnaire raisonné des sciences, des arts et des métiers*, ed. Denis Diderot and Jean le Rond d'Alembert, University of Chicago: ARTFL Encyclopédie Project (Spring 2016 edition), ed.

Robert Morrissey and Glenn Roe, http://encyclopedie.uchicago.edu/ (accessed 20 December 2016).

Sewall, Richard B. (1938), 'Rousseau's Second Discourse in England from 1755 to 1762', *Philological Quarterly*, 17, 97–114.

Valihora, Karen (2013), 'The Judgement of Judgement: Adam Smith's *Theory of Moral Sentiments*', *British Journal of Aesthetics*, 41, 138–61.

Whately, Thomas (1982) [1770], *Observations on Modern Gardening*, New York: Garland Publishing.

Willis, Peter (1972), 'Rousseau, Stowe, and *Le Jardin anglais:* Speculations on Visual Sources for *La Nouvelle Héloïse*', *Studies on Voltaire and the Eighteenth Century*, 90, 1791–8.

Winch, Donald (1996), *Riches and Poverty: An Intellectual History of Political Economy in Britain, 1750–1834*, Cambridge: Cambridge University Press.

9

Sentimental Conviction: Rousseau's Apologia and the Impartial Spectator

Adam Schoene

In contrast to the pernicious impact of *amour-propre* that Rousseau details in his conjectural history *Discours sur l'origine et les fondements de l'inégalité parmi les hommes* (1755), he sets out to view himself through the eyes of another in *Rousseau juge de Jean-Jacques, Dialogues* (1776). Rousseau embarks upon this painstaking endeavour in order to pass judgement on his actions and to unveil the true nature of 'Jean-Jacques', false victim of a universally entrenched conspiracy. In the introductory remarks of this autobiographical fiction, Rousseau writes:

> I had necessarily to say how, if I were someone else, I would view a man such as myself. I have tried to discharge such a difficult duty equitably and impartially . . . by explaining simply what I would deduce about a constitution like mine carefully studied in another man. (Rousseau 1990: 6/OC I: 665)[1]

Before Rousseau, Adam Smith also confronted this challenge of how to objectively judge oneself in *The Theory of Moral Sentiments* (1759) with his conception of the impartial spectator, a theory of conscience in which moral judgement is cultivated through sympathy and imagination.[2] I will trace a Smithian sentiment that I perceive in the radical division of the self dramatised in the *Dialogues*, with particular emphasis on Rousseau's attempt to liberate his own gaze, enabling it to render an unbiased judgement.

Where Smith extends the domain of the spectator beyond the ocular realm and claims that 'we must become the impartial spectators of our own character and conduct' (TMS III.ii.2: 114),

Rousseau also attempts to probe beyond the visual surface to examine through careful study the 'constitution' of another, who is actually himself. Yet ultimately Rousseau does not seem to position himself as impartial in the *Dialogues*, but instead occupies the role of his worst enemies, viewing himself in 'the most deplorable and cruel position in the world' (Rousseau 1990: 6/OC I: 665). I take as a point of departure Jean Starobinski's (1989: 16) interpretation of Rousseau's self-directed gaze as inward condemnation projected outwards by the imagination, a self-defence mechanism that shifts inner conflict, re-establishing the unity of the ego by obliging it to confront an all-encompassing enemy. Venturing beyond this ego-based analysis of Rousseau's masochistic adoption of the persecutory perspective of his most malevolent detractors, I will argue that in critically assessing his own conduct through the apologetic dialogue form, Rousseau also expresses a desire for an apparatus kindred to that of Smith's impartial spectator, which would serve to cast a judicious gaze on both his character and his writing. By integrating Smith's theory with Rousseau's apologia, my aim is to offer new inroads to navigating the often obscured and misjudged *Dialogues*.

While the influence of Rousseau upon Smith has become an area of increased recent investigation, I will invert this emphasis to examine how Smith's *Theory of Moral Sentiments* might further elucidate certain elements of Rousseau's conception of justice. Charles Griswold (2010) has comprehensively laid the groundwork for this exploration by crafting an imaginary interlocution between Rousseau and Smith that compellingly demonstrates an ultimate divergence in their ideas of *pitié*, sympathy and spectatorship. In the rich dialogue that Griswold stages, he identifies a tension between Smith's ocular model of sympathetic spectatorship and the narrative dimension underlying *The Theory of Moral Sentiments*, with an interpretive process at work through its chronicles with competing claims to adjudicate. Griswold postulates that Rousseau would consider Smith's impartial spectator almost like a character in a narrative, and would therefore contend that such a 'story' about impartial spectating in the guise of theory playing down its rhetorical side would not be ethically or politically beneficial, but would serve merely as a fictionalised social standard of perfect perspective, with theory as a kind of 'gaze' concealing a constructed tale (Griswold 2010: 77). As Griswold perceptively emphasises, Rousseau's autobiographical writings attest to a sentiment that human interaction is characterised by a mutual 'unnarratability', but I will underscore a simultaneous yearning for understanding and vindication that persists in the *Dialogues*. My intervention does not stand in opposition to Griswold's assessment that Rousseau would refute the possibility of a full-fledged Smithian sympathy, but rather interrogates how the ardent impetus behind the *Dialogues* might also be more cogently understood alongside Smith's spectator. Although Rousseau does not write in discourse with Smith in the same manner that Smith responds directly to him, he applies a strikingly similar rhetorical device to the spectator within the dialogic structure of his autobiographical apologia; thus we may find Smithian strains in Rousseau by turning to the *Dialogues*.

Written in a discontinuous process between 1772 and 1776 in the context of solitude and isolation during Rousseau's final stay in Paris, *Rousseau juge de Jean-Jacques* has often been disregarded or characterised as a work of madness or paranoia. Its frequent digressions and repetitions, along with predominant themes of imprisonment, conspiracy, darkness and surveillance, have helped to fuel such portrayals (Lilti 2008: 58). The text is composed of three dialogues between the protagonists: 'Rousseau', a Swiss 'foreigner', similar but not exactly identical to Rousseau himself; 'the Frenchman', defined predominantly by his nationality, lacking much further character description; and 'Jean-Jacques', an author who is the victim of a plot first devised by his enemies, but that eventually spreads to include all those close to him, in ubiquitous persecution, with the intent of destroying his reputation by challenging the authenticity of his character and writing. Autobiographical references abound, with Rousseau's works all attributed to Jean-Jacques by their real titles, along with frequent mention of actual conflicts with Diderot, Hume and others. Rousseau's relationship with the public and the reader also shifts from the confident mood of the *Confessions* to one of defence, further fuelling its adversarial reception.

Rousseau notes that his second autobiographical effort is propelled by a failure on the part of his readers to correctly understand his *Confessions*, and it serves as an attempt to illustrate how to seek out the truth and justice required to properly read the rest of his works; yet the style in which he composes the *Dialogues* may only have even further estranged him from his audience.[3] His dissatisfaction with the public's consideration of his soul-baring

Confessions as a work to be read for mere pleasure is reflected in the drastically different form of the *Dialogues*, with his shift to the role of both judge and accused, a splitting of the self that is also prone to much critique as evidence of a mind obscured by paranoia. In contrast to this prevalent perspective, Kelly and Masters (Rousseau 1990: xiv) observe that Rousseau's division of himself into multiple characters, while often cited as evidence of his insanity, is a frequent feature of Platonic dialogue in the illustration of philosophic issues, thus likening Rousseau to the misunderstood Socrates of the *Apology*, who also both judges and is judged. In his 1962 *Dialogues* introduction, Michel Foucault (1962: vii–xxiv) likewise mounts a defence against charges of pure madness, describing the work as, by definition, 'non-madness', and an important part of Rousseau's autobiographical trilogy, stressing its hidden rigour and coherence.[4] However, as Antoine Lilti suggests, even Foucault seems to stumble into a similar interpretive trap as that in which Rousseau implicates his guilty readers, since in conducting a purely semiotic reading, Foucault breaks with 'the existential suffering and demand for recognition at the heart of the text', treating it entirely as a literary work, when it is 'first and foremost intended as an action – one meant entirely as a denunciation of injustice' (Lilti 2008: 57). This active dimension of the *Dialogues* lies both in its trenchant defence of Rousseau's system and in its moral education of the reader, who may then better understand Rousseau's character and judge his works accurately, in a similar manner to the instructive function of Smith's spectator.

A Smithian sentiment is perceptible from the opening remarks of the *Dialogues*, with a comparable blurring of both the visual and narrative components of spectatorship. In *The Theory of Moral Sentiments*, Smith draws inspiration from the 'moral sense' tradition of Hutcheson and Hume, but adopts a pluralistic approach to morality with his concept of 'sympathy', describing sentimental feelings of a manifold nature when a spectator imaginatively reconstructs the situation of another.[5] By imagining ourselves in the shoes of another through a sympathetic correspondence of sentiments, we are able to access a more approximate awareness of motive and intention, which enables us to better judge the other's action. Smith describes how we also scrutinise the propriety of our own conduct through sympathy, acting as spectators of our behaviour by viewing ourselves as if through the eyes of others.

Similarly, at the beginning of the *Dialogues*, Rousseau laments: 'The humiliating role of my own defence is too much beneath me, too unworthy of the feelings that inspire me for me to enjoy undertaking it . . . but I could not examine the public's behavior regarding me without viewing myself in the most deplorable and cruel position in the world' (Rousseau 1990: 5/OC I: 664).[6] Starobinski (1989: 17) suggests that the mechanisms of projection lead Rousseau to misconstrue the intentions of others into invented hostilities from a failure to recognise the internal nature of his own guilt, but in the *Dialogues*, Rousseau seeks a way to better judge himself. While he must endure a painful and laborious undertaking in adopting the perspective of his most incendiary detractors to help reveal the true nature of 'Jean-Jacques', Rousseau sets out to view himself through the eyes of others in order to pass judgement on his actions and to ensure that they are not shaped merely by self-interest, as he calls into question the relativity of perception through the narrative that he constructs.

As with the ocular and narrative tension that Griswold identifies in Smith's impartial spectator, Rousseau, too, seems attuned to this aporia in his *Dialogues*. An emphasis upon the visual component is evident in 'Rousseau's' insistence that the Frenchman should go and 'see' Jean-Jacques in person in order to form an accurate opinion of the author's character: 'What I saw is better seen than said. What I saw suffices for me, who saw it, to determine my judgement, but not for you to arrive at yours on the basis of my report. For this has to be seen to be believed' (Rousseau 1990: 105/OC I: 797).[7] Jean-Jacques never actually appears in the text apart from discussions between 'Rousseau' and the Frenchman, who does not end up 'seeing' the author in person, but gets to 'know' him nonetheless by reading his works and listening to 'Rousseau'. While *voir* is the most frequent verb in the text, the world of the *Dialogues* is a sensory space that extends far beyond the visual horizon, with seeing juxtaposed with a deeper quest for knowledge, or *savoir*, and truth.[8] Although sight may work to deceive us or we might be unable to see amid darkness, we still hold evidence of our inner experience and feeling, which serves to reveal a deeper, more visionary truth.

In the first dialogue, 'Rousseau' explains to the Frenchman the importance of reading the works of the author before judging him to be 'monstrous' based upon hearsay alone, and thus of approaching Jean-Jacques' work with an impartial spirit. 'Don't even think of the Author as you read', writes Rousseau, 'and without any bias either in favor or against, let your soul experience the impressions it will receive. You will thus assure yourself of the intention behind the writing of these books' (Rousseau 1990: 31/OC I: 699).[9] The Frenchman becomes a sort of impartial spectator in his reading of the works, which is a unique and empathetic form of evaluation enabling the well-disposed reader to gain access to the genuine intentions or 'situation' of the author; although the works are considered as separate from the author so that they may be studied objectively, they are inextricably related in that they enable access to his moral disposition. This method of reading is different from a critical one ensnared by arguments and contradictions, as it entails confirmation with Smith's 'man within the breast' to decipher the sentiments of the author, as the Frenchman recounts:

> I didn't apply myself to picking apart a few scattered and separate sentences here and there, but rather consulting myself both during these readings and as I finished them, I examined as you desired the dispositions of soul into which they placed and left me, judging as you do that it was the best means to penetrate through to that of the Author when he wrote them and the effect he proposed to produce. (Rousseau 1990: 209/OC I: 930)[10]

'Rousseau's' position as a foreigner, along with the fact that he has read the author's works, establishes him as a less-biased judge than the Frenchman, who has not initially read them, but 'Rousseau' must also first determine the character of Jean-Jacques. It is only upon 'Rousseau's' meeting with Jean-Jacques along with the Frenchman's reading of his books that they may affirm their overall coherence in line with the authorial intent.

Rousseau's defence of the intention and character of the author in the *Dialogues* is also parallel in certain ways with Smith's rooting of justice in sympathy and sentiment, as opposed to abstract rights or reasoned principles.[11] Where 'Rousseau' deplores the Frenchman's inquiry: 'You ask what harm there would be, when the crime is evident, in putting the accused on the rack without hearing him?' (Rousseau 1990: 59/OC I: 735),[12] Smith may follow up with related trepidation: 'Though our brother is on the rack, as long as we ourselves are at our ease, our senses will never inform us of what he suffers' (TMS I.i.1.2: 9). These mutual sentimental concerns illustrate a shared departure from a reason-based theory of justice, which may best be understood within Rousseau's *Du contrat social* (1762) construct of the heteronomic Legislator. Rousseau's political ideal is that of a silent citizenry that looks inward to *feel* the general will, rather than engaging in any form of public debate, and it is through the sublime and lyrical eloquence of the Legislator as opposed to rational argument that the will is persuasively internalised within the people.[13] The Legislator is unable to use either force or reasoning, but must have recourse to another order of authority, which he would use to win over without violence and persuade without convincing. Might it be possible to consider Smith's impartial spectator as a supplemental juridical figure to Rousseau's *Du contrat social* Legislator, after the foundational groundwork of persuading without convincing is complete?[14] While there may be common ground within their sentimental concerns, Griswold's imaginary dialogue between Rousseau and Smith regarding the impartial spectator suggests greater discord,[15] with Rousseau critiquing the fictionalised social standard of perfect perspective it embodies, seeing the theory acting as a sort of concealing gaze (Griswold 1999: 7). Rousseau and Smith share a sentiment-based system of justice, yet Rousseau sees his case as incapable of being judged impartially, since no one may truly understand his inner feelings or nature; thus all of his efforts to redeem himself fall short.

The prospective deficiencies of a non-rational system of justice are evident in the precarious 'situation' in which we first meet Jean-Jacques, and his fraught tale ends on similarly tenuous grounds, since as the Frenchmen and 'Rousseau' begin to blend into one another (and even adopt the same language), their character differences dissipate, and they eventually seem to become one. As the Frenchman initially professes: 'Even if J.J. had not committed any crime, he would be no less capable of them all. He is not being punished for one offense or for another, but he is abhorred for harboring them all in his heart. I see nothing that is not just in that' (Rousseau 1990: 62/OC I: 740).[16] In spite of the forbidding case against him, Jean-Jacques finds a staunch advocate in 'Rousseau'; victim himself of the misfortune of 'errors of opinion' in the 'sweet chimera of friendship', 'Rousseau' had withdrawn from society, but living exclusively between himself and nature, tasted 'an infinite sweetness' in the thought that he was not alone, that he was 'not conversing with an insensitive, dead being' (Rousseau 1990: 52/OC I: 727).[17] This is evocative of sympathy with the dead, which Smith offers both as a shocking limit case and as 'the great restraint upon the injustice of mankind' (TMS I.i.2.1: 13). Yet 'Rousseau' is not entirely alone, as he finds in the books of Jean-Jacques one who shares feelings compatible with his own, a 'portrayer of nature and historian of the human heart . . . the man he found in himself' (Rousseau 1990: 52/OC I: 728).[18] In his defence of Jean-Jacques, he rails against the cruelty of the Frenchman's charges, which reveal a twisted sentimental system of law:

> You have founded the system that is followed with regard to him on duties of which I have no idea, on virtues which inspire horror in me, on principles which in my mind reverse all principles of justice and morality. Picture people who start by each putting on a well-attached mask, who arm themselves to the teeth with swords, who then take their enemy by surprise, grab him from behind, strip him naked, tie up his body, his arms, his hands, his feet, his head so that he cannot move; put a gag in his mouth; poke out his eyes, stretch him out on the ground, and finally spend their noble lives massacring him slowly for fear that if he dies of his wounds, he will stop feeling the pain too soon. (Rousseau 1990: 75/OC I: 756)[19]

Physical pain is fleeting for Smith, whereas insults or fear induced from bodily pain evoke greater sympathy, since the imagination is triggered in a more intensive way. As the haunted tone of the *Dialogues* conjures in this scene, the painful form of a sentimental jurisprudence may be horrific, but 'Rousseau' succeeds in his quest to arouse sympathy in the Frenchman; he reads Jean-Jacques' books and comes to recognise coherence in his system, based upon the main principle that nature made man happy and good, but that society depraves him and makes him miserable. While Jean-Jacques is acquitted in the eyes of 'Rousseau' and the Frenchman, the trio ultimately shrink to what Antoine Lilti (2008: 67) has called 'a single sovereign solitude', which leads into the monologue of the *Rêveries*.

For Smith, 'solitude is still more dreadful than society' (TMS II.ii.2.3: 84), with nothing more likely to dissolve the human bonds of reverence and compassion than silence. While Rousseau would probably adopt an opposing stance, the silence in which the *Confessions* ends ('I concluded my reading this way and everyone was silent' (Rousseau 1995b: 550/OC I: 656))[20] is the very reason he first embarks upon the *Dialogues*, in the hope that he might teach his readers to understand his work, a task that Rousseau never fully seems to relinquish, as he inevitably winds up in the street handing out anonymous leaflets entitled 'To All Frenchmen Who Still Love Justice and Truth' (Rousseau 1990: 251/OC I: 984).[21] While people refuse to accept or read the pamphlets, there nonetheless remains a glimmer of hope amid a seemingly doomed situation that his writing may someday find itself in the hands of a sympathetic audience, like that of 'Rousseau' and the Frenchman. As the awareness of the Smithian spectator's sympathy brings an agent relief by integrating with the original suffering the pleasure afforded by the sympathy, we might say that a fictional Jean-Jacques has at least found something like this in his two allies, with the caveat that they embody imaginary, disjointed parts.[22] Politics, for Smith, is about improving our capacity to judge ourselves and others through refined conversation, and in a musical metaphor that Rousseau might have appreciated (or abhorred, given his steadfast preference for melody over harmony), pleasure emerges out of this dialogue from 'a certain harmony of minds, which like so many musical instruments coincide and keep time with one another. But this most delightful harmony cannot be obtained unless there is a free communication of sentiments and opinions', as no man can fail to please 'if he has the courage to utter his real sentiments as he feels them, and because he feels them' (TMS: VII.iv.27: 337). Although marked differences separate many of their political conceptions, the moral theories of Smith and Rousseau are in concord in their shared sentimental conviction.

Sophie de Grouchy, Madame de Condorcet, offers one of the earliest visions for how one might read Smith in relation to Rousseau in her *Lettres sur la sympathie* (1798), while also introducing her own new ideas on morality and conceptions of law and justice. Well known for her marriage to Nicolas de Condorcet, Sophie de Grouchy maintained her own influential identity as a salon hostess and writer, with her letters attempting to develop sympathy in the context of French philosophical thought. They were included in her translation of *The Theory of Moral Sentiments*, a work she began on the eve of the Revolution, with her reading of Smith undoubtedly inflected by the nature of the revolutionary experience, espousing different views in relation to the significance of physical pain and introducing a view of sympathy moderated by reason. De Condorcet reads Smith as an amalgam between Voltaire's critical spirit and Rousseau's sentimentalism, here illuminating her distinction between the two:

> Rousseau spoke more to conscience, Voltaire to reason. Rousseau established his views on the strength of his sensibility and his logic; Voltaire by the biting charms of his wit ... The former will renew enthusiasm for freedom and virtue for ages to come; the latter will awaken every century to the sinister effects of fanaticism and credulity. (Grouchy Condorcet 2008: 145)

In contrast with the Voltairean style of exoneration before the tribunal of public opinion, as in the famous cases of Jean Calas and François-Jean Lefebvre de la Barre, Rousseau appeals to the heart of his readers to sympathise and acquit him of the libellous charges.

De Condorcet's amalgamation of Rousseau and Voltaire in reading Smith is furthermore fitting in that Smith's final recorded comment on Rousseau was to the French traveller Barthélemy Faujas de Saint-Fond in 1782, who claims that Smith spoke to him of Rousseau with a kind of religious respect:

> 'Voltaire,' said he, 'sought to correct the vices and the follies of mankind by laughing at them and sometimes even getting angry with them; Rousseau, by the attraction of sentiment and the force of conviction, drew the reader into the heart of reason. His *Contrat social* will in time avenge him for all the persecutions he suffered.' (Saint-Fond 1907: 246)

If read in a straightforward manner, Smith seems to be speaking to the brilliance of *Du contrat social*, but this remark may also be interpreted ironically, falling more in line with his earlier criticism of Rousseau as a 'hypocritical Pedant' (Corr. 93: 112–13) in his correspondence with Hume.[23] However, *Du contrat social* was the cause of real persecution against Rousseau, and he crafts a true apologetic epistolary dialogue of it in his *Lettres écrites de la montagne*, written in exile after renunciation of his Geneva citizenship. While his writing and citizenship inexorably lie at the very heart of this controversy, Rousseau removes himself from the centre of the debate, in contrast to the *Dialogues*, to emphasise the severity of this key moment for the well-being of Geneva:

The crisis you are in requires another deliberation of which I am no longer the object . . . Your rights claimed and attacked can no longer remain in doubt. They must either be recognized or abolished, and it is their obviousness that places them in danger. The torch should not have been brought close during the storm. But today, the house is on fire. (Rousseau 2001: 134/OC III: 687)[24]

Yet as the *Dialogues* suggest, Rousseau's personal life is rarely far from the political context, as having escaped to Môtiers in Switzerland following the warrant issued for his arrest in France, Rousseau is once again forced to flee from local minister Montmollin's excommunication crusade, in which he rallies the public against Rousseau with sermons likening him to the Antichrist, culminating in the dramatic stoning of his home in 1765.

As Rousseau is accused of madness in his writing of the *Dialogues*, and author Jean-Jacques is deemed a monster within this text, Adam Smith's thought has likewise often been misconstrued, with its critics frequently situating it within a false context.[25] Both Smith and Rousseau fall victim to a discourteous public incapable of acceptance or understanding, unable to grasp the keys that reside within their works to reach a more just interpretation of them. *The Theory of Moral Sentiments* offers a guide to sympathetic impartiality through the figure of the spectator, and the *Dialogues* are a cry for due process through an appeal to the sentiments to sympathise with a falsely accused victim. Rousseau also falls victim to his own excessive sensibility, which drives him into further isolation and seems to contribute to the masochistic position he adopts. What I have tried to illustrate is that underlying this self-punitive tenor is a deeper yearning for an impartial interlocutor, one that achieves its strongest articulation in *The Theory of Moral Sentiments*. Reading Rousseau alongside Smith might help to situate the *Dialogues* not as a work of madness or failure, but as a persistent struggle for justice. Although Rousseau fails to adopt a truly unbiased perspective, 'Jean-Jacques' discovers a degree of faith in the possibility of redemption by future readers, and Rousseau succeeds in depicting the fictional nature of the self through the dialogic form. Smith and Rousseau are often placed on opposing theoretical poles, and they remain perhaps most clearly distinguished by their differences. Nonetheless, a careful reading of their works discloses certain similarities in the realm of moral theory, revealing a mutual sentimentality amid tensions within the interplay of spectatorship and narrative. Smith differentiates between the perspectives of the grammarian and the critic in his distinction between justice and the other virtues, with the rules of justice compared to those of grammar, and the rules of the other virtues to those 'which critics lay down for the attainment of what is sublime and elegant in composition' (TMS III.6.11: 175). Reading Rousseau's *Dialogues* alongside Smith further complicates this opposition, illustrating how literature and theory might work in tandem, rather than in conflict, as with divided author Jean-Jacques and philosopher Rousseau, in search of Smith's impartial spectator.[26]

Notes

1. 'Il falloit nécessairement que je disse de quel œil, si j'étois un autre, je verrois un homme tel que je suis. J'ai tâché de m'acquitter équitablement et impartialement d'un si difficile devoir . . . en expliquant simplement ce que j'aurois déduit d'une constitution semblable à la mienne étudiée avec soin dans un autre homme.' I will use OC to refer to *Œuvres complètes de Jean-Jacques Rousseau*.

2. For a critical discussion and historical situation of the impartial spectator, see Raphael (2007).

3. See Kelly and Masters, 'Introduction' (Rousseau 1990: xvii).

4. See also Bellhouse (2013). Bellhouse further develops resonance with Foucault in arguing that Rousseau adopts the device of disassociating himself into several fictional characters to resist disempowerment as an object under surveillance, and to teach his readers about such objectification.

5. TMS I.i.1.2: 9: 'As we have no immediate experience of what other men feel, we can form no idea of the manner in which they are affected, but by conceiving what we ourselves should feel in the like situation. Though our brother is on the rack, as long as we ourselves are at our ease, our senses will never inform us of what he suffers. They never did, and never can, carry us beyond our own person, and it is by the imagination only that we can form any conception of what are his sensations.'

6. 'Le rolle humiliant de ma propre défense est trop au dessous de moi, trop peu digne des sentiments qui m'animent pour que j'aime à m'en charger . . . Mais je ne pouvais examiner la conduite du public à mon égard sans me contempler moi même dans la position du monde la plus déplorable et la plus cruelle.'

7. 'Ce que j'ai vu est meilleur à voir qu'à dire. Ce que j'ai vu me suffit, à moi qui l'ai vu, pour déterminer mon jugement, mais non pas à vous pour déterminer le votre sur mon rapport; car il a besoin d'être vu pour être cru.'

8. For more on the tension between *voir* and *savoir*, see Jones (1991: 144). Jones highlights how the *Dialogues* are about revealing the truth regarding Jean-Jacques, as well as uncovering the nature of truth more broadly.

9. 'Ne songez point à l'Auteur en les lisant, et sans vous prévenir ni pour ni contre, livrez votre âme aux impressions qu'elle en recevra. Vous vous assurerez ainsi par vous-même de l'intention dans laquelle ont été écrits ces livres.'

10. 'Je ne m'attachai pas à éplucher çà et là quelques phrases éparses et séparées, mais me consultant moi-même et durant ces lectures et en les achèvent, j'examinois comme vous l'aviez désiré, dans quelles dispositions d'âme elles me mettoient et me laissoient, jugeant comme vous que c'étoit le meilleur moyen de pénétrer celle ou étoit l'Auteur en les écrivant, et l'effet qu'il s'étoit proposé de produire.'

11. See Kelly and Masters (Rousseau 1990: xx), who reference Rousseau's defence of *Du contrat social* (1762) in the *Lettres écrites de la montagne* (1764) as his clearest example of the importance of authority given by character. In this text, Rousseau outlines three different 'proofs' of Christian doctrine: miracles, of least significance; the doctrine itself, understood by few; and of most significance, the character of those who preach the doctrine.

12. 'Vous demandez quel inconvénient il y auroit, quand le crime est évident à rouer l'accusé sans l'entendre.'

13. In his *Essai sur l'origine des langues* (1755), Rousseau similarly notes that the first language would employ aphorisms instead of arguments, represent without reasoning, and persuade without convincing, mirroring the expression he uses in *Du contrat social* to describe the non-rational persuasive force of the Legislator in inducing shared feelings within the citizens.

14. In addition to the Legislator, another possible parallel to the impartial spectator could be the divine and natural internally guiding voice embodied in the figure of the Savoyard Vicar in *Émile, ou De l'éducation* (1762), for which Rousseau was also condemned. The Savoyard Vicar offers the alternative conception of a form of deity within, epitomised by an interior voice and sustained as if by an unwritten or moral law. Dolar thus describes the Savoyard Vicar as Rousseau's 'own private Socrates, man of no written work,

supported by mere voice and following his own inner voice', which possesses a 'divine spark' that is absent in mere reason and understanding alone, as well as in other competing forms of voice (Dolar 2006: 86). While Dolar sees the mechanism of voice at its purest in the figure of the Vicar, he also describes how it could become entangled with the voice of the Other, as illustrated in the relationship between Émile and his tutor.

15. See also Hont (2015: 55–6). Hont maintains that, like Rousseau, Smith creates a natural history of justice and society to explain the origin of law and politics, yet refuses to make use of the idea of contract as a constitutive element in forming his account of the birth of legality. Also helpful in contrasting Smith's spectator in relation to Rousseau's contract and general will are Boyd (2015) and Stimson (2015).

16. 'Quand J.J. n'auroit commis aucun crime, il n'en seroit pas moins capable de tous. On ne le punit ni d'un délit ni d'un autre, mais on l'abhorre comme les couvant tous dans son cœur.'

17. 'Revenu de cette douce chimère de l'amitié dont la vaine recherche a fait tous les malheurs de ma vie, bien plus revenu des erreurs de l'opinion dont je suis la victime . . . Je me suis retiré au dedans de moi, et vivant entre moi et la nature, je goutais une douceur infinie à penser que je n'étois pas seul, que je ne conversois pas avec un être insensible et mort.'

18. 'J'y puisois des sentimens si conformes à ceux qui m'étoient naturels, j'y sentois tant de rapport avec mes propres dispositions que seul parmi tous les auteurs que j'ai lus il étoit pour moi le peintre de la nature et l'historien du cœur humain. Je reconnoissois dans ses écrits l'homme que je retrouvois en moi.'

19. 'Vous avez fondé le sistème qu'on suit à son égard sur des devoirs dont je n'ai nulle idée, sur des vertus qui me font horreur, sur des principes qui renversent dans mon esprit tous ceux de la justice et de la morale. Figurez-vous des gens qui commencent par se mettre chacun un bon masque bien attaché, qui s'arment de fer jusqu'au dents, qui surprennent ensuite leur ennemi, le saisissent par derrière, le mettent nud, lui lient le corps, les bras, les mains, les pieds, la tête, de façon qu'il ne puisse remuer, lui mettent un bâillon dans la bouche, lui crèvent les yeux, l'étendent à terre, en passant en fin leur noble vie à le massacrer doucement de peur que mourant des ses blessures il ne cesse trop tôt de les sentir.'

20. 'J'achevai ainsi ma lecture et tout le monde se tut.'

21. '*A tout François aimant encor la justice et la vérité.*'

22. Karen Pagani follows James F. Jones in situating the ending of the *Dialogues* as 'just the beginning of what will be an ongoing struggle to reconcile the demands of his bifurcated existence, and it is yet another example within Rousseau's corpus of an ending that is, in essence, a nonending' (Pagani 2015: 96).

23. In Letter 93 from Smith to Hume on 6 July 1766, Smith writes: 'By endeavouring to unmask before the Public this hypocritical Pedant, you run the risk, of disturbing the tranquillity of your whole life' (Corr. 93: 112–13).

24. 'La crise où vous êtes exige une autre délibération dont je ne suis plus l'objet . . . Vos droits réclamés et attaqués ne peuvent plus demeurer en doute; il faut qu'ils soient reconnus ou anéantis, et c'est leur évidence qui les met en péril. Il ne falloit pas approcher le flambeau durant l'orage; mais aujourd'hui, le feu est à la maison.' The fire is in reference both to the state of religion, which had become discredited by philosophy in Rousseau's eyes, losing its ascendancy over the people, as well as the constitutional crisis resulting from the government's usurpation of power in Geneva. See Kelly's 'Introduction' to Rousseau (2001: xv).

25. See Rasmussen (2008). Rasmussen describes how both defenders and critics alike of Smith tend to inaccurately paint him as a 'free-market ideologue', when his defence of commercial society is actually of a 'pragmatic and prudential' nature (2008: 160).

26. I am grateful to Jason Frank, Nicholas Huelster, Tracy McNulty, and especially to Neil Saccamano and the editors of this volume for their invaluable insight and support in helping me to explore Rousseau and Smith together in the development of this chapter. It also benefited greatly from remarks by participants in the Cornell University Political Theory Writing Colloquium, Brown University's 'Equinoxes', the Sciences Po 3rd Graduate Political Theory Conference, and 'Themes from Smith and Rousseau' at the University of Glasgow in 2015.

Bibliography

Bellhouse, Mary (2013), 'Rousseau under Surveillance: Thoughts on a New Edition and Translation of *Rousseau, Judge of Jean-Jacques: Dialogues*', *Interpretation: A Journal of Political Philosophy*, 21.2, 169–79.

Boyd, Richard (2015), 'Justice, Beneficence, and Boundaries: Rousseau and the Paradox of Generality', in James Farr and David Lay Williams (eds), *The General Will: The Evolution of a Concept*, New York: Cambridge University Press, 247–69.

Dolar, Mladen (2006), *A Voice and Nothing More*, Cambridge, MA: MIT Press.

Foucault, Michel (1962), 'Introduction', in *Rousseau juge de Jean-Jacques, Dialogues*, Paris: A. Colin, coll., Bibliothèque de Cluny, vii–xxiv.

Farr, James, and David Lay Williams (2015), *The General Will: The Evolution of a Concept*, New York: Cambridge University Press.

Griswold, Charles L. (1999), *Adam Smith and the Virtues of Enlightenment*, Cambridge: Cambridge University Press.

Griswold, Charles L. (2010), 'Smith and Rousseau in Dialogue: Sympathy, *Pitié*, Spectatorship and Narrative', in Vivienne Brown and Samuel Fleischacker (eds), *The Philosophy of Adam Smith: The Adam Smith Review, volume 5: Essays Commemorating the 250th Anniversary of The Theory of Moral Sentiments*, New York: Routledge, 59–84.

Grouchy Condorcet, Marie-Louise-Sophie de (2008) [1798], *Letters on Sympathy (1798): A Critical Edition*, trans. James E. McClellan, Transactions of the American Philosophical Society, vol. 98, part 4, ed. Karin Brown, Philadelphia: American Philosophical Society.

Hont, Istvan (2015), *Politics in Commercial Society: Jean-Jacques Rousseau and Adam Smith*, ed. Béla Kapossy and Michael Sonenscher, Cambridge, MA: Harvard University Press.

Jones, James F. (1991), *Rousseau's Dialogues: An Interpretive Essay*, Geneva: Librairie Droz.

Lilti, Antoine (2008), 'The Writing of Paranoia: Jean-Jacques Rousseau and the Paradoxes of Celebrity', *Representations*, 103, 53–83.

Pagani, Karen (2015), *Man or Citizen: Anger, Forgiveness, and Authenticity in Rousseau*, University Park: Pennsylvania State University Press.

Raphael, D. D. (2007), *The Impartial Spectator: Adam Smith's Moral Philosophy*, New York: Oxford University Press.

Rasmussen, Dennis C. (2008), *The Problems and Problems of Commercial Society: Adam Smith's Response to Rousseau*, University Park: Pennsylvania State University Press.

Rousseau, Jean-Jacques (1959), *Œuvres complètes de Jean-Jacques Rousseau, I: Les Confessions, autres textes autobiographiques*, ed. Bernard Gagnebin and Marcel Raymond, Paris: Gallimard.

Rousseau, Jean-Jacques (1964), *Œuvres complètes de Jean-Jacques Rousseau, III: Du contrat social – Écrits politiques*, ed. Bernard Gagnebin and Marcel Raymond, Paris: Gallimard.

Rousseau, Jean-Jacques (1969), *Œuvres complètes de Jean-Jacques Rousseau, IV: Émile – Éducation – Morale – Botanique*, ed. Bernard Gagnebin and Marcel Raymond, Paris: Gallimard.

Rousseau, Jean-Jacques (1990), *Rousseau, Judge of Jean-Jacques: Dialogues*, ed. Roger D. Masters and Christopher Kelly, trans. Judith R. Bush, Christopher Kelly and Roger D. Masters, Hanover: University Press of New England.

Rousseau, Jean-Jacques (1995a), *Œuvres complètes de Jean-Jacques Rousseau, V: Écrits sur la musique, la langue et le théâtre*, ed. Bernard Gagnebin and Marcel Raymond, Paris: Gallimard.

Rousseau, Jean-Jacques (1995b), *The Confessions and Correspondence, Including the Letters to Malesherbes*, ed. Christopher Kelly, Roger D. Masters and Peter G. Stillman, trans. Christopher Kelly, Hanover: University Press of New England.

Rousseau, Jean-Jacques (2001), *The Collected Writings of Rousseau: Letter to Beaumont, Letters Written from the Mountain, and Related Writings*, ed. Christopher Kelly and Eve Grace, trans. Christopher Kelly and Judith R. Bush, Hanover: University Press of New England.

Saint-Fond, Barthélemy Faujas de (1907), *A Journey through England and Scotland to the Hebrides in 1784*, vol. 2, trans. Sir Archibald Geikie, Glasgow: Hugh Hopkins.

Starobinski, Jean (1989), *The Living Eye*, trans. Arthur Goldhammer, Cambridge, MA: Harvard University Press.

Stimson, Shannon C. (2015), 'The General Will after Rousseau: Smith and Rousseau on Sociability and Inequality', in James Farr and David Lay Williams (eds), *The General Will: The Evolution of a Concept*, New York: Cambridge University Press, 350–81.

Part IV

Commercial Society
and Justice

10

Being and Appearing: Self-falsification, Exchange and Freedom in Rousseau and Adam Smith

Charles L. Griswold

Man is least himself when he talks in his own person. Give him a mask, and he will tell you the truth.

Oscar Wilde (2007: 185)

Adam Smith remarks in *An Inquiry into the Nature and Causes of the Wealth of Nations* that once the division of labour has taken hold and interdependence is the norm, 'Every man thus lives by exchanging, or becomes in some measure a merchant, and the society itself grows to be what is properly a commercial society.'[1] To be a merchant is not just to sell goods, one might claim, but to sell oneself. It is not difficult to imagine exchange as an invitation to manipulative and debased relations not just in a commercial context but also in a broad range of interactions in society.

In this essay I will focus on one of the ways in which Rousseau articulates what he takes to be a key problem that besets society (particularly one devoted to commerce), and on Smith's contrasting take on the issue. That problem concerns a split between 'to be' and 'to appear' (DI 1997a: 170.2/OC III: 174) that involves deception about who or what one is, as well as play-acting of which even the actor may be unaware. The matter involves a distinction, indeed contrast, between the self as it truly is and how the self appears to others (and possibly even to oneself). I will refer to this multifaceted problem as 'self-falsification'. It turns out that, for Rousseau, self-falsification corrodes freedom (a contested notion that will therefore draw my attention here as well). Remarkably, two of the three passages from the *Discourse on the Origin and the Foundations of Inequality among Men* that Smith translated in his *Letter to the Authors of the Edinburgh Review* discuss the being/appearing theme.[2] Modern interpreters too have frequently focused on those passages.[3]

On one occasion Smith speaks of 'commerce' in the broad sense of the term, as meaning social exchange (TMS I.ii.4.1: 39). In that sense commerce has always been with us. In the narrower sense of the term evident in the quotation from *The Wealth of Nations* at the start of this essay, commerce would seem to be characteristically modern, though of course it exhibits features that are also evident in commerce (that is, exchange) in the broad sense. This raises the issue of periodisation. Is Rousseau saying in the two *Discourses* and *Preface* that self-falsification (as I am calling it) is coeval with society, or that it is especially grave in modern society, or that it occurs only in commercial society?[4] I am taking what I think is the most conservative view of the matter, namely that on Rousseau's view the self-falsification problem is especially grave in modern commercial society but is also evident in society as such. Consequently, his self-falsification thesis should make sense in the context of modern commercial society, if it makes sense anywhere. But since the core problem exhibited by commercial society is implicit in post-lapsarian social relations as such (and is explicit once *amour-propre* is present), I will generally refer to 'exchange' rather than 'commerce' so as to include social interchange, communication, as well as more narrowly commercial relations.

Self-falsification, Being and Appearing: Rousseau's Argument Unfolds

Our first text is from the *First Discourse* (1751) where Rousseau complains that 'One no longer dares to appear what one is [*On n'ose plus paroître ce qu'on est*]' (FD 1997a: 8.13/OC III: 8). The main thought in the passage from which I quote here seems to be that because of the pressure of conformism, one is obliged to hide who one is. Let us call this the *conformity thesis*. At first glance it does not seem particularly deep or persuasive. Even if conformity is a pervasive feature of social life, that does not entail that there is a hidden or genuine self, so much as that one could 'be' many different things, depending on the circumstances. The passage as a whole clearly implies that conformity is a kind of strategy. As a generalisation, that too seems unconvincing. If the thesis reduces to the requirements of 'politeness' (mentioned in the passage from which I have just quoted), the tie to self-falsification would seem rather weak, for one could be both polite and true to oneself: moreover, one could be polite and do what is right.

Let us turn to Rousseau's next formulation of the issue, published several years later in the *Preface* (1753). Rousseau there writes: 'From now on we must take care never to let ourselves be seen as we are [*Il faut désormais se garder de nous laisser jamais voir tels que nous sommes*]: because for every two men whose interests coincide, perhaps a hundred thousand oppose them, and the only way to succeed is either to deceive or to ruin all those people' (1997a: 100.28/OC II: 968). The idea that self-falsification is a deliberate strategic stance is even more pronounced in the passage from which I have just quoted. But Rousseau also moves here beyond the conformity thesis to something new. Borrowing a phrase used by Rousseau in the *Second Discourse* (1997a: 171.27/ OC III: 175), I will call it the *conflict of interests thesis*. On this view, self-falsification is necessary as a means to survival, and perhaps also to one's flourishing (as subjectively defined), given the implicitly competitive game for scarce goods. The result may or may not be conformism, and in any case conformism is not the driving force. As Rousseau presents it, the conflict of interests is unavoidable (as is implied by the use of 'only' and 'never' in the sentences quoted).[5]

The passage raises a variety of questions. First, it is unclear why the game is zero-sum, or indeed, negative-sum.[6] Secondly, it is unclear why opposition rather than cooperation is entailed by competition. And thirdly (and importantly for our present purposes), it is unclear why self-falsification – in the sense of never letting ourselves be seen 'as we are' – is the necessary result of opposition. Most importantly, the notion of who we really are behind the mask is still left obscure.

In the *Second Discourse* (1755) Rousseau returns several times to the self-falsification theme and offers a more compelling version of the idea that there is a split between being and appearing. By this stage of his narrative, metallurgy, agriculture and other arts have been invented, and inequality has taken hold. In the course of a paragraph that was translated and quoted by Smith in the *Letter*, Rousseau says:

> Here, then, are all our faculties developed, memory and imagination brought into play, amour propre interested ... Here are all natural

qualities set in action ... and, since these are the only qualities that could attract consideration, one soon had to have or to affect them; for one's own advantage one had to seem other than one in fact was. To be and to appear became two entirely different things [*Etre et paroître devinrent deux choses tout à fait différentes*] ... Looked at in another way, man, who had previously been free and independent, is now so to speak subjugated by a multitude of new needs to the whole of Nature, and especially to those of his kind ... (DI 1997a: 170.27/OC III: 174–5)

Here the plot has thickened. While relations between these self-interested agents are conflictual (Rousseau mentions the 'conflict of interests' further on in this same paragraph), 'advantage' seems not to be understood merely in terms of survival or force, but also in terms of recognition for one's qualities (aesthetic, inter alia). The reference to *amour propre* suggests that comparison is at play, and hence self-image. So one thought is that in order to receive what now feels to be very important, namely appropriate recognition from one's *semblables*, one has to present oneself to them in a way that does just that, that is, to frame oneself in terms acceptable to them. And thus their (favourable) 'consideration' comes to seem necessary to one's conception of oneself. One's self-conception is now at stake – neither the conformity thesis nor the conflict of interests thesis explicitly involved *that* – and self-conception is entangled with the agent's conception of how the agent appears to others (cf. Starobinski 1988: 249).

There is a further thought that Rousseau now makes explicit, namely that because our interdependence is closely tied to the creation of 'new needs', we are each more reliant on others than ever.[7] This somehow makes it necessary to deceive others if (as the paragraph from which I am quoting makes clear) one cannot get what one wants by appealing to their self-interest. And this in turn provides a bridge to a thought that was not explicit in the two passages quoted earlier: what is lost in this being/appearing split is *freedom*.[8] This suggests that the self behind the appearance or mask is a 'free' self in some sense of the term, whereas the deceiving or appearing self, however strategically deployed, is unfree. The various strands of thought in the passage in question include, then, what I will call the *loss of freedom thesis*. Taken as a whole, the passage implies that deception and self-falsification will be part of any system of interdependence, and further that what is being falsified is what one is qua free agent.

Does Adam Smith offer a sound reply to this multifaceted critique to the effect that 'to be' and 'to appear' have come apart – a critique, let us recall, to which he calls our attention by translating and quoting, in the *Letter*, several pertinent passages of the *Second Discourse*?

A Reply to Rousseau: Smith's *Wealth of Nations* on Exchange

Smith famously writes that:

> It is not from the benevolence of the butcher, the brewer, or the baker, that we expect our dinner, but from their regard to their own interest. We address ourselves, not to their humanity but to their self-love, and never talk to them of our own necessities but of their advantages. Nobody but a beggar chuses to depend chiefly upon the benevolence of his fellow-citizens. (WN I.ii.2: 26–7)

In the passage from which I quote, Smith tells us that the propensity to exchange is an exercise in persuasion in a context of vast interdependence. Further, as in the conflict of interests thesis passage of the *Preface* and the loss of freedom thesis passage of the *Second Discourse* from which I quoted above, exchange is a matter of appealing to another's 'self-love' (which, for present purposes, I will take to be synonymous with 'self-interest').

But not only do deception, falsification of self, presenting an appearance of self as opposed to who one really is and vice have no explicit role in exchange, the scene as Smith paints it may, on the contrary, be interpreted as one that exemplifies a highly ethical and respectful reciprocity. This is precisely the interpretation put forth by Samuel Fleischacker and also developed by Stephen Darwall.[9] Smith characterises exchange (commerce in the narrow sense of the term) not only as probably derived from speech and rationality (commerce in the broader sense), but also as involving norms of fairness. And the capacity to reason certainly suggests that we are not mere creatures of instinct and to that extent suggests that we are free (as noted by Fleischacker 2004: 94).

Persuasion through exchange is being implicitly contrasted here with the application of force. In exchange, the independence and moral standing of both parties is implicitly recognised.

Neither party *has* to say yes to the proposal (as noted in Darwall 2006b: 48). The goods in the possession of each are securely so. In Fleischacker's elegant summary: 'The virtues of commerce include not just peace among nations, but the moral bases of individual freedom and mutual respect' (Fleischacker 2004: 94; cf. WN IV.iii.c.9: 493).[10] If we picture Smith's tradespeople as fitting the description of what he calls 'the prudent man' (TMS VI.i.7: 213), then there is all the more reason to think that the hypocrisy and vices that Rousseau takes to be present here need not be. This is not to say, of course, that Smith is oblivious to the possibility of deception in exchange (WN IV.iii.c.8, 10: 493–4; cf. TMS I.iii.3.7: 64, VI.i.8: 214; see Rasmussen 2008: 79–81).

The freedom through interdependence that Smith is sketching here is contrasted with a demeaning dependence, namely that of the beggar. *That* relationship would certainly be more conducive to the pathologies of self-falsification that Rousseau is describing (see Rasmussen 2008: 124–5). But even that degree of dependence does not seem to *require* appearing other than one is, either for strategic reasons or as a consequence of the nature of that relationship. The conformity thesis, conflict of interests thesis and the loss of freedom thesis don't seem particularly compelling when confronted with Smith's famous passage.

To be 'Within' rather than 'Outside' Oneself: Rousseau on Freedom

Let us cycle back to Rousseau, this time to two further passages from the *Second Discourse*. The first introduces a thought that has so far been mostly implicit; namely that the desire for social standing 'almost always keeps us outside ourselves [*nous tient presque toûjours hors de nous mêmes*]' (DI 1997a: 184.52/OC III: 189). The next text comes from the second to last paragraph of the *Second Discourse*. In Smith's translation:

> For such in reality is the true cause of all those differences: the savage lives in himself; the man of society, always out of himself [*le Sauvage vit en lui-même; l'homme sociable toûjours hors de lui*]; cannot live but in the opinion of others, and it is, if I may say so, from their judgment alone that he derives the sentiment of his own existence. It belongs not to my subject to show, how . . . every thing being reduced to appearances, every thing becomes factitious and acted [*tout devient*

factice et joüé]; . . . how in one word always demanding of others what we are [*ce que nous sommes*], and never daring to ask ourselves the question . . . (Letter: 253; for Gourevitch's translation, see DI 1997a: 187.57/OC III: 193)

It doesn't seem that being 'factitious' is necessarily strategic in character; rather, it seems deeply rooted in what it means to be social. This passage is pointing to (among other things) what one might call the *social constitution thesis*, that is, the thesis to the effect that the self we now recognise is socially constituted.[11] Taken together, the *Second Discourse* passages from which I have quoted emphasise that, as a result of our acquired social constitution, something has gone deeply awry such that we no longer live 'within' ourselves and have become unfree.[12] We have lost track of who we are, and in so doing have become 'Happy slaves' (FD 1997a: 7.9/OC III: 7). How should we understand the links between these various ideas?

Part of the answer lies in '*tout devient factice et joüé*'. Gourevitch's 'play-acting' is a nice translation of that last word (Smith's translation, quoted above, also preserves the relevant resonance). The suggestion is that our other-directedness leads us to play out our assigned parts in a social script, as well as to accept its norms, prescribed roles and distribution of rights, privileges, responsibilities and resources with little to no reflection.[13] Self-forgetfulness and appearing to others as we imagine they think we should are now conjoined. So it is true, at one level, that people become merely appearances of themselves and are not really *being* themselves.

But if something like that is happening, what is the true self that is now occluded?[14] How are we to understand the freedom that agents immersed in the appearance-driven script have forgotten?

Despite the implication of the passages in which Rousseau characterises the 'savage' as free (including at DI 1997a: 187.57/OC III: 192), reversion to the state of 'natural man' (DI 1997a: 127.8/OC III: 125) is neither possible nor desirable. Rousseau cannot be saying – not with any hope of convincing us – that our inner savage is the true self which the current appearing self is covering over or falsifying (see Griswold 2016). But then, to reiterate, what is the 'free' self that is now submerged in the socially constituted self?

There may not be a single answer, at least within or implied by the texts under discussion here, especially as we want to understand the 'free' self in ways that somehow mesh with the distinctions between what is within and outside, and between being and appearing. Let me sketch five possible ways to understand the relevant contrasts, or rather, aspects of this 'free' self that is 'within' or behind its appearance.[15]

To begin with, Rousseau may be saying that to live 'outside' oneself in an unfree manner is to be dependent for one's self-esteem on what one takes to be the esteem of others. So this is a matter of poor self-esteem. Such a person would be rather like Smith's 'vain man' who 'in the bottom of his heart, is very seldom convinced of that superiority which he wishes you to ascribe to him' (TMS VI.iii.36: 255). The connection between low self-regard, dependence on others for one's esteem and alienation from oneself is certainly familiar to interpreters of Rousseau.[16] It is also an ancient and well-known thought.

Next, Rousseau's contrast between living 'within' and 'outside' oneself may be understood as a contrast between an agent's first-personal perspective and a spectatorial, third-personal perspective. The constitution of self as divided between inside and outside, actor and spectator, need not of itself entail that, qua actor, one govern oneself from the standpoint of the spectator that is 'the other'. If that is so, then part of Rousseau's complaint may be that in defining oneself from the standpoint of the spectator, one may no longer be oneself because the agent's 'sentiment of his own existence' is wrongly trumped by the spectatorial perspective. What might that mean?

To adopt a spectatorial perspective is, for Smith, to acquire distance, a kind of cool, third-personal detachment (consider TMS I.i.4.7: 21, I.ii.3.8: 38, I.ii.4.1: 39, II.i.2.2: 69, II.ii.2.4: 85, III.4.3, 4: 157, VI.iii.5: 238). Rousseau might agree but then infer that to live by Smith's spectator standard would be to live 'outside' oneself in a way that makes it difficult to identify with and espouse one's own experiences, beliefs, projects and such, in all their fullness. Many examples could be offered, such as religious ecstasy and erotic or romantic passion. These are felt experiences whose meaning for the agent might be diminished when filtered through the eyes of a non-agential spectator (indeed, Smith says that romantic love looks 'ridiculous' to the spectator; TMS I.ii.2.1: 31).[17] So adopting a particular kind of spectatorial perspective – one that places us 'outside' ourselves as distinguished from whatever distance from self is required for self-awareness – might augment our alienation from ourselves and thereby diminish our freedom.

Thirdly, the primacy of the actor's perspective may connect with another thought about freedom, inspired by Hegel and articulated by Robert Pippin with reference to the sentence that begins the second excerpt at the start of this section (DI 1997a: 187.57/OC III: 193). Pippin writes:

> We can thus now see that the underlying problem pointed to – the normative status of mine in all its senses – appears as the problem of freedom, understood broadly as the ability to see myself in my own deeds, to experience such deeds as the products of my will, not the forces of social necessity; in a word *as mine*. (Pippin 2008: 219)[18]

Pippin's topic here is not Rousseau, but his phrase 'products of my will' is nonetheless helpful because the idea of *authorship* seems closely tied, for Rousseau, to the ideas of both freedom and authority, and so to the idea of self-legislation.

A fourth aspect of freedom possibly in play here is predicated on malleability or possibility or what Rousseau calls 'the faculty of perfecting oneself' (DI 1997a: 141.17/OC III: 142), in conjunction with what he refers to as the distinctly human 'property of being a free agent' (DI 1997a: 141.16/OC III: 141). On this interpretation, what 'civilized man' (DI 1997a: 187.57/OC III: 192) has given up is the consciousness of his own freedom to choose different roles, or at least the meaning thereof; he therefore fails to recognise that nobody is just this or that role or even an assemblage of roles. That would, of course, be a Sartrean reading of what Rousseau is saying here, and as such would not commit Rousseau to holding that there is some inner, authentic self, waiting to be (re)discovered.[19]

These four aspects of free agency imply that the self-falsification Rousseau is pointing to is not simply a cognitive error, or a question of false belief, or about unnecessary desires, or self-deception. Rosen, Ignatieff, Starobinski and Gauthier variously refer to the role of 'false consciousness', 'bad faith' or 'false identity' in Rousseau's theory (Rosen 1996: 92–3, 99–100; Ignatieff 1984: 122; Starobinski 1988: 38; Gauthier 2006: 153–4). These interpretations suggest that the self-falsification that Rousseau is painting concerns an individual's cognitive, affective, dispositional and desiderative capacities taken together.

A fifth aspect of the lost freedom is quite closely connected to the fourth. It concerns the obscuring of the notion that even an unjust society is 'authorised' (Rousseau's term at DI 1997a: 131.2/

OC III: 131) by its participants. This means, as Neuhouser tells us, that they wrongly believe in its 'legitimacy or naturalness' and are responsible for their error (Neuhouser 2014: 19).

Putting together these five aspects of the free or real self to which our present untrue self is being contrasted, a relevant question suggests itself. How can it be that we 'authorise' our own self-falsification, such that our deeds are no longer 'our own', such that we are not 'within' ourselves and no longer truly free?

By way of sketching an answer, I will draw here on an essay by Rae Langton, summarising parts of her complex discussion all too briefly. In 'Projection and Objectification', Langton sets out a theory of projection that helps to explain how people come to treat each other (and, presumably, themselves) as less than free, as (among other things) reified and commodified. Casting people into certain roles (in particular, gender and sexual roles) can play a part in that process. As pornography (mentioned by Langton 2004: 288) illustrates, the 'projective process' (2004: 287) may come with significant moral, not to mention cultural, economic and political implications. What Langton calls the 'epistemology of objectification' (2004: 287) is at work in this phenomenon. Key to this epistemology is the idea that certain beliefs are driven by desires, contrary to the usual 'rules of direction of fit' (Langton 2004: 287).

Drawing on Hume, Langton first describes a form of 'desire-driven projection' that she calls the *phenomenological gilding of desired objects'* (2004: 289). The basic idea is that desire can make its object seem, phenomenologically, to have 'independent qualities that justify, demand, or legitimate the desire, making it almost literally *appear* to have independent value' (Langton 2004: 291). A second form of projection is 'wishful thinking', and it too is inspired by Hume. Here the desirer forms the belief that, for example, the desired person has a 'matching desire', that is, that the desire is reciprocated (Langton 2004: 292–3; the context remains that of 'sexual objectification'). People who are objectified and commodified are no longer understood from within *their* experience – it is all appearance, from the outside, from the perspective of the desiring person. Langton also specifies a third form of projection (which can be generated by 'any datum about oneself', desire included), that is, 'pseudo-empathy' (2004: 298). To paraphrase: wishful thinking posits that since I desire that the other desire X, the other person does desire it; pseudo-empathy posits that since I desire X, the other person does too. The second and third forms of projection may work together and be difficult to distinguish (Langton 2004: 298).

As Langton argues in her concluding section, projection understood in these ways has remarkable features. First, the 'genesis of the projective belief' is made 'invisible' (2004: 300), such that the projected belief looks to the believer 'to be aiming to fit the world'. Secondly, one's projected beliefs seem to 'make counter-evidence disappear' by explaining it away (2004: 300–1). Further, false views become social facts, to the point that even the oppressed affirm them. Consequently, 'If the world changes, so that it fulfills the projective belief' (2004: 302), the counter-evidence really has disappeared from sight. That sounds very close to the kind of complaint about society, especially modern society, that Rousseau is making. Hence his opening claims in the *Second Discourse* about the difficulty of self-knowledge, the ways in which even the greatest philosophers have unknowingly projected their socially formed false beliefs on to human nature, and the implicit point that those who live 'outside' of themselves have no idea that they are doing so. Self-deception clearly forms part of self-falsification brought about through a 'projective process' of this sort.

A Rousseauian Critique of the *Wealth of Nations* on Exchange

A Rousseauian critique of Smith's description of exchange in *The Wealth of Nations* now gains traction. Re-imagine the seemingly innocent scene that Smith paints. You approach the baker, not as beggar but nonetheless as having insufficient funds to feed your family adequately; each party plays his or her assigned role, seemingly respectful of the other. It is understood that the portly baker will make out well, in these scarce times, and that you and yours will not. No questions are raised, no force is applied; the social script conveys that the rules are 'fair' in spite of any such results. Is the seemingly personal, face-to-face interaction between client and baker masking an ugly reality? Perhaps the baker is a front for a corporation, a prop to give the illusion of local enterprise; is he, along with the smile and greeting required of all employees of the corporation, also fake?

Consider next the brewer. He would seem to stand for desires felt as needs – just the sort of phenomenon Rousseau complains of. Why is alcohol felt to be necessary by its consumers? Are the economically hard-pressed expending a disproportionate amount of their resources on it? Is the rate of alcoholism much higher among the poor? Are these expenditures voluntary?[20] Should the consumption of alcohol be permitted at all?[21]

As to the butcher: Smith elsewhere characterises that job as 'a brutal and an odious business', albeit usually more remunerative (WN I.x.b.2: 117). Presumably nobody undertakes it except out of a kind of duress and obduracy, as one must put up with what Smith there implies is its 'disgrace' in order to earn superior returns. Why are things structured such that people have to assume jobs of that sort? Smith also points out that meat is not really a necessity for decent nutrition (WN V.ii.k.15: 876). Is the question of the ethical status of animals occluded in the social script? Operative in the background is the expanding sphere of wants about which Rousseau complains, wants that come to be experienced as perfectly normal needs by those subject to them. In sum, simply accepting social facts – being 'outside' oneself in that way – dampens critical reflection on how social structures shape who we are, thereby limiting our freedom.

Of course, people will see each other as responsible for having chosen the roles they find themselves in, at least where the free market operates. Strikingly, in the passage from *The Wealth of Nations* discussed above, Smith speaks of the beggar as 'choosing' to depend on the benevolence of others. One has to wonder what sort of agency is being exercised by the actors in this scene.

Are the tradespeople (like the beggar) in Smith's famous scene all male? Imagine an affirmative answer, and also imagine that the answer goes without saying because it is another strand in the un-self-knowing social script. Where then are the women?[22] Imagine a longer list of employments in the urban scene in question; include, in view of the topic of Langton's essay, prostitutes. It is safe to say that they are likely to be women. As objects of desire, prostitutes are obvious candidates to illustrate the projective and objectifying process Langton describes. Correspondingly, prostitution might be seen as a 'natural' part of the script, and prostitutes as deserving or choosing their lot. I am not accusing Smith of indifference to prostitution or, for that matter, to beggars; any such accusation would be grossly inaccurate. Yet it is interesting that he has relatively little to say about prostitution. By contrast, in a passage of the *Confessions* whose capital importance he explicitly signals,

Rousseau describes his encounter with a courtesan. The point of the story he recounts has everything to do with the phenomena of projection, false consciousness and ideology thanks to which the victim gets blamed for her lot.[23]

In view of all this, it may initially come as a surprise that Smith is perfectly well aware of the issue of projection, and indeed its connection with the drive to acquire wealth and power. We pursue wealth so as 'To be observed, to be attended to, to be taken notice of with sympathy, complacency, and approbation' (TMS I.iii.2.1: 50). That sounds like what Rousseau describes as living outside ourselves. The desirability of acquiring wealth is premised on the assumption that those who have wealth gain happiness by virtue of the attention it brings. So a desire (for attention) generates a (false) belief. In Smith's strikingly Humean formulation (recall Langton on 'gilding'), 'When we consider the condition of the great, in those delusive colours in which the imagination is apt to paint it, it seems to be almost the abstract idea of a perfect and happy state' (TMS I.iii.2.2: 51). These 'prejudices of the imagination' have enormous social consequences in founding the social hierarchy (TMS I.iii.2.2, 3: 52–3). Our needs and imagination have created a world in which false beliefs have become 'true' social facts. This bespeaks collective participation in what Smith calls a 'deception' of the imagination (TMS IV.1.10: 183).[24] One could also point to passages about sympathy in which Smith seems to be talking about the 'invisible' (to borrow Langton's term) work of the projective imagination in regard to the dread of death (TMS I.i.1.13: 12–13; cf. 'illusive sympathies' at II.i.5.11: 78).

It may also be surprising that Smith grants that a social system predicated on 'bettering our condition' (TMS I.iii.2.1: 50) – by what amounts to living 'outside ourselves' – does sometimes have deleterious effects, and not just in terms of moral corruption (about which, see TMS I.iii.3: 61–6; IV.1.8: 181–3). Smith famously describes them at WN V.i.f.50: 781–2 (cf. WN I.xi.p.8, 9: 265–6). It is hardly inconceivable that the labour of the baker, brewer and butcher may be repetitive in a way that yields these stupefying and degrading results. Smith does indicate that antidotes to the alarming situation of the benumbed workers are very much worth pursuing.[25] And yet – here is another source of surprise – he thinks that agential freedom and self-falsification may coexist under some conditions. Let me turn next to that thought.

Being 'Outside' Oneself, Self-falsification and Agency: Smith on Freedom

For Smith, viewing ourselves from the outside, as in a mirror, is constitutive of having a self at all. Samuel Fleischacker (2011: 82) argues that Smith's 'metaphor of the mirror is misleading' in that it implies that the mirrored self is there waiting to be perceived, whereas Smith's thesis is stronger: there is nothing there to be perceived in the absence of the mirror. So this is the social constitution thesis, full on; crucially, though, it is not contrasted with a 'true self' or with the 'natural man' of Rousseau's narrative. How is this deep sociality or mirroring structure of self-awareness, along with the deception, illusion and projection it may bring in its train, compatible with freedom or agency (political and economic liberty to one side)?

While Smith does often speak of 'the agent' (for example, at TMS III.i.6: 113), 'agency' is a term he uses rarely and not in connection with freedom (e.g. in WN V.i.f.24: 767, with regard to the gods). More importantly, Smith almost never uses phrases such as 'free will' or its equivalent (for a rare exception, see TMS II.ii.1.5: 79).[26] Smith generally avoids speaking of the human will as a faculty, especially a moral faculty. And yet he certainly knew of the elaborate discussions of free will in the works of Hume and Locke, for example. One explanation for his near complete silence is simply that he accepted Hume's compatibilism, and, consequently, Hume's skeptical recasting of the free will/necessity debate altogether. Smith never says so explicitly, however, and for that reason (among others) it is questionable whether he is simply treading in Hume's footsteps here.[27]

Further, Smith does not point to anything like a Sartrean story about freedom, so far as I can tell. Next, for Smith there is no 'natural' self that is the 'original' of the 'artificial' self, if the former is taken to be the self of the pre-lapsarian human and the latter (i.e. the 'artificial') a merely derivative or deficient version thereof. So for Smith, the contrast between the self as free and unfree does not align with an asocial (or pre-social)/social contrast. Although talk about 'nature' abounds in Smith, he is not a social contract theorist in any sense that he or Rousseau would recognise.[28] Smith also doesn't have a Rousseauian notion of 'natural freedom' to which he can appeal (notwithstanding Smith's own talk of a 'system of natural liberty'; WN IV.ix.51: 687), and does not put forward a theory of freedom as self-legislation. By contrast, in the *Second Discourse* Rousseau connects freedom with knowing obedience to the (moral) law (DI 1997a: 127.8/OC III: 125) and famously comments in the *Social Contract* that 'obedience to the law one has prescribed to oneself is freedom' (SC 1997b: I.8.3/OC III: 365).[29] So far as I know, Smith does not speak of freedom or liberty in those terms. Let me flesh this out a bit by looking briefly at his theory of the impartial spectator, for arguably it is there that a relevant notion of freedom is at work.

As an emendation of the standpoint of the spectator, the imagined impartial spectator necessarily reflects a division *within* the agent between agential and spectatorial perspectives (TMS III.1.6: 113). For Smith, this dividedness is not in principle a lamentable loss of integrity or agency; it is simply a structural feature of selfhood that has the potential for both self-degradation and self-emendation. The 'real man of virtue' regulates himself by the impartial spectator's standpoint (TMS VI.iii.18: 245). To the extent to which we successfully identify (for the verb, see TMS III.3.25, 28: 147, 148; III.4.4: 158) ourselves with the standpoint of the impartial spectator and mould our sentiments, characters and actions accordingly, we are presumably to be described as being true to our (best) selves and as achieving a kind of unity of agency. Smith does not, to my knowledge, characterise this self-regulation as a form of freedom. But he says enough to suggest that successful self-regulation in his sense is freedom from being ruled by impulsive passion, from internal conflict, and from the agonies of self-doubt (TMS VI.iii.50: 261; cf. TMS I.iii.2.1: 51). It does involve practical reason. At its heart, this is a classical conception of self-regulation as freedom, one that recalls Rousseau's talk of 'moral freedom' (SC 1997b: I.8.3:54).[30] Brown thus seems to be entirely right when, in her discussion of Smith's view of agency in *The Theory of Moral Sentiments*, she argues that Smith's model of the impartial spectator points to a notion of 'deliberative independence' as a crucial part of agency (2009: 62). Smith tells us explicitly that the project of becoming perfectly virtuous is never-ending and challenging (TMS VI.iii.23–5: 247–8). Rational self-regulation is an achievement, and indeed is connected in complex ways to the surrounding social, economic and political world.[31]

That said, the standpoint of the impartial spectator does not seem to be, for Smith, one of 'obedience to the law one has prescribed to oneself' or of knowing submission to law. Smith does not seem to be working with Pippin's Hegelian notion of freedom, and does not describe morality as a matter of (human) authorship, or at least not as only that. Why is that?

One answer may be that, for Smith, the level of rationality required for something like freedom as self-legislation is simply too demanding and does not capture what we are actually doing when arriving at moral rules. On Smith's philosophical account, to be sure, morality is sourced in human nature. But he insists that general rules are arrived at inductively over time and are grounded in 'immediate sense and feeling' exercised in particular instances (TMS VII.iii.2.6–7: 319–20). His particularism plays a role in his view as to the source of morality. That view fits poorly with the idea that rational agents author or legislate morality. Neither the judgements arrived at by the impartial spectator nor moral rules or laws (TMS III.5.6: 165–6) seem to be 'products of my will', to recall the passage quoted from Pippin above.[32] Moreover, Smith also indicates that morality is not experienced in that way. That is, the authority (and so the source) of norms is taken to be external to oneself.[33] So while the phenomenology (as he describes it) does not mirror his theory as to the source of morality, it does not line up with the notion of morality as rational self-legislation either. And Smith does not want to sacrifice the phenomenology.

One might argue that Smith rejects the notion of freedom as self-legislation for yet another reason as well, namely a fear of a kind of fanaticism, that is, a fear of an overly rigoristic 'absurd idea of duty' that such a law- and will-driven conception might generate (TMS III.6.12: 176; consider too the reference in that paragraph to Voltaire's *Mahomet*). Still further, he may wish to avoid the notion of freedom as self-legislation on the ground that such a conception of freedom invites the dangerous idea that some agents should be 'forced to be free' (to borrow Rousseau's famous phrase; SC 1997b: I.7.8: 53/OC III: 364).

There may be at least one more reason why Smith does not go along with Rousseau's conception of agential freedom as self-legislation. Stephen Darwall remarks in 'Norm and Normativity' that 'If guidance by norms is essential to agency, then maybe the validity of norms – normativity itself – can somehow be explained by this very fact. This was the possibility seized upon, first in broad outline, by Rousseau, and then, in systematic detail, by Kant' (Darwall 2006a: 1015). As Darwall goes on to suggest, 'Like the rationalists', Rousseau's picture of self-determining agency crucially included regulation by universal norms' (2006a: 1017). But why are norms binding and in what do they consist? For the rationalists, Darwall continues, 'the validity of norms does not itself depend on agency in any way' (2006a: 1017). By contrast, 'The central Rousseauan move was to hold that laws could bind (in the political realm, anyway) only if they expressed the general will' (2006a: 1017). Correspondingly, Rousseau points ahead to Kant's idea that 'normativity must itself ultimately be rooted in self-determining practical reason' (2006a: 1017). If the rationalist position is associated with the idea that an impartial spectator takes itself to be looking at norms that are independent of it, then it would be natural for Rousseau (if interpreted along the lines Darwall sketches) to view the privileging of the spectatorial standpoint as an abdication of freedom and in that sense as self-falsification. It would also be natural for Rousseau to think of freedom qua self-legislation as expressing a privileged position of the agent qua actor (rather than spectator). So Rousseau and Smith may disagree about how a norm comes to be and about why it is binding on the agent, with the result that their conceptions of both (non-political) freedom and of the role of self-falsification diverge.

I mentioned at the end of the preceding section of this essay that Smith is well aware of the phenomenon of projection, as his reference to the 'deception' of the imagination indicates, and have also just discussed Smith's notion of spectator-based agency. Smith seems to hold that agents can govern themselves 'under the character of a spectator' (TMS III.1.6: 113) while also accepting systems of norms and social roles unreflectively and to that extent without understanding the possibility of a better, freer mode of existence. The same holds when it comes to views about one's fundamental goals in life, one's conception of happiness – of the human good, one might say. This seemingly unlikely combination is made possible not only by Smith's rejection of Rousseau's notion of freedom as self-legislation in favour of a notion of self-regulation and by Smith's construal of the social constitution thesis (there being no asocial 'self' to oppose to the socially constituted self, for Smith), but also by Smith's implicit view (as I read it) that the impartial spectator is not a systematic philosopher or theorist. The impartial spectator doesn't seem to correct, or perhaps even perceive the existence of, the large-scale deception imposed upon us by the imagination, and we ordinary agents 'rarely view' the imagination's delusive projection 'in this abstract and philosophical light', that is, *as* a 'deception' (TMS IV.1.9, 10: 183; cf. I.iii.2.8: 57, I.i.1.13: 13).

It would therefore be perfectly possible for Smith's baker, butcher and brewer to regulate their private morals by the standard of the impartial spectator – in that sense freely and without being deceived – and yet also to be subject to fantasies of projection that are structurally similar to those that Langton examines – in that sense unfreely and while being deceived. To 'identify' oneself with the impartial spectator is not to undo the 'delusive colours' or 'prejudices' or 'deception' of the imagination that recommend wealth-getting and status-seeking inter alia. For the reasons I have discussed, agential freedom is compatible, for Smith, with those extraordinarily consequential deceptions and delusions.[34]

I imagine that, for Rousseau, all this would amount to confirmation that Smith doesn't have a genuine solution to the problem of living 'outside' oneself and of the corresponding loss of agency. Rousseau can grant that living 'within' oneself does not preclude being a spectator (even of oneself) and also hold that it entails exercising one's freedom in the sense of authorship or self-legislation – in *that* sense, he might say, his view is fundamentally actor-centred, not spectator-centred. Rousseau might add the point about the inaccessibility to the spectator, even by Smith's account, of some essential human experiences such as that of romantic passion. He can also argue that if Smithian moral agents do not occupy a deliberative standpoint from which they might assess the justice of their political and social system as a whole, then Smith is effectively endorsing a distinctly conservative, passive and unreflective acceptance of social hierarchy, social roles and a conception of the good life – in short, the social script as historically formed (see TMS VI.ii.1.20: 226).[35]

By way of a response to some of these points, Smith could argue that whatever else the impartial spectator does, it corrects for one kind of potentially disastrous deception, namely the 'delusions of self-love' (TMS III.4.7: 159). Those delusions are clearly tied to anxieties of self-esteem that, according to Rousseau, stem from reliance on the spectatorial standpoint. Stephen Darwall argues that the phenomenon of self-deception 'is related, in short, to lack of a kind of self-respect'. Darwall continues: 'Unable to maintain an acceptable self-image, one turns to others in the desperate hope that they can provide for one what one cannot provide acceptably for oneself – a self' (Darwall 1988: 418).[36]

Smith emphasises the importance of the matter when he says, in reference to the 'mysterious veil of self-delusion' (TMS III.4.4: 158): 'This self-deceit, this fatal weakness of mankind, is the source of half the disorders of human life' (TMS III.4.6: 158). Fleischacker remarks in his discussion of Smith on self-deceit that, for Smith, there 'may be no purely internal way of getting ourselves out of that condition [of self-deceit]' (Fleischacker 2011: 90). In Fleischacker's concluding paragraph, playing off a line from T. S. Eliot, he remarks:

> Smith, I suggest, thinks that we cannot be authentic in any sense – true to ourselves – *unless* we prepare a face to meet the faces that we meet . . . We *are* the faces we prepare, to meet the faces that we meet. (2011: 91)

The passages examined above suggest that, for Rousseau, this is actually a description of the nightmare into which we have descended: a hall of mirrors in which there is nothing real or substantial. Rousseau might point out that the entire community may be subject to the 'mysterious veil of self-delusion' – indeed, that is in effect what he is saying in the *Second Discourse* passages we have examined.[37] Moreover, we cannot just *be* the faces we prepare, for who is doing the preparing?

There is another issue too. As Fleischacker notes in the essay just cited (2011: 79), Smith isn't clear about the relation between self-deceit and the deception that leads us to be industrious (TMS IV.1.10: 183). I suggest that this may create something of a dilemma for Smith. On the one hand, if the 'deception' that nature or the imagination imposes on us is self-deception, then correcting self-deception would presumably correct the other deception as well, and vice-versa. On the other hand, while Smith clearly thinks that self-deception is always to be avoided, he tells us (in a context that then offers an indirect reply to Rousseau; see n. 24 above) that the 'deception' that nature imposes on us is a good thing (TMS IV.1.10: 183). He never suggests that correcting the 'delusions of self-love' (TMS III.4.7: 159) also corrects errors of imagination that support social hierarchy (TMS I.iii.2.2: 51–2). So correcting the source of 'half the disorders of human life' seems to leave intact the other half – probably including those typical of a society organised around these cognitive and affective distortions. The Rousseau examined here would probably view this as a serious problem for Smith, not least because what we are self-deceived about, especially when it is the result of self-love, is dependent on our image of others' image of us, and thus is infected by the socially embedded false beliefs that accompany the delusions in question. But that is just to say that the unfreedom that comes with self-deceit is inseparable from the unfreedom that comes with the identity-forming and spectator-centric 'play-acting' to which Rousseau strenuously objects.[38]

Consider once more the reference to persuasion in the butcher/baker/brewer passage from *The Wealth of Nations*. As I mentioned, Smith offers persuasion as a seemingly attractive alternative to the use of force. Rousseau, I think, sees its darker possibilities; persuasion as rhetoric designed to confuse and control, to render unfree.[39] By contrast, Smith sees the 'desire of being believed' as deeply and felicitously human (TMS VII.iv.25: 336) and describes how one would 'die of despair' if one were never believed (TMS VII.iv.26: 336). The desire to be believed is rooted our nature as sociable and sympathetic beings, and so is not simply strategic for Smith (TMS VII.iv.28: 337). What lies within – one's self as agent – can be affirmed by the process of accommodation and communication, so long as the agent is (as Smith says in the passage just referred to) free. Rousseau smells fakeness, pretence, fantasy and coercion in Smith's description there of what 'We all desire': who is this 'we'? But then Rousseau, unlike Smith, seems left with anxiety and despair, as well as with a dream of solitude without those emotions – a dream of a tranquil 'savage', a mythic figure that Rousseau does not harbour as an inner self, a figure he would not become even if he could.[40]

Notes

1. WN I.iv.1: 37. Cf. the reference to 'commercial countries' in TMS VI.ii.1.13: 223.
2. See Letter: 252–4. Smith translated and quoted more of Rousseau's text than the parts on which I am focusing. My citations of Rousseau's texts (other than SC) are by page and paragraph numbers (the latter are supplied in the Gourevitch translations I am using (1997)). I use the following abbreviations: *First Discourse* or FD = *Discourse on the Sciences and Arts*; *Preface = Preface to 'Narcissus'*; *Second Discourse* or DI = *Discourse on the Origin and the Foundations of Inequality Among Men*; SC = *The Social Contract*. For the French edition of

Rousseau's writings, I rely on the *Oeuvres complètes* (OC). I have occasionally interpolated the French in brackets when quoting.

3. Jean Starobinski's influential *Jean-Jacques Rousseau: Transparency and Obstruction* pretty much begins with the relevant passage from the *First Discourse* (Starobinski 1988: 5).

4. In the *First Discourse*, 'commerce' is mentioned four times but only once (1997a: 18.41/OC III: 19) in the narrow economic sense. In the *Preface*, commerce (in the narrow sense) is mentioned immediately before the being/appearing issue is described (1997a: 100.27/OC II: 968), and then is singled out in a long footnote (1997a: 101/OC II: 969–70). At the start of Part II of the *Second Discourse*, property and the accumulation thereof are a source of great evil (1997a: 161.1/OC III: 164). The theme is then taken up again and connected with the rise of inequality (1997a: 171.27/OC III: 175). Commerce is mentioned at 1997a: 174.33/OC III: 178. See also 1997a: 184.52/OC III: 189.

5. See Rasmussen's (2008: 30–5, 40) helpful discussion of the being/appearing theme. In those pages he notes the 'role-playing' that Rousseau is condemning and rightly suggests that commercial society exacerbates the problem, for Rousseau, because it relies so heavily on self-interest. The link between self-falsification or dissimulation and un-selfconscious role-playing is noted by Melzer (1990: 75–7). However, Melzer's interpretation stresses the foundational role of 'disunity of soul' (1990: 63) for Rousseau. That does not underlie my account here.

6. I am hardly the first to characterise Rousseau's picture as 'zero-sum'. See, for example, Anderson (2016: 163) (with reference to the *Second Discourse*). I am indebted to Christopher Kelly for suggesting to me that the picture is actually negative-sum.

7. Did Rousseau mean to present his thinking about self-falsification as unfolding from publication to publication? The answer is not essential to my case, but he does suggest that he revealed his 'system' in steps (see *Confessions* VIII, at OC I: 388, together with 'Preface of a Second Letter to Bordes' (1997a: 110.9, 10/OC III: 106)). My thanks to Christopher Kelly for pointing this out to me. I do not pretend to any chronological sequence as my discussion progresses (*The Wealth of Nations*, for example, was published over two decades after the *Second Discourse*).

8. In the *Second Discourse* Rousseau emphasises the crucial moral value of freedom and free will at 1997a: 178.41 and 179.42/OC III: 183–4; and at 1997a: 140–1.15–16/OC III: 141–2. His narrative also tells us that once things have progressed far enough, 'natural

freedom' is 'irreversibly destroyed' and property as well as inequality are fixed by law (1997a: 173.33/OC III: 178).

9. Fleischacker (2004: 90–103; 1999: 154–6) and Darwall (2006b: 46–8). See also Rasmussen (2008: 79), on the lack of suggestion in the butcher/brewer/baker passage that deception is at stake. Rasmussen also remarks (2008: 82, 89–90) that Smith does not follow Rousseau in emphasising 'the problem of role playing' and does not generalise it to everyone in commercial society.

10. In an excellent article, Thomas J. Lewis makes some of these same points (Lewis 2000; see p. 288 in particular). See also Ignatieff (1984: 121).

11. Neuhouser offers a version of the social constitution thesis in Neuhouser (2008: 84) and (2014: 149–50). See also the remarks by Blaise Bachofen and Bruno Bernardi in Rousseau (2008: 253–4 n. 140), as well as Starobinski (1988: 251). Other interpreters have commented along similar lines. As will be discussed below, Rousseau's version of the social constitution thesis comes with this unSmithian twist, namely, that the constituted self is 'artificial', the result of a departure from 'original man' (DI 1997a: 186.57/OC III: 192).

12. For the sake of clarity, where Smith translates 'in' and 'out of' in the first sentence of the passage just quoted, I will continue to use Gourevitch's 'within' and 'outside'.

13. I offer some discussion of this matter in Griswold (2014).

14. I am using 'true self' to refer to the '*ce que nous sommes*' of DI 1997a: 187.57/OC III: 193 (see the block quotation immediately above). It is an imperfect gloss on Rousseau's phrase but is very familiar in Rousseau scholarship, not to mention in ordinary language. For similar reasons, I will refer to 'alienation', although Rousseau does not use the term.

15. Let me also note that my purpose here is not to catalogue every sense of freedom present in the texts under review. Certainly issues of economic inequality would have to be addressed, for example, in a comprehensive discussion.

16. However, see Neuhouser's remarks about the relation between existing outside oneself and self-estrangement or alienation (2008: 82–5) (he is particularly insistent there that alienation is not the same as living outside oneself) and (2014: 184–5).

17. For discussion, see Griswold (1999: 96–9, 109–12, 148–55), and the sources cited therein. There exists scholarly controversy as to why, for Smith, the agent's erotic and romantic love as such is so difficult for the spectator to sympathise with.

18. See Neuhouser's excellent discussion of Rousseau's 'ideal of free agency' as 'determining oneself what to do, or obeying only oneself' (2014: 128). Elsewhere Neuhouser rightly underlines that one component of freedom for Rousseau is that free agents be aware of their status as free (2000: 80–1). Similarly, see Brooke (2012: 205) and Cooper (1999: 157–8). Cf. DI 1997a: 127.8/OC III: 125.

19. Sartre (1992: 96–116, 584–5, 640). The thought that Rousseau's notion of freedom may be related to Sartre's is noted by Neuhouser (2008: 41). See also Jaffro (2014: 165, 168–9).

20. Of relevance is Smith's detailed discussion of taxes, including on 'malt, hops, beer, and ale' (WN V.ii.k.42: 887 and the thirteen subsequent paragraphs). That Smith's three examples here of tradespeople concern the production of food and drink certainly raises the question as to where the line between necessity and luxury lies.

21. The enormous cultural role of alcohol (or its absence) is described by Osborne (2013).

22. Edith Kuiper offers several relevant observations about this issue (2002: 78–80). Harkin (2013: 502–4) notes that a number of interpreters have remarked on the relative absence of women from *The Wealth of Nations*.

23. In the works that Smith published, he refers to prostitutes once (WN I.xi.b.41: 177; he is discussing nutrition). Prostitution also comes up in the *Lectures on Jurisprudence*, in the context of a discussion of slavery (which Smith is at pains to criticise); see LJA: 178–9 and 193. With regard to Rousseau, I refer to his narrative in the *Confessions* Book VII (OC I: 316–22) about his encounter with Zulietta. See Christopher Kelly's illuminating remarks (1987: 182–3).

24. The next sentence in Smith's text resonates with a passage in the *Second Discourse* that Smith had translated in the *Letter*, as has long been noted by, inter alios, the editors of *The Theory of Moral Sentiments* and by Ignatieff (1984: 111–12). In Griswold (1999: 222, 262–6), I argue that in *The Wealth of Nations* Smith did not abandon this idea of deception. That interpretation is contested by Fleischacker (2004: ch. 6). For a discussion of the controversy that argues for a position that, as I understand it, is close to mine, see Rasmussen (2008: 132–40).

25. For discussion, see Griswold (1999: ch. 7.3). Harpham (2000: 225) notes the 'limited' range of 'Smith's educational proposals'.

26. Cf. TMS III.5.6: 166 and VI.ii.2.18: 234. At TMS III.6.12: 176 Smith writes of 'the will of the Deity' (cf. TMS III.6.1: 171) and at TMS VII.iii.2.2: 318 of the 'arbitrary will of the civil magistrate',

and he speaks of the agent as 'willing' to do X (e.g. TMS VI.ii.3.3: 235) and of 'good-will' (e.g. TMS VI.ii.3.1: 235). See also TMS I.iii.2.1: 51, II.ii.1.3: 79, and VII.iv.28: 337.

27. I am grateful to Aaron Garrett for discussion of that possibility. Brown (2009: 58–62) argues that Smith is not following Hume here. Fleischacker (2004: 167) notes that 'Smith has no philosophical account of freedom', but suggests that Smith may not need one if (as Fleischacker maintains) he is a 'common-sense philosopher'. That characterisation of Smith is contestable.

28. An argument has recently been made that Smith is a 'special kind of contractarian'; see Thrasher (2015: 195). But the kind of contractarianism Thrasher is attributing to Smith is not, I would argue, one that Smith or Rousseau would have in mind. See also Rasmussen (2014: 120–1).

29. The quoted words will be found at Rousseau (1997b: 54). 'I.8.3' refers to SC Book I, Chapter 8, paragraph 3.

30. The connection, in Smith, between freedom and self-command is nicely set out by Harpham (2000: 228–31). See also Fleischacker (1999: 156–60) and Hanley (forthcoming). Cf. Otteson (2002: 238–9), Griswold (1999: 115, 130–1, 196, 214) and Carrasco (2012).

31. For an excellent and wide-ranging discussion, see Schmidtz (2016). See also Herzog (2013: 122–8, 134–6).

32. Smith does say that, after relevant experience, we may 'lay down to ourselves a general rule' (TMS III.4.7: 159; see also III.4.12: 160–1), and the rule functions as a sort of substitute for identification with the impartial spectator. But these rules are not expressions of the will. They are rooted in the particulars, are initially directed to regulating one's own behaviour, and are defeasible. Smith also describes how one can be self-deceived in applying such a rule, thanks to what he calls 'refinements', that is, rationalisations (TMS III.6.10: 175).

33. Smith is pretty clear that the authority attached to the 'sacred regard to general rules' (TMS III.5.2: 163) is commonly felt as external to oneself (TMS III.5.2–6: 163–6). See also Griswold (1999: 144–6, 160–73) for support of the interpretation I am sketching here. I note that Smith does speak of the '*Author* of our nature' (TMS III.5.10: 169, emphasis added; cf. TMS III.5.7: 166).

34. For a discussion of the relation between deception or self-deceit and economic exchange, see Gerschlager (2001). See also Kelly (2011: 117–72). Kelly attributes a notion of 'persuasive agency' (2011: 119–21, 171–2) to Smith, and also offers some helpful remarks

about the relation between Smith and Rousseau that intersect with the argument in the present essay (2011: 121–8). Kelly concludes that Smith thought that the 'propriety of liberty' (i.e. 'persuasive agency', if I understand Kelly correctly) is compatible with 'the realities (and psychological traumas) of self-deception and imaginative delusion that commercial society promotes' (2011: 171). See also Griswold (1999: 262–6).

35. See also TMS I.iii.2.1–3: 50–3, I.iii.3.2: 62, VI.iii.30: 252–3, and WN V.i.b.3–12: 710–15.

36. The magnitude of the threat that self-deception presents to the sort of view of agency proposed by Smith is explained by Darwall (1988: 407–10, 419–20, 424–5 and 427–8 n. 13).

37. The metaphor of the 'veil' is used by Rousseau too, and is emphasised by Starobinski (1988: 4–5, 9–11, 41–2). Cf. WN V.i.g.24: 802–3.

38. For discussion from a different angle of the problematic relation between belief, truth and freedom, see Griswold (2015).

39. For discussion that takes a number of Rousseau's texts into account, see Garsten (2006: ch. 2). Certainly, Smith too recognises the fact of groundless persuasion (e.g. TMS VI.iii.27: 249).

40. This essay was originally delivered as a set of remarks at 'The Enduring Challenge of Rousseau's Thought: Tercentenary Conference', held by The Colorado College and the Rousseau Association (2012). Drafts were presented at Boston College (Clough Center, 2013), the College of the Holy Cross (McFarland Center, 2014), Yale University (Center for the Study of Representative Institutions, 2015), the University of Glasgow (2015, as the plenary address of a joint meeting of the International Adam Smith Society and the Rousseau Association) and the Catholic University of America (2015). I am grateful to participants in those events for their questions and comments. I am especially indebted to Christopher Kelly and to Steven Smith for their commentaries at Boston College and Yale respectively. I also thank Christopher Berry, Remy Debes, Douglas Den Uyl, Ryan Hanley, Paul Katsafanas, Marina McCoy, Robert Pippin, Dennis Rasmussen and Susanne Sreedhar for their thoughts about drafts of the paper or for discussion, and Aaron Garrett for stimulating conversation about Rousseau and Smith. I would also like to express my thanks to the editors of this volume for their comments, and to Getty Lustila and Valerie Williams for their very helpful editorial assistance. This essay is drawn from my *Jean-Jacques Rousseau and Adam Smith: A Philosophical*

Encounter, and is reprinted here by permission of Routledge. Dennis Rasmussen kindly read a draft of the book chapter from which this essay is drawn, and I am indebted to him for his comments on it as well. The present essay builds on and occasionally draws from Griswold (1999). I gratefully acknowledge Fellowships from the American Council of Learned Societies and the Boston University Humanities Foundation, as well as a summer Fellowship Research Grant from the Earhart Foundation, that supported my work on the project from which this essay stems.

Bibliography

Anderson, Elizabeth (2016), 'Adam Smith on Equality', in Ryan P. Hanley (ed.), *Adam Smith: His Life, Thought, and Legacy*, Princeton: Princeton University Press, 157–72.

Brooke, Christopher (2012), *Philosophic Pride: Stoicism and Political Thought from Lipsius to Rousseau*, Princeton: Princeton University Press.

Brown, Vivienne (2009), 'Agency and Discourse: Revisiting the Adam Smith Problem', in Jeffrey T. Young (ed.), *Elgar Companion to Adam Smith*, Cheltenham: Edward Elgar, 52–72.

Carrasco, Maria (2012), 'Adam Smith, Self-command, Practical Reason and Deontological Insights', *British Journal for the History of Philosophy*, 20, 391–414.

Cooper, Laurence D. (1999), *Rousseau, Nature, and the Problem of the Good Life*, University Park: Pennsylvania State University Press.

Darwall, Stephen (1988), 'Self-Deception, Autonomy, and Moral Constitution', in Brian P. McLaughlin and Amélie O. Rorty (eds), *Perspectives on Self-deception*, Berkeley: University of California Press, 407–30.

Darwall, Stephen (2006a), 'Norm and Normativity', in Knud Haakonssen (ed.), *The Cambridge History of Eighteenth-Century Philosophy*, Cambridge: Cambridge University Press, vol. II, 987–1025.

Darwall, Stephen (2006b), *The Second-Person Standpoint: Morality, Respect, and Accountability*, Cambridge, MA: Harvard University Press.

Fleischacker, Samuel (1999), *A Third Concept of Liberty: Judgment and Freedom in Kant and Adam Smith*. Princeton: Princeton University Press.

Fleischacker, Samuel (2004), *On Adam Smith's Wealth of Nations: A Philosophical Companion*, Princeton: Princeton University Press.

Fleischacker, Samuel (2011), 'True to Ourselves? Adam Smith on Self-deceit', *The Adam Smith Review*, 6, 75–92.

Garsten, Bryan (2006), *Saving Persuasion: A Defense of Rhetoric and Judgment*, Cambridge, MA: Harvard University Press.

Gauthier, David (2006), *Rousseau: The Sentiment of Existence*, Cambridge: Cambridge University Press.

Gerschlager, Caroline (2001), 'Is (Self-)Deception an Indispensable Quality of Exchange? A New Approach to Adam Smith's Concept', in Caroline Gerschlager (ed.), *Expanding the Economic Concept of Exchange: Deception, Self-Deception and Illusions*, Boston: Kluwer, 27–51.

Griswold, Charles L. (1999), *Adam Smith and the Virtues of Enlightenment*, Cambridge: Cambridge University Press.

Griswold, Charles L. (2014), 'Narcissisme, amour de soi et critique sociale. *Narcisse* de Rousseau et sa *Préface*', trans. Christophe Litwin, in Blaise Bachofen, Bruno Bernardi, André Charrak and Florent Guénard (eds), *Philosophie de Rousseau*, Paris: Classiques Garnier, 289–304.

Griswold, Charles L. (2015), 'Liberty and Compulsory Civil Religion in Rousseau's *Social Contract*', *Journal of the History of Philosophy*, 53, 271–300.

Griswold, Charles L. (2016), 'Genealogical Narrative and Self-knowledge in Rousseau's *Discourse on the Origin and the Foundations of Inequality among Men*', *History of European Ideas*, 42, 276–301.

Hanley, Ryan Patrick (forthcoming), 'Freedom and Enlightenment', in David Schmidtz and Carmen Pavel (eds), *The Oxford Handbook of Freedom*, Oxford: Oxford University Press.

Harkin, Maureen (2013), 'Adam Smith on Women', in Christopher J. Berry, Maria P. Paganelli and Craig Smith (eds), *The Oxford Handbook of Adam Smith*, Oxford: Oxford University Press, 501–20.

Harpham, Edward J. (2000), 'The Problem of Liberty in the Thought of Adam Smith', *Journal of the History of Economic Thought*, 22, 217–37.

Herzog, Lisa (2013), *Inventing the Market: Smith, Hegel, and Political Theory*, Oxford: Oxford University Press.

Ignatieff, Michael (1984), *The Needs of Strangers*, New York: Picador.

Jaffro, Laurent (2014), 'Comment produire le sentiment de l'existence?', in Jean-François Perrin and Yves Citton (eds), *Jean-Jacques Rousseau et l'exigence d'authenticité: une question pour notre temps*, Paris: Classiques Garnier, 153–69.

Kelly, Christopher (1987), *Rousseau's Exemplary Life: The Confessions as Political Philosophy*, Ithaca, NY: Cornell University Press.

Kelly, Duncan (2011), *The Propriety of Liberty: Persons, Passions and Judgement in Modern Political Thought*, Princeton: Princeton University Press.

Kuiper, Edith (2002), 'Dependency and Denial in Conceptualizations of Economic Exchange', in Caroline Gerschlager and Moniko Mokre (eds), *Exchange and Deception: A Feminist Perspective*, Boston: Kluwer Academic, 75–90.

Langton, Rae (2004), 'Projection and Objectification', in Brian Leiter (ed.), *The Future of Philosophy*, Oxford: Clarendon Press, 285–303.

Lewis, Thomas J. (2000), 'Persuasion, Domination and Exchange: Adam Smith on the Political Consequences of Markets', *Canadian Journal of Political Science*, 33, 273–89.

Melzer, Arthur M. (1990), *The Natural Goodness of Man: On the System of Rousseau's Thought*, Chicago: University of Chicago Press.

Neuhouser, Frederick (2000), *Foundations of Hegel's Social Theory: Actualizing Freedom*, Cambridge, MA: Harvard University Press.

Neuhouser, Frederick (2008), *Rousseau's Theodicy of Self-Love: Evil, Rationality, and the Drive for Recognition*, Oxford: Oxford University Press.

Neuhouser, Frederick (2014), *Rousseau's Critique of Inequality: Reconstructing the Second Discourse*, Cambridge: Cambridge University Press.

Osborne, Lawrence (2013), *The Wet and the Dry: A Drinker's Journey*, New York: Broadway Books.

Otteson, James (2002), *Adam Smith's Marketplace of Life*, Cambridge: Cambridge University Press.

Pippin, Robert (2008), 'Recognition and Politics', in Robert Pippin, *Hegel's Practical Philosophy: Rational Agency as Ethical Life*, Cambridge: Cambridge University Press, 210–38.

Rasmussen, Dennis C. (2008), *The Problems and Promise of Commercial Society: Adam Smith's Response to Rousseau*, University Park: Pennsylvania State University Press.

Rasmussen, Dennis C. (2014), *The Pragmatic Enlightenment: Recovering the Liberalism of Hume, Smith, Montesquieu, and Voltaire*, Cambridge: Cambridge University Press.

Rosen, Michael (1996), *On Voluntary Servitude: False Consciousness and the Theory of Ideology*, Cambridge, MA: Harvard University Press.

Rousseau, Jean-Jacques (1959–95), *Oeuvres complètes*, ed. Bernard Gagnebin and Marcel Raymond, 5 vols, Paris: Gallimard, Bibliothèque de la Pléiade.

Rousseau, Jean-Jacques (1997a), *The Discourses and Other Early Political Writings*, ed. and trans. Victor Gourevitch, Cambridge: Cambridge University Press.

Rousseau, Jean-Jacques (1997b), *The Social Contract and Other Later Political Writings*, ed. and trans. Victor Gourevitch, Cambridge: Cambridge University Press.

Rousseau, Jean-Jacques (2008) [1755], *Rousseau: Discours sur l'origine et les fondements de l'inégalité parmi les hommes*, ed. Blaise Bachofen and Bruno Bernardi, Paris: Flammarion.

Sartre, Jean-Paul (1992) [1943], *Being and Nothingness*, trans. Helen Barnes, New York: Washington Square Press.

Schmidtz, David (2016), 'Adam Smith on Freedom', in Ryan Hanley (ed.), *Adam Smith: His Life, Thought, and Legacy*, Princeton: Princeton University Press, 208–27.

Starobinksi, Jean (1988), *Jean-Jacques Rousseau: Transparency and Obstruction*, trans. Arthur Goldhammer, with an Introduction by Robert J. Morrissey, Chicago: University of Chicago Press. This edition of *Transparency* includes seven essays by Starobinski.

Thrasher, John (2015), 'Adam Smith and the Social Contract', *Adam Smith Review*, 8, 195–216.

Wilde, Oscar (2007) [1891], 'The Critic as Artist', in *The Complete Works of Oscar Wilde*, ed. Josephine M. Guy, Oxford: Oxford University Press, vol. IV, 123–206.

11

Citizens, Markets and Social Order: An Aristotelian Reading of Smith and Rousseau on Justice

Jimena Hurtado

Adam Smith and Jean-Jacques Rousseau agree that justice is the cornerstone of society, and they disagree in their appraisal of commercial society on the grounds of justice. Their disagreement goes beyond their beliefs about whether justice can be achieved or not in this society: it has to do with what exactly they understand by the term 'justice', and which sense of justice they consider indispensable for social order. In general, justice has to do with the regulation of social interactions, but looking into the details of this allows us to understand that there are different types of justice, which entail different kinds of regulations.

Even if neither of them accomplished their avowed project of completing a whole system of jurisprudence (Hanley 2008a), both Rousseau and Smith thought it was of the utmost importance for the good government of a well-ordered society. Smith considered natural jurisprudence to be the most important part of the science of ethics for social order, as it aims at establishing precise rules for behaviour, and in particular deals with the study of justice, 'the only virtue with regard to which such exact rules can be properly given' (TMS VII.iv.7: 329–30). These rules guarantee the preservation of society because without justice 'the fabric of human society . . . must in a moment crumble into atoms' as 'a man would enter an assembly of men as he enters a den of lions' (TMS II.ii.3.4: 86). Along the same lines, Rousseau gives justice a fundamental role in promoting the greatest good for all, that is, freedom and equality for all citizens as members of the general will (DCS OC III: 391).[1] In his *Lettres écrites de la montagne* he says 'the first and greatest interest of the public is always justice. They all want conditions to be the same for all, and justice is this equality' (OC III: 891). Justice and truth, according to Rousseau, are the first duties (*Lettre à M. d'Alembert* OC V: 3) of citizens so they may enjoy their rights (DCS OC III: 363).

Rousseau and Smith agree that the law, or positive jurisprudence, should establish the rules of justice, and that government exists to enforce them. The rule of law then makes society viable when it creates a just institutional framework. However, the justice that they speak of is not the same. In book VII, on Systems of Moral Philosophy, of *The Theory of Moral Sentiments*, Smith explains that there are three different but related meanings of justice (TMS VII.ii.1.10: 269): commutative justice, distributive justice and a third one, which he does not name, but which could be called estimative justice.[2] He defines each in turn, and declares that in *The Theory of Moral Sentiments* he has dealt with the first type of justice because it is the one necessary to uphold social order. It is a negative virtue where members of society refrain from hurting each other. In his *Lettre à M. d'Alembert*, Rousseau talks about two types of justice: universal and particular. A just society needs both, a universal justice that regulates the relationship between citizens as part of the general will, and a particular justice that regulates interactions between individuals.

In order to compare their typologies of justice, I turn to Aristotle, not only because he presents all the meanings of justice that both Smith and Rousseau speak of, but also because, in particular, Smith refers to Aristotle regarding justice, and to the connection between their moral systems. My intention is not to assess whether Rousseau or Smith are in any way Aristotelian[3] or not, but rather to use Aristotle as a common ground to understand the type of justice they are advancing. In book V of the *Nicomachean Ethics*, Aristotle explains in detail the virtue of justice, and states there are varieties of this virtue. As with any other virtue, justice is an intermediate between two extremes, and it is, at the same time, a virtue and a part of virtue. A just person is someone who is lawful and fair (1999: 68, 1129b1); a person who complies with the law, that which 'requires actions in accord with the other virtues, and prohibits actions in accord with the vices' (1999: 68, 1129b20–5); one who uses wealth correctly, and is not an over-reacher (1999: 68, 1129b5). These two attributes of a just person allow us to distinguish general from special justice, and to understand why justice is 'complete virtue in relation to another'

(1999: 69, 1129b30). As in Rousseau and Smith, justice regulates social interactions and is 'the only virtue that seems to be another person's good' (1999: 69, 1130a5). That is why Aristotle argues that justice can be understood as virtue but only 'insofar as virtue is related to another' (1999: 69, 1130a10): a view that Rousseau and Smith would share.

Nevertheless, the specific type of justice they regard as fundamental varies. Rousseau is more concerned with general justice, whereas Smith advocates special justice, and not necessarily in all its meanings, to guarantee social order. Moreover, Rousseau believes that unfairness is inherent to commercial society while Smith suggests that the market can regulate over-reaching behaviour (Walraevens 2014). Therefore, for Rousseau, justice is, at least, incomplete in commercial society, while for Smith, it is regulated through different but complementary institutions (i.e. the law and the market).

In the next four sections I present Rousseau's and Smith's views on justice, comparing them with Aristotle's, in order to understand the differences and coincidences between them. The first section presents the idea of justice as the regulation of social interactions between individuals in search of mutual recognition, or justice as 'another person's good'. The next section follows Smith's classification of justice as presented in book VII of *The Theory of Moral Sentiments* in order to assess the differences between commutative, distributive and estimative justice, and their relation with general, special, universal and particular justice. The third section concentrates on justice in exchange, and the possibilities for a commercial society to be just. The final section presents some concluding remarks and future lines of research.

Justice, Virtue and Social Interactions

The love, admiration and consideration of others is what every individual seeks. Beyond providing for physical needs, society promotes and satisfies psychological and emotional needs and desires. Rousseau and Smith recognise as much (Hont 2015; Hanley 2008b), and are also well aware of the risks that this entails. Rousseau describes the society he lives in as a society of appearances, where competition, envy, jealousy and rivalry prevail as the result of the loss of the love of oneself, and the rise of self-love (SD OC III: 175). Everyone wants to be loved and admired more than their fellow beings, and is unable to respond to others' demands for their approval and recognition, losing their selves in this permanent game of being and appearing. Society becomes a comedy where individuals live for the approval of public opinion.

Even if Smith does not share this view of society, he is well aware of the possible negative effects of self-love and self-interest on social order. Self-interest makes individuals unreliable; their search for recognition and admiration blinds them to the needs of others, and makes them selfish and unfair because they feel so little for each other, and so much for themselves (TMS III.3.3: 135). This is why he agrees with Rousseau on the need for justice as a regulator of interested behaviour which is derived from social passions (Calkins and Werhane 1998: 47). In this sense, both agree that it is possible to cure the evils that modern society might cause (Fleischacker 2004: 59). Justice is this remedy, and it has individual and social qualities: it 'induces an individual to protect life, property, and the rights of others', and its first concern 'with the protection of society's welfare and integrity' makes it 'the premier of social virtues' (Calkins and Werhane 1998: 48–9).

Human beings cannot survive without society (TMS II.ii.3.1: 85) because they cannot live without others to satisfy their material and spiritual needs. According to Rousseau, 'society has made man weaker, not only by taking from him the right he had over his own force, but mostly making it insufficient' to provide for his needs (*Émile* OC IV: 309). Human beings in society enjoy an imperfect freedom because they cannot act at will, as they stand in constant need of the assistance of others: 'The only one who does as he wills is the one who does not need to have the arms of another as an extension of his own in order to do so' (*Émile* OC IV: 309). In society, desires always exceed individual ability to secure them, and this constant and mutual need makes individuals weak and miserable (*Émile* OC IV: 310).

Rousseau asserts this as the source of all the contradictions of the social system, which can be overcome if we come to understand that there are two kinds of dependence: a natural dependence on things, and a social dependence on other human beings, which contrary to the first, entails moral relations. These moral relations can be disorderly, as they are mediated by self-love and a permanent search for the recognition of others. Like Smith, Rousseau recognises that humans' foremost desire is to be loved and admired. However, for the citizen of Geneva, this desire leads to a change in the nature of the love of oneself, which is directed to conservation and to self-love, a relative feeling that implies inter-personal comparison and competition to be more highly valued in the eyes of others.

It is well known that Rousseau denounces this as a step towards the society of appearances, where pretending and seeming to be something are more important than what the person really is. Living in the eyes of others makes individuals lose themselves, hence Rousseau's permanent call to remain within oneself and find self-realisation in our inner world. But this is his educational project, which has to go hand in hand with the regulation of social dependence in order to avoid the negative consequences of the unenlightened self-love that Smith also recognises.

Rousseau's solution is to

> substitute the law for man, and to arm the general will with a real force superior to the action of any particular will. If the law of nations could have, as those of nature, the inflexibility that no human force could ever vanquish, the dependence between men would become that of things, and it would unite into the Republic all the advantages of the natural state and those of the civil state, it would unite the freedom that keeps men from vices and the morals that rise them to virtue. (*Émile* OC IV: 311)

This way, individuals would enjoy what they were looking for when they formed civil societies: to preserve their goods, their lives and their freedom through the protection of all (DEP OC III: 248). The challenge then is to find how to make citizens defend some-one's freedom without trespassing on that of the rest, and how to provide for public needs without disturbing their own property (DEP OC III: 248). The answer is the law of the general will.

This law regulates social interactions in a way that Smith would not appreciate: it puts distance between individuals and makes them aware of being part of a greater whole. But it does so in a way that Rousseau would not recognise as increasing physical or social distance. Rousseau is also aware of the negative effects of distance: 'It seems that the sentiment of humanity evaporates and weakens when it is extended over the earth and that we would not be touched by the calamities of the Tartars or Japan as by those of a good European people' (DEP OC III: 254). It is rather the source of dependence that Rousseau aims at changing, because the law diminishes mutual dependence among citizens, and reinforces each citizen's dependence on the social body (DCS OC III: 394).

This change also shows a crucial difference in the way that Rousseau and Smith conceive justice. Rousseau advocates a kind of justice that regulates interactions between individuals by regulating the relationship between the citizen and the whole social body, or between individuals as citizens and members of the general will. This explains the difference between universal justice and particular justice (*Lettre à M. d'Alembert* OC V: 61). Universal justice has to do with our duties as members of society, and refers to our morals; particular justice regulates our individual relationships with others as determined by the law. Universal justice demands reciprocity (DCS OC III: 378–9) and equal treatment, which implies treating our fellow citizens with the respect and consideration they deserve. In the next section, we will deal with these different types of justice.

Types of Justice

Aristotle observed that 'The just is spoken of in more ways than one' (1999: 68, 1129a.25), and Smith, in particular follows this approach and traces three different but related meanings of the word justice (TMS VII.ii.1.10: 269): commutative, distributive and estimative justice. The first means abstaining from hurting others; the second, 'which consists in proper beneficence, in the becoming use of what is our own, and in applying it to those purposes either of charity or generosity' (TMS VII.ii.1.10: 269–70); and the third, valuing an object in its full worth, and pursuing self-interest with appropriate attention (TMS VII.ii.1.10: 270). Commutative justice corresponds to a negative virtue as it requires no specific action, and can be respected by sitting still and doing nothing; distributive justice 'comprehends all the social virtues'; and estimative justice 'comprehends in it, not only the offices of commutative and distributive justice, but of every other virtue, of prudence, fortitude, of temperance . . . the perfection of every sort of virtue' (TMS VII.ii.1.10: 269–70).

Estimative justice would seem to come closer to Aristotle's general justice as 'general virtue' but 'in relation to another' (1999: 69, 1129b27). According to Aristotle, justice can be general, referring to compliance with the law, or special, referring to fairness, and aiming at filling the gaps of general justice. Special or particular justice is divided into distributive and corrective justice. The former has to do with the allocation of goods, respecting proportionality, and the latter, with the restoration of equality. Justice is necessary to regulate interactions but, especially, to regulate the desire for life, which is infinite, and therefore disorderly; and to show citizens the difference between this infinite desire, and the desire for the good life, which is limited to happiness as defined in the city. Thus, individuals learn justice as citizens, in their political debates, within the perfect association where the good, the useful and the just are united.

Commutative Justice

At the end of *The Theory of Moral Sentiments*, Smith declares that he has dealt with commutative justice, which may be shown to be the fundamental type of justice necessary for the adequate functioning of society. As no impartial spectator will ever go along with harming an innocent victim, refraining from hurting someone in their person or property or breaching contract become actions that can be demanded by force from any member of society, and anyone can be punished if they engage in such behaviour. Any prudent individual can comply with these rules, which prevent society from becoming a den of lions where each member is guided only by a limited and egotistical self-interest.

> Mere justice is, upon most occasions, but a negative virtue, and only hinders from hurting our neighbour. The man who barely abstains from violating either person, or the estate, or the reputation of his neighbours, has surely very little positive merit. He fulfils, however all the rules of what is peculiarly called justice, and does everything which his equals can force him to do, or which they can punish him for not doing. We may often fulfil all these rules of justice by sitting still and doing nothing. (TMS II.ii.1.9: 81–2)

In this sense, justice is related to what Smith identifies in his *Lectures on Jurisprudence* as perfect rights.[4] Life, property and contract are the three main perfect rights, and justice should protect them. Refraining from violating another's life, property or breaching contract would then be enough to be just. Any prudent individual can accomplish this, and, as prudence takes the place of honour in Smith's explanation of virtues (McCloskey

2006), justice, while it may be hard to know (Aristotle 1999: 82, 1137a10), is not difficult to understand, because 'even the most stupid and unthinking, abhor fraud, perfidy, and injustice, and delight to see them punished' (TMS II.ii.3.9: 89). Indeed, 'The whole virtue of justice, therefore, the most important of all virtues, is no more than the discreet and prudent conduct with regard to our neighbours' (TMS VII.ii.2.11: 297).

Therefore, for Smith, virtue is excellence, but as excellence cannot be generally expected (TMS VII.ii.3.18: 305), propriety and decency are enough for people to act justly (Waszek 1984: 594). Sympathetic human beings can act with justice, understood as 'abstaining from what is another's, and in doing voluntarily whatever we can with propriety be forced to do' (TMS VII.ii.1.10: 269). This is why justice can be precise in its rules (TMS III.6.10: 175), and its violation can be punished (TMS II.ii.1.9: 81), but also why it requires no particular action, and 'does no positive good' (TMS II.ii.1.9: 82).

Distributive Justice

The second sense of justice Smith describes has to do with our consideration of others:

> We are said not to do justice to our neighbour unless we conceive for him all that love, respect, and esteem, which his character, his situations, and his connection with ourselves, render suitable and proper for us to feel, and unless we act accordingly. (TMS VII.ii.1.10: 269)

This second sense corresponds to 'proper beneficence, in the becoming use of what is our own, and in the applying it to those purposes either of charity or generosity' (TMS VII.ii.1.11: 270). This justice is associated with imperfect rights or those 'which ought to be performed to us by others but which we have no title to compel them to perform; they having it entirely in their power to perform them or not' (LJA: 9). No one can be forced to use their property in any way, and even if social interactions might be more pleasant when each complies with the duties associated with their direct relation to others – for example, parents and children – society will not crumble because individuals fail to do so. Beneficence embellishes society but it is not its foundation;

hence, according to Smith, distributive justice is not a fundamental part of social order.

Rousseau, on the other hand, puts these duties at the centre of a government's duties in the society of the general will. He states that what seems most necessary and most difficult for any government is to guarantee justice for all, and especially to protect the poor against the tyranny of the rich (DEP OC III: 258). Inequality is a violation of the social contract, which establishes the same conditions and rights for all (DCS OC III: 374). Equality of rights is essential to social order, and material inequality threatens it. The rich are above the law and the poor fall through the gaps (DEP OC III: 258). When the law reflects a social pact between the rich and the poor (DEP OC III: 273) rather than the general will of equal citizens, it protects the possessions of the wealthy and leaves the poor with barely what they need to survive (DEP OC III: 271). This means that all the advantages of society are enjoyed by the rich and powerful, and the rules of justice protect them rather than the poor (DEP OC III: 271–2), ignoring the fact that 'the loss of the poor can be much less easily repaired than those of the rich, and that the difficulty in acquiring always increases with need' (DEP OC III: 272).

Material inequality puts individuals in the disorderly dependence Rousseau warns about, because it makes them, rich and poor, renounce their own wills to satisfy their desires by satisfying those of others (SD OC III: 174–5). This situation is contrary to the common good that Rousseau identifies as the end of any system of legislation: liberty and equality (DCS OC III: 391).

Moreover, what Rousseau calls mediocrity of fortune is necessary for law to be effective as the regulator of social interactions. Therefore, one of the government's most important tasks is to prevent the extreme inequality of fortunes 'not by taking treasures from their owners, but taking away from all the means to accumulate such treasures, nor by building hospitals for the poor but guaranteeing citizens will never become poor' (DEP OC III: 258).

The government then must ensure the conditions needed for each citizen to be able to satisfy their needs with their labour. So, citizens have the right to work but also the duty to do so. The first communities were formed in this way, and the society of the general will recovers this characteristic of human societies as communities of shared labour, and of humans as workers. Citizenship, which means equality of rights and duties, also means reducing material inequality and putting material well-being within everyone's reach (DEP OC III: 262). But it also means equal treatment of citizens by the government and between themselves. In this sense, distributive justice is a means to this equal treatment as the recognition of equal rights and duties for all. Therefore, it is part of the citizens' duties as prescribed by the law they have given themselves, and which expresses their own will. According to Rousseau, if citizens do not comply with this law, with the contract they have passed among themselves as members of the general will, not only do they act against their own will, they are also unjust (DCS OC III: 363).

Therefore, the exercise of distributive justice is part of a citizen's duties, which he or she can only come to know and understand in his or her participation in public debate. As in Aristotle, only the citizen has access to knowledge about virtue; consequently, he or she will know what is the proper use of things or 'the becoming use of what is our own' (TMS VII.ii.1.11: 270). The correct use of goods, their use according to virtue, is part of striving at happiness, humans' ultimate end, because it 'is impossible or it is not easy to perform good actions if one has no resources' (Aristotle 1999: 11, 1099a32–3).

Moreover, the correct use of goods implies knowing who and what they are good for. An unjust individual 'will be concerned with goods – not with all goods, but only with those involved in good and bad fortune, goods which are [considered] without qualification, always good, but for this or that person not always good' (Aristotle 1999: 68, 1129b1–4). Only the citizen can attain this knowledge; hence his or her participation in the life of the city is central to the correct development of his or her faculty to use and acquire goods: that is, to economics.

Rousseau follows Aristotle closely in defining economics (moral and political) as 'the wise and legitimate government of the household, for the common good of the whole family' (DEP OC III: 241). Aristotle states that economics corresponds to the management of the household, which includes the good use of domestic resources (*Pol.* 1256a10–12). There is a direct connection between the art of governing the household and that of governing the city because the necessary knowledge of how to correctly acquire and use goods comes from politics (*Pol.* 1259a33–6). The administrator of the city also has to know how to acquire and correctly use the goods needed to sustain the good life. In this sense, economics is part of the architectonic science of politics, and it is also subordinated to it. As what Rousseau intends to discuss is the administration of the state, he uses the term political economy (DEP OC III: 241). Like Smith, Rousseau places political economy within the science of the legislator, much in the same way as Aristotle deals with the economy and economics as part of the administration of the city, and therefore of political science.

The fact that politics is the art and science of knowing and updating the ultimate good of the city, and hence of its citizens, and that economics is subordinate to politics, means that justice, in all its senses, has to be exercised in the acquisition and use of material goods (Hurtado and Melo 2015). In this sense, it is possible to understand why Rousseau would include distributive justice within universal justice, and thus as the foundation of civil society.

Estimative Justice

Smith accounts for a third sense of justice 'more extensive than either of the former, and very much akin to' distributive justice (TMS VII.ii.1.11: 270). In this third sense, justice means valuing things according to their appropriate 'degree of esteem, or to pursue [them] with that degree of ardour which to the impartial spectator it may appear to deserve or to be naturally fitted for exciting' (TMS VII.ii.1.11: 270). It coincides with the exact and perfect propriety of conduct, and hence includes commutative and distributive justice, as well as every other virtue of prudence, fortitude and temperance (TMS VII.ii.1.11: 270).

Estimative justice then synthesises, so to speak, the core message of those systems that make virtue consist in propriety. The main difference between those systems and Smith's is that he includes something that the others lack: the measure of propriety (Berns 1994). Only one other system proposed a measure, and that was the one that placed virtue in utility (TMS VII.ii.3.21: 305–6). Both systems, like Aristotle's, assert that 'virtue consists not in any one affection, but in the proper degree of all affections', but Smith's makes 'sympathy, or the correspondent affection of the spectator, the natural and original measure of this proper degree' (TMS VII. ii.3.21: 306). Therefore, Smith places his own system in line with Aristotle's, and considers that he has improved on it.

There is, however, an important difference between the systems that brings Rousseau closer to Aristotle. Valuing things according to their appropriate degree of esteem or pursuing something with the appropriate degree of enthusiasm requires a particular knowledge about what, precisely, constitutes such an appropriate degree. For Smith, this corresponds to the degree that the impartial spectator would approve of, a degree that individuals learn through the sympathetic process, which is instantaneous and depends upon the community that the person belongs to. For Aristotle, this would have to do with the difference between justice as excellence or virtue and particular justice.

Estimative justice seems related to general, universal or whole justice; that justice which individuals learn and practise as citizens: the one that tells them the difference between the desire for life and the desire for the good life. Everyone might desire life for itself, a limitless desire because it can never be satisfied; a desire that can be associated with the ambitious or grasping person, whose main motivation is the pleasure of gain. But only the citizen desires the good life, a limited desire because the good life is guided by the ultimate good as defined in the city and captured in the law.

Rousseau talks about universal justice, referring to that which regulates the interactions between the general will and its members, beyond particular justice, which regulates interactions between individuals. Universal justice aims at promoting the greatest good for all, which requires equality among citizens (DCS OC III: 391) in order for civil liberty to prevail, that is, 'regulated freedom under the law of the general will'. This way, each citizen will 'be in a perfect independence from all others, and in excessive dependence on the State . . . because the force of the State makes the freedom of its members' (DCS OC III: 394). Justice then is directly related to the life of the city, and for Rousseau, this life, when it is legitimate, expresses the will of citizens as members of the general will.

In the city, following Aristotle, individuals debate about the good life, and learn that

> For even if the good is the same for the city as for the individual, still the good of the city is apparently a greater and more complete good to acquire and preserve. For while it is satisfactory to acquire and preserve the good even for an individual, it is finer and more divine to acquire and preserve it for a people and for cities. (Aristotle 1999: 2, 1094b8)

Citizens will learn how to deal with their desire for recognition, and the like desires of others, through the study and practice of politics and political science or the art of the citizen. They will understand that the use and acquisition of goods, that is economics, is part of this art, and cannot be separated from it, lest it turns into vice.

Rousseau, like Aristotle, makes justice equivalent to virtue, and necessary for political life. In the society guided by the general will, citizens contract among themselves in order to guarantee life, property and freedom. This contract implies that each member has equal rights and duties that they must observe as the expression of their own will as a citizen. The foundation of equality of rights and duties is equality of treatment among citizens, which requires controlling inequality of wealth. Therefore, a just citizen is someone who is lawful and fair, and a good system of jurisprudence is one that establishes equality before the law, and promotes mediocrity of fortunes so no one will ever be above or beneath the law, and will only use his or her wealth for the good, that is, for happiness as defined in the city.

Universal justice implies mutual engagements as citizens, as members of the general will, and is general in its object and essence, for it loses its rectitude when dealing with particular objects (DCS OC III: 373). In this sense, universal justice goes beyond individual relationships among neighbours, which would correspond to Smith's distributive justice. It implies the recognition of equality resulting from an individual sense of value, and the same rights for all resulting in equal dignity. This engagement among citizens is reciprocal (DCS OC III: 378–9) and connects love of justice and love of humankind (*Émile* OC IV: 547), which would not be possible if citizens were not trustworthy and were guided only by their self-love. The law makes material the agreement to comply with these mutual engagements as free and equal citizens (DCS OC III: 248). Only when pity extends from individuals to humankind do individuals develop a sense of justice, the 'virtue that most contributes to [its] common good' (*Émile* OC IV: 548). Extended pity is the basis for the law, which aims at the common good and, again following Aristotle, is just because 'in one way what we call just is whatever produces and maintains happiness and its parts for a political community' (1999: 68, 1129b17–19). A virtuous and just person will obey the law of the general will, following its commands, as Aristotle says, 'which are prescribed from the point of view of excellence taken as a whole ... with a view to education for the common good' (1999: 70, 1130b20–9). Therefore a just person will also be a good citizen, knowledgeable in the art of politics (1999: 70, 1130b20–9), just as Rousseau would have it.

For Rousseau, universal justice would be the only way to stop individuals from trying to impose their will on others, just as children do. Precisely this comparison with childhood shows how Rousseau believes that the existing social pact puts individuals in the same state as children: 'We were made to be men, the laws and society have put us back into childhood' (*Émile* OC IV: 310). Each child wants others to do as he or she wishes; they strive to submit others to their will, but their relative weakness makes this impossible and they end up doing as others tell them with rage and frustration. The same happens with adults in an unregulated or ill-regulated society. Each member wants others to do as he or she wishes, and especially to recognise and praise his or her superiority. They see others as the source of recognition but, at the same time, as the obstacle to this recognition. The law then should establish the impossibility of submitting to others, and the general will should be the only source of recognition for its citizens.

This universal justice, and the general engagement it implies, does not seem possible for Smith. Any individual's concern for the whole 'is made up of the particular regards which we feel for the different individuals of which it is composed' (TMS II.ii.3.10: 89–90). This explains why, for Smith, universal justice 'is no more that the general fellow-feeling which we have with every man merely because he is our fellow-creature' (TMS II.3.10: 90). Besides, as Calkins and Werhane (1998) and Hanley (2006) show, Smith, as opposed to Aristotle and Rousseau, is silent about the ultimate good, and redefines the flourishing life 'as one of social cooperation rather than self-perfection' (Hanley 2006: 19) because 'he does not agree with Aristotle's idea of virtue as having a pre-conceived ultimate end or perfection' (Calkins and Werhane 1998: 51). Therefore, Smith makes justice a practical virtue; it is

a habit with respect to [individual] fairness and proportionality for practical matters and the order that follows once society is protected from harm. It is a commutative construct and it does not promote social or individual welfare beyond certain negative requirements. (Calkins and Werhane 1998: 53)

Rather than relying on mutual engagement or the love of humankind and the love of justice, Smith relies on humans' natural tendency to sympathise as the basis for that justice which guarantees rights and regulates social interactions. Through the sympathetic process, a process of moral education, individuals learn to control their passions and develop self-love under the rule of reason (TMS III.3.4: 137). When individuals 'practise truth, justice and humanity' they are certain of obtaining 'the confidence, the esteem, and the love of those' they live with (TMS III.5.8: 166–7). Prudence, justice and beneficence are, according to Smith, the proper actions of those who follow 'the sentiments of the supposed impartial spectator, of the great inmate of the breast, the great judge and arbiter of our conduct' (TMS VI.concl.1: 267).

The sympathetic process has been presented as an elaboration of Aristotelian ethics, especially its sentimental side, allowing us to flesh out how the golden mean or the propriety of sentiments is achieved (Berns 1994). Smith himself classifies his system within those that make virtue consist in propriety (TMS VII.ii.1.1: 267), where he also classifies Plato, Aristotle and Zeno. According to these philosophers, 'virtue consists in the propriety of conduct, or in the suitableness of the affection from which we act to the object which excites it' (TMS VII.ii.1.1: 267). A virtuous individual enjoys a 'perfect and complete harmony of the soul' identified with 'good temper, or sobriety and moderation' (TMS VII.ii.1.8: 268). Such an individual is just inasmuch as they exercise this moderation in their relations with others, acting when reason and passions coincide and according to the situation.

However, the complexity of social interactions in commercial society might hinder this process of moral education, and therefore a system of positive jurisprudence becomes more necessary to maintain social order. Justice, as a negative virtue, describes actions that refrain from hurting others, but requires no specific action from the individual or any particular regard for others. It entails compliance and punishment in case of its violation because it is the necessary condition for the preservation of social life. In an extended society, where people grow increasingly further apart, and have ever-diminished personal relationships with most of society's other members, the information that the sympathetic process requires is harder to acquire. Individuals know less and less about each other because social and psychological distance increases, making the sympathetic process insufficient to guarantee social order, let alone social cohesion.

In small circles, defined by the physical and psychological distance between their members, the sympathetic process is enough to regulate interactions. The ease in identification, as members of such circles have enough information about each other, the pleasure of mutual sympathy and the greatest human aspiration of being loved and regarded with consideration lead individuals to relationships of mutual respect. But as physical and psychological distance increases, the possibility of identifying with others decreases, and self-love can overcome any other feeling. When this happens, the individual will only take into consideration his or her own interest, with little or no regard for others with whom he or she cannot identify and whose approbation he or she cannot enjoy.

Smith here recognises the destructive power of self-love, and the need for justice to curb it. Justice, in this first sense, is 'the main pillar' of society: 'If it is removed, the great, the immense fabric of human society, that fabric which to raise and support seems in this world, if I may say so, to have been the peculiar and darling care of Nature, must in a moment crumble into atoms' (TMS II.ii.3.4: 86). Without justice, strangers cannot trust each other; it is as if they could only expect harm from each other. This would make society unsustainable because it 'cannot subsist among those who are at all times ready to hurt each other' as 'the prevalence of injustice must utterly destroy it' (TMS II.ii.3.3: 86).

Both Rousseau and Smith agree on the need of a system of positive jurisprudence, even if they do not agree on the justice it should advance. As Hanley (2008b) points out, Rousseau and Smith consider that such a system should adapt general principles to particular circumstances, making the science of the legislator a combination of system and practical knowledge (Haakonssen 1981). The difference between them is that whereas Smith shows confidence in the natural order, Rousseau believes justice needs positive institutions (Hanley 2008a: 224–31). This would explain why Smith does not deal with universal or general justice, as natural order will take care of itself; whereas Rousseau intends to restore or rather recreate such justice. In this sense, Rousseau advances artificial justice, and Smith advocates for natural justice.

Even if Smith is less radical, as he believes that the natural order can impose itself, simply because his account of human psychology shows that nothing can replace personal and social interactions in our search for recognition and belonging, he would agree with the need for external regulation, that is, for a positive system of jurisprudence. Such a system would gather and materialise the rules of justice, guaranteeing security from injury and providing the foundation of civil government (LJB: 398). It would reinforce the voice of the impartial spectator, and extend the rules that we would naturally observe with those who are physically and psychologically close to us. Positive rules of justice take the place of 'the soft power of humanity', 'the feeble spark of benevolence which Nature has lighted up in the human heart', and will help this stronger power counteract 'the strongest impulses of self-love' (TMS III.3.4: 137).

The first, and for Smith, the main part of this system of jurisprudence is commutative justice, which guarantees perfect rights: 'those which we have a title to demand and if refused to compel an other to perform' (LJA: 9), and they refer to the preservation of life, property, reputation and contract. This type of justice means 'we are said to do justice to our neighbour when we abstain from doing him any positive harm, and do not directly hurt him, either in his person, or in his estate, or in his reputation' (TMS VII. ii.1.10: 269). This meaning coincides with Aristotle's commutative justice 'which consists in abstaining from what is another's, and in doing voluntarily whatever we can with propriety be forced to do' (TMS VII.ii.1.10: 269).

Commutative justice would coincide with Rousseau's particular justice, which is insufficient to guarantee a legitimate social order. In Aristotle's definition of justice it is clear that it goes beyond a negative virtue. 'Justice is the only virtue that seems to be another person's good, because it is related to another; for it does what benefits another' (1999: 69, 1130a4–5). In order to put order into social dependence, universal justice is required, and this justice seems to come closer to Aristotle's complete justice, and to include distributive and estimative justice, as Smith defined them.

Justice in Exchange

In commercial society individuals stand at all times in need of each other. According to Rousseau, in this society individuals are completely dependent on each other, and they strive to convince each other that working together is for their mutual benefit. Just as with Smith (WN I.ii.2: 26–7), Rousseau also believes that individuals address themselves to others' self-interest in order to satisfy their needs. However, for Rousseau, this has the sad result of 'isolating each one in their self-love, and of protecting herself behind a deceitful appearance' (Starobinski 1971: 37). They build their selves by searching for exterior signs of their superiority and this explains the race for wealth. Individuals come together to satisfy their needs, and, at the same time, they draw each other apart because self-love leads to a society of enemies highly dependent on each other. Such individuals see each other as instruments for their own vanity, and use their fellows just as they are used by them (DCS OC III).

The apparent principle of our institutions, says Rousseau, is the division of labour (*Émile* OC IV). Through exchange individuals can profit from each other's talents, and the division of labour will allow gains in productivity, leading to greater quantities and higher quality goods. Smith agrees with this view, but instead of stating that it is only an apparent principle, it is presented as the foundation of a commercial society, where each one participates and enjoys the wealth of society precisely because of their participation in the division of labour. The difference between them is that, contrary to Smith, Rousseau considers commercial society to be essentially a monetary economy, and money, more than a common measure, corrupts everything. Money, says Rousseau, allows comparisons of value and, in this sense, it can be said to be the true social link (*Émile* OC IV); it is a conventional sign, but members of commercial society have forgotten this, and they seek money for itself, for its infinite purchasing power, for its ability to substitute goods, and to make them apparently completely independent from each other (*Émile* OC IV); money is desired as a sign of inequality. Money, following Aristotle's characterisation of a just person, makes people unfair. Some are unjust because they have too much and others suffer injustice because they have too little (Aristotle 1999: 76, 1133b30).

Instead, Smith argues that commercial society depends on the virtue of prudence, and should work within an institutional framework that requires its members to be fair even to strangers (Calkins and Werhane 1998: 55–7). Following Walraevens (2014), markets observe the conditions of justice because they favour certain behaviours associated with individual virtues, especially prudence, making individuals moderate the intensity of their passions in order to persuade others to exchange with them (Walraevens 2014: 245).

However, the institutional framework must guarantee markets. In commercial societies, where there is no mutual love and affection but only relationships between merchants through 'a mercenary exchange of good offices according to an agreed valuation' (TMS II.ii.3.2: 86), justice is particularly needed. Indeed:

> men, though naturally sympathetic, feel so little for another, with whom they have no particular connexion, in comparison of what they feel for themselves; the misery of one, who is merely their fellow-creature, is of so little importance to them in comparison even of a small conveniency of their own; they have it so much in their power to hurt him, and may have so many temptations to do so, that if this principle did not stand up within them in his defence, and overawe them into a respect for his innocence, they would, like wild beasts, be at all times ready to fly upon him; and a man would enter an assembly of men as he enters a den of lions. (TMS II.ii.3.4: 86)

Commercial society is unjust, for Rousseau, because it is a monetary economy where people act unfairly and do not respect distributive justice. It is as if Rousseau considered commercial society necessarily to be the materialisation of bad chrematistics. Individuals use their wealth incorrectly to isolate themselves from others, satisfy their self-love and show off their apparent superiority. The market, instead of providing the basis for mutual interdependence among equals, reinforces the dynamics of inequality. Rousseau's social project stands on the opposite side: striving for equality in dignity, the society of the social contract requires more than commutative justice. Each member of the general will must be just by promoting and recognising equal dignity in his or her fellow citizens. Therefore, distributive and estimative justice are also necessary, but general justice, as complete virtue in regard to another, is fundamental.

Rousseau believes that such justice must be constructed as the result of a mutual and reciprocal engagement among citizens. He proposes an artificial system of justice where the law comes before justice. Smith, on the contrary, advocates natural justice, and thinks that justice comes before the law. They both recontextualise Aristotle's virtue in a commercial society, and are well aware of its effects on individual behaviour. Rousseau adheres to Aristotle's view of justice as complete virtue in relation to another, whereas Smith presents justice as a practical virtue of avoiding harming another.

Nevertheless, taking a closer look at Aristotle when he explains justice in exchange, it is possible to find reasons for Smith's confidence in commercial society, and its possibilities for justice. Even if Aristotle says that reciprocity does not really fit justice (1999: 74, 1132b25), he also argues that 'in communities of exchange, however, this way of being just, reciprocity, that is proportionate rather than equal, holds people together for a city is maintained by proportionate reciprocity' (1999: 74, 1132b30). Exchange means returning good for good, and as long as exchange is proportionate, it will hold people together and be just. For this to happen, things must be in some way equal, that is, comparable, and so they 'must be measured by some one measure' (1999: 75, 1133a25). This measure is need, 'which holds everything together: for if people needed nothing, or needed things to different extents, there would be either no exchange or not the same exchange. And currency has become a sort of pledge of need, by convention' (1999: 75, 1133a28–9). Therefore, we have here both of the things that Rousseau feared: exchange and currency. But they are not presented in a negative light, bringing us closer to Smith and the possibility of a just monetary economy.

Conclusion

Aristotle's main concern is for the end of the state, as it is something more complete and greater than a human being: 'for though it is worth while to attain the end merely for one man, it is finer and more godlike to attain it for a nation or for city-states' (1999: 3, 1094a18–1094b11). The order of the different associations also allows us to understand this priority. Human beings are sociable; they live in communities as members of their household, their village and their city. In order to understand the end of each of these associations, and thus the end of human beings, we must understand each one of them but as part of something more perfect precisely because it is the whole. This means that it is only possible to understand the highest good or the ultimate end of human beings as part of this more perfect whole that is the city. Through the citizens' participation in public debate they will come to this knowledge which must be permanently updated, and which is directly linked to the understanding and practice of virtue, and therefore of justice. Hence, the rules of conduct of virtuous individuals, the appraisal of their virtuous character and conduct, depend upon this public knowledge and upon the practice of citizenship.

Rousseau would agree that the source of the rules of justice is to be derived from public debate among citizens, as members of the general will. The most universal rules and certain rules 'sur lesquelles on puisse juger d'un bon ou d'un mauvais gouvernement, et en général, de la moralité de toutes les actions humaines' are the product of this common person that citizens form in political society (DEP OC III: 245). Human beings owe justice and freedom to the law, as the expression of the general will (DEP OC III: 248).

Smith radically changes this, or, at least, public debate and citizenship seem much less present in his analysis. Being a good citizen is certainly related to the 'wish to promote, by every means in his power, the welfare of the whole society of his fellow-citizens' (TMS VI.ii.2.11: 231), but the citizen's concern for their fellow citizens arises from the sympathetic process and not, for example, from the 'love of mankind' (TMS VI.ii.2.4: 229):

> It is not the love of our neighbour, it is not the love of mankind, which upon many occasions prompts us to the practice of those divine virtues. It is a stronger love, a more powerful affection, which generally takes place upon such occasions; the love of what is honourable and noble, of the grandeur, and dignity, and superiority of our own characters. (TMS III.3.5: 137)

It would be as if human beings simply did not have the cognitive power to conceive of the whole; and acknowledging this limit leads also to recognising that the mechanisms that explain social life are consistent with Rousseau's maxim of taking human beings as they are, and not as philosophers wish them to be. Therefore, Smith allows us to consider the possibility of a society made up of less than virtuous individuals. For Aristotle and Rousseau, virtue and hence the three types of justice are necessary for social order, whereas for Smith, only commutative justice is indispensable.

Notes

1. All references to Rousseau's works are to his *Oeuvres complètes*, éditions La Pléiade. Translations are by the author. The following abbreviations have been used: DCS = *Du contrat social*; DEP = *Discours sur l'économie politique*; FD = *Discours sur les sciences et les arts*;

SD = *Discours sur l'origine et les fondements de l'inégalité parmi les hommes.*

2. I follow Daniel Klein's suggestion in using this term.

3. Much has been written especially on the possible influence of Aristotle or other Classical writers on Smith, and on Smith as a virtue ethicist (cf. Vivenza 2001; Fleischacker 2004; McCloskey 2008; Hanley 2009; Pack 2010; Levy and Peart 2013, among many others); this debate lies beyond the scope of this chapter. Here, I will follow Vivenza (2010: 300), who suggests that Smith's elaboration on justice, in spite of its references to Classical philosophers, 'is expressed in such a way that we can attribute it to Smith himself: the reference to the different meaning [*sic*] of the word in Greek and in other languages, and the comment on the "natural affinity among those various significations" suggest that it is a personal reflection'.

4. Fleischacker (2004) and Salter (2012) discuss this aspect of Smith's view of justice, and its possible relation with more modern meanings of distributive justice. See also Vivenza (2010).

Bibliography

Aristotle (1999), *Nichomachean Ethics*, trans. Terence Irwin, 2nd edn, Indianapolis: Hackett.

Berns, Laurence (1994), 'Aristotle and Adam Smith on Justice: Cooperation between Ancients and Moderns?', *The Review of Metaphysics*, 48.1, 71–90.

Broadie, Alexander (2010), 'Aristotle, Adam Smith and the Virtue of Propriety', *Journal of Scottish Philosophy*, 8.1, 79–89.

Calkins, Martin J., and Patricia H. Werhane (1998), 'Adam Smith, Aristotle, and the Virtues of Commerce', *Journal of Value Inquiry*, 32, 43–60.

Fleischacker, Samuel (2004), *On Adam Smith's 'Wealth of Nations': A Philosophical Companion*, Princeton: Princeton University Press.

Griswold, Charles L. (1999), *Adam Smith and the Virtues of Enlightenment*, Cambridge: Cambridge University Press.

Haakonssen, Knud (1981), *The Science of a Legislator: The Natural Jurisprudence of David Hume and Adam Smith*, Cambridge: Cambridge University Press.

Haakonssen, Knud (1996), *Natural Law and Moral Philosophy: From Grotius to the Scottish Enlightenment*, Cambridge: Cambridge University Press.

Hanley, Ryan Patrick (2006), 'Adam Smith and Virtue Ethics', in

L. Montes and E. Schliesser (eds), *New Voices on Adam Smith*, New York: Routledge, 17–39.

Hanley, Ryan Patrick (2008a), 'Enlightened Nation Building: The "Science of the Legislator" in Adam Smith and Rousseau', *American Journal of Political Science*, 52.2, 219–34.

Hanley, Ryan Patrick (2008b), 'Commerce and Corruption. Rousseau's Diagnosis and Adam Smith's Cure', *European Journal of Political Theory*, 7.2, 137–58.

Hanley, Ryan Patrick (2009), *Adam Smith and the Character of Virtue*, Cambridge: Cambridge University Press.

Herzog, Lisa (2014), 'Adam Smith on Markets and Justice', *Philosophy Compass*, 12.12, 864–75.

Hont, Istvan (2015), *Politics in Commercial Society. Jean-Jacques Rousseau and Adam Smith*, ed. B. Kapossy and M. Sonenscher, Cambridge: Cambridge University Press.

Hurtado, J. (2016), 'On the Possibility of Justice in Commercial Society according to Jean-Jacques Rousseau and Adam Smith', working paper, Documento CEDE 20, Bogotá: Facultad de Economía, CEDE, Universidad de los Andes.

Hurtado, J., and S. Melo (2015), 'Economía y crematística en los comentarios de Juan Ginés de Sepúlveda a la Política de Aristóteles', in F. Castañeda and A. Lozano-Vásquez (eds), *Grupo de traducción de latín Universidad de los Andes, Aristóteles. Sobre la República – Libro I. Según la traducción latina y escolios de Juan Ginés de Sepúlveda*, Bogotá: Ediciones Uniandes, 233–72.

Levy, David M., and Sandra J. Peart (2013), 'Adam Smith and the State: Language and Reform', in C. J. Berry, M. Paganelli and C. Smith (eds), *The Oxford Handbook of Adam Smith*, Oxford: Oxford University Press, 372–92.

McCloskey, Deirdre (2006), *The Bourgeois Virtues: Ethics for an Age of Commerce*, Chicago: University of Chicago Press.

McCloskey, Deirdre (2008), 'Adam Smith, the Last of the Former Virtue Ethicists', *History of Political Economy*, 40.1, 43–71.

Pack, Spencer J. (2010), *Aristotle, Adam Smith and Karl Marx. On Some Fundamental Issues in 21st-Century Political Economy*, Cheltenham: Edward Elgar.

Rackham, H. (1932), *Aristotle: Politics*, Cambridge, MA: Harvard University Press.

Rasmussen, Dennis C. (2008), *The Problems and Promise of Commercial Society. Adam Smith's Response to Rousseau*, University Park: Pennsylvania State University Press.

Ross, W. D. (1957), *Aristotelis Politica*, Oxford: Clarendon Press.

Rousseau, Jean-Jacques (1959–95), *Œuvres complètes*, ed. B. Gagnebin and M. Raymond, 5 vols, Paris: NRF, Gallimard.

Salter, John (1994), 'Adam Smith on Justice and Distribution in Commercial Societies', *Scottish Journal of Political Economy*, 41.3, 299–313.

Salter, John (2012), 'Adam Smith on Justice and the Needs of the Poor', *Journal of the History of Economic Thought*, 34.4, 559–75.

Saunders, T. J. (1995), *Aristotle: Politics Books I and II*, Oxford: Clarendon Press.

Schneider, J. G. (1809), *Aristotelis Politicorum Libri Octo Superstites*, Frankfurt: Libreria Academica.

Starobinski, Jean (1971), *Jean-Jacques Rousseau, la transparence et l'obstacle*, Paris: Gallimard.

Vivenza, Gloria (2001), *Adam Smith and the Classics. The Classical Heritage in Adam Smith's Thought*, Oxford: Oxford University Press.

Vivenza, Gloria (2010), 'Justice as a Virtue – Justice as a Principle in Adam Smith's Thought', *Revista Empresa y Humanismo*, XIII.1, 297–332.

Walraevens, Benoît (2014), 'Vertus et justice du marché chez Adam Smith', *Revue économique*, 65, 419–38.

Waszek, Norbert (1984), 'Two Concepts of Morality: A Distinction of Adam Smith's Ethics and its Stoic Origin', *Journal of the History of Ideas*, 45.4, 591–606.

Part V

Politics and Freedom

12

Smith, Rousseau and the True Spirit of a Republican

Dennis C. Rasmussen

One of Adam Smith's earliest writings, a letter to the *Edinburgh Review* published in 1756, concludes with an extended analysis of Jean-Jacques Rousseau's recently released *Discourse on Inequality* (see Letter: 250–4). Much of Smith's review is dedicated to high-lighting a number of unexpected parallels between Rousseau and Bernard Mandeville, the notorious defender of commercial vice.[1] After praising Rousseau's writing style in fulsome terms, Smith's appraisal culminates in the claim that 'it is by the help of this style, together with a little philosophical chemistry, that the principles and ideas of the profligate Mandeville seem in [Rousseau] to have all the purity and sublimity of the morals of Plato, and to be only the true spirit of a republican carried a little too far' (Letter: 251). I have argued elsewhere that the curious phrase 'philosophi-cal chemistry' is an implicit reference to Rousseau's fundamental doctrine of the natural goodness of humanity, meaning both that human beings are naturally well-ordered, self-sufficient and hence happy (they are good for themselves), and that they naturally have little inclination or reason to harm other people and are averse to seeing them suffer (they are good for others) (see Rasmussen 2008: 64–6).[2] I did not examine the last part of Smith's statement – that is, his reference to Rousseau embodying 'the true spirit of a republican carried a little too far' – mostly, I confess, because of its manifest ambiguity. The term 'republican' had a host of meanings in the eighteenth century, as it does today. Thus, it is not immedi-ately clear what Smith meant by 'the true spirit of a republican', or in what sense he thought Rousseau carried this spirit too far. The present chapter rectifies the omission in my earlier discussion by exploring these questions. Along the way, it also considers Smith's and Rousseau's conceptions of liberty, arguing that their views are nearly diametrically opposed, but not (only) in the way that is generally assumed.

There is now a sizeable and growing literature dedicated to myriad aspects of the Smith–Rousseau connection.[3] Many scholars who have explored this connection have quoted Smith's claim about Rousseau carrying the true spirit of a republican a little too far, but the precise *meaning* of the claim has very rarely been considered. Those scholars who *have* moved beyond mere quotation of this line have generally been quick to assume that Smith's 'a little too far' was in reference to Rousseau's 'republican' or 'positive' understanding of liberty, according to which true freedom is realised in and through collective self-government and obedience to the general will. For instance, Eric Schliesser interprets Smith's statement as drawing an implicit contrast between Rousseau's 'extremist republicanism', according to which freedom requires a public-spirited citizenry, agrarianism and self-sufficiency, and Smith's own 'modern, moderate republicanism', which rests instead on the negative virtue of justice and the so-called bourgeois virtues (Schliesser 2006: 347; see also 345–6). Similarly, Donald Winch construes Smith's statement as an allusion to Rousseau's 'republican conception of liberty', as opposed to 'the commercial alternative', although he does not elaborate the point much further (Winch 1995: 8). Indeed, I myself offered a similar reading in another work – without thinking the matter through sufficiently, I now realise – writing that

> it is not surprising that in his letter to the *Edinburgh Review* Smith had proclaimed that Rousseau's writings embody 'the true spirit of a republican *carried a little too far*.' Whereas Rousseau sees true freedom as a matter of collective self-government, Smith . . . sees it as consisting instead in a sense of security and personal independence. (Rasmussen 2013: 68)

I now believe this reading is mistaken: when Smith declares that Rousseau carries the true spirit of a republican a little too far, he is *not* – or at least not primarily – referring to Rousseau's 'positive' conception of liberty. The one scholar who has interpreted Smith's claim correctly thus far, to my knowledge, is Pierre Force. Throughout his book Force emphasises the parallels between Smith and Rousseau, particularly with respect to the principal themes of civic humanism: critique of the corrupting influence of luxury and wealth, praise of poverty and virtue. In the conclusion of his review of the *Second Discourse*, Smith characterized Rousseau's book as manifesting 'the true spirit of a republican carried a little too far.' In other words, Smith saw Rousseau as someone who shared his republican values, but expressed them in an extremist fashion. (Force 2003: 159)

As I have indicated elsewhere, I believe that Force drastically over-states the extent to which Smith shared Rousseau's values (see Rasmussen 2008: 64–5; 2013: 55–6; 2014: 286). For all of Smith's awareness of the potential drawbacks of commerce and commercial society, in the end there is no doubt that he is a proponent of both. Smith does not believe that luxury and wealth are inherently 'corrupting', and he most certainly does not 'praise' poverty, as Force claims; indeed, his entire political economy is dedicated to combating it. While Force's overall reading of Smith is flawed, however, I will argue that his interpretation is on the mark with respect to the specific issue of what Smith meant in stating that Rousseau carries the true spirit of a republican a little too far: this line is not a reference to Rousseau's 'positive' conception of liberty, but rather to his view that commerce is invariably corrupt and corrupting.

Smith and the Term 'Republican'

There has been a great deal of debate in the Smith literature regarding whether, or to what extent, Smith himself can properly be described as a 'republican'.[4] Those who hold that Smith *was* a republican in some sense have generally taken their cue from John Rae's influential biography of Smith, first published in 1895, which declares – immediately after a brief discussion of Smith's review of the *Discourse on Inequality* – that 'he seems to have been always theoretically a republican' (Rae 1965: 124). Rae's claim on this score appears to rest in turn on the (perhaps not entirely reliable) authority of Smith's self-described 'disciple', the Earl of Buchan, who asserted in an obituary that Smith 'approached to republicanism in his political principles'.[5] This position has gained added force in recent decades from the more categorical claim of the editors of the Glasgow edition of *The Theory of Moral Sentiments* that Smith 'was always a staunch republican in spirit'.[6]

Yet the precise meaning of such claims remains uncertain given that the term 'republican' had, as Winch notes, 'a fairly elastic meaning during the second half of the eighteenth century' (Winch 1978: 42; see also 41–4 more generally). Often it was used simply to refer to popular or representative governments, such as those of Holland or Geneva, as opposed to monarchies, or else to those who admired such governments. It was widely believed that this type of government was viable only in relatively small, egalitarian and homogeneous communities, so 'republican' sometimes implied (support for) one or all of these characteristics, as well.[7] In the British context, the term was frequently applied to those who believed that the balance of the mixed constitution had shifted too far towards monarchy. At other times, it was used to denote one or another aspect of the 'civic republican' (or, alternatively, 'classical republican' or 'civic humanist') tradition that has been brought to the fore by J. G. A. Pocock and others, according to which the truest or highest form of freedom is instantiated in a republic of virtuous citizens who dedicate themselves to the common good through political participation and military defence.[8] This latter meaning of the term, much more than the others, tends to entail a wariness of commerce, luxury and their corrupting effects. (This is the way Force generally uses it.) Given the many different meanings of the term, Duncan Forbes is right to maintain that in the end 'to describe Smith . . . as "always theoretically a republican", is not saying very much' (Forbes 1975: 195).

Leaving that issue aside, the obvious place to begin an inquiry into what Smith meant when he described Rousseau as a 'republican' is to examine how he uses the term elsewhere in his corpus. Unfortunately, such an examination does not prove particularly helpful, as Smith appears to use it in all of the different senses alluded to above, and does not always make his precise meaning explicit.[9] In his jurisprudence lectures, Smith divides governments into monarchies (ruled by a single person), aristocracies (ruled by a nobility) and democracies (ruled by the people as a whole) and follows Montesquieu in labelling both of the latter two as 'republican' (see especially LJA: 200, 404).[10] Accordingly, he most often uses the term as an adjective to describe the governments of ancient Greece and Rome, modern Switzerland and the Netherlands, and England during the Commonwealth period. He also uses it at least once to refer to the Whig party in Britain (LJA: 327; see also 318–19).

In *The Wealth of Nations*, Smith uses the term 'republican' only seven times. Four of these are straightforward descriptions of the governments of Switzerland and the Netherlands (see WN III. ii.20: 395; V.ii.k.80: 906, where Smith uses the term twice; and V.iii.3: 909). Another two appear in a discussion of the American colonies, although here Smith uses the term to describe not just the colonial governments but also the people's egalitarian 'manners'. After noting the lack of a hereditary nobility in America and the fact that colonial legislatures were held closely responsible to their constituents, he writes: 'there is more equality, therefore, among the English colonists than among the inhabitants of the mother country. Their manners are more republican, and their governments . . . have hitherto been more republican too' (WN IV.viii.b.51: 585).[11] The final appearance in *The Wealth of Nations* is the one where Smith comes closest to the civic republican sense of the term. In a prominent passage, he notes that 'men of republican principles have been jealous of a standing army as dangerous to liberty' (WN V.i.a.41: 706). He goes on to argue, in opposition to such 'republican principles', that as long as the military is subservient to the civil authorities, 'a standing army can never be dangerous to liberty', and in fact that it 'may in some cases be favourable to liberty', insofar as 'the security which it gives to the sovereign renders unnecessary that troublesome jealousy, which, in some modern republicks, seems to watch over the minutest actions, and to be at all times ready to disturb the peace of every citizen' (WN V.i.a.41: 706–7). In other words, Smith believed that those who worried about the dangers of standing armies – who included, it should be noted, many of his friends[12] – carried the spirit of a republican a little too far, much as he claimed Rousseau did in his *Letter to the Edinburgh Review*. This broadly 'civic' use of the term 'republican', then, would appear to shed the most light on his claim about Rousseau, although no clear or definite inference can be drawn here, given that the passages appeared almost two decades apart and that Rousseau does not so much as mention the idea of a standing army in the *Second Discourse*.

Ultimately, then, a review of Smith's use of the term 'republican' throughout his other writings offers only the smallest of clues as to what he meant when he claimed that Rousseau embodied 'the true spirit of a republican carried a little too far'. Given, however, that *all* of the different senses of this term are connected in one way or another to the (equally ambiguous) notion of 'liberty', the next logical step is to examine Smith's and Rousseau's respective understandings of this latter concept.

Smith and Positive Liberty

Smith and Rousseau are generally assumed to have adopted diametrically opposed views of liberty. Smith is almost universally seen as an archetypal advocate of the 'negative' concept of liberty, according to which freedom consists simply in the absence of restraints or interference from others, while Rousseau is just as widely considered one of the most powerful modern exponents of 'positive' liberty, according to which true freedom consists instead in (individual or collective) self-government – mastery of the passions, obedience to the general will, and the like.[13] This conventional view has considerable merit with respect to these thinkers' political ideals, but on the level of the individual it oversimplifies matters greatly. In fact, I will argue that Smith advocates something akin to positive liberty as a central feature of his moral theory and that Rousseau advocates negative liberty for all of those who are healthy enough to avoid abusing it.

There can be little question that Smith's political thought rests on a basically negative understanding of liberty.[14] He equates 'the liberty of every individual' with 'the sense which he has of his own security' (WN V.i.b.25: 722–3), and he famously advocates leaving 'every man ... perfectly free to pursue his own interest his own way', at least 'as long as he does not violate the laws of justice' (WN IV.ix.51: 687; see also IV.ix.3: 664). Book III of *The Wealth of Nations* draws a contrast between commercial liberty and the direct, personal dependence characteristic of the feudal age, when the serfs had little discretion about things such as where to live, what occupation to practise, how to use their property, and even whom to marry. It was only after people gained freedom of choice about these kinds of matters, Smith writes, that they 'became really free in our present sense of the word Freedom' (WN III.iii.5: 400). Of course, he does believe that the state has a significant role to play in providing for national defence, administering justice and establishing certain public works (see WN IV.ix.51: 687–8). Unlike, say, Jeremy Bentham in his extreme moments,[15] Smith recognises that not every law undermines liberty, and in fact that liberty is *advanced* by predictable rules of fair play and by the government's protection of individuals from each other and from other outside forces.[16] Nor does Smith's embrace of negative liberty lead him to advocate atomistic individualism. Society may be able to 'subsist' where people merely abstain from harming one another, he says, but it will not 'flourish' or be 'happy' unless the citizens 'are bound together by the agreeable bands of love and affection, and are, as it were, drawn to one common centre of mutual good offices' (TMS II.ii.3.1–3: 85–6).[17]

Smith denies emphatically, however, that people can attain true freedom only in and through politics or collective self-government. On the contrary, he depicts participatory republics of the kind found in ancient Greece and Rome as significant *threats* to freedom. He notes, first of all, that the self-government of the citizens depended on slavery: the only reason the citizens 'had it in their power to attend on publick deliberations' was that they 'had all their work done by slaves' (LJ: 410; see also 226, 242–3).[18] He also laments the tendency of these republics to subordinate the interests of individuals to the state's glory and military success. As Samuel Fleischacker (2004: 250; see also 250–7 more generally) writes, Smith holds that individuals 'should not identify their worth with their nation's glory, both because that has nothing to do with their individual worth and because such identification is the source of one of the greatest of human evils: war'. Smith does show some support for representation and a widespread franchise, but his reason for doing so is that elections serve as an important check on power, not that participating in politics allows people to attain freedom through collective self-government (see WN IV.vii.b.51: 584–5; LJ: 270–4, 422, 524). He in fact tends to speak of the desire to participate in politics in fairly derogatory terms, writing for instance that 'men desire to have some share in the management of publick affairs on account of the importance which it gives them' (WN IV.vii.c.74: 622) and that the 'prudent man ... has no taste for that foolish importance which many people wish to derive from appearing to have some influence in the management of [the affairs] of other people' (TMS VI.1.13: 215). And like David Hume before him and James Madison after him, Smith expresses deep concern about the 'rancorous and virulent factions which are inseparable from small democracies' (WN V.iii.90: 945).

Yet for all of his support for negative liberty – and opposition to positive liberty – *in politics*, Smith advocates something akin to positive liberty on the level of the individual. Self-command is, after all, in many ways the crowning virtue of *The Theory of Moral Sentiments*. Smith proclaims that 'self-command is not only itself a great virtue, but from it all the other virtues seem to derive their principal lustre' (TMS VI.iii.11: 241). This is so because almost all of the virtues that he discusses throughout the book require people to check their momentary passions and to moderate their self-love to the level with which an impartial spectator would sympathise (see TMS VI.iii.1: 237). 'Without the restraint which this principle imposes', Smith writes,

> every passion would, upon most occasions, rush headlong ... to its own gratification. Anger would follow the suggestions of its own fury; fear those of its own violent agitations. Regard to no time or place would induce vanity to refrain from the loudest and most impertinent ostentation; or voluptuousness from the most open, indecent, and scandalous indulgence. (TMS VI.concl.2: 262–3)

Self-command is, in other words, a necessary – although not sufficient – condition of living a moral life.[19] Admittedly, Smith never uses the language of liberty in making this point; that is, he never speaks of achieving 'freedom from one's passions', or the 'freedom of rational self-direction'. There is, in fact, no sustained or systematic discussion of liberty in the entirety of *The Theory of Moral Sentiments*. Yet the *idea* of positive liberty is clearly present in these passages; the notion of restraining or commanding one's passions is central to the positive conception of liberty in almost all of its various manifestations (see Berlin 1998: 203). Indeed, Edward Harpham goes so far as to declare that 'although Smith may have lacked the modern terminological distinctions, *The Theory of Moral Sentiments* is, for all intents and purposes, an inquiry into the question of positive liberty' and that 'a notion of positive liberty lies at the heart of' Smith's moral theory (Harpham 2000: 226, 229).

Many proponents of positive liberty – including Rousseau – extend this idea to the political sphere, believing that individual self-government depends on (or can be realised through) collective self-government. Smith, to repeat, does not. While he sees self-command as a prerequisite of a truly moral life, he does not believe that politics is the sole arena in which this virtue can be realised, or even that the state can effectively promote it. The state is, after all, administered by politicians, and Smith evinces a rather cynical view of these 'insidious and crafty animal[s]', repeatedly depicting them as partial, corrupt and grossly overconfident of their ability to effect change without producing unintended consequences (WN IV.ii.39: 468). Thus, he is sceptical about the capacity of governments to cultivate the moral character of their citizens directly.[20] One of the central purposes of *The Theory of Moral Sentiments* is to locate an alternative means of reaching this goal, one that does not require heavy-handed regulations on the part of the political (or ecclesiastical) authorities. Smith seeks to show that people will *naturally* tend to moderate their passions and seek to act so that an impartial spectator would approve of them, in the absence of coercive measures, thanks to the workings of sympathy, and that internal and social motivations are often far more effective than legal ones. Ironically, then, for Smith, 'governments foster virtue best where they refuse, directly, to foster virtue at all: just as they protect economic development best where they refuse, directly, to protect development' (Fleischacker 2002: 518–19).

Rousseau and Negative Liberty

Just as the conventional view of Smith as an advocate of negative liberty is accurate with respect to his *political* thought, the conventional view of Rousseau as an advocate of positive liberty is accurate with respect to *his* political thought.[21] Rousseau's stated aim in *The Social Contract* is to show how people can be united in society and placed under the rule of law while remaining as free as before, and his seemingly paradoxical solution to this problem is 'the total alienation of each associate with all of his rights to the whole community' (Rousseau 1997c: 20). This kind of 'total alienation' preserves people's freedom, according to Rousseau, because it ensures that they obey not another individual or group but the will of the community as a whole – the community of which they are an integral part – which means that they obey only laws that they themselves have chosen or willed. Because the citizens are themselves the author of the general will, they achieve freedom through collective self-government. They trade an utterly precarious 'natural freedom' – the ability to do and take whatever they desire – for a far more secure 'civil freedom' (Rousseau 1997c: 53–4). Hence, in stark contrast to Smith, Rousseau sees participatory republics on the model of ancient Sparta and Rome – as well as (an idealised version of) modern Geneva – as models of freedom. In the *Discourse on Political Economy* he puts the point succinctly: 'The fatherland cannot endure without freedom, nor freedom without virtue, nor virtue without citizens' (Rousseau 1997a: 50).

Moreover, Rousseau insists that the liberal regimes of modern Europe, which purported to protect people's negative liberties, in fact produced a great deal of *unfreedom*. He holds that this is true, in the first place, because extensive commerce, and the massive inequalities it engenders, fosters the dependence of the poor on the rich and the dependence of all on material goods and on opinion.[22] Further, Rousseau holds that even a government of this sort that starts out limited will ultimately grow to be despotic, since 'the same vices that make social institutions necessary make their abuse inevitable'. In other words, he claims that it is next to impossible, in the long run, to 'contain men without changing them' – that is, to prevent people from harming and exploiting one another without transforming them into virtuous citizens (Rousseau 1997b: 182; see also 185–6). More generally, Rousseau argues that even if people's negative liberties *were* adequately protected in such societies, both from the state and from each other, the people would still suffer from an even more profound form of enslavement: enslavement to their own passions, above all to *amour-propre* and all of the harsh, bitter feelings it produces. Hence his famous claim that 'the impulsion of mere appetite is slavery, and obedience to the law one has prescribed to oneself is freedom' (Rousseau 1997c: 54). For the vast majority of people in the modern world, whose passions or appetites would lead them far astray, freedom can be found only in self-mastery or obedience to a self-imposed law.

Yet however impracticable Rousseau deems negative liberty as a *political* ideal, he sees this kind of liberty as a supreme good for certain individuals.[23] After all, the innocent, happy, self-sufficient inhabitants of the 'pure' state of nature in the *Second Discourse* enjoyed what is perhaps the most negative form of liberty imaginable: complete independence and freedom from interference, unhampered even by the rule of law (see especially Rousseau 1997b: 157–9). Negative liberty was healthy in the state of nature, according to Rousseau, because *people* were healthy in the state of nature; they did not have the passions that would lead them to abuse it. Similarly, Rousseau favours negative liberty for those rare individuals of the modern world who are somehow able to retain or restore their natural goodness. In *The Reveries of the Solitary Walker*, he admits that he himself was far from a virtuous citizen and that he found it nearly impossible to overcome his inclinations and act out of a sense of duty (Rousseau 1992: 77). Yet he claims that his state of moral and intellectual isolation allowed him to (largely) avoid the ills associated with *amour-propre*, and thus that he too was able to enjoy negative liberty without the myriad problems that so often attend it. Indeed, he goes so far as to claim in this context that 'man's freedom' consists in 'never doing what he does not want to do; and that is the freedom I have always laid claim to' (Rousseau 1992: 83–4). For most people, he goes on to reiterate, a mere lack of compulsion would *not* render them truly free: 'busy, restless, ambitious, detesting freedom in others', they would 'torment themselves their whole life long by doing what is loathsome to them' and 'omit nothing servile in order to command' (Rousseau 1992: 84). But for certain rare individuals like himself, it seems, negative liberty *is* true liberty. A similar phenomenon is visible in *Emile*: for most of the book, the title character enjoys a kind of negative liberty: he feels no dependence on others and is given no duties that oppose his inclinations, yet his education in toughness, moderation and self-sufficiency keeps him healthy and happy.[24]

Of course, in Rousseau's eyes the individuals who are able to enjoy negative liberty without abusing it are exceptional in every sense of the term: the extreme primitiveness of natural man, the extreme isolation of his own life as a solitary walker, and the extremely painstaking education of Emile are not easily replicated. Indeed, Rousseau himself regarded the first and last of these models as *impossible* to replicate in the modern world, and he acknowledged that his own example would be unsuitable for the overwhelming majority of people (see Rasmussen 2008: 40–1, 44–7). Still, the fact that he considered negative liberty to be healthy for healthy individuals makes the contrast with Smith even starker.

On the level of politics, as is well known, Smith advocated negative liberty and stressed the dangers of positive liberty, while Rousseau advocated positive liberty and stressed the dangers of negative liberty. Conversely, on the level of the individual, Smith regarded a kind of positive liberty (self-command) as a necessary component of a moral life, while Rousseau regarded negative liberty as a supreme good for those who are sufficiently free of destructive passions that they will refrain from abusing it.

Carrying the Spirit of a Republican Too Far

We are now finally in a position to clarify what Smith meant when he claimed in his *Letter to the Edinburgh Review* that Rousseau embodied 'the true spirit of a republican carried a little too far'. It seems unlikely, first of all, that Smith used the term 'republican' here to refer to Rousseau's advocacy of a popular or representative form of government, as opposed to a monarchy. After all, he was referring to the *Second Discourse*, and Rousseau devotes very little attention to the subject of regime type in this work outside of the effusive dedication to the republic of Geneva.[25] And it is fairly clear that Smith did *not* believe that Rousseau carried his praise of Geneva too far, as later in his review he describes Rousseau's dedication as 'an agreeable, animated, and I believe too, a just panegyric' that 'expresses that ardent and passionate esteem which it becomes a good citizen to entertain for the government of his country and the character of his countrymen' (Letter: 254).[26] Thus, while in the rest of his corpus Smith uses 'republican' most often to denote popular or representative governments (and those who admired them), this does not seem to be the sense with which he applied the term to Rousseau.

It seems more probable, then, that Smith's description of Rousseau as a 'republican' was meant to point to some aspect of the civic republican outlook. (This was, recall, also the way he used the term in one prominent passage in *The Wealth of Nations*: see WN V.i.a.41: 706.) However, contrary to my own earlier assumption (see Rasmussen 2013: 68), it appears unlikely that Smith was referring to what we might call the 'constructive' side of the civic republican tradition, meaning the claim that true freedom is found only in and through politics – more specifically, in Rousseau's case, in obedience to the general will. Smith would surely oppose this side of Rousseau's outlook, but, once again, Rousseau's case for this conception of liberty is found not in the *Second Discourse* but rather in *The Social Contract* and his other political works.[27] Indeed, we have just seen that in the *Second Discourse* Rousseau generally employs and applauds a *negative* conception of liberty, painting an attractive picture of the 'natural freedom' enjoyed by the inhabitants of the 'pure' state of nature. And it is fairly clear that Smith noticed this aspect of the work, as it appears (at least obliquely) in each of the three lengthy passages that Smith translated for the readers of the *Edinburgh Review*.[28]

By a process of elimination, then, it seems most likely that Smith's reference was to what we might call the 'critical' side of the civic republican tradition – in this case, Rousseau's critique of commerce as invariably corrupt and corrupting. Of the principal threads of the *Second Discourse* (leaving aside, once again, the dedication), this is the aspect of the work that best fits the appellation 'republican'. And Smith's appreciation of this aspect of the work is unambiguous: the passages that he translates in his review centre on what are arguably Rousseau's three fundamental critiques of commercial society.[29] The first passage conveys Rousseau's claim that commercial society creates massive inequalities, thereby pitting people against one another; the second passage focuses on his claim that commercial society encourages personal dependence and *amour-propre*, thereby gravely corrupting morality; and the third and final passage highlights his claim that commercial society expands people's desires immensely, thereby inducing them to spend their entire lives toiling and striving in a vain attempt to attain a happiness that will always elude them (see Letter: 251–4). One of the main burdens of my book on these two thinkers was to show that Smith sympathised to a surprising degree with each of these Rousseauian critiques, but also offered a number of counter-arguments and pointed to a number of counter-measures for each of them.[30] All of this, of course, squares perfectly with the idea that Smith was referring to Rousseau's critique of commerce when he declared that Rousseau embodied 'the true spirit of a republican carried a little too far': for Smith, a true republican would recognise the potential dangers and drawbacks of commerce, but in his eyes Rousseau carries this spirit too far. Thus, while I did not examine (or even quote) this statement in my book, I now think that, properly interpreted, it could have served as the book's thesis statement.

Notes

1. For a much fuller examination of Smith's review, see Rasmussen (2008: 59–70).
2. For a slightly different but related suggestion, see Melzer (1990: 25–6). David Hume (1998: 91) also uses the phrase 'philosophical chymistry', although he employs it to describe the misguided attempts of 'an Epicurean or a Hobbist' to subsume all passions into self-love.

3. See the editors' introduction to this volume.

4. For citations to some of the literature on both sides of this question, see Hanley (2009: 32 n. 27).

5. Buchan wrote the obituary under the pen name 'Ascanius': see Ascanius (1791: 164–5). For a comment on the general unreliability of Buchan's testimony, see Viner (1965: 22–3).

6. See D. D. Raphael and A. L. Macfie's introduction in TMS: 19.

7. On the 'small-republic thesis' and the various challenges to it in the eighteenth and early nineteenth centuries, see Levy (2006).

8. See especially Pocock (1975; 1985). For Pocock's view of the Scottish Enlightenment in relation to the civic republican tradition, see Pocock (1983). Pocock portrays Rousseau as falling squarely within this tradition and even claims that 'Rousseau was the Machiavelli of the eighteenth century' (Pocock 1975: 504).

9. Smith's use of the term 'republican' is restricted almost exclusively to the *Lectures on Jurisprudence* (where he uses the term some thirty-five times) and *The Wealth of Nations* (seven times). He never uses the term in his correspondence, in his lectures on rhetoric and *belles lettres*, or in any of the pieces collected in *Essays on Philosophical Subjects* other than the reference to Rousseau under consideration in this chapter. It appears only once in *The Theory of Moral Sentiments*, in a passage that was added in the sixth edition (1790), where he offhandedly mentions the 'republican party' of Rome in the context of a discussion of suicide (see TMS VII.ii.32: 286).

10. Smith does not follow Montesquieu, however, in distinguishing monarchy (in which one person rules through fixed laws) from despotism (in which one person rules based on his own will or caprice). For Montesquieu's typology, see Montesquieu (1989: 10).

11. On the basis of this passage Forbes maintains that 'what "republicanism" seems to mean, above all, in *The Wealth of Nations* is the "equality" which is the result of freedom from aristocratic privilege and oppression, and along with this goes a more representative or democratic or "republican" government' (Forbes 1975: 196).

12. Most of the leading figures of the Scottish Enlightenment – the Moderate literati – championed the reinstitution of a Scottish militia with universal (male) conscription as a means of promoting civic and martial virtue, with the significant exceptions of Smith and Hume, both of whom expressed more doubts and worries than hopes on this score. See Robertson (1985: chs 3, 7 and 8) and Sher (1985: ch. 6).

13. The *locus classicus* of the distinction between negative and positive liberty, Isaiah Berlin's famous essay, places Smith and Rousseau

firmly in these opposing camps. See Berlin (1998: 198, 208, 216, 219, 233–4).

14. Samuel Fleischacker has argued that Smith in fact upheld a 'third concept of liberty' that focuses neither on a simple lack of interference nor on collective self-government, but rather on the individual exercise of judgement (Fleischacker 1999: chs 6–8). The brief overview offered here is, I believe, compatible with Fleischacker's nuanced and much more detailed analysis.

15. Bentham goes so far as to claim at one point that 'every law is an evil, for every law is an infraction of liberty' (Bentham 1914: 65).

16. As Emma Rothschild rightly notes, throughout his writings Smith is concerned that the government be *strong* enough to defend individuals against the sometimes oppressive measures of 'churches, parish overseers, corporations . . . masters, proprietors' and the like. This is an important and under-appreciated point: 'The criticism of local institutions, with their hidden, not quite public, not quite private powers, is at the heart of Smith's politics' (Rothschild 2001: 71, 108; see also 32).

17. Given that a degree of reciprocal concern among fellow citizens is indispensable for a society to truly thrive, Smith holds that it is within the state's purview to promote the moral character of its citizens, writing that 'the civil magistrate . . . may prescribe rules . . . which not only prohibit mutual injuries among fellow-citizens, but command mutual good offices to a certain degree' (TMS II.ii.1.8: 81; see also WN V.i.f.61: 788). He warns, though, that 'of all the duties of a law-giver . . . this, perhaps, is that which it requires the greatest delicacy and reserve to execute with propriety and judgment. To neglect it altogether exposes the commonwealth to many gross disorders and shocking enormities, and to push it too far is destructive of all liberty, security, and justice' (TMS II.ii.1.8: 81).

18. Smith maintains that republican governments are less likely to abolish slavery, and republican peoples less likely to treat their slaves humanely, than are monarchs and their subjects (see especially LJA: 181–5, 255; and WN IV.vii.b.55–6: 587–8).

19. Far from claiming that self-command is *sufficient* for living a moral life, Smith stresses the danger inherent in the fact that we tend to admire self-command even when it is employed for the sake of pernicious ends: see TMS VI.iii.12: 241–2; and VI.concl.7: 264. This point has been stressed by Hanley (2009: 169–70).

20. While Smith is sceptical about the ability of governments to cultivate virtue directly, through coercive measures, he regards compulsory,

state-supported education as an important means of fostering it indirectly, in a less forceful way. In his view, education helps to render people 'less liable ... to the delusions of enthusiasm and superstition', 'more decent and orderly' and 'more disposed to examine, and more capable of seeing through, the interested complaints of faction and sedition' (WN V.i.f.61: 788).

21. While I concur with Isaiah Berlin – and countless others – that Rousseau's political thought places him squarely in the positive liberty camp, I do not mean to imply agreement with Berlin's claim that he was therefore 'one of the most sinister and most formidable enemies of liberty in the whole history of modern thought' (Berlin 2002: 49).

22. This theme pervades Rousseau's corpus, but see especially Rousseau (1997b: 170–1, 183–4).

23. Although I do not claim to have canvassed the entirety of the vast Rousseau literature on this point, the closest anticipation of this argument that I know of can be found in Wokler (2012: esp. 161–4).

24. Of course, the fact that Emile *feels* no dependence on others is made possible only by the constant vigilance and manipulation of his governor, Jean-Jacques, but he at least has the *experience* of negative liberty. It is also interesting to note that as he approaches adulthood Emile seems to achieve a kind of positive liberty – that is, he chooses or wills to obey Jean-Jacques, even when the governor's commands thwart his present inclinations, precisely in order to protect himself from his own passions – although I cannot pursue the implications of this point here (see especially Rousseau 1979: 325). An even clearer model of a healthy individual enjoying negative liberty in this work comes in a digression at the end of Book 4, where Rousseau describes how he would live if he were rich. For analysis of this passage, see Rasmussen (2015).

25. Indeed, there is only a single paragraph devoted to the subject of regime type in the body of the *Second Discourse*; see Rousseau (1997b: 181).

26. For further discussion of this statement, see Rasmussen (2008: 66–8).

27. There are only the smallest of hints at Rousseau's positive conception of liberty in the body of the *Second Discourse*, such as his fleeting reference to a 'true' social contract in which the people 'united their wills into a single one' (Rousseau 1997b: 180).

28. Smith quotes Rousseau as claiming that before the rise of the division of labour, people 'lived free, healthful, humane and happy ...

and continued to enjoy amongst themselves the sweets of an independent society' (first passage); that people were originally 'free and independent' (second passage); and that 'the savage breathes nothing but liberty and repose' (third passage). See Letter: 252–3.

29. I have made this case at much greater length in Rasmussen (2008: 25–40, 68–70).

30. For Smith's sympathy with these critiques, see Rasmussen (2008: ch. 2). For the counter-arguments and counter-measures, see Rasmussen (2008: chs 3–4).

Bibliography

Ascanius [Earl of Buchan] (1791), letter to the editor of *The Bee, or Literary Weekly Intelligencer*, 8 June 1791.

Bentham, Jeremy (1914) [1840], *The Theory of Legislation*, Oxford: Oxford University Press.

Berlin, Isaiah (1998), 'Two Concepts of Liberty', in Isaiah Berlin, *The Proper Study of Mankind: An Anthology of Essays*, ed. Henry Hardy and Roger Hausheer, New York: Farrar, Straus and Giroux, 191–242.

Berlin, Isaiah (2002), *Freedom and Its Betrayal: Six Enemies of Human Liberty*, Princeton: Princeton University Press.

Fleischacker, Samuel (1999), *A Third Concept of Liberty: Judgment and Freedom in Kant and Adam Smith*, Princeton: Princeton University Press.

Fleischacker, Samuel (2002), 'Adam Smith', in Steven Nadler (ed.), *A Companion to Early Modern Philosophy*, Oxford: Blackwell, 505–26.

Fleischacker, Samuel (2004), *On Adam Smith's Wealth of Nations: A Philosophical Companion*, Princeton: Princeton University Press.

Forbes, Duncan (1975), 'Sceptical Whiggism, Commerce, and Liberty', in Andrew S. Skinner and Thomas Wilson (eds), *Essays on Adam Smith*, Oxford: Clarendon Press, 179–201.

Force, Pierre (2003), *Self-Interest before Adam Smith: A Genealogy of Economic Science*, Cambridge: Cambridge University Press.

Hanley, Ryan Patrick (2009), *Adam Smith and the Character of Virtue*, Cambridge: Cambridge University Press.

Harpham, Edward J. (2000), 'The Problem of Liberty in the Thought of Adam Smith', *Journal of the History of Economic Thought*, 22.2, 217–37.

Hume, David (1998) [1751], *An Enquiry Concerning the Principles of Morals*, ed. Tom L. Beauchamp, Oxford: Clarendon Press.

Levy, Jacob T. (2006), 'Beyond Publius: Montesquieu, Liberal Republicanism and the Small-Republic Thesis', *History of Political Thought*, 27.1, 50–90.

Melzer, Arthur M. (1990), *The Natural Goodness of Man: On the System of Rousseau's Thought*, Chicago: University of Chicago Press.

Montesquieu, Charles de Secondat, baron de (1989) [1748], *The Spirit of the Laws*, trans. Anne M. Cohler, Basia C. Miller and Harold S. Stone, Cambridge: Cambridge University Press.

Pocock, J. G. A. (1975), *The Machiavellian Moment: Florentine Political Thought and the Atlantic Republican Tradition*, Princeton: Princeton University Press.

Pocock, J. G. A. (1983), 'Cambridge Paradigms and Scotch Philosophers: A Study of the Relations between the Civic Humanist and the Civil Jurisprudence Interpretation of Eighteenth-Century Social Thought', in Istvan Hont and Michael Ignatieff (eds), *Wealth and Virtue: The Shaping of Political Economy in the Scottish Enlightenment*, Cambridge: Cambridge University Press, 235–52.

Pocock, J. G. A. (1985), *Virtue, Commerce, and History: Essays on Political Thought and History, Chiefly in the Eighteenth Century*, Cambridge: Cambridge University Press.

Rae, John (1965) [1895], *Life of Adam Smith*, with introductory guide by Jacob Viner, New York: Augustus M. Kelley.

Rasmussen, Dennis C. (2008), *The Problems and Promise of Commercial Society: Adam Smith's Response to Rousseau*, University Park: Pennsylvania State University Press.

Rasmussen, Dennis C. (2013), 'Adam Smith and Rousseau: Enlightenment and Counter-Enlightenment', in Christopher J. Berry, Maria Pia Paganelli and Craig Smith (eds), *The Oxford Handbook of Adam Smith*, Oxford: Oxford University Press, 54–76.

Rasmussen, Dennis C. (2014), *The Pragmatic Enlightenment: Recovering the Liberalism of Hume, Smith, Montesquieu, and Voltaire*, Cambridge: Cambridge University Press.

Rasmussen, Dennis C. (2015), 'If Rousseau Were Rich: Another Model of the Good Life', *History of Political Thought*, 36.3, 499–520.

Robertson, John (1985), *The Scottish Enlightenment and the Militia Issue*, Edinburgh: John Donald.

Rothschild, Emma (2001), *Economic Sentiments: Adam Smith, Condorcet, and the Enlightenment*, Cambridge, MA: Harvard University Press.

Rousseau, Jean-Jacques (1979) [1762], *Emile, or On Education*, trans. Allan Bloom, New York: Basic Books.

Rousseau, Jean-Jacques (1992) [1782], *The Reveries of the Solitary Walker*, trans. Charles E. Butterworth, Indianapolis: Hackett.

Rousseau, Jean-Jacques (1997a) [1755], *Discourse on Political Economy*, in *The Social Contract and Other Later Political Writings*, ed. Victor Gourevitch, Cambridge: Cambridge University Press.

Rousseau, Jean-Jacques (1997b) [1755], *Discourse on the Origin and Foundations of Inequality Among Men*, in *The Discourses and Other Early Political Writings*, ed. Victor Gourevitch, Cambridge: Cambridge University Press.

Rousseau, Jean-Jacques (1997c) [1762], *Of the Social Contract*, in *The Social Contract and Other Later Political Writings*, ed. Victor Gourevitch, Cambridge: Cambridge University Press.

Schliesser, Eric (2006), 'Adam Smith's Benevolent and Self-Interested Conception of Philosophy', in Leonidas Montes and Eric Schliesser (eds), *New Voices on Adam Smith*, New York: Routledge.

Sher, Richard B. (1985), *Church and University in the Scottish Enlightenment: The Moderate Literati of Edinburgh*, Edinburgh: Edinburgh University Press.

Viner, Jacob (1965), 'Guide to John Rae's *Life of Adam Smith*', in John Rae, *Life of Adam Smith*, New York: Augustus M. Kelley, 5–145.

Winch, Donald (1978), *Adam Smith's Politics: An Essay in Historiographic Revision*, Cambridge: Cambridge University Press.

Winch, Donald (1995), 'Mandeville, Rousseau, and the Paradox in Favour of Luxury', Carlyle Lecture delivered at Oxford University, http://www.intellectualhistory.net/donald-winch (last accessed March 2015).

Wokler, Robert (2012), 'Rousseau's Two Concepts of Liberty', in Bryan Garsten (ed.), *Rousseau, the Age of Enlightenment, and Their Legacies*, Princeton: Princeton University Press, 154–84.

13

Left to Their Own Devices: Smith and Rousseau on Public Opinion and the Role of the State

Jason Neidleman

Once the people become sovereign – as they ostensibly have in today's self-described democracies – public opinion must play some role in determining the legitimacy of sovereign power.[1] In standard treatments of democratic politics, public opinion – the will of the people – is widely assumed to be the origin of public policy. While empirical studies may call into question the extent to which public policy does *in fact* reflect public opinion (Gilens and Page 2014; Enns 2015; Bashir 2015), there is no debate among normative theorists of democracy that public policy *ought* to reflect public opinion. There may be disagreement about how, how much, and subject to which constraints public opinion ought to be reflected in public policy, but there is a general consensus that respect for public opinion is essential to the legitimate exercise of sovereign power (Fishkin 1997; Urbinati 2014).[2]

Public opinion derives from a variety of sources, far too numerous to list and probably impossible to fully catalogue. One of those sources – the one that will be explored in this essay – is the government itself, through an activity that is referred to variously as statesmanship, nation building, civic education or simply government. How (and how much) the government influences public opinion is not clear but has recently become a subject of sustained interest among political scientists (Bullock 2011; Matsubayashi 2012; Boudreau and MacKenzie 2013). Rousseau for his part believed that the effect was substantial: 'It is certain that the people are in the long run what the government makes them' (PE OC III: 251; *Collected* III: 148).[3] Whether this is the case or not, it *is* clear is that political elites attempt – and often have no better option than to attempt – to manage public opinion. This essay explores the role of the state in the formation of public opinion in the works of Adam Smith and Jean-Jacques Rousseau.

For ancient political thinkers, the management of public opinion was the government's chief function. The government's success or failure in this regard was the measure of its success or failure generally, and the project itself was normatively unproblematic, because they in no way believed that the exercise of sovereign power needed to be justified *via* a notion of the will of the people. By contrast, for Enlightenment thinkers, including Smith and Rousseau, the project of managing public opinion was fraught with justificatory dilemmas. The very entity that is meant to execute the will of the people is also at the same time charged with forming it. While Smith and Rousseau recognised the urgency of the endeavour, they were worried about sanctioning a role for the government in the formation of public opinion. Enlightenment models of political legitimacy presupposed that the relationship between public opinion and governance moves from the former to latter, as the sovereign people embody their will in government. And yet Smith and Rousseau – the latter far more than the former – acknowledged the necessity of the inverse as well. That is, they envisioned a role for the government in the process of opinion formation. Smith, for example, described 'management and persuasion' as the 'easiest and the safest instruments of government' (WN V.i.g.21: 799), while Rousseau identified the 'talent of a leader' as the ability to 'disguise his power to make it less odious' or, famously, 'to persuade without convincing' (PE OC III: 250; *Collected* III: 147; SC OC III: 383; *Collected* IV: 156).

Smith and Rousseau treated this dimension of politics as essential, but, in our own time, the only people interested in articulating a role for the government in managing public opinion are confined to bastions of the cultural right and a very few narrow concerns on the cultural left. Academic philosophers and political theorists are mainly interested in exposing the ways in which public opinion is subverted, distorted, or, as Nadia Urbinati puts it, 'disfigured' by attempts to influence the manner by which the 'will of the people' is constituted or construed.[4] There is much less interest in developing a *normative* account of nation building – of what leaders ought to do enlighten public opinion – because such a project seems unavoidably elitist or anti-democratic. In fact, in approaching this topic through the writings of Smith and

Rousseau, we get a good sense of how and why this question became problematic. It is a story about how subjects became sovereign, a story about democratic or popular sovereignty. If we temporarily permit ourselves to have recourse to concepts that I hope to complicate in this essay – liberalism and republicanism – we can sketch a preliminary account of the difference between the two figures on the question of nation building. Because Smith's overriding political impulses were *liberal*, his concerns about the project of enlightened will-formation revolved around the dangers to individual liberty associated with concentrating power in the government. Rousseau's overriding political impulses were, by contrast, *republican*, and so he was concerned not only about how individual liberty might be subverted by a powerful government but also about how to justify government intervention into the process of will-formation. In short, in making the people sovereign, Rousseau increased the urgency of nation building while simultaneously undermining its legitimacy.

In this essay I primarily emphasise the differences between Smith and Rousseau, but, as will become clear, there are many similarities as well. These have been ably described by Ryan Hanley (2008) in an essay called 'Enlightened Nation Building: The "Science of the Legislator" in Adam Smith and Rousseau', from which I have appropriated much for purposes of this essay, including the phrase 'enlightened nation building'. Hanley shows how, in spite of their differences, Rousseau and Smith share similar concerns about the forces that threaten modern societies and adopt similar strategies with respect to protecting society from those forces.[5] Supplemented with Istvan Hont's lectures on Smith and Rousseau (see below), this gives us a good account of the symmetries in the two philosophers' diagnoses of the problem and their prescribed remedies. Rather than rehearse these readings in this essay, I build on them by specifying what differences remain once the similarities have been cancelled out and by explaining what accounts for those differences. In short, it is neither the diagnosis nor the solution that most distinguishes Smith from Rousseau; it is rather 1) the *magnitude* of the dangers they identify and 2) the *stakes* they associate with failing to overcome those dangers. For Rousseau, failure to overcome the problems posed by commercial society vitiates the republican project itself; for Smith, by contrast, the consequences of failure are borne by individuals in the form of an impoverished inner life, but the political project remains viable for him even if the excesses of commercial society are allowed to proliferate.

My argument proceeds in three stages. The first section of the essay describes *what* distinguishes Smith from Rousseau with respect to the role of the government in the formation of public opinion. The second section explains *why* the two differ in the ways that they do on this subject. The final section assesses the legitimacy of the nation-building project and then offers a Rousseauian corrective to Smith and a Smithian corrective to Rousseau, the combination of which could be helpful in re-animating this dormant corner of democratic theory.

The Role of the State in Guiding Public Opinion

Given that Smith is so closely associated with liberal, market-oriented, proto-capitalist political theory and Rousseau with republican, autarchic, proto-socialist political theory, it is perhaps surprising to discover that they not only share similar diagnoses of the problems associated with commercial society but that they are quite close with respect to the public policy they favour as a response to those problems. Istvan Hont's lectures on Smith and Rousseau offer a good entry point for understanding how this could have been the case. Particularly helpful is Hont's choice to situate Smith and Rousseau within the context of commercial society – to see them as writing in reaction to a specific set of historical developments broadly understood as the displacement of involuntary bonds of kinship or social class by voluntary relations based in rationality and self-interest.[6] In reading them through the lens of commercial society, we are able to put them into more productive conversation than we might be able to do given their otherwise quite distinct points of emphasis and departure. Hont prompts us to think about Smith and Rousseau as proposing distinct answers to the same question – namely, what was the right type of state for the kind of society that was emerging across Europe in the eighteenth century?

For Hont, Smith and Rousseau were optimists, inasmuch as they believed in the possibility of political redemption, in the power of the state to solve (or at least come close to solving) the problems posed by commercial society. They both believed that we have it in us to solve our problems. Their optimism, Hont argues, is to be situated against the prevailing view of Jansenists such as Pierre Nicole, for whom this world was irredeemably flawed, and for whom the state could only temper the fallen nature of human beings so as to produce moments of intermittent peace. For the Jansenists, true redemption could only come later, while, for Smith and Rousseau, this world was itself redeemable (Hont 2015: 54). That said, with respect to the project of enlightened nation building, the path to redemption was much more treacherous for Rousseau than it was for Smith. For Smith, the government should act to smooth out the rough edges of public opinion, but it need not undertake – as Rousseau will argue – a transformation of human nature.

For Smith, the first obligation of the magistrate with respect to the policing of public opinion is to ensure that criminals are identified, prosecuted and punished appropriately. Though we normally think of punishment as a way of controlling behaviour, for Smith punishment is equally important as a way of influencing public opinion, particularly with respect to resentment. Resentment spurs within each person a desire for the righting of wrongs, a desire to see that justice is done (TMS II.ii.1.4: 79). Resentment can become dangerous when it is allowed to develop into hatred and a desire for revenge, but within the constraints of a legal apparatus it provides the affective support for the formal apparatus of crime and punishment (TMS III.i.5.7: 76). While the dangers Smith associated with resentment usually emerge from its excesses, when resentment is too little felt so too will be the corresponding desire to see that justice is done. So, the government must apply the law consistently and fairly so as to ensure that resentment is expressed and constrained in ways that are conducive to the common welfare.

Secondly, and here we see the most resonant affinities with Rousseau, Smith envisioned a role for the state in honouring certain forms of esteem. Smith, like Rousseau, believed that a desire for the approval of others – the desire for 'approbation' as Smith called it – was among our most basic moral sentiments. People are so enamoured of esteem, Smith wrote in *The Theory of Moral Sentiments*, that they are often willing to forsake that which is estimable or *worthy* of esteem in favour of that which *brings* honour or esteem (TMS VII.ii.4.10: 310–11). Given that this is the case, it becomes important that citizens esteem the right things. Accolades must be awarded for behaviour that serves the public interest or that is at least not inconsistent with the public interest. While Smith was a liberal, his liberalism was not grounded in a principled opposition to government participation in the formation of civic virtue. It was much more pragmatic, as Dennis Rasmussen (2014) has argued. It was much more about the advantages that could be derived from respecting the liberty of individuals. But Smith was very willing to acknowledge that there are also perils associated with the unconstrained interaction of individuals upon one another. This allowed him to be friendly to some of the nation building that we typically associate with Rousseauian republicanism.

The greatest cause of corruption for our moral sentiments, Smith wrote, is the disposition to admire, and 'almost to worship', the rich and the powerful and to 'despise' or at least to 'neglect' the poor (TMS I.iii.3.1: 61). Smith also worried that the idleness of merchants would lead them to 'riot and debauchery'. He worried that commerce would extinguish the 'martial spirit', and that this would in turn necessitate a professional class of warriors to provide for the common defence (LJB: 540–1). And then there are the problems associated with the division of labour: worldviews have a tendency to narrow when a person's time is occupied with the highly specialised tasks required of them in differentiated economies, as 'when a person's whole attention is bestowed on the 17th part of a pin or the 80th part of a button' (LJB: 549). In words that echo Rousseau, Smith contrasted modern human beings with 'our ancestors' who were 'brave and warlike' because 'their minds were not enervated by cultivating arts and commerce' (LJB: 549). The result, Smith feared (in language so desperate that it rivals Rousseau's darkest moments), would be that citizens may reach the point where they are 'incapable of defending [their] country in war' and 'incapable of exerting [their] strength with vigour and perseverance, in any other employment than that to which he has been bred' (WN V.i.f.50: 782). And so Smith envisioned a role for government here: 'The great body of the people', Smith wrote, will fall into 'torpor' and become as 'stupid and ignorant as it is possible for a human creature to become . . . unless the government takes some pains to prevent it' (WN V.i.f.50: 782).

Smith's liberalism did not prevent him from assigning to the government the formal authority to participate in enlightened nation building. Indeed, for the reasons given above, he believed it to be an affirmative obligation. As for precisely *how* the government should carry out this responsibility, Smith was vague. He wrote that education is useful for overcoming the stultifying ignorance caused by the division of labour in commercial society, that it can dissuade people from the 'delusions of enthusiasm and superstition' which 'occasion the most dreadful disorders', and that it can instil the judgement required to resist what Smith calls 'wanton or unnecessary' opposition to the state (WN V.i.f.g.61: 788). But he acknowledged that further remedies would be required to address the problem of feebleness – both with respect to individual character and the collective defence. While he refers to the 'ancient institutions of Greece and Rome' which were effective at maintaining the 'martial spirit' of the people, he does not seem to think there exists an equivalent for modern, commercial societies. Neither does he specify precisely how the government might act to temper the tendency among citizens in a commercial society to become overly enamoured of the rich and powerful and to neglect the suffering of the poor and the powerless.

The third element of the magistrate's role with respect to the management of public opinion concerns the power of factions, the Church in particular. The 'animosity of hostile factions' was, for Smith, a greater threat than even the animosity of hostile nations: 'Of all the corrupters of moral sentiments, therefore, faction and fanaticism have always been by far the greatest' (TMS III.3.43: 156). Smith was not hostile to religion itself, which he in fact lauded for its power to turn principles of morality into a sacred duty. However, he was extremely concerned about religion's tendency towards zealotry and superstition, and, especially, the commingling of earthly and spiritual power, what he called the 'temporal power of the clergy' (WN V.i.g.25: 803). Direct persecution of the clergy backfires, as it only drives people in greater numbers to the persecuted priest: 'Fear is in almost all cases a wretched instrument of government'; it serves only to confirm the opposition of the priests and their followers, where a more gentle approach could get them to soften (WN V.i.g.19: 798). Instead, the state should encourage two things: education and public diversions. Science, Smith wrote, is the 'great antidote' to the 'poison of enthusiasm and superstition'. And public diversions, such as painting, poetry, music and dancing – which have historically been so derided by those fearful of 'popular frenzies' – serve to dissipate the 'melancholy and gloomy humour which is almost always the nurse of popular superstition and enthusiasm' (WN V.i.g.15: 796). The arts are to be encouraged – in spite of Smith's concerns about

their effect on martial spirit – as they counteract religious superstition; satire is to be supported in particular as it subjects deviancy
to ridicule and tends towards the 'reformation of manners and
the benefit of mankind' (LRBL i.v.116: 47). Ultimately, Smith
was confident that 'the gradual improvements of arts, manufactures, and commerce' would result in a waning of ecclesiastical
authority (WN V.i.g.24–5: 803). The magistrate should encourage
these things, but the key is to allow them to operate of their own
accord, to insinuate themselves into the culture. Indeed, Smith was
generally optimistic about the emergent commercial societies of
eighteenth-century Europe, and this optimism is reflected in the
significant but limited role he assigns to the state in the cultivation
of salutary public opinions.

For Rousseau, the threats posed by commercial society were
more serious. Consequently, Rousseau's government must do all
of the things Smith recommends, but it must do more than that.
The task of aligning public opinion with public policy is so onerous
that Rousseau frequently expressed doubt as to whether it could
be done, at one point suggesting that there was only a single place
in Europe – Corsica – that could manage it. While both men may
have been optimists when put alongside the Jansenists, Rousseau,
contra Hont, was not the optimist that Smith was. Smith thought
us fortunate that there is a symmetry between the virtues of the
good person and the virtues required for commerce to flourish.
The symmetry is not perfect but neither are the two inherently at
odds. Moreover, with respect to the desire for approbation, there
was for Smith an internal, self-regulating constraint in the form
of an equally strong desire to be worthy of approval. The 'most
sincere praise', Smith wrote, 'gives little pleasure, without praiseworthiness' (TMS III.2.4: 114). For Rousseau, by contrast, the
desire for approval, which he called *amour-propre*, had no such
tethering mechanism and tended to attach itself to the corrupt
vagaries of popular taste. The government could not allow for
an invisible hand of the marketplace, because, left to their own
devices, the people would pursue personal rather than civic ends.
The drive for distinction must be directed towards civic ends and
away from personal ones.

Moreover, the consequences of failing to constrain the desire
for approval were greater for Rousseau, whose republic of virtue
would stand or fall based on its capacity to control and redirect
amour-propre. For Rousseau, personal ambition was at odds with

the common good unless it could be transformed into a general-ised form of *amour-propre* – love of self based on that which is shared with others rather than love of self based on that which distinguishes us from others and therefore separates us from our compatriots.[7] For Smith, enlightened nation building was needed to counteract the ill effects of an unconstrained marketplace. It worked to smooth out the rough edges of commercial society. But Rousseau's project of nation building was much more thorough-going, much more radical: 'Whoever gets involved in founding a people ought to know how to dominate opinions and govern men's passions by them' (GP OC III: 95–6; *Collected* XI: 179). It is not enough to smooth out commercial society's rough edges; Rousseau's republic of virtue requires a wholesale transforma-tion. Smith's nation-building activities were corrective and inter-mittent. Rousseau's were ongoing; indeed they were the chief function of government.

Like Smith, Rousseau was worried about factions. He was worried about them for all of the reasons Smith was worried about them, but also for reasons that went further. Particularity itself was a concern for Rousseau because it interfered with the people's ability to express its collective interest, which Rousseau conceptualised through his famous idea of the general will. And so Rousseau's magistrate or Legislator must work to curb the influ-ence of 'partial societies' over the deliberative process. Particularity is an inevitable outgrowth of liberty; it cannot be eliminated, and any attempt to eliminate it would compromise personal liberty. But its influence over *political* deliberation must be controlled. This is the meaning of Rousseau's insistence that there be 'no partial society *in the state*, and that each citizen give only his own opinion' (SC OC III: 372; *Collected* IV: 147–8, italics added). If there are partial societies, the best approach, as Smith also counselled, is that 'their number must be multiplied and their inequality prevented, as was done by Solon, Numa, and Servius' (SC OC III: 372; *Collected* IV: 148). This was important for Rousseau not only because it would prevent the usurpation of power or the fracturing of society, but also – and it is here that Rousseau's austerity *vis-à-vis* Smith becomes apparent – because particularity subverts attempts to for-mulate the general will (SC OC III: 421; *Collected* IV: 186).

Rousseau's magistrate, again like Smith's, must to work reori-ent citizens' imagination away from a love of wealth and luxury. And, again, the project for Rousseau is more radical that it was for

Smith, because the threat is greater and the need to overcome the threat is more urgent: 'Luxury corrupts everything, both the rich person who enjoys it and the wretch who covets it' (O OC III: 51; *Collected* II: 49). For Rousseau, commercial society was not a safe harbour for the passions, as it generally was for Smith. For Smith, the moral effects of commercial society were mainly benign, with excesses occurring around the edges. For Rousseau, by contrast, the very viability of a republican society was contingent upon reorienting the citizens' desire for wealth and luxury. In his advice to Poland, he wrote:

> I should like all the patriotic virtues to be given luster by means of honors, the citizens to be kept ceaselessly occupied with the father-land, it to be made their most important business, it to be kept inces-santly before their eyes. In this way they would have less, I admit it, opportunity and time for getting rich, but they would also have less desire and need to do so: their hearts would learn to know a different happiness than that of fortune, and that is the art of ennobling souls and of making them into an instrument and more powerful than gold. (GP OC III: 962; *Collected* XI: 176)[8]

In thinking through the problem of commercial society, Rousseau and Smith were interested in the conditions that would be required in order for the ordinary activity of commercial society, the ongoing, reciprocal activity of citizens upon one another, to be conducive to virtue. As long as societies remained simple, agrar-ian and small, Rousseau was confident that the reciprocal activity of citizens upon one another would be conducive to civic virtue. *But*, once societies turned to commerce, a series of transforma-tions occurred, and while Smith viewed these transformations with a mixture of optimism and chagrin – tending more towards optimism – Rousseau viewed them in overwhelmingly negative terms. We might put it this way: Rousseau's political science is designed to save citizenship from commercial society itself, while Smith's need only spare us from its excesses.

There are several areas in which Rousseau's advice to the mag-istrate goes well beyond Smith's.[9]

1) Whereas Smith was generally sanguine about the effects of the arts and sciences on public morality, Rousseau famously argued that the public's exposure to the arts and sciences – the theatre in particular – should be limited: 'All the eloquence of Demosthenes

could never revive a body enervated by luxury and the arts' (DAS OC III: 10; *Collected* II: 8).[10] Rousseau believed that the arts and sciences subvert the foundations of republican government, principally religion and patriotism.[11]

2) The government must instil in citizens a respect for ancient laws, customs and traditions. Rousseau advised Poland, for example, to 'never lose sight of the important maxim of not changing anything without necessity, neither to cut back not to add' (GP OC III: 985; *Collected* XI: 194).

3) The government must instil in citizens a love of the fatherland. For Rousseau, this meant expanding citizens' *amour-propre* such that it would include a love of their compatriots. Smith extolled the virtues (and acknowledged the dangers) of patriotism in *The Theory of Moral Sentiments*, but he did not assign the state a role in its cultivation (TMS VI.ii.2.2–3: 227–9). Rousseau's Legislator, by contrast, is tasked with the onerous responsibility of expanding citizens' affection beyond themselves, but not so far beyond themselves that it transcends national boundaries and thereby risks becoming dissolute. The Legislator must avoid the twin problems of particularity and cosmopolitanism and orient citizens' affections specifically towards the *patria* (E OC IV: 248–9; *Collected* XIII: 163–4, GP OC III: 958; *Collected* XI: 173, GM OC III: 286–7; *Collected* IV: 80–1).

4) The government must instil a civil religion. While Smith and Rousseau were both hostile to the Church, Rousseau was far more sanguine about religion itself, going so far as to endorse a quasi-establishment of religion in the form of the civil religion proposed at the end of the *Social Contract*. Rousseau regarded Christianity as 'contrary to the social spirit' (primarily because of its cosmopolitanism), but he also maintained that no state has ever been founded 'without religion serving as its base' (SC OC III: 465, 464; *Collected* IV: 220, 219). The reason for this was religion's capacity – also acknowledged by Smith – to sacralise civic obligations. And so Rousseau imagined an ecumenical civic faith that would be broad enough to include the basic principles of Christianity (in all of its denominations) as well as non-Christian religions and which could revive the ancients' religious devotion to the *patria*.

5) The government must censor opinions contrary to the general will: 'Just as the general will is declared by the law, public judgement is declared by censorship' (SC OC III: 458; *Collected* IV: 214). Rousseau advocated the use of a censorial tribunal, not to

form or alter mores, but to maintain them by preventing opinions from becoming corrupt.

In sum, the citizen must be transformed from an individual who 'by himself is a perfect and solitary whole' into a citizen who is 'part of a larger whole from which this individual receives ... his life and his being' (SC OC III: 381; *Collected* IV: 155). Some of this is achieved through the formal apparatus of the social contract itself, but much of it occurs through the activity of the government, which must, in Denise Schaeffer's felicitous phrase, 'reorient the political imagination' (Schaeffer 2010: 396).

An Explanation of the Difference

Why is Rousseau's position so much more austere than Smith's? Part of the explanation is a difference of opinion about commercial society. For Rousseau, the large commercial republics emerging in the eighteenth century could not succeed, because republican principles are compromised by the selfishness and materialism that accompany commerce and by the complexity and detachment that accompany expansive states. Smith, by contrast, regarded the emergence of commercial societies as on balance a positive development and was broadly sanguine about the moral dispositions that tend to accompany commercial society.

There is, for example, the well-known argument – sometimes referred to as the invisible hand – from *The Wealth of Nations* about the fortuitous symmetry between the self-interested actions of individual economic actors and the collective interest of society as a whole. There is the accompanying argument – sometimes referred to as *doux commerce* – that manners become softened and refined in commercial societies.[12] But, for Smith, our moral psychology *itself* inclines us towards propriety and civic virtue. Human beings have, he writes, a 'natural abhorrence for vice' (TMS I.ii.3.4: 36). When we feel ourselves succumbing to those sentiments that lead away from virtue, there is an even stronger inclination pulling us back:

> Hatred and anger are the greatest poison to the happiness of a good mind. There is, in the very feeling of those passions, something, harsh, jarring, and convulsive, something that tears and distracts the breast, and is altogether destructive of that composure and tranquillity of mind which is so necessary to happiness, and which is best promoted

by the contrary passions of gratitude and love ... If we yield to the dictates of revenge, it is with reluctance, from necessity, and in consequence of great and repeated provocations. (TMS I.ii.3.7–8: 37–8)

Smith was aware that there are those who will opt for anger and revenge over gratitude and love, but he did not worry that those divisive or destructive passions would displace the positive ones that we know to be more conducive to our own happiness and more amenable to the impartial spectator – the arbiter of propriety that resides innately within the gaze of every reasoning person. The sentiment of love is, 'in itself, agreeable to the person who feels it' (TMS I.ii.4.2: 39). It is as though there is a happy, peaceful state of being to which moral agents seek to return, a 'healthful state of the human constitution' as Smith puts it, which inclines us to linger in the 'agreeable and becoming' passions and to temper those that are disagreeable and destructive (TMS I.ii.4.2: 39, I.ii.3.8: 38). Even the resentment that fuels anger and revenge when it is unconstrained serves a salutary social function when it is properly 'guarded and qualified'. But all of this occurs within the moral psychology of the individual. There is not much that the government can do to ennoble our moral sentiments. Indeed, Smith seems to suggest precisely the opposite when he writes, 'Magnanimity, or a regard to maintain our own rank and dignity in society, is the only motive which can ennoble the expressions of this disagreeable passion [revenge]' (TMS I.ii.3.8: 38). In this area there is little that the government can do, but neither is there much that the government needs to do.

In short, there are a series of inherent affinities between the moral psychology of human beings and the practical requirements of the state and society, particularly the commercial societies emerging in eighteenth-century Europe. For Smith, there is a fortuitous 'utility', as Smith describes it, with respect to the constitution of human nature: 'It is thus that man, who can subsist only in society, was fitted by nature to that situation for which he was made' (TMS II.ii.3.1: 85). And this affinity goes beyond even the Aristotelian notion of human beings as social animals, able to find fulfilment only in society. There is also, Smith adds, a desire in human beings to delight in contemplating the activity of a mechanism fulfilling its purpose. Just as we admire the healthy growth and reproduction of plants and animals, the digestion of food, the circulation of blood and so forth, so do we take a kind of aesthetic pleasure in participating in the 'orderly and flourishing state of society' (TMS II.ii.3.7: 88).[13] This translates into a desire to see that the laws are obeyed and that crimes are punished.

For Smith, there are both personal and social forces at work in a free society that tend through their own action and inertia to purge the citizenry of harmful opinions and to incline them towards good citizenship. But, as we have seen, Smith and Rousseau were actually closer than one might think with respect to their criticisms of commercial society. While Smith's criticisms did not approach the severity of Rousseau's, substantively they were remarkably similar. So, there is probably more involved in Rousseau's posture of relative austerity with respect to the government's role in public-opinion formation. This points towards the question of the *stakes* associated with the nation-building project. For Rousseau, the stakes were high, not only because the threats posed by commercial society were greater, but also because he envisioned a society in which citizens would participate directly in their own governance. For Smith, there was less inherent tension between the good judgement of citizens and the effects of commercial society, and, because the requirements of active citizenship were not as austere, there was also less at stake politically in the failure of citizens to develop good judgement. Moral turpitude did not automatically destroy the fabric of society. Indeed, commercial society was largely conducive to good citizenship for Smith. David Reisman (1976: 20) goes so far as to say 'there is no conflict of interest between the individual and the group'. The consequences of commercial society's brutish, venal excesses were mainly confined to the sphere of the personal, could be satisfied largely by the market, and would not generally constitute a danger to political order and stability. They ought to be combated of course, and there is a role for the government to play in this process, but the urgency is at the level of the individual rather than the political.

This is not to deny the political implications associated with Smith's programme of enlightened nation building. For Smith, self-command was the goal for moral agents. Though he generally thought about self-command with respect to personal morality and personal moral development, there were political implications as well. In particular, individuals could only develop their capacity for self-command within a context of relative individual autonomy. This meant that the state would need to restrain the influence of the greatest threat to self-command – the Church. But

Smith was also wary of concentrating power in the state. So the question then became, if order is not produced out of submission to either the Church or the state, from where does it emerge? In his study of Smith, Joseph Cropsey (2001: 101) – placing perhaps even more trust in commercial society than did Smith himself – answers that order emerges 'through the dilution of ecclesiastical authority by means available to a society unencumbered with enthusiasm and superstition, viz. humanized, civilized commercial society'. Put slightly differently, we could say that order emerges in commercial society through the emancipation of the individual to self-command, driven by a desire for the honour and respect of his or her fellow citizens and the corresponding refinement of manners that follows. This requires some direct action on the part of the state, but largely action, as we have said, around the edges, intended not to counteract the effects of commercial society but to curb its excesses and to constrain threats to its free development.

The difference between Smith and Rousseau lies in the difference between self-command and self-government. Smith's citizens must be capable of self-command, of subordinating their selfish desires to the demands of shared social values. Rousseau's, by contrast, must both obey *and* define those values. Smith envisioned a republic in which citizens would be governed by elected representatives, while Rousseau's republicanism demanded citizens capable of governing themselves. This greater political responsibility borne by citizens implies a corresponding responsibility borne by those charged with managing public opinion. For Rousseau, unlike for Smith, the people must legislate for themselves, and, in order to legislate well, the public must be taught to 'know what it wants' (SC OC III: 380; *Collected* IV: 154). Political legitimacy for Rousseau requires that the will of the people be sovereign; it requires self-government. But Rousseau did not believe that the people were themselves always a reliable judge of their own interests:

> The general will is always right, but the judgment that guides it is not always enlightened. It must be made to see objects as they are, or sometimes as they should appear to be; shown the good path it seeks; safeguarded against the seduction of private wills; shown how to assimilate considerations of time and place; taught to weigh the attraction of present, tangible advantages against the danger of remote hidden ills. Private individuals see the good they reject; the public

wants the good it does not see. All are equally in need of guides. The former must be obligated to make their wills conform to their reason. The latter must be taught to know what it wants. (SC OC III: 380; *Collected* IV: 154)

The purpose of the nation-building activities outlined in the previous section is to create a cultural backdrop against which the people will be able to see the good that it wants. For Rousseau, this meant privileging the interests that we hold in common and subordinating or privatising those are not shared with our fellow citizens. While each individual can, 'as a man', have 'a private will contrary to or differing from the will he has as a citizen', the people must speak in unison – or as close to unison as they can come – with respect to matters of political deliberation. They must, as Bronislaw Baczko (1982: 91) puts it, form *'une parole collective'* (a collective voice). Failure to do so will result in political failure, a dissolution of the social bond and a resurgence of those interests we hold separate from others or, worse yet, those that can only be satisfied at the expense of the common interest. While Smith saw patriotism as admirable and socially useful, Rousseau regarded it as absolutely essential to a free society. 'The state should be considered lost', Rousseau wrote, as soon as someone says, 'What do I care?' with respect public affairs (SC OC III: 429; *Collected* IV: 192).

If we want to understand the full picture, we need to think about democratic sovereignty, which Rousseau (unlike Smith) regarded as an essential component of political legitimacy. The gap between Smith and Rousseau on the question of public opinion must be understood not only through the lens of the *dangers* posed by commercial society but also and equally through the lens of the *responsibility* assigned to citizens. Rousseau's citizens were to be tasked with formulating legislation, with the responsibility to participate actively in their own governance. Both Smith and Rousseau were interested in combating the effects of commercial society on citizens, but only Rousseau believed that the very survival of free societies depended on their ability to succeed in this regard. Rousseau's model of citizenship was consequently much more austere than Smith's. You will have no 'freedom without virtue', Rousseau wrote in the *Discourse on Political Economy* (OC III: 259; *Collected* III: 154). Citizens will be needed for Rousseau, and it is not at all clear that this was the case for Smith. In fact, it was probably statements like the one just cited that prompted Smith to characterise Rousseau as an 'extreme advocate' of republican principles, one who, in Smith's words, had carried those principles 'a little too far' (Letter: 251). Smith's citizen must be 'decent and orderly', as he put it in *The Wealth of Nations* (WN V.i.f.61: 788), but Rousseau's must be brimming with love of the *patria* and ready to make sacrifices for it. The republic dies, according to Rousseau, with the 'slackening of the social bond', while, for Smith, the cost of moral corruption is largely limited to the personal sphere and does not threaten the foundation of the political system.

Both Smith and Rousseau were concerned to supplant the aristocratic face of virtue with a republican one, but Rousseau's concerns were weighted more towards the political and Smith's more towards the personal. Smith was concerned about moral virtue, because he believed it to be the thing that validates a life well-lived, but he was less concerned about explicitly *civic* virtues, or, perhaps it is better to say, his threshold for good citizenship was much lower than Rousseau's. With respect to politics, Smith was primarily concerned to keep citizens from interfering in the just administration of sovereign power. This passage from *The Wealth of Nations* captures the contrast between the two thinkers:

> An instructed and intelligent people . . . feel themselves . . . more likely to obtain the respect of their lawful superiors, and they are therefore more disposed to respect those superiors. They are more disposed to examine, and more capable of seeing through, the interested complaints of faction and sedition, and they are, upon that account, less apt to be misled into any wanton or unnecessary opposition to the measures of government. (WN V.i.f.61: 788)

What is striking in this passage is Smith's very different sense of the role or virtue of the citizen. Where Smith sees the virtue of the citizen as intelligent perception, Rousseau saw it as the active construction and maintenance of the general will. While intellect may be the key to seeing through the 'interested complaints' that worried Smith, the formulation of the general will requires probity as well as criticality. Smith's political virtues – perception and intelligence – were cultivated largely in the left side of the brain, while Rousseau's – passion and duty – had to be both directed by reason *and* felt by the heart.

Whither the Nation-building Project?

Smith and Rousseau both recognised the dangers of a state-sponsored project of opinion formation. Rousseau supported such a project, while at the same time seeming to reject the premises on which that very project could be justified – a problem that is often referred to as the Legislator's paradox, or simply the paradox of politics.[14] Smith encouraged the magistrate to enact 'rules' which, as he put it, 'command mutual good offices to a certain degree', but he hastened to add that, of all of the magistrate's duties, this one 'requires the greatest delicacy' (TMS II.ii.1.8: 117). However, with respect to the question of the legitimacy of the project, Smith had two resources not available to Rousseau. First, as we have seen, Smith was relatively sanguine about the judgements of common people in commercial society. Not so Rousseau. Sometimes Rousseau spoke as a revolutionary, sometimes as a traditionalist, but he never talked about society the way Smith did. Society must either transform itself or restore itself, but all will not be well if the people are left to their own devices. Vigilance against threats to the general will must be ongoing. As he put it in the *Social Contract*, 'the private will acts incessantly against the general will' and 'the government makes a continual effort against sovereignty' (SC OC III: 421; *Collected* IV: 186). Secondly, Smith invoked knowledge of the 'rules of natural justice' as the animating force of the science of the legislator (TMS VII.iv.36: 341). This allowed him recourse to an authority higher than the people, to which he could appeal in order to justify the role of the legislator in nation building. Rousseau believed in the idea of natural justice (which he called natural right), but he regarded the general will as the sole legitimate source of sovereign power.

Rousseau confronted a problem here – one that remains at the centre of democratic theory. Because he believed in popular sovereignty, Rousseau could not have recourse to natural right as a justification for the actions of the government. And because he did not believe that the people saw the good that is their own, there was no question of excluding the government from the activity of managing public opinion. Baczko (1982: 90) frames the problem this way: 'There is no intermediary between the people that speaks and the people that listens.' Maurizio Viroli (1988: 99) formulates it as follows: 'Rousseau's project is to provide a theoretical definition of the most suitable ways in which men's views can be altered and to make them moderate and temperate, without forsaking the principle that the individual acts only in accord with what he judges to be his interest.'

For Smith, the science of the Legislator was almost entirely pragmatic. He was concerned to properly derive the principles of legislation from the rules of natural justice, but he was not concerned about justifying the project itself. Rousseau, on the other hand, was always also worried about the question of legitimacy. Given the demands of political right or legitimacy – namely, that the people must govern themselves – how, Rousseau was compelled to ask, can the project of enlightened nation building be justified? Who carries out the project? Is it the people themselves? Anything else would seem to violate the very principle (self-rule) upon which the republican project is based. But if the people were competent to carry out this task, the task itself would not be necessary in the first place.

This question is one of the most significant and most difficult in Rousseau studies. Here I can only summarise its relevance for the issue I have raised in this chapter. In sum, Rousseau does not acknowledge anything other than the will of the people as the legitimate basis for the exercise of *either* sovereign power or government power. However, while he insists that sovereignty be exercised democratically, he makes no such demand of government, condoning a variety of arrangements, with some kind of enlightened aristocracy probably preferable to the others. This elected government is tightly bound by the constraints of the general will and is charged to act only insofar as those actions can be justified as enacting the general will. Here there is a contrast with Smith, for whom it is natural justice that acts as the justification and inspiration for state action. While Rousseau accepted the existence of natural justice, he rejected the invocation of any authority other than the general will with regard to state action or public policy. Natural justice or natural right, as he called it, could be too easily invoked as a justification for the subversion of the general will. So, this leaves Rousseau's government in the position of having to justify all of its actions as directly enacting the general will or at least as necessary to its enactment.

And in formulating the problem in this way, Rousseau changed forever the way we think about the justification for the state's role in the education and management of public opinion. What had historically been justified by an appeal to authority, now had to be reconciled with democratic principles. Towards this end, I conclude by offering one Rousseauian corrective to Smith and one Smithian corrective to Rousseau, with an eye towards contemporary democratic theory. The Rousseauian corrective to Smith runs as follows: all systems of government wrestle with the relationship between public opinion and public policy, but democracy places more authority in the former; the fundamental problem of governance does not change – but it must now be approached under the constraints of the paradox of politics. The problem of justifying the management of public opinion was more straightforward when subjects were simply subjects. Once they became sovereign as well, this question became far more complicated. Now the same results must be achieved (perhaps the people must be even more enlightened given their new responsibility), but the moral authority by which the project was justified prior to the Enlightenment has disintegrated.

And, finally, I offer a hopeful Smithian corrective to Rousseau. Among Smith's great innovations was the idea that enlightened public opinions could emerge organically in societies that engage in commerce and protect personal liberty from the incursions of interested factions. If this is the case, then the people, left to their own devices, through the steady action of one upon another, may elicit from each other some of the virtues that Rousseau thought could only be found in the republics of antiquity, in simple, agrarian societies like Corsica, or in the improbably engineered society of the *Social Contract*. As Anna Stilz (2009) has shown, there are, even within Rousseau's account of socialisation and social life, internal resources that approximate or resemble the externally imposed socialisation of the Lawgiver or the government.[15] If Stilz is correct, if the steady action of society upon itself produces the kinds of virtues that Rousseau expected of citizens, then the paradox of politics may not be such a paradox after all.

Notes

1. In fact, public opinion always plays *some* role in legitimising sovereign power – as the events of the so-called Arab Spring demonstrated – even where the people are not formally sovereign, but that is a matter for another occasion.

2. As I sat down to write, members of the Democratic Party in the US House of Representatives were conducting a direct action to

stop the majority from conducting business. Their justification for doing so was opinion polling that showed that vast majorities of the American electorate favoured public policy on gun control. And as I returned to this note, Britain was exiting the European Union based on a referendum.

3. Citations of Rousseau are, first, to *œuvres complètes*, Paris: Bibliothèque de la Pléiade, 1959–96, and, secondly, to *The Collected Writings of Rousseau*, Hanover: University Press of New England, 1990–2010. I have used the following abbreviations: Cor *Constitutional Project for Corsica*; DAS *Discourse on the Arts and Sciences*, also referred to as the *First Discourse*; DI *Discourse on the Origin and Foundations of Inequality Among Men*, also referred to as the *Second Discourse*; LDA *Letter to d'Alembert on the Theatre*; LM *Letters Written from the Mountain*; O *Observations [to Stanislas, king of Poland]*; PE *Discourse on Political Economy*; SC *Social Contract*.

4. Jürgen Habermas's *Structural Transformation of the Public Sphere* (1989) lays out what is probably the seminal framework for the way in which this question is approached in contemporary political theory. Nadia Urbinati's more recent *Democracy Disfigured* (2014) presents a penetrating and far-reaching inventory of the ways in which the government (and other forces) influence the process of democratic will-formation.

5. Istvan Hont's (2015) lectures on Smith and Rousseau are also useful in framing the similarities and differences between Smith and Rousseau on this subject, as I discuss below.

6. Rasmussen (2008) also approaches Smith and Rousseau through the lens of their responses to commercial society.

7. There is now a substantial literature on the various manifestations of *amour-propre*. For a good account of the role of the state in the transformation of *amour-propre* into *amour de la patrie*, see Engel (2005).

8. See also Cor. OC III: 935–6; *Collected* XI: 152.

9. I have left out of this account policies that have an indirect effect on public opinion, such as an agrarian economy and territorial limits, which Rousseau believed were conducive to inculcating republican mores.

10. This argument can be found principally in the first *Discourse* and in the *Letter to d'Alembert on the Theatre*.

11. In an argument that operates as a microcosm of the one he makes in 'Enlightened Nation Building', Hanley (2006) argues that Smith and

Rousseau turn out to be rather close with respect to their views on the moral effects of the theatre. Rousseau famously summarised his view of the theatre with the remark that it was bad for a good people and good for a bad people (LDA OC V: 59–60; *Collected* X: 298). Hanley argues – persuasively – that Smith held a similar view. Indeed, for both Smith and Rousseau, theatre was not itself morally edifying but could serve a useful moral end by occupying the time and energy of people who might otherwise be engaged in something much worse. However, even if Smith and Rousseau shared a broadly similar interpretation of the moral effects of the theatre, they had very different views of the moral requirements of *justice*. This compelled Rousseau (as we will see below) to assign the state an active role in securing conditions that Smith could afford to treat as merely preferable.

12. 'Whenever commerce is introduced into any country, probity and punctuality always accompany it' (LJB: 538).

13. 'The fitness of any system or machine to produce the end for which it was intended, bestows a certain propriety and beauty upon the whole' (TMS IV.1.1: 179).

14. This problem – that citizens must be 'prior to the laws what they ought to become by means of laws' – is much discussed in the scholarship on Rousseau (SC OC III: 383; *Collected* IV: 156). Bonnie Honig's treatment (2007) is particularly insightful.

15. I develop an interpretation in this vein in chapter 5 of *Rousseau's Ethics of Truth*.

Bibliography

Baczko, B. (1982), 'La cité et ses langages', in R. A. Leigh (ed.), *Rousseau after Two Hundred Years*, Cambridge: Cambridge University Press, 87–108.

Bashir, O. S. (2015), 'Testing Inferences about American Politics: A Review of the "Oligarchy" Result', *Research & Politics*, 2.4, 1–7.

Boudreau, C., and S. A. MacKenzie (2013), 'Informing the Electorate? How Party Cues and Policy Information Affect Public Opinion about Initiatives', *American Journal of Political Science*, 58.1, 48–62.

Bullock, J. G. (2011), 'Elite Influence on Public Opinion in an Informed Electorate', *American Political Science Review*, 105.3, 496–515.

Cropsey, J. (2001), *Polity and Economy*, South Bend, IN: St. Augustine's Press.

Engel, S. (2005), 'Rousseau and Imagined Communities', *The Review of Politics*, 67.3, 515–37.

Enns, P. K. (2015), 'Relative Policy Support and Coincidental Representation', *Perspectives on Politics*, 13.4, 1053–64.

Fishkin, J. S. (1997), *The Voice of the People: Public Opinion and Democracy*, New Haven, CT: Yale University Press.

Gillens, M., and B. I. Page (2014), 'Testing Theories of American Politics: Elites, Interest Groups, and Average Citizens', *Perspectives on Politics*, 12.3, 564–81.

Habermas, J. (1989), *The Structural Transformation of the Public Sphere: An Inquiry into a Category of Bourgeois Society*, Cambridge, MA: MIT Press.

Hanley, R. P. (2006), 'From Geneva to Glasgow: Rousseau and Adam Smith on the Theater and Commercial Society', *Studies in Eighteenth-Century Culture*, 35.1, 177–202.

Hanley, R. P. (2008), 'Enlightened Nation Building: The "Science of the Legislator" in Adam Smith and Rousseau', *American Journal of Political Science*, 52.2, 219–34.

Honig, B. (2007), 'Between Decision and Deliberation: Political Paradox in Democratic Theory', *American Political Science Review*, 101.1, 1–17.

Hont, I. (2015), *Politics in Commercial Society: Jean-Jacques Rousseau and Adam Smith*, Cambridge, MA: Harvard University Press.

Matsubayashi, T. (2012), 'Do Politicians Shape Public Opinion?', *British Journal of Political Science*, 43.2, 451–78.

Muller, J. Z. (1992), *Adam Smith in His Time and Ours: Designing the Decent Society*, New York: The Free Press.

Neidleman, J. (2017), *Rousseau's Ethics of Truth: A Sublime Science of Simple Souls*, New York: Routledge.

Rasmussen, D. C. (2008), *The Problems and Promise of Commercial Society: Adam Smith's Response to Rousseau*, University Park: Pennsylvania State University Press.

Rasmussen, D. C. (2014), *The Pragmatic Enlightenment: Recovering the Liberalism of Hume, Smith, Montesquieu, and Voltaire*, Cambridge: Cambridge University Press.

Reisman, D. A. (1976), *Adam Smith's Sociological Economics*, London: Croom Helm.

Rousseau, Jean-Jacques (1959–96), *Œuvres complètes*, ed. B. Gagnebin and M. Raymond, 5 vols, Paris: NRF, Editions Gallimard

Rousseau, Jean-Jacques (1990–2010), *The Collected Writings of Rousseau*, 13 vols, Hanover: University Press of New England.

Schaeffer, D. (2010), 'Realism, Rhetoric and the Possibility of Reform in Rousseau's Considerations on the Government of Poland', *Polity*, 42.3, 377–97.

Stilz, A. (2009), *Liberal Loyalty: Freedom, Obligation, and the State*, Princeton: Princeton University Press.

Urbinati, N. (2014), *Democracy Disfigured: Opinion, Truth, and the People*, Cambridge, MA: Harvard University Press.

Viroli, M. (1988), *Jean-Jacques Rousseau and the 'Well-Ordered Society'*, Cambridge: Cambridge University Press.

14

'Savage Patriotism', Justice and Cosmopolitics in Smith and Rousseau

Neil Saccamano

In *Politics in Commercial Society*, originally given as the Carlyle Lectures at Oxford University and published posthumously, Istvan Hont compares the usually contrasted writings of Adam Smith and Jean-Jacques Rousseau on a range of issues including sympathy and pity, sociability, morality, law, government, revolution and commerce, and he concludes his discussion by noting their shared recognition of the need to address the problems posed by nationalism, especially with regard to war. Both writers, Hont remarks, acknowledged 'a tension between global and national societies and their attendant social psychologies' (2015: 132) that led them to plan future works to respond to these conflicts. As we know, Rousseau's *Social Contract* was to comprise the first part of a treatise entitled *Political Institutions*, the second part of which presumably would have addressed international law and the rights of war and commerce.[1] Although, after extracting the *Social Contract*, Rousseau burned the remainder of his writing for this book, some of the political fragments, particularly *The State of War*, along with the first two chapters of the *Geneva Manuscript* (the initial draft of the *Contract*) and, more significantly, the Digest and Judgement on the Abbé de Saint-Pierre's *Perpetual Peace* have been taken to indicate the issues Rousseau would have developed in the unfinished project. In the case of Smith, the proposed work was a discourse on 'natural jurisprudence, or a theory of the general principles which ought to run through and be the foundation of the laws of all nations', as he announces it in the last paragraph of *The Theory of Moral Sentiments* (TMS VII.iv.37: 341). The papers for this unfinished study, too, were consumed by flames at the author's behest; yet his *Lectures on Jurisprudence* survive in the form of student notes, and sections of *The Wealth of Nations* and especially *The Theory of Moral Sentiments* have been considered to provide sufficient evidence of Smith's views on war, and international justice and morality. Indeed, Charles Griswold (1999: 258), for one, contends that the general principles with which Smith wanted to found the laws of nations could be nothing other than the moral and intellectual sentiments he had already presented in the latter work, given the historical basis of his philosophy. With some of these texts furnishing a frame of reference, Hont draws his comparative study of Rousseau and Smith to a close by emphasising another of their commonalities: their joint failure to elaborate a transnational politics:

> It is quite convenient to finish on a note of failure by both Rousseau and Smith on this issue. The aim is to show that they failed in the same place, and that their arguments are often more similar than we tend to assume. Further, it is not clear whether we have gotten that much further. This year [2009], I hope that I will be forgiven more easily for being a bit skeptical about our theoretical progress. (Hont 2015: 132)

Where Hont ends his lectures I would like to begin my essay. Taking his conclusion as a point of departure, I want to examine in sharper focus the place at which both writers apparently reach a limit in their thinking and their projects go up in smoke. Rousseau's and Smith's political philosophies may founder on the question of how effectively to prevent states of war and acts of hostility, yet they approach nationalism with very different assessments and with conflicting perspectives on the desirability and salutary effects of supranational political institutions. That Smith advocates for global flows of commerce in opposition to both mercantilism and international politics as a means to temper state hostilities is well known: when denouncing what he considers the malignant enmity of a 'savage patriotism' (TMS VI.ii.2.3: 228), for instance, Smith does not turn to natural jurisprudence and to mediating judicial instruments, but hopes, as Fonna Forman-Barzilai has remarked, that 'free, self-interested commercial intercourse among nations might mitigate aggression and cultivate international peace without goodwill or coercion, produce cosmopolitan ends without cosmopolitan intentions, balance national wealth with global "virtue"'

(2010: 212). With respect to Rousseau, on the other hand, 'savage patriotism' could aptly name the normative – even constitutive – effect of civic virtue on which he relies in his republican model of political community: 'every patriot is harsh to foreigners' because, as the wise legislator must acknowledge, 'patriotism and humanity are . . . two virtues incompatible in their energy' (E *Collected* XIII: 163/OC IV: 248–9; LM *Collected* IX: 144n./OC III: 706n.).[2] The decision to destroy the manuscript of *Political Institutions* would seem then, in this context, to indicate that his notion of republican virtue compels him 'to put an end to international society', as Georg Cavallar (2002) sums up the consensus on Rousseau's approach to cosmopolitanism. Nonetheless, Cavallar, Grace Roosevelt and others have also argued that Rousseau takes seriously the possibility of transnational political institutions to bring about peace; his doubts about that possibility have less to do with the inefficacy of political institutions than of the means necessary to realise them. As we will see, the obstacle to attaining 'perpetual peace' for Rousseau is the force and agency that must be calculatedly exercised in the absence of a non-providential or non-teleological conception of history.

The different reasons why Rousseau and Smith fail to move through (if not beyond) the politics of the nation-state are worth considering more extensively, first of all, so that we have a fuller, more intricate comparative account of their understandings of inter-state relations and war. But these reasons might also prove instructive about the current state of international politics – when war and occupation continue to ravage the Middle East and kill, oppress and displace millions; when the European Union faces nationalist challenges, particularly in response to the influx of migrants and refugees across 'external' and 'internal' borders (Brexit); when populist, racist and xenophobic ideologies and parties vigorously reassert themselves in the US and individual European nations in reaction to globalisation (Trump, the French National Front, the Danish People's Party, the Austrian Freedom Party); when United Nations' humanitarian and peacekeeping interventions have become politically suspect; when the outgoing Secretary General denounces UN member states not just for failing to protect civilian populations but for actively contributing to the atrocities of war (in Syria), and the new US president dismisses the UN as a global club where people come together just to talk; and when South Africa and Gambia withdraw from the International

Criminal Court, repudiating it as the International Caucasian Court for decisions taken at the Hague and aimed at Africa, to mention only these instances. Of course, the limited wars between sovereign states addressed by eighteenth-century cosmopolitanisms have been historically exceeded, as Jürgen Habermas has succinctly detailed, by a variety of wars or hostilities that have correspondingly enlarged cosmopolitan rights and norms to include war itself as a crime.[3] Yet the difficulties that Rousseau and Smith encounter when they try to imagine an end to war remain of interest to us, as current challenges to the sovereignty and the very idea of a nation-state have 'opened a space for an active revival of cosmopolitanism as a way of approaching global political-economic, cultural, environmental, and legal questions' (Harvey 2009: 78).[4]

Still pertinent to us today is their shared assumption that morality and politics must be understood in relation to feelings, sentiments or affects constitutive of community and as essential to justice as the prevention and alleviation of violence and suffering – especially the relationship between love of country and love of humanity, or what I will call *philopatria* and *philanthropia*. In fact, one fault-line in contemporary debates about cosmopolitanism lies in the tension between a politics that relies on legal and deliberative international institutions to guarantee moral universal rights, and one that acknowledges 'the crucial role played by passions and affects in securing allegiance to democratic values' and that facilitates ensembles of extralegal practices and institutions so as to produce 'collective forms of identification' and subjectivity, as Chantal Mouffe (2000: 95–6) puts it. Mouffe's scepticism about the moral universal claims made for judicial and deliberative institutions to achieve peace through consensus without being based on 'forms of life' that could facilitate political acts of contestation – indeed, bypassing politics altogether – leads her to critique cosmopolitanism for reasons not dissimilar to Rousseau's own worry about supranational political institutions.

Since love has everything to do with morality and politics for Smith and Rousseau, we should begin by recalling their accounts of the affectivity of social relations and civic bonds. As Smith himself observed in his brief commentary on the *Discourse on the Origins of Inequality*, Rousseau, like Hobbes and Mandeville, rejects natural sociability, but in its place endows human beings in the state of nature with the universal sentiment of pity to temper the principle of self-preservation and to anticipate the emergence in the civil state of such social virtues as benevolence, mercy, generosity and friendship, which follow from it.[5] Pity, for Rousseau, is a passion provoked specifically by scenes of suffering; it 'puts us in the position of the one who suffers' and, through this identification of the witness or spectator with the afflicted creature, we are carried without reflection, 'heedlessly' (*étourdiment*), to the aid of others, thereby also helping to preserve the entire species. Consequently, Rousseau names pity the 'first sentiment of humanity'. Yet 'pity' or 'humanity' is not solely a feeling in the state of nature, since it necessarily compels the 'savage' to relieve suffering and, in so doing, couples sentiment and benevolent action as if they together comprise an almost instinctual response to tragic spectacles. In his hypothetical history, Rousseau stresses the inseparability of affect and action in the state of nature so as to narrate the arrival in the civil state of the possibility of deliberate moral action or virtue proper, which, however, coincides with the fall of pity into merely a sentiment, if it exists at all. Stifled in the social state by emergent passions organised around self-love (*amour-propre*), pity or humanity, whose 'gentle voice' no one was 'tempted to disobey', must be replaced by 'laws, morals [*moeurs*], and virtue' nationally, and the law of nations internationally, to overcome the ensuing hostilities of war (DOI *Collected* III: 37/ OC III: 155–6). Although Rousseau claims, at one point in the *Second Discourse*, that natural pity might still be found in 'a few great cosmopolitan souls who surmount the imaginary boundaries that separate Peoples . . . and embrace the entire human Race in their benevolence' (DOI *Collected* III: 54/OC III: 178), he more often locates common vestiges of pity in the theatre, where it has become practically inhumane in being decoupled from action. In the *Discourse*, Rousseau ironically refers to the sight of weeping spectators at a tragic drama as a sign that natural pity cannot be completely destroyed by the 'depraved morals' of society, for these moved spectators in the theatre would, in the tragic tyrant's place, actually 'aggravate his enemy's torments even more' (DOI *Collected* III: 36/OC III: 155). The pity to be found in a theatre is 'a sterile pity' – we could call it an aesthetic sentiment – 'which feeds on a few tears and which has never produced the slightest act of humanity', Rousseau comments in the *Letter to d'Alembert*. And as if anticipating the critique of a sentimental humanism sometimes associated with his work, Rousseau admonishes theatrical spectators for confusing moral with aesthetic pity insofar as we imagine that 'we have satisfied all the rights of humanity [*droits de l'humanité*] without having to give anything more of ourselves' than a few tears (LD *Collected* X: 268–9/OC V: 23).

Although he forcefully narrates the fall of natural pity into an aesthetic sentiment that takes the place of acting on the rights of humanity, we should be aware that the persistence of natural pity in the social state would not, of itself, be morally sufficient for Rousseau. Precisely because its identifications and actions to alleviate suffering are performed *étourdiment* in response to those near us, natural pity needs to be corrected and regulated by reflection and reason for the sake of justice. As he notes in *Emile*, a pity that could persist in the civil state has to be prevented from 'degenerating into weakness' on account of our tendency to act heedlessly and contingently, with partiality or 'blind preference', and to extend care primarily to those 'immediately involved with us'. A judgement concerning the moral character and situation of the person suffering is not a condition of natural pity, and thus this 'first sentiment of humanity' can itself be inhumane or cruel: 'pity for the wicked is a very great cruelty to men'. To moralise pity in society, it must become 'enlightened and wise' (*éclairé et sage*), 'generalised and extended to the whole of mankind' and yielded to 'only insofar as it accords with justice'. This is evidently the pity that ought to belong to the exceptional cosmopolitan souls of the *Second Discourse* – and to Emile and presumably his tutor, as well. 'For the sake of reason', Rousseau asserts, 'we must have pity for our species still more than for our neighbor [*prochain*]', because 'the love of mankind is nothing other than the love of justice' (E *Collected* XIII: 409–10/OC IV: 548).

The complicated relationship between pity and justice is not peculiar to Rousseau but is symptomatic of a difficulty found in accounts of morality and politics by philosophical psychology from Shaftesbury's moral-aesthetic sense forward to Kant's rejection of such approaches as issuing in pathology, not universal morality. In Smith, too, a similar difficulty troubles the relation between sympathy and morality and concerns the desirability and even possibility of an impartial or de-particularised conception of justice that might sustain ethical community but also extend beyond national-cultural borders to international judicial and political institutions. As Dennis Rasmussen (2008: 63) has helpfully spelled out, Smith's sympathy differs from Rousseau's pity in a number of ways, an important one being the broader scope of sympathy as a mechanism enabling non-self-interested fellow-feeling.[6] Although Smith opens *The Theory of Moral Sentiments* by citing pity or compassion as his first example of sympathetic identification, and he often turns to scenes of suffering to describe the efforts required by the spectator 'to put himself in the situation of the other and to bring home to himself every little circumstance of distress' so as to produce, if possible, a 'correspondence of sentiments' (TMS I.i.4.6: 21), he also explicitly employs the term sympathy 'to denote our fellow-feeling with any passion whatever' (TMS I.i.1.3: 10). In addition, there is the tendency to contrast Rousseau's pity, as only ever an immediate response of the spectator, with sympathy, as conditioned by the spectator's and actor's awareness of their irreducible difference, by the acknowledged 'imaginary' act of exchanging their positions, and by the reciprocal, self-regulating adjustments required to produce a harmony of sentiments, which unintentionally also help to sustain social life. 'Mankind, though naturally sympathetic, never conceive', Smith observes, 'that degree of passion which naturally animates the person principally concerned' but only 'a passion somewhat analogous to what is felt' by others (TMS I.i.4.7: 21–2); consequently, those who seek sympathy – and the non-utilitarian desire for sympathy as the approbation of others is a psychological datum or starting point in Smith – must imagine themselves in the position of their own spectators and conform at least the signs of their passion to the norms and conventions of propriety that generally do and should elicit sympathy. In these mutual accommodations, the spectator and object of sympathy mediate their relations to themselves through others, who eventually become the abstracted and internalised third-person other, the normative point of view of the impartial spectator. As Smith puts it with regard specifically to justice, the virtue distinctively connected to sympathy with the suffering and resentment of others and hence the virtue closest to pity or compassion: every person, who 'naturally prefers himself to all mankind' and especially to those 'with whom [he has] no particular connexion', must nonetheless view himself as others will view him and recognise that 'to them he is but one of a multitude in no respect better than any other in it'; to obtain the sympathy of an 'impartial spectator', 'which is what of all things he has the greatest desire to do', he must therefore 'humble the arrogance of his self-love and bring it down to something which other men can go along with' (TMS II.ii.2.2: 83). In this way, we do and should feel sympathy with the misery of others and we do and should restrain ourselves from causing the ruin of another person.

For Rousseau, the desire for the approbation of others is the catastrophe of the social state insofar as it drives individuals 'outside' themselves, compelling them to draw the very 'sentiment of their own existence' from the opinion of others, to which they must at least appear to conform and for which they are in competition and rivalry (DOI *Collected* III: 66/OC III: 193). Hence, law, civic virtue and an enlightened pity (if possible) are needed to replace natural pity. In Smith, on the other hand, the overwhelming desire for sympathy appears to countervail the individual's self-love and contributes to social concord as long as something like an 'impartial' or impersonal norm presides over sympathetic identification. Yet in Smith, too, the virtue of justice, and in the last resort the force of law, must intervene in the absence of sympathy for humanity in general:

> Men, though naturally sympathetic, feel so little for another, with whom they have no particular connexion, in comparison of what they feel for themselves, the misery of one, who is merely their fellow-creature, is of so little importance to them in comparison even of a small inconveniency of their own; they have it so much in their power to hurt him, and may have so many temptations to do so, that if this principle [of justice] did not stand up within them in his defence, and overawe them into a respect for his innocence, they would, like wild beasts, be at all times ready to fly upon him; and a man would enter an assembly of men as he enters a den of lions. (TMS II.ii.3.3: 86)

Although Smith appears to rely on sympathy for social and ethical self-regulation, he also acknowledges its contingency and limits and must resort to fear of violent death – punishment as legal retaliation – to found and sustain a well-ordered society. This helps explain, perhaps, why Smith initially and frequently exemplifies sympathy by pity or compassion in response to violence and why the discussion of sympathy with the dead in the first chapter concludes with a comment on the regulative function of 'the dread of death' as 'the great restraint upon the injustice of mankind, which, while it afflicts and mortifies the individual, guards and protects the society' (TMS I.i.1.10: 13). Without the 'negative virtue' of justice as abstention from violence, 'the immense fabric of human society . . . would crumble into atoms'. Hence, justice as 'the guard of the life and person of our neighbour' is paramount. In both writers, then, what corrects, regulates or manages 'partiality' and its potentially disastrous effects in the name of justice is essential for the constitution and continuation of society (TMS II.ii.1.10; II.ii.2–4: 82–6).[7]

Smith's Theodicy and the Humility of Borders

To help move us further towards Rousseau's and Smith's views on moral and political cosmopolitanism, we need, however, to clarify what sorts of communities justice upholds. For Smith's phrase 'the immense fabric of human society' does not suppose that all individuals are members of one organised society but, rather, that they belong to diverse societies, each of which would collapse without justice. The meaning and function of the term 'neighbour' in their texts can serve to guide our elucidation of this issue. Is justice due only to our 'neighbour', to those near to us? Should anyone near us be considered a 'neighbour'? And how is nearness or closeness to be measured and determined: contiguity, similarity, belonging or kinship, intimacy or affection? In what we have cited of Smith thus far, it would seem that justice must intervene to preserve the neighbour as one in our proximity but with whom we have no 'particular connexion' other than the similarity of being a 'mere fellow-creature', apparently even if belonging to the same nation. A neighbour is a stranger, in this respect. Justice is necessary for there to be any human society at all in Smith precisely because we do not both love and act benevolently towards human beings as such, but are disposed, like predatory animals, to destroy those for whom we have no affection. And affection for others, including our relatives, is 'in reality nothing but habitual sympathy', which results from 'being placed in situations which naturally create' it; only in 'tragedies and romances' do we find a 'mysterious affection' supposedly – but 'ridiculously', says Smith – based on 'the force of blood' (TMS VI.ii.1.7–10: 220–3). Although the desire for sympathy tends to normativise and promote social concord, Smith also recognises that society must be able to function without strong affective communal bonds and proposes a strictly contractual model: 'Society may subsist among different men, as among different merchants, from a sense of its utility, without any mutual love or affection . . . it may still be upheld by a mercenary exchange of good offices according to an agreed valuation' (TMS II.ii.3.2: 86).

In fact, indifference (at best) to the neighbour who remains a stranger unloved and 'of so little importance' also shadows Smith's discussions of national belonging and *philopatria* and even forms part of his critique of war. As we know, Smith – or, rather, the author of nature – places spatial limits on sympathy and the active or positive virtue of beneficence. After the care a man naturally has for himself comes care for those 'who usually live in the same house with him, his parents, his children, his brothers and sisters are naturally the objects of his warmest affections' (TMS VI.ii.1.2: 219).[8] And since the house containing our loved ones is 'comprehended within' the state in which we live, the latter is the 'greatest society upon whose happiness or misery, our good or bad conduct can have much influence' and is, 'accordingly, by nature, most strongly recommended to us' (TMS VI.ii.2.2: 227). As a consequence, we develop a love for our country's 'constitution or form of government' and wish to be a 'good citizen' who acts to 'promote, by every means in his power, the welfare of the whole society of his fellow-citizens' (TMS VI.ii.2.11: 231).[9] Yet since Smith takes as a datum that beneficence cannot be practised beyond the border of the state, he argues that the globe does not comprise a sphere of active virtue, even though we supposedly love humanity as a whole.

> The love of our own country seems not to be derived from the love of mankind. The former sentiment is altogether independent of the latter, and even seems sometimes to dispose us to act inconsistently with it . . . We do not love our country merely as part of the great society of mankind: we love if for its own sake, and independently of any such consideration. The wisdom which contrived the system of human affections, as well as that of every other part of nature, seems to have judged that the interest of the great society of mankind would be best promoted by directing the principal attention of each individual to that particular portion of it, which was most within the sphere both of his abilities and of his understanding. (TMS VI.ii.2.4: 229)

As I have already remarked, what Smith calls here 'the great society of mankind' refers to humanity as already organised into diverse nations, which the 'system of human affections', by divine contrivance, cannot much influence: 'It very rarely happens . . . that our good-will towards such distant countries [as Japan or China] can be exerted with much effect' (TMS VI.ii.2.5: 230). Our 'good-will is circumscribed by no boundary, but may embrace the immensity of the universe', he observes; but universal benevolence does not carry with it 'effectual good offices', which can 'seldom be extended to any wider society that our own country' (TMS VI.ii.3.1: 235). We do not love and care for our fellow citizens because we love humanity; we love and care for human beings because they are our compatriots or neighbours. Since national residence makes possible a particular connection to others, our country is the natural and proper sphere of our public benevolence. Active virtue or acts of humanity practically coincide with the territorial nation-state. *Philopatria* is a psychological given that Smith must acknowledge in principle so as not to dispute the divine order. He cannot but generally endorse patriotism as pride in the superiority of the nation whose 'prosperity and glory seem to reflect some sort of honour upon ourselves' (TMS VI.ii.2.2: 227).

Yet just as Smith hedges the natural disposition towards sympathy with conditions so as to align it with the impartial spectator's normative position, so too must he qualify the preference expressed in *philopatria*. A politics, as well as an ethics, derived from a psychology of passions demands that the natural particularity or partiality of love of self and love of country be calibrated with justice. Of course, war is the critical issue to be treated in this context. Interestingly, among the various reasons why Smith opposes war (including its economic effects) is one that seems to suspend the active virtue of beneficence as well as the negative virtue of justice, which follow upon a sense of national belonging. There is a tension between the indifference to strangers in the contractual model of society, in which others are 'merely fellow-creatures' whose protection ultimately requires force when the negative justice associated with pity or compassion fails, and the wish to promote actively or benevolently the welfare of the entire society and the happiness of fellow citizens as neighbours. This tension can be glimpsed in a passage from *The Wealth of Nations* in which Smith exposes a structural social division and bitterly attacks the partiality of the sacrifices offered up in national wars:

> In great empires the people who live in the capital, and in the provinces remote from the scene of action, feel, many of them scarce any inconveniency from the war; but enjoy, at their ease, the amusement of reading in the newspapers the exploits of their own fleets and armies. To them this amusement compensates the small difference between the

taxes which they pay on account of the war, and those which they had been accustomed to pay in time of peace. They are commonly dissatisfied with the return of peace, which puts an end to their amusement, and to a thousand visionary hopes of conquest and national glory from a longer continuance of the war. (WN V.iii.37: 920)

Samuel Fleischacker (2004: 255) has drawn attention to these remarks to explain Smith's refusal to endorse most wars – mercantilist wars, civil wars and foreign wars, whether 'lamented as national tragedies' or 'acclaimed as national triumphs'. In a way tantamount for Fleischacker to an accusation of treason, Smith denounces the social-spatial distance between members of the same nation: those who live remote from the scene of action and whose lives are not at risk have little regard for the horrors suffered by their fellow citizens, who remain merely fellow creatures. War here exposes the willingness of one part of the nation to sacrifice another part as if they were apart from the nation, more like foreigners than strangers or neighbours.

I would also call attention to Smith's critical mention in this passage of the press as a medium that does at least two things. First, it seems to aestheticise war such that, even if violence and suffering were 'brought home' to the reader by the newspaper accounts, the resulting pity or compassion would be entangled with a kind of aesthetic pleasure or 'amusement' divorced from both the atrocities of war and any acts to put an end to it; this pity would be 'sterile', to recall Rousseau's attack on the moral effects of tragic theatre. War mediatised through journalism takes the form of a cultural commodity – like an epic poem or heroic drama – worth the price of purchase to those with the economic means and social standing to occupy the position of cultural consumer (spectator or reader). For Smith, that the newspapers reporting on war only distance its pains indicates not only the indifference of readers to the lives of their neighbours, but also the depravity of their desire to have war waged so as to experience the pleasure of self-aggrandising national glory.

Secondly, the medium of journalism enables 'visionary hopes of conquest and national glory', not only by distancing readers from action (of war itself and of any benevolent reaction to it) but also by mediating these readers with each other so that they might imagine themselves as belonging to the same nation in the first place. In this way, what Benedict Anderson (1991) has called 'print capitalism' works to construct national identity among those strangers who have no habitual contact and might as well consider each other foreigners residing in the same territory. National glory here is 'visionary' in the sense of purely imaginary because it is effectively founded on a 'fictive' identity which, according to Étienne Balibar, designates the 'nationalization of societies and peoples and thus of cultures, languages, genealogies' as a process that entails the confrontation and reciprocity between two notions of the people: '*ethnos*, the "people" as imagined community of membership and filiation, and *demos*, the "people" as the collective subject of representation, decision-making, and rights' (2004: 8). Although in contrast to Rousseau, as we will see, Smith does not much emphasise *ethnos* or the cultural constitution of community, his naturalisation of patriotism does accord with Balibar's sense that nationalism requires the 'subjective interiorisation of the idea of a border – the way individuals represent their place in the world to themselves' (Balibar 2004: 8). In Smith's critique of the phantasmatic or visionary hope of national glory through war, the borders distinguishing nations and orienting individuals to the world are also revealed to be internal to the mediatised nation where one group decides to send their neighbours to their deaths, as if treasonably at war with itself.[9]

Moreover, if we return to the critique of *philopatria* in *The Theory of Moral Sentiments*, we can observe Smith's stress on its pathology and examine the conceptual difficulties it prompts as he tries to correct for its partiality: in this account, justice paradoxically becomes injustice. Take the example of 'the patriot who lays down his life for the safety, or even the vain-glory' of his society. Smith notes that we naturally tend to view him, along with our other warriors and statesmen, with an admiration that is 'partial' and to rank him 'sometimes most unjustly' above those of other nations. On the other hand, the injustice of our *philopatria* conflicts with the 'perfectly just and proper' sacrifice of the patriot who indeed personifies justice by identifying with the 'impartial spectator' and regarding himself 'as but one of the multitude' obliged to promote 'the glory of the greater number' through his 'heroic virtue'. Since the impersonal 'multitude' in this instance consists not of 'human society' but only of his fellow citizens, however, the nationally heroic and just action of the patriot is internationally unjust or inhumane. Furthermore, when read in conjunction with the passage in *The Wealth of Nations* on the domestic politics of war conducted for the phantom of national glory – here echoed by Smith's mention of 'vain-glory' – these remarks suggest that 'heroic virtue' functions ideologically (WN VI.ii.2.2: 227–8).

Smith also criticises the pathological effects of *philopatria* in the system of human passions for its tendency to give rise to 'malignant jealousy and envy' of any prosperous neighbouring nation. In his well-known formulation: 'Each nation foresees, or imagines it foresees, its own subjugation in the increasing power and aggrandisement of any of its neighbours; and the mean principle of national prejudice is often founded upon the noble one of the love of our own country.' As with self-loving individuals in relation to their fellow citizens, national self-love is the cause of hatred and war against neighbours. The analogy of individuals and the state that governs views of international politics in Smith and other political philosophers of the period inevitably leads to the problem of how the bellicosity of 'savage patriotism' can be regulated.[11] Justice requires the force of law in the last instance, the fear of violent death as retaliation by the state, in the absence of pity or compassion. Sympathetic attunement between the sovereigns and between individual citizens of neighbouring states is foreclosed by the supposed impenetrability of affective and territorial borders. 'Continual dread and suspicion' are the result of such borders; statesmen and sovereigns neither expect justice nor extend it to each other. In addition, there is 'no common superior' to resolve conflicts, and the 'laws of nations', to which sovereign states declare themselves obligated, are 'very little more than mere pretense' and 'either evaded or directly violated' every day (TMS VI.ii.2.3: 228). Smith reaches a political limit here.

In response to the lack of multinational legal institutions and political communities cutting across sovereign borders, Smith does not envisage the possibility of cosmopolitical practices that might work to realise a de-nationalised justice.[12] Instead, he makes moral pronouncements. This tactic is evident in his discussion of the conflicting views of Marcus Cato and Scipio Nascia over the fate of conquered Carthage. For Smith, the elder Cato's conclusion to every speech that 'Carthage ought to be destroyed' is 'the natural expression of the savage patriotism of a strong but coarse mind, enraged almost to madness against a foreign nation'; in contrast to this patriot's madness, Scipio Nascia's concluding counter-demand to spare Carthage is 'the liberal expression of a more enlarged and enlightened mind, who felt no aversion to the prosperity even of an old enemy, when reduced to a state which could no longer be formidable to Rome'. Echoing Scipio's liberality, Smith then comments that, while France and England 'may have some reason to dread the increase of the naval and military power of the other', it is 'surely beneath the dignity of two such great nations' to envy the prosperity, manufacturing and commercial advances, and progress of arts and sciences of each other because these ennoble 'human nature'. Since, for Smith, these improvements serve humanity, each nation 'ought . . . from the love of mankind' to promote, not obstruct, the progress of its neighbours; these improvements are the 'proper objects of national emulation, not of national prejudice or envy' (TMS VI.ii.2.3: 228–9).

Although the 'enlightened' politics advocated here seems to be founded on *philanthropia* as a moral sentiment that corrects for the savagery of *philopatria*, there are some complications that we should address in this account – not least being Smith's qualification that Scipio's liberality depends on the reduction of Carthage 'to a state which could no longer be formidable to Rome'. In his analogy to France and England, Smith consequently takes care to distinguish between a neighbour's advance in military power, which presumably is the proper object of national dread, and its progress in economic, cultural and other non-military areas. *Philanthropia* extends to other states only if they are rendered incapable of waging war, whether aggressively or defensively. And since this incapacity must be actively maintained indefinitely into the future unless one nation is permanently disarmed or destroyed so as never to possess a greater power in comparison, an effectual state of war (if not continual hostile acts) remains the condition of possibility of the philanthropic encouragement of a neighbouring nation.

But a further complication attends Smith's declaration that each nation 'ought' to act benevolently towards past or potentially future enemies: what basis in practice does this moral duty possess? What is the force of this statement of obligation to respect the dignity of other nations? Just as we underlined the necessity of the force of law for justice to strangers within the state, Smith imagines that, to prevent even a 'paltry misfortune to himself', a European might be willing 'to sacrifice the lives of millions of his brethren, provided that he had never seen them', and that such savagery can be prevented not through the 'love of mankind' and the 'soft power of humanity' but through 'reason, principle, conscience' represented by the impartial spectator, who shows us 'the deformity of injustice' and reminds us 'we are but one of a multitude' (TMS III.3.4: 137). If sovereign states merely profess to be obligated by the law of nations, which is powerless to punish aggression and dispense justice, and if the active virtue of benevolence naturally ends at a border, then Smith may speak as and for the impartial spectator with his imperative to act philanthropically, but he cannot and does not claim to present moral and political actuality: he asserts that the lives and persons of the multitude of humanity cannot be protected by justice in the same way as those of the multitude of fellow citizens. Indeed, we should recall in this context that the 'liberal' perspective of Scipio did not prevail politically and that Rome, in fact, waged a war to destroy Carthage, a war of annihilation that Ben Kiernan has called the first genocide.[13]

In addition, this imperative to act benevolently towards neighbour states, even if the condition of their perpetual vulnerability to our military power were met, seems to contradict the divine wisdom that limits the force of justice and moral practice to nation-states as the best way to promote 'the interest of the great society of mankind'. In this respect, we might describe Smith's rhetorical strategy in the chapter on universal benevolence in *The Theory of Moral Sentiments* as a kind of lure for those inclined to venerate the wise man, such as Marcus Aurelius, who is 'principally occupied' in the 'sublime contemplation' of the benevolence of the divine being and to consider him superior to 'the most active and useful servant of the commonwealth' (TMS VI.ii.3.5: 236). We might even suspect Smith to be here deflecting the possible accusation that his earlier remarks on the benevolence owed to neighbouring states resemble the preoccupation of the Stoic Marcus with 'philosophical speculations' on cosmopolitan humanity to the neglect of the welfare of the Roman Empire itself (TMS VI.ii.3.6: 237). For, as Smith proceeds in his discussion, he seems to invite the reader to identify both with the wise man who is willing to sacrifice private interests to the interests of society, and those social interests to the 'great interest of the universe' administered by God (TMS VI.ii.3.1: 235), and with patriot-soldiers who similarly 'sacrifice their own little systems to the prosperity of a greater system' as directed by their commanding officers. Yet Smith's ironic strategy in invoking these two figures of self-sacrifice consists in claiming that 'the great Conductor of the universe' commands the wise man, in effect, to retreat to the national border and follow the model of the soldier's patriotism: he must 'humble' his vain ambition to act philanthropically and must calibrate his will to 'the weakness of his powers'. Soon after remarking on the injustice of *philopatria* and apparently affirming universal benevolence, Smith brings the reader up short: 'The administration of the great system of the universe, however, the care of the universal happiness of all rational and sensible beings, is the work of God and not man.' In Smith's theodicy, the so-called wise man is commanded to renounce his willingness to sacrifice national self-interest when necessary, as if such philanthropic acts were motivated by an impious pride, and to submit to the due degree of weakness (to echo Pope) that divinely circumscribes his moral sphere to 'the care of his own happiness, of that of his family, his friends, his country' (TMS VI.ii.3.4–6: 236–7). The rest (including the effects of global commerce) is in the hands of providence.

Rousseau's History and the Violence of Transnational Politics

Rousseau and Smith share as their starting point the view that the sentiment of pity or compassion naturally extends to those with whom we have some particular and proximate connection and whose lives alone, it is assumed, can be affected by our acts. For Rousseau, what Smith calls 'human society' or the 'great society of mankind' also does not exist in a strict social sense, as he makes clear in his reflections on Diderot's *Encyclopedia* entry on 'Natural Right'. In an effort to regulate the unjust actions of the purely self-interested individual whom he considers 'the enemy of the human race', Diderot postulates a general will of the entire species (and, in principle, of animality) that determines laws of justice; naturally gaining access to this will through reason, we thereby derive rules that govern the conduct of members of the same society to each other, their relations to their own particular society, and the interaction of societies among themselves (OC III: 136–8). For Rousseau, however, 'the term *human race* suggests only a purely collective idea which assumes no real union among the individuals who constitute it'. To be more than merely an 'idea', a general human society would need to exist as a 'moral person having – along with a feeling of common existence [*sentiment d'existence commun*] which gives it individuality and constitutes it as one – a universal motivation which makes each part act for an end that is general and relative to the whole'. This 'common feeling is humanity', he observes, and it would need to be animated and directed by 'natural law [as] the active principle of the entire machine'. Rousseau objects that a common sense or sensibility unifying a social body – its 'central nervous system' – cannot exist because the 'development of society stifles humanity in men's hearts by awakening personal interest, and that concepts of the natural law, which should rather be called the law of reason, begin to develop only when the prior development of the passions renders all its precepts impotent [*impuissans*]' (GM *Collected* IV: 78/OC III: 283–4). Self-interested passion and reason thwart the emergence of a common sense, without which so-called natural laws have no power to move aggregates of individuals to act collectively.[14] Hence Rousseau's recourse to the social compact to supersede the inefficacy of natural law by putting in its place the general will of a particular people through which they give the law to themselves and conventionally constitute a 'moral being' with a common sense and ability to act.

Rousseau further counters with the historical argument that the notion of humanity as 'the brotherhood of all men' was only generalised rather late by Christianity, and that the Romans, whose ancestors considered the words 'stranger' and 'enemy' to be synonymous, legally authorised 'acts of violence not only against declared enemies but also against anyone who was not a subject of the Empire'; consequently, 'the humanity of the Romans extended no further than their domination' (GM *Collected* IV: 81/OC III: 287). In other words, 'humanity' is coextensive with an existing political order and the legal protection only it can provide to subjects and citizens. Rousseau, in fact, reverses the causality of Diderot's account by arguing that the empty idea of general human society based on natural law is actually the effect of living within political communities: 'We conceive of the general society on the basis of [*d'après*] our particular societies; the establishment of small republics makes us think about the large one, and we do not really begin to become men until after we have been citizens.' Although he once praised the universal benevolence of a few great cosmopolitan souls, he attacks cosmopolitanism here (as he does elsewhere) in the name of *philopatria*: 'It is apparent from this what should be thought of those professed cosmopolites who, justifying their love of the homeland [*patrie*] by means of their love of the human race, boast of loving everyone in order to have the right to love no one' (GM *Collected* IV: 81/OC III: 287). As with Smith's discussion of universal beneficence, Rousseau affirms *philopatria* as the social affection that gives rise to moral practice: if we act humanely, out of love, we do so only towards our compatriots. And again, as in Smith, Rousseau explains this circumscription of moral practice within national borders by attesting to our affective weakness. 'The feeling of humanity evaporates and weakens as it is extended over the whole world' and must 'be confined and compressed to be activated', he observes in the *Discourse on Political Economy*; only in being 'concentrated among fellow citizens' does it become 'useful' (DPE *Collected* III: 151/OC III: 254–5). He puts the consequences of the identification of humanity and citizenry even more starkly in *Emile*:

> Every particular society, when it is narrow and unified, is estranged from the all-encompassing society. Every patriot is harsh to foreigners [*étrangers*]. They are only men. They are nothing in his eyes . . . The essential thing is to be good to the people with whom one lives. Abroad, the Spartan was ambitious, avaricious, iniquitous. But disinterestedness, equity, and concord reigned within his walls. Distrust those cosmopolitans who go to great length in their books to discover duties they do not deign to fulfill around them. A philosopher loves the Tartars so as to be spared having to love his neighbours. (E *Collected* XIII: 163–4/OC IV: 248–9)

Foreigners or strangers cannot be the beneficiaries of acts of humanity precisely because to patriots they are merely 'human', members of the species, and hence 'nothing', vulnerable to being treated with iniquity. Equity and justice cannot and should not cross national borders for they would thereby disappear from the earth. The globe is not a territorial state and human society is not a *patrie*. In contrast to Smith's equivocations concerning *philopatria*, Rousseau here unapologetically affirms the international injustice of republican virtue as a kind of 'savage patriotism' enabling social concord and justice to reign within the walls of the state. Otherwise, however, Rousseau shares Smith's dismissal of universal or cosmopolitan beneficence as mere philosophical (perhaps Stoic) speculation, since it is not only unrealisable but disposes us to neglect our moral responsibilities to our neighbours – the sole kind of virtue possible and necessary.[15]

Although Rousseau repeatedly invokes republican virtue as the norm of ethical community, he also realises, of course, that it is a historical anachronism in relation to the political institutions of contemporary Europe (with the possible exception of Geneva). In his version of classical republicanism, the naturally autonomous self is integrated into 'the common unity' so that each person 'no longer feels except within the whole': 'A citizen of Rome was neither Caius nor Lucius; he was a Roman. He even loved his country exclusive of himself.' In modern Europe, on the other hand, such civic integration is no longer possible and results in a contradictory person who is neither an autonomous individual nor a citizen; a contemporary Englishman or Frenchman is merely 'a bourgeois' – 'nothing' (E *Collected* XIII: 164/OC IV: 249–50). Without distinct national institutions to subjectivise individuals and form civic identity, 'there are only Europeans' with 'the same tastes, the same passions, the same morals', to whom national location matters little, as long as they can satisfy their passion for gold (CGP *Collected* II: 175/OC III: 960).

On the ethical character of modern nations, Rousseau and Smith might agree, especially if we recall Smith's acknowledgement that 'mutual love and affection' may be replaced by utility, self-interest and the 'mercenary exchange of goods' in society. They certainly do agree about the weakness of moral cosmopolitanism or *philanthropia* to issue in acts of benevolence towards foreigners and about the counter-productive effects of such vain humanitarian affection on the concord and moral practice of one's own society. Furthermore, Rousseau also does not simply accept that a state of war must prevail internationally as long as one has peace and equity at home, for national and international politics are interdependent. The obstacles to perfecting government 'are born less from its constitution than from its external relations' because the primary domestic priority must be the maintenance of force capable, at the very least, of resisting foreign hostile acts by nations from whom justice cannot be expected and, at worst, of rendering them no longer formidable, as Smith put it. For Rousseau, too, argues that national strength is relative; a state 'feels itself to be weak as long as there are any stronger than it' and therefore, to preserve itself, will continually increase its size and force to 'make itself more powerful than all its neighbours' (SW *Collected* II: 67/OC III: 605). 'War is born from peace', he paradoxically observes (SW *Collected* II: 62/OC III: 610). Hence, in *The Plan for Perpetual Peace* he explores a way to mitigate the unavoidable consequence that 'by uniting ourselves to several men', we have 'forestalled private wars only to ignite general ones, which are a thousand times more terrible', and thereby 'we really become the enemies of the human race' (PP *Collected* II: 28/OC III: 564). Or as he concedes elsewhere: the general will as 'the rule of what is just and unjust' is 'infallible [*sûre*] in relation to all citizens [but] can be defective with foreigners' as members of 'the large city of the world' (DPE *Collected* III: 143/OC III: 245). Surprisingly, given the normativity of heroic republican virtue in Rousseau, the citizen becomes the enemy when seen from the perspective of foreign nations, as occurs with Smith's provisional adoption of universal benevolence as a lens that brings the violence of patriotism into sharper focus.

Both writers confront the bellicosity that results from the unjust justice of national politics, but both dismiss the law of nations as illusory and ineffectual since it has force only insofar as it accords with the self-interest of a nation and is otherwise violated with impunity. 'Justice' for Rousseau is merely an 'empty word', lacking a historical referent in international relations and functioning only as 'the safeguard of violence' (SW *Collected* II: 62/OC III: 610). Unlike Smith, however, Rousseau does not fall back on providence to care for humanity behind the backs of moral or political actors – 'to produce cosmopolitan ends without cosmopolitan intentions', to recall Forman-Barzilai's formulation (2010: 235). Rather, Rousseau tends to think dialectically. If republican citizens have been historically succeeded by nationally deracinated, 'bourgeois' individuals who are merely 'Europeans', then Rousseau considers whether these Europeans might have a collective *ethos* that can also constitute the *demos* of a transnational political community. This is surely the appeal of Abbé de Saint-Pierre's proposal of a European federation that could be founded on common connections among nations previously under the domination of the Roman Empire. Through conformity in their customs and the bonds formed by the Christian religion, morals, commerce and 'the invention of the Printing Press and the general taste for Letters, which has given them a community of studies and of knowledge', Europeans are not 'divided Peoples', nor, on the other hand, simply an 'ideal' or speculative unity, but a 'real society' spanning the borders of territorial states (PP *Collected* II: 31/OC III: 567). Of course, a European federation of states, which always respects their national sovereignty, is by no means a cosmopolis. Yet by praising the Abbé's plan to erect a transnational legal-political institution on common sociocultural and historical grounds – he claims 'no more useful Plan has ever occupied the human mind' – Rousseau tries to move politically beyond Smith's moral imperatives and reliance on providential care (PP *Collected* II: 27/OC III: 563). In Grace Roosevelt's words: 'Rousseau's political and educational writings indicate that the divergent values of patriotism and humanitarianism are not mutually exclusive in the long run ... Nations ... can eventually mature into political bodies willing to join with others to promote a more general will through international law' (Roosevelt 1990: 81).

In Rousseau's judgement (a rather sanguine one, in historical hindsight), if a European republic could be made 'real for a single day [it] would be enough to make it last forever, so much would each [prince and his people] find by experience his private profit in the common good' (PP *Collected* II: 53/OC III: 591). But Rousseau does have doubts; they concern, however, not the longevity of a European republic but the means and conditions necessary for its institution. In the *Geneva Manuscript*, he imagines the possibility of establishing 'a general Society of which the State gives us an idea' and of extending the civility and beneficence practised in a *patrie* to strangers and foreigners (GM *Collected* IV: 113/OC III: 328–9). Yet he takes issue here with the Abbé's 'simplicity' in supposing that the rationality and common good of the plan would, in itself, be persuasive enough to make nations 'willing to join with others', in Roosevelt's phrasing. 'Like a child', the Abbé assumed that 'all that was necessary was to gather together a Congress, to propose his articles there, that they were going to be signed, and that everything would be accomplished' (PP *Collected* II: 56–7/OC III: 595). The discursive force of public reason (like Smith's enlightened moral declaration) is powerless to convince sovereigns, who are primarily occupied with 'extending their domination abroad and making it more absolute at home', to reach a consensus and to implement this plan (PP *Collected* II: 54/OC III: 592). Moreover, even if princes could possibly be thought benevolently disposed, Rousseau objects that a historical 'moment favorable for the execution of the system' would be almost impossible to find, because there would need to be such a concurrence of wisdom and interests 'that one must hardly hope for the fortuitous harmony of all the necessary circumstances from chance' (PP *Collected* II: 56/OC III: 595). Since he does not fall back on providence (or, as Kant would, on a teleological plan of nature) to supply the necessary historical conditions for founding a transnational political body, the possibility of putting an end to war seems almost hopelessly contingent.

Yet instead of hoping against hope for these conditions to arrive at some moment in a non-providential history, Rousseau uneasily turns to the agency of war itself. In the absence of a harmony of circumstances, 'force is the only thing that can take its place', and persuasion must give way to military coercion. If war is born of peace, then peace might be born of the power of war to give a European republic a historical chance. Such a chance already has, in fact, historical precedent in the actions of Henri IV (1553– 1616) who, according to Rousseau, sought to establish a Christian republic and to bring about 'immortal peace' by waging a 'final' war to end war (PP *Collected* II: 56, 60/OC III: 595, 599). Henri in this regard replaces Smith's God not only because he attempts through *virtù t*o shape the course of history, but also because he, too, must act in a mysterious and cunning way. To form a coalition of national powers, Henri did not appeal to a common interest, 'which is never that of anyone', or expressly declare perpetual peace to be the aim, 'about which few would have cared'. Instead, he kept his plan a 'profound secret' from the European sovereigns who joined forces to defeat the common enemy of Spain out of their own particular interests, while they unknowingly cooperated to implement his design (PP *Collected* II: 58/OC III: 597–8). By this means, Henri hoped to realise a cosmopolitical end without the other actors' cosmopolitical intentions.

Ironically, Henri's life was cut short by an accident of fortune that prevented him from accomplishing his goal. In Rousseau's admittedly ambivalent response to this loss and failure, however, we finally come up against the limit of his cosmopolitical approach to peace. For, if public good is never the primary interest and willed object of sovereigns, then Rousseau suspects that Henri might well have made himself the 'foremost potentate of Europe', had he been successful. And if all sovereigns seek to extend their domination abroad, then the European federation under Henri could not but globally continue the state of war it was established to end. Put differently, multinational institutions claiming to dispense justice out of humanity cannot escape a particularised political and potentially unjust relation to those strangers beyond

their borders. Furthermore, the contradiction entailed in using violence to eliminate violence also prompts Rousseau to hesitate over
embracing the only historical means he considers available to help
realise a cosmopolitical humanity. Hence, he recommends that we
admire the beauty of the proposal (*un si beau plan*) and yet refrain
from executing it by means so 'violent and formidable to humanity': 'One does not see federative Leagues established by any way
other than revolutions, and on this principle who among us would
dare to state whether this European League is to be desired or to
be feared?' (PP *Collected* II: 60/OC III: 600).

In conclusion, Rousseau's unanswered question concerning the
revolutionary violence needed to create and conserve a binding
'law of nations' marks a limit in his cosmopolitical thought that
unexpectedly brings him nearer to Smith, but even closer to our
own historical situation. For Smith, too, had suspicions about the
political consequences of a 'public spirit which is founded upon
love of humanity' but mixed with 'a spirit of system'. Although he
directs his critique to the social and political 'innovations' introduced within a state by a vain, misguided *philanthropia*, yet he also
repudiates the 'great violence' wielded for the cause of justice in
place of a discursive reason incapable of persuasively forming consensus, and he also acknowledges the 'beauty of an ideal system'
of universal justice which must remain an aesthetic object, not a
political project to be realised (TMS VI.ii.2.15: 232–3). Rousseau
arrives at a similar place but from an approach that speaks more
directly to current concerns with the politics of deploying force
in the name of the moral sentiment of humanity to deliver justice
to suffering others – for example, the violence of humanitarian
interventions that aid others who cannot act for themselves, and
that are carried out by a limited number of powerful states, often
the former Western colonisers of the victims, under the aegis of
the UN but promoting these states' particular interests. Even his
suspicion about the inevitable partial or interested actions of a
potent European republic resonates with current critiques of the
politics involved in the very claim to represent a transnational
humanity: for some, the realisation of the cosmopolitan project
'could only signify the world hegemony of a dominant power'
which, 'identifying its interests with those of humanity, would
treat any disagreement as an illegitimate challenge to its "rational"
leadership' (Mouffe 2005: 106–7).[16] Instead of renouncing as self-
righteous such philanthropic political efforts, Rousseau lays out

contradictions in the politics of implementing justice that still remain with us.

Notes

1. See Bernard Gagnebin's introduction to Rousseau's *Oeuvres complètes*, III, xv–xvi, and *The Confessions* (*Collected* V: 339–40, 432).
2. English citations of Rousseau's works are taken from the volumes of the *Collected Writings* (1990–2010) and abbreviated as follows: CGP *Considerations on the Government of Poland*; DOI *Discourse on the Origin of Inequality*; DPE *Discourse on Political Economy*; E *Emile*; GM *Geneva Manuscript*; LD *Letter to d'Alembert*; LM *Letters Written from the Mountain*; PP *Plan for Perpetual Peace*; SC *Social Contract*; SW *State of War*. The Pléiade edition is hereafter abbreviated OC, and English translations are occasionally modified.
3. 'Kant is thinking here [in *Perpetual Peace*] of spatially limited wars between individual states or alliances, not of world wars. He is thinking of wars conducted between ministers and states, but not yet of anything like civil wars. He is thinking of technically limited wars that still permit the distinction between fighting troops and the civilian populations, and not yet of anything like guerrilla warfare and the terror of bombardment. He is thinking of wars with politically defined aims, and not yet of anything like ideologically motivated wars of destruction and expulsion ... Now that wars are unlimited, the concept of peace has also been correspondingly expanded to include the claim that war itself, in the form of a war of aggression, is a crime that deserves to be despised and punished. For Kant, however, [there are crimes committed during war but] there is not yet a crime *of* war' (Habermas 1997: 115). We will have occasion later to suggest that Smith's reference to Cato's rage towards Carthage raises the spectre of war as destruction.
4. See all of chapter 8 (Harvey 2009: 77–97) for Harvey's critique of much new cosmopolitan theory as 'arid' universalism that does not take into account the determinations of geographical space. For an excellent account of ways to move from a moral cosmopolitanism to a cosmopolitics that involves transnational practices by individuals and groups as agents rather than nations and international courts, see James D. Ingram's (2013) *Radical Cosmopolitics: The Ethics and Politics of Democratic Universalism*.
5. Letter: 242–54; also see Rousseau (DOI *Collected* III: 37/OC III: 155).

6. 'First, [sympathy] denotes a correspondence with any kind of feeling, not just suffering or sorrow; second, it is a *mechanism* or a correspondence between feelings rather than a feeling or sentiment itself; third, it is what the *spectator* feels in any given situation for Smith's system of morality, not what the actor feels; and finally, since Smith's sympathy is a rather complicated process that sometimes requires elaborate assessment, it is stronger and more refined in civilized people than in savages' (Rasmussen 2008: 63).

7. Forman-Barzilai (2010: 235) focuses her efforts to locate a universalistic element in Smith on justice as a negative virtue and also aligns it with Rousseau's pity. What she stresses, however, is the immediacy of compassion, in which 'the human heart leaps unmediated to the suffering victim' on account of a 'visceral affinity with the victim of cruelty'. As I have noted, however, Rousseau argues for the need to overcome precisely the unreflective and immediate character of natural pity in relation to justice, since the indiscriminate heart could itself be cruel by pitying the wicked; on the other hand, even pity and compassion must also be mediated or enlightened in Smith by knowledge of the victim's situation. For instance, in the opening pages of *The Theory of Moral Sentiments*, he seems to present the spectator's compassion for the victim of torture as similar to what some might call a Humean contagion – 'the passions, upon some occasions, may seem to be transfused from one man to another, instantaneously, and antecedent to any knowledge of what excited them in the person' – but, in fact, this is not the case: 'General lamentations, which express nothing but the anguish of the sufferer, create rather a curiosity to inquire into his situation, along with a disposition to sympathize with him, than any actual sympathy that is very sensible. The first question which we ask is, What has befallen you? Till this be answered . . . our fellow-feeling is not very considerable' (TMS I.i.1.6–9: 11–12). Although this issue would require a more extended analysis, my sense is that Smith insists on the condition of knowledge in order to align sympathy with justice from the very beginning of his account, to avoid specifically the possible cruelty of sympathy, and to make possible a theory of moral sentiments more generally.

8. Notably absent from this list and the ensuing ranking of family members and friends in our affections is the wife or mother. Carole Pateman's (1988: 45–50; see also Hobbes 1996: 142) arguments concerning the marriage contract as structuring liberal political theory might be interesting to recall in this context. She has

focused on a similar absence of a wife or a mother in Hobbes's definition of the traditionally heterosexual family in *Leviathan*, which she interprets to mean that, since women have no political rights, they have been consigned to the status of servants in Hobbes's understanding of a family, whether it 'consist of a man and his children; or of a man and his servants; or of a man, and his children, and servants together: wherein the Father or Master is the Soveraign [*sic*]'.

9. In the *Treatise of Human Nature*, Hume makes a more explicit analytical effort to explain the apparent gap between empirical face-to-face contact with others as a condition of sympathy and a sympathetic identification with a country: it has to do with the generation of the passion of pride via the intermediary idea of a 'relation' to the self, and especially 'property'. See Book II.9–10 of the *Treatise*.

10. My mention of 'print capitalism' and Balibar's of 'imagined community' refer, of course, to Benedict Anderson's *Imagined Communities: Reflections on the Origin and Spread of Nationalism* (1991).

11. See Tuck (1999: 78–108) on Grotius, where the analogy serves to justify war between trading states and colonialism.

12. Nor does he envisage Henry Fielding's (2005: 237) embrace of theatre itself as an alternative: 'We cannot suppress a pious Wish, that all Quarrels were to be decided by those Weapons only, with which Nature, knowing what is proper for us, hath supplied us; and that cold Iron was to be used in digging no Bowels, but those of the Earth. Then would War, the Pastime of Monarchs, be almost inoffensive, and Battles between great Armies might be fought at the particular Desire of several Ladies of Quality; who, together with the Kings themselves, might be actual Spectators of the Conflict. Then might the Field be this Moment well strewed with human Carcasses, and the next, the dead Men, or infinitely greatest Part of them, might get up like Mr. *Bayes's* Troops, and march off either at the Sound of a Drum or Fiddle.'

13. Ben Kiernan claims that the annihilation of Carthage, most of its inhabitants (civilian and military) and its culture 'fits the modern legal definition of the 1948 United Nations Genocide Convention: the intentional destruction "in whole or in part, [of] a national, ethnical, racial or religious group, as such"' (2004: 28). I cannot help but imagine that Cato's rationale for destruction was known to Smith: Cato 'insisted on Roman military domination. "The Carthaginians are already our enemies; for he who prepares everything against me, so that he can make war at whatever time he

wishes, he is already my enemy even though he is not yet using arms"' (Kiernan 2004: 28).

14. Rousseau distinguishes an 'aggregation' (or what we might now call a 'multitude'), which 'has neither public good nor body politic', from an 'association' (SC *Collected* IV: 137/OC III: 359).

15. See Rorty (1996: 352–3) for a discussion of Rousseau's relation to Stoicism, especially on cosmopolitanism. See also Brooke (2012: 181–208).

16. From among the many current critiques of a politics based on humanity and human rights, also see Didier Fassin (2012), who takes aim at how moral sentiments support what he calls contemporary forms of 'humanitarian government', and Samuel Moyn (2010, 2014).

Bibliography

Anderson, Benedict (1991), *Imagined Communities: Reflections on the Origin and Spread of Nationalism*, New York: Verso.

Balibar, Étienne (2004), *We, the People of Europe? Reflections on Transnational Citizenship*, Princeton: Princeton University Press.

Brooke, Christopher (2012), *Philosophic Pride: Stoicism and Political Thought from Lipsius to Rousseau*, Princeton: Princeton University Press.

Cavallar, Georg (2002), *The Rights of Strangers; Theories of International Hospitality, the Global Community, and Political Justice since Vitoria*, Aldershot: Ashgate.

Fassin, Didier (2012), *Humanitarian Reason: A Moral History of the Present*, trans. Rachel Gomme, Berkeley and Los Angeles: University of California Press.

Fielding, Henry (2005) [1749], *The History of Tom Jones, a Foundling*, New York: Penguin.

Fleischacker, Samuel (2004), *On Adam Smith's Wealth of Nations: A Philosophical Companion*, Princeton: Princeton University Press

Forman-Barzilai, Fonna (2010), *Adam Smith and the Circles of Sympathy: Cosmopolitanism and Moral Theory*, New York: Cambridge University Press.

Griswold, Charles (1999), *Adam Smith and the Virtues of Enlightenment*, New York: Cambridge University Press.

Habermas, Jürgen (1997), 'Kant's Idea of Perpetual Peace, with the Benefit of Two Hundred Years Hindsight', in James Bohman and Matthias Lutz-Bachmann (eds), *Perpetual Peace: Essays on Kant's Cosmopolitan Ideal*, Cambridge, MA: MIT Press.

Harvey, David (2009), *Cosmopolitanism and the Geographies of Freedom*, New York: Columbia University Press.

Hobbes, Thomas (1996) [1651], *Leviathan*, New York: Cambridge University Press.

Hont, Istvan (2015), *Politics in Commercial Society: Jean-Jacques Rousseau and Adam Smith*, ed. Béla Kapossy and Michael Sonenscher, Cambridge, MA: Harvard University Press.

Ingram, James D. (2013), *Radical Cosmopolitics: The Ethics and Politics of Democratic Universalism*, New York: Columbia University Press.

Kiernan, Ben (2004), 'The First Genocide: Carthage, 146 BC', *Diogenes*, 203, 27–39.

Mouffe, Chantal (2000), *The Democratic Paradox*, London: Verso.

Mouffe, Chantal (2005), *On the Political*, New York: Routledge.

Moyn, Samuel (2010), *The Last Utopia: Human Rights in History*, Cambridge, MA: Harvard University Press.

Moyn, Samuel (2014), *Human Rights and the Uses of History*, New York: Verso.

Pateman, Carole (1988), *The Sexual Contract*, Stanford, CA: Stanford University Press.

Rasmussen, Dennis C. (2008), *The Problems and Promise of Commercial Society: Adam Smith's Response to Rousseau*, University Park: Pennsylvania State University Press.

Roosevelt, Grace G. (1990), *Reading Rousseau in the Nuclear Age*, Philadelphia: Temple University Press.

Rorty, Amélie Oksenberg (1996), 'The Two Faces of Stoicism: Rousseau and Freud', *Journal of the History of Philosophy*, 34, 335–56.

Rousseau, Jean-Jacques (1959–96), *Œuvres complètes*, ed. B. Gagnebin and M. Raymond, 5 vols, Paris: NRF, Editions Gallimard

Rousseau, Jean-Jacques (1990–2010), *The Collected Writings of Rousseau*, 13 vols, Hanover: University Press of New England.

Tuck, Richard (1999), *The Rights of War and Peace: Political Thought and the International Order from Grotius to Kant*, Oxford: Oxford University Press.

Notes on Contributors

Tabitha Baker is a PhD candidate in the Department of History at the University of Warwick. She is currently working on a joint doctoral project with the University of Warwick and the Victoria and Albert Museum entitled 'The Embroidery Trade in Eighteenth-Century France'. Her research interests also include comparative Rousseau and Smith studies, and the influence of Smithian thought on eighteenth-century French literature.

Christel Fricke holds a PhD in philosophy and a habilitation from Heidelberg University, Germany. She is Professor of Philosophy at the University of Oslo, Norway and was the founding director of the Centre for the Study of Mind in Nature. Her research focuses on human morality and its natural foundations, the question of how to bridge the gap between a descriptive (psychological or sociological) discourse and a normative discourse about morality. She has published on moral theory and its history. Her recent publications include *Intersubjectivity and Objectivity in Adam Smith and Edmund Husserl* (co-edited by Christel Fricke, Ontos Verlag, 2012), *The Ethics of Forgiveness* (edited by Christel Fricke, Routledge, 2011) and *Adam Smith and the Conditions of a Moral Society* (co-edited by Christel Fricke, *The Adam Smith Review* VI, 2011).

Charles L. Griswold is Borden Parker Bowne Professor of Philosophy at Boston University. His teaching and research address various themes, figures and historical periods. The latter include ancient philosophy and eighteenth-century philosophy. His publications include *Adam Smith and the Virtues of Enlightenment* (Cambridge University Press, 1999), *Forgiveness: A Philosophical Exploration* (Cambridge University Press, 2007) and *Jean-Jacques Rousseau and Adam Smith: A Philosophical Encounter* (Routledge, 2017).

Ryan Patrick Hanley is Mellon Distinguished Professor of Political Science at Marquette University. He is the author of *Adam Smith and the Character of Virtue* (Cambridge University Press, 2009) and *Love's Enlightenment: Rethinking Charity in Modernity* (Cambridge University Press, 2017), and editor of *Adam Smith: His Life, Thought and Legacy* (Princeton University Press, 2016) as well as the Penguin edition of Adam Smith's *Theory of Moral Sentiments* (2010).

Mark Hill is a Fellow at the London School of Economics working as a political theorist and intellectual historian. He received his DPhil from the University of Oxford, where he wrote a dissertation on the ideas of founding and re-founding political regimes in thought of Jean-Jacques Rousseau. In addition to the history of political thought, he is also currently working on the methodological implications of computer-aided textual analysis for researchers working with historical sources.

Mark Hulliung is Professor of History at Brandeis University. He has published widely on topics concerning intellectual, cultural and political history, both European and American, including interactions between Europe and America. He is a historian and a political theorist, and his work is interdisciplinary in nature, cutting especially across history, political science and literary studies. His works include *The Autocritique of Enlightenment: Rousseau and the Philosophes* (Harvard University Press, 1994).

Jimena Hurtado is Associate Professor in the Economics Department, Universidad de los Andes, where she teaches the history of economic thought and is involved in exploring methods to further civic education. Her main area of research is economic philosophy, and she has worked especially on Jean-Jacques Rousseau and Adam Smith, which has led her to study the Colombian tradition in economic thought and education, trying to retrace the link between liberal political philosophy and political economy.

John McHugh received his PhD from Boston University. He is currently Visiting Assistant Professor of Philosophy at Denison University and does research on early modern moral theory, with a particular focus on Adam Smith, David Hume and Francis Hutcheson.

Jason Neidleman is Professor of Political Science at the University of La Verne, where he teaches political theory. His wide-ranging work on Rousseau includes *Rousseau's Ethics of Truth: A Sublime Science of Simple Souls* (Routledge, 2017) and *The General Will is Citizenship: Inquiries Into French Political Thought* (Rowman & Littlefield, 2001).

Maria Pia Paganelli is an Associate Professor of Economics at Trinity University. She works on Adam Smith, David Hume, eighteenth-century monetary theories and the links between the Scottish Enlightenment and behavioural economics. She is the book review editor for the *Journal of the History of Economic Thought* and co-edited the *Oxford Handbook of Adam Smith*.

Dennis C. Rasmussen is Associate Professor of Political Science at Tufts University. He is the author of *The Infidel and the Professor: David Hume, Adam Smith, and the Friendship That Shaped Modern Thought* (Princeton University Press, 2017), *The Pragmatic Enlightenment: Recovering the Liberalism of Hume, Smith, Montesquieu, and Voltaire* (Cambridge University Press, 2014) and *The Problems and Promise of Commercial Society: Adam Smith's Response to Rousseau* (Penn State University Press, 2008).

Neil Saccamano is Associate Professor of Comparative Literature and English at Cornell University. He has published on British and French literature and political and aesthetic philosophy in the eighteenth century, as well as on contemporary theory that addresses the legacy of the Enlightenment. Most recently, he has written on aesthetics and property in Hume and on faith, reason and Enlightenment in Derrida, and he has co-edited a collection of essays on *Politics and the Passions* from Machiavelli to Bentham.

Michael Schleeter is Associate Professor of Philosophy at Pacific Lutheran University. He regularly teaches courses in ethics, social and political philosophy, and business ethics, as well as courses in early modern philosophy, nineteenth- and twentieth-century continental philosophy and the philosophy of race. His areas of scholarly interest include political philosophy, political economy, German Idealism and phenomenology.

Adam Schoene is a doctoral candidate in the Department of Romance Studies at Cornell University. He is the author of recent articles on Rousseau, and his dissertation interrogates the political force of silence in eighteenth-century French literature.

Craig Smith is the Adam Smith Senior Lecturer in the Scottish Enlightenment at the University of Glasgow. He is the author of *Adam Smith's Political Philosophy: The Invisible Hand and Spontaneous Order* (Routledge, 2006) and is one of the editors of the *Oxford Handbook of Adam Smith*.

Index